VINTAGE

Ladies' Compacts

IDENTIFICATION & VALUE GUIDE

ROSELYN GERSON

The current values in this book should be used only as a guide. They are not intended to set prices, which vary from one section of the country to another. Auction prices as well as dealer prices vary greatly and are affected by condition as well as demand. Neither the Author nor the Publisher assumes responsibility for any losses that might be incurred as a result of consulting this guide.

Searching For A Publisher?

We are always looking for knowledgeable people considered to be experts within their fields. If you feel that there is a real need for a book on your collectible subject and have a large comprehensive collection, contact Collector Books.

Photography by Alvin Gerson
Cover Design by Beth Summers
Book Design by Sherry Kraus & Michelle Dowling

On the Cover: Lower Left: *Pygmalion goldtone compact designed to resemble grand piano; interior puff reads "Sonato"; mother-of-pearl lid; sticker on interior mirror reads "Marhill Genuine Mother-of-Pearl"; collapsible legs; 2¼" x 2¾" x 1½". NPA*

Upper Right: *Vanitie goldtone compact/bracelet combination; lid of compact has onyx disc decorated with goldtone filigree and with a pearl in the center; cut out designs on side of cuff; 1¼". $225.00 – 300.00.*

Upper Left: *Ivorene and maroon plastic fan/compact combination; incised sunburst design on fan; maroon handle incorporates compact; interior reveals mirror and puff; exterior mirror on reverse side of compact; tassel; 7" x 11½", compact 2⅛" dia. NPA.*

Lower Right: *Lucien Lelong round polished goldtone compact designed to resemble tambourine; lid decorated with incised birds; disc with Lucien Lelong logo and eight moveable rings on outer rim of compact; interior mirror, powder compartment and puff; 2½" dia. $175.00 – 275.00.*

Center Right: *Originals by Roberts dresser vanity polished goldtone armchair/compact combination; legs, arms and back heavily engraved; filigree on back and skirt of chair elaborately decorated with pearls and rhinestones; lid of chair opens to reveal mirror, puff, and powder compartment; paper label affixed to compact mirror reads "Fabulous Boutique Originals by Roberts"; 2½" dia x 5" high. $250.00 – 350.00.*

Dedication

ROSELYN GERSON

Roselyn Gerson, affectionately referred to as "The Compact Lady" by compact collectors and dealers, is the founder of the Compact Collectors Club and editor and publisher of the newsletter, *Powder Puff*. She is the author of the first book written on, and devoted solely to ladies' compacts, entitled *Ladies' Compacts of the Nineteenth and Twentieth Centuries*, which is a Jewelry Book Club selection. She has also written *Vintage Vanity Bags & Purses*, the first book devoted exclusively to bags/purses which incorporate compacts. She has been an avid researcher and collector since 1976 and has completed the Appraisal Studies Certification course at New York University. She works for a number of private clients as a compact research consultant and lectures widely. She is on the Board of Advisors, Accessory Division, of the Museum of Vintage Fashion, California. Gerson is a professional Member of The National Writers' Club, and has written numerous articles on compacts and vanity bags/purses. She is a member of the Costume Society of America, the Society of Jewelry Historians, U.S.A., and the Long Island Professional Antiques Dealers Association. She is on the Board of Advisors for both *Warman's Americana & Collectibles* and *Warman's Antiques and their Prices*. She is also the ladies' compact advisor to the *Schroeders Antiques Price Guide* and their companion book *Flea Market Trader*. Gerson is listed as "Compact Expert" in the CIC *Antiques & Collectibles Resource Directory*.

Gerson is an active fund-raiser for the Leukemia Research Foundation and is past president of the South Nassau (New York) Chapter of the Nassau Center for Emotionally Disturbed Children, Inc.

Acknowledgments

My heartfelt thanks to the many wonderful compact collectors for their continued friendship, support, encouragement, and enthusiasm. My grateful appreciation to them also for sharing their experiences, valued resources, and research information. I also wish to express my sincere appreciation to the following people: Joan Orlen, Barbara Schwerin, Ruth Wacker, and Cynthia Fleck for graciously allowing their valued "one-of-a-kind" compacts to appear in this book; to Lenore Regan, Terri La Mothe, Mike and Sherry Miller, Steve Gelfand, Molly Kluppell, and Louanne Balcerak, for generously sharing their beautiful vintage catalog ads; to Peggy Gilges and Roberta Maneker of Christy's for permission to reproduce material; to Lois and Bob Widder of Snap Shot; and a special thanks to Laurel Mae and Laurel Lynn Bailey, Marion Cohen, Kitty Foster, Bosha Lipton, Rachel Marks, and Ellen Foster. I am also appreciative to my editor, Lisa Stroup for her encouragement, enthusiasm, and confidence in me.

To my dearest children Roy, Ira and Gayle, and Robin and Denis and wonderful grandchildren, Ilyse, Sarah, Shayna, Katerina, and Andrew.

And most of all to my best friend and photographer extraordinaire, Alvin.

Pricing Information

It is impossible to give absolute prices for articles as varied as compacts. Dealers' retail prices are determined by a number of factors:

Condition: Mint? Scratched, dented, cracked, or chipped? Mirror intact? Original puff, mirror, chain, and powder sifter? Original pouch and presentation box?

Production: Handmade? Mass produced? Hand painted? Commissioned Personalized? Limited Edition?

Decoration: Precious metals, gold, silver? Silver plate, base metals? Precious stones — diamonds, rubies, emeralds, sapphires? Gemstones? Synthetic stones? Enameled? Man-made materials?

Maker or Manufacturer?

Date of Manufacture?

Place of Purchase: Demand and selection varies from one part of the country to another.

This is merely an "average price range" value guide and not a price list. Prices may be higher or lower than listed depending on the above conditions. Values given for items in mint condition, with original parts and presentation box.

NPA: No Price Available. Not enough examples of specific items evaluated to obtain fair median value. There may also be a large disparity of prices for identical items — prices for these items not yet stabilized.

Contents

Foreword

by Al Gerson

Antiquing...That's the one word that made me cringe. The weekend would begin with my wife's favorite request, "Let's go antiquing; it's fun." I always begged off saying that I had work that had to be ready for Monday.

I never found out what "fun" she had until the summer of 1976. It was the bi-centennial and we went to a July 4th celebration in Sparrowbush, NY. There were antique vendors and flea market booths offering all kinds of "bargains." Now, don't get me wrong, I like a bargain as well as the next guy, but spending $25.00 for an old cake plate was not my idea of fun (or a bargain either, for that matter).

As I wandered from table to table watching the excitement on the face of my wife, I noticed a box with some small trinkets that were being sold as "collectibles." While my wife looked at the articles that were "bigger than a breadbox," I rummaged through the small items. That's when it happened! Here they were, the answer to my space problems (antiques take up a lot of room) and a way to save money.

"Look at these great collectibles," I shouted. She put down the item she was ready to purchase and came to see the "specials" I had discovered.

They were two ladies' compacts. One was black enamel and the other was silver with a cloisonné center. The price was right, since the enamel was 50 cents and the silver was 25 cents. Not only were these inexpensive, but how much room would a little compact need? I had to convince her to give up antiquing and take up collecting.

"Let me buy these for you as the start of your new collection and let's see if we can add to them at other markets," I pleaded. I was happy when she agreed. Look at how much money and room I saved just in that one trip alone. LITTLE DID I KNOW!

Here we are almost 20 years later and we now have compacts displayed on walls, in cases, and in trays. So much for the room saving. I also defy anyone to find a silver or enamel compact for 50 cents today.

But I have to admit this small venture into the land of antiques and collectibles has changed our lives for the better. Now I look forward to spending my weekends with my lovely wife traveling from market to market in search of that one elusive different compact. In the past two decades we have traveled to many parts of the U.S. and enjoyed each other's company and mutual interests.

There are other benefits as well...I can honestly say that I am having "fun" and the work I saved for the weekend now gets done at the office.

Speaking of benefits, I have the sole distinction of being called "Mr. Compact Lady."

Preface

In 1989 *Ladies' Compacts of the Nineteenth and Twentieth Centuries*, the first book devoted solely to compacts was published. It was received enthusiatically and warmly by compact collectors, dealers, costumers, historians, fashion designers, museums, and students of vintage fashion. After a while, fellow compact collectors again strongly encouraged me to do a larger book, with additional pictures of compacts in color. I have acquired or have access to many more beautiful and unusual compacts since writing the first book, so of course I was thrilled to do this. However, I could not write a completely new book because there is very little additional historical information available regarding compacts. Most of the manufacturers of ladies' vintage compacts are no longer in existance. Unfortunately, there were little or no records kept by these manufacturers. Many of these firms moved, changed hands, or were absorbed by other companies, and if there were any records they were lost in the shuffle. Information and data relating to compacts was compiled from catalogs, magazines, advertisments, articles appearing in antique papers, antique books, the dictionary, encyclopedia, patents, trademarks, and also from sources that were totally unrelated to compacts. Also researched were museums, libraries, auction houses, and antique shows. There are many compacts that have no identifying marks such as patent numbers, manufacturer's name, or place of origin on them. In order to determine the date of these compacts; their designs, mirrors, backs, clasps, powder sifters, puffs, composition, and motifs were examined and compared with similiar examples of compacts whose date was known. Many compact manufacturers spanned two or three decades and rather than speculate on the exact date a specific compact was manufactured, only the name of the manufacturer, if known, was listed. Therefore, I felt it was necessary to retain the important and pertinent compact information that appeared in the first book on compacts. However, throughout this book, I have added more patents and ads, additional information and hundreds of compacts in full color, most of them have never before appeared in print.

Compact collecting has become so popular in the last few years that many compact articles, listed in the bibliography, have appeared in magazines, trade papers, and newspapers in both the United States and Europe. There are also other books on compacts that have been published, since the first book.

In recent years, compact collecting has become recognized as a separate collectible category area. Price guides now have a "Compact" category listing. In fact, in 1994 for the first time, the Texas State Fair had a separate category for "Compacts" in its Antique Round-up. Because the interest in compact collecting was so intense, in 1987, *Powder Puff* the Compact Collectors Chronicle was created! This quarterly newsletter for compact collectors has an international readership and also sponsors an annual Compact Collectors Convention.

Vintage compacts are now being featured in prestigious auction houses. On February 27, 1995, Phillips, London, had a compact auction of over 350 compacts; December 6, 1994, Christie's, NY, had a jewelry sale and auctioned off a gold Flato compact and original color drawings of Flato's vanities and compacts; in the spring of 1988 Sotheby's, NY, auctioned off 24 of Andy Warhol's compacts, and on June 16, 1988, Christie's East, NY, had a compact auction.

And, the first museum vintage compact exhibition "Compacts of Character" featuring vintage compacts manufactured by Stratton, Kigu, and U.S. manufacturers was held from July 1 through July 31, 1994, at The Manor House Museum, Honey Hill, Bury St. Edmunds, Suffolk, England.

Compacts have been recognized by yet other authorities in popular trends. Enesco and Hallmark, manufacturers of collectible Christmas ornaments that parallel the changing interests, hobbies, and needs of the public, have created and introduced limited editions of adorable Christmas compact ornaments.

Vintage compacts and vanity cases are one of the most sought after new collectibles today by both men and women. Men who collect ladies' compacts are usually interested in their intricate mechanicisms or in the secondary accessory that the compact might be combined with, i.e. watches, music boxes, compasses, etc. or if the motif of the compact touches on their primary collection, Empire State Building, World's Fair, Ships, etc. The combination compacts are also eagerly sought by the secondary accessory enthusiast.

Vintage compacts are especialy desirable since their workmanship, design, technique, and materials used in the execution of these compacts would be very expensive and virtually impossible to duplicate today. Vintage compacts are reminders of another era, they have a history, uniqueness, and patina. They are a nostalgic romantic link in miniature with the past. They were made in a myriad of shapes, styles, materials, and motifs. They were made of precious metals, base metals, fabrics, plastics, and in almost every conceivable natural or man-made medium imaginable. Commemorative, premium, patriotic, figural, combination compacts,

Art Deco, and enamel compacts are a few examples of the most desirable collectible vintage compacts. Collectible also are compacts whose lids are decorated with hand-painted reproductions of priceless paintings by famous artists. Some of the subjects of the Louvre compact series; Romeo and Juliet, Wood by the Winds, A Gallant Gentleman, April Showers, etc. A hand-painted reproduction of the French artist Hardouin Coussin's rendition of Napoleon Bonaparte's sister, Marie Pauling also graced many lids of the popular Mondaine compacts.

History once again repeats itself, the "old" compacts are the "new" collectibles. Vintage compacts are becoming more and more precious and are rapidly appreciating in value and desirability. As for the contemporary future collectibles, many of the giants of the beauty industry are featuring lovely compacts. Estee Lauder has one of the most beautiful, affordable lines of compacts filled with her cosmetics, many of them made in limited editions. Yves St. Laurent's heart shaped compacts with matching lipsticks, feature a different colored center stone each year. Stratton continues to manufacture lovely compacts and purse accessories. Many firms commission artists to create compacts for them. Robert Lee Morris created a new line for Elizabeth Arden. In fact, would you believe, Tweety Bird and Sylvester compacts made exclusively for Warner Bros. stores and Minnie and Mickey Mouse compacts made exclusively for Disney stores are very collectible. Perhaps, some of these compacts will be future collectibles, especially the ones made in limited editions.

I hope that you will enjoy this book as much as I enjoyed collecting, researching, and writing on one of my favorite subjects, compacts.

A History of Compacts

Dating back to the ancient civilizations of the world, the use of cosmetics and cosmetic containers was commonplace in all climes and sections of the globe. The word cosmetics is derived from the Greek word kosmein, meaning to decorate or adorn. Cosmetics were used as an artificial means to enhance and embellish the natural beauty of both men and women. The oldest known surviving cosmetic is powder which was originally made by pulverizing flowers and fragrant leaves.

The predecessors of the present day powder compact were the Oriental ointment container, the Egyptian kohl-pot *(Figure 1)*, the Etruscan cosmetic jar, the French unguent jar, and the English sweet coffer. Although cosmetics originated in the Orient, the Egyptian tombs yielded the first evidence of the use of cosmetics. In the days of antiquity it was customary for kings and queens to be buried with their personal artifacts and most valued possessions. When Egyptian tombs were excavated, archaeologists discovered cosmetic containers known as kohl pots and applicators known as cosmetic spoons. Kohl pots or containers were found in various sizes and were

Figure 1 — Egyptian kohl-pots, obsidian with gold mountings, Twelfth Dynasty. Courtesy of Metropolitan Museum of Art, Purchase, Rogers Fund, and Henry Walters Gift, 1916 (16.33–35).

made of onyx, glass, ivory, bone, alabaster, steatite, and wood. Kohl was a black mineral substance used to embellish the lashes and lids of the eyes. The kohl was applied with an elab-

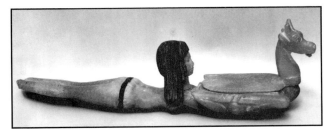

Figure 2 — Egyptian covered cosmetic spoon, alabaster and slate, c. Eighteenth Dynasty. Courtesy of the Metropolitan Museum of Art, Rogers Fund, 1926 (26.2.47).

orately carved ivory or wood cosmetic spoon *(Figure 2)* or kohl-stick. In addition to being used as a cosmetic, kohl protected the eyes from insects which caused eye diseases and shielded the eyes from the desert's glaring sun.

In ancient Greece, Rome, and China, carbonate of lead was used to whiten the face and alkanet was used for rouge. Queen Jezabel is believed to have introduced cosmetics to the Hebrews. In India, both men and women used cosmetics after the bath.

Cosmetics were used throughout the Middle Ages. The Crusaders returning to Britain brought back cosmetics from the harems in the East. Cosmetics were used extensively by men and women alike in Renaissance Italy and France. In Britain during Queen Elizabeth's reign cosmetics were in fashion and were kept in sweet coffers that were restricted to the boudoir.

In the late eighteenth century the use of cosmetics in England was so widespread, Parliament passed a law that made the use of cosmetics and other seductive ploys akin to witchcraft:

"That all women of whatever age, rank, profession, or degree, whether virgins, maids, or widows, that shall, from and after such Act, impose upon, seduce, and betray into matrimony, any of His Majesty's subjects, by the scents, paints, cosmetic washes, artificial teeth, false hair, Spanish wool, iron stays, hoops, high heeled shoes, bolstered hips, shall incur the penalty of the law in force against witchcraft and like misdemeanors, and that the marriage, upon conviction, shall stand null and void."

Women who used cosmetics were suspected of being "ladies of the night" and it was suggested in "Eve's Glossary" by the Marquise de Fontenoy in 1897 that women, instead of using harmful artificial and poisonous substances, use only natural substances, such as the ingredients in the following three recipes.

The first recipe, *Baume des Sultanes*, a balm for the skin, was used in Oriental harems to mask skin imperfections.

BAUME DES SULTANES
Incorporate in 4 ounces of
sweet almond oil
320 grains melted white virgin wax
320 grains whale white
100 grains finely powdered benzoin
60 grains tincture of ambergris
320 grains pulverized rice feculae
15 grains pure carmine.

The second recipe for powder was handed down from a celebrated beauty at the Court of Louis XIV, of France.

POUDRE D'AMOUR
Scrape six juicy raw carrots and half a pink beet-root, squeeze the juice out through a muslin bag and put it aside. Take 3 ounces finely powdered corn-starch, mix it with the carrot and beet juice, expose it to the sun and stir occasionally until the fluid evaporates, leaving the tinted starch dry. Sift through a piece of silk gauze and add:
Powdered Venetian talc, 300 grains
Powdered lycopodium, 300 grains
Powdered bergamot, 45 grains
Powdered bismuth, 7 grains
Sift again and keep in a sandalwood box.

The third recipe is for rouge :

MOUSSE DE FRAISES
(strawberry foam)
Take three quarts of fine ripe strawberries, put them in a wide-mouthed, thick glass bottle together with a pint of distilled water. Place the bottle in a large saucepan of water on a slow fire and let it boil for two hours. Strain through an extra fine hair-

sieve and set aside. When absolutely cool, add:
4 drops attar of roses
2 drops attar of neroli
12 ounces deodorized spirit
15 grains pure carmine and
30 grains best Russian isinglass which has been previously melted. Keep in a glass jar in a cool place. Apply with a fine sponge.

In the late nineteenth century, the use of cosmetics in Europe, particularly in France, Italy, and Austria experienced a revival...The most precious, stunning, and exquisitely executed compacts were made in Europe at the turn of the century. Italy produced sterling silver compacts with a robust gilt

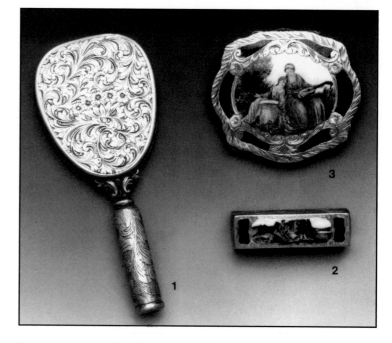

Figure 3 — 1. Sterling Silver stylized floral engraved compact designed as hand mirror with coral cabochon thumbpiece, lipstick in handle.
2. Antiqued sterling-silver enameled lipstick case; painted scene on lid lifts to reveal mirror, Italy, c. 1900s.
3. Antiqued sterling-silver enameled compact with painted scene on lid and gilded interior, Italy, late 19th century.

overlay and colorful painted enamel scenes on the lids *(Figure 3)*, and also produced engraved sterling silver compacts resembling hand mirrors with a lipstick concealed in the handle *(Figure 3)*. French compacts or vanity cases were finished in a matte gilt and encrusted with gems or stones set in prongs, with either a wrist chain or finger ring chain attached. Austrian compacts were elaborately made enamels with a finger ring, chain, or lipstick attached *(Figure 4)*.

Figure 4 — Matte goldtone-finish vanity case with enameled lid encrusted with pronged blue and pink cabochon stones; carrying chain and tassel, goldtone interior, and compartment for powder, lipstick, and eye makeup, France, turn of the century.

During the Victorian era the use of artificial beauty aids was frowned upon in polite society, a conservative attitude that was also adopted in America. Before World War I the use of make-up was considered immoral. Instead, proper diet, fresh air, and exercise were recommended as the only way to improve on nature. In the early twentieth century women were advised to pinch their cheeks to obtain a natural, rosy glow. In 1923 the Dorothy Gray cosmetic firm introduced the face patter to stimulate circulation and thereby make the cheeks naturally pink *(Figure 5)*.

Attitudes regarding cosmetics changed drastically in the first quarter of the twentieth century. The use of make-up during the day became accepted and was no longer looked upon with disdain. The practice had finally achieved an element of respectability and acceptability. The trend-setting silver screen stars played an important part in the acceptance of make-up. The word "make-up" was in fact coined by Max Factor, beauty consultant to the stars. Women began to recognize the importance of personal beauty and opted to adopt a "modern" image aided by the use of cosmetics. As women became "liberated" and as more women entered the business world, the use of cosmetics became a routine and necessary part of a woman's grooming. Subsequently, compacts, portable containers for cosmetics became a necessity. Because of this, the basic compact, an easy-to-carry container for cosmetics, complete with mirror and cosmetic applicator or puff, emerged.

Before World War I, women smoking in public was universally frowned upon. In fact, an Italian composer, Ermanno Wolf-Ferrari, wrote an opera in 1909 called "Il Segreto di Susanna" (The Secret of Susanna). Susanna's secret was not that she was unfaithful to her husband, but rather that she smoked cigarettes without her husband's knowledge. After the war, when it became acceptable and fashionable for women to smoke and wear makeup publicly, accessories that accommodated both makeup and cigarettes emerged. Ronson, Elgin-American, Evans, Volupte, Richard Hudnut, and others made these compact/cigarette cases in a variety of combinations, designs, and materials. These cases not only conserved space in a purse but also allowed a woman to light a cigarette and at the same time have access to her compact.

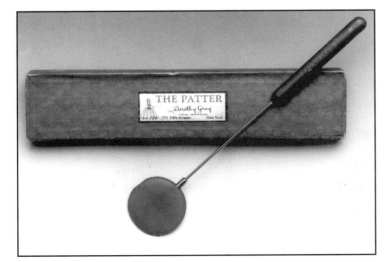

Figure 5 — Dorothy Gray "Patter" with description on lid: "A specially contrived instrument for applying stimulation to the facial muscles without irritating the skin"; original patter box, patented 1923.

The umbrella term "compact" is usually used to designate a portable cosmetic container. The nomenclature soon broadened for the various styles of cosmetic containers in addition to "compact":

COMPACT: A small portable make-up box *(Figure 6)* containing a mirror, puff, and powder with either screw-top, slip-cover, or piano-hinge lid.

Figure 6 — Elgin American satin and gilt hand-engraved compact with plastic beading around edge and center monogram, c. 1950s.

VANITY CASE: A powder compact *(Figure 7)* that also contains rouge and/or lipstick.

Figure 7 — Black plastic vanity case with rhinestone geometric design on lid; front opens to reveal mirror an powder and rouge compartments, back contains coin pocket; black carrying cord with lipstick concealed in tassel, c. 1920s.

VANITY BAG: A dainty evening bag *(Figure 8)*, usually made of mesh, incorporating a compact as an integral part of the bag.

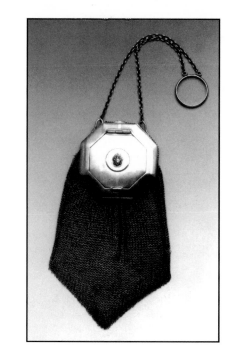

Figure 8 — Sterling silver hallmarked octagonal mesh vanity bag with goldtone interior and finger ring chain.

VANITY CLUTCH: A small clutch bag *(Figure 9)* with specific compartments for compact, lipstick, and rouge. These cases can be removed and replaced.

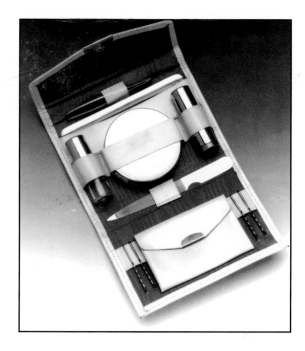

Figure 9 — Rumpp beige cowhide vanity clutch lined in red moiré; compartments for compact, lipstick, perfume, tweezers, nail file, bobby pins, and change purse.

VANITY PURSE: A leather, fabric, metal, or beaded purse that contains a vanity case as an integral part of the purse.

VANITY RETICULE: A bag with designated compartments for compact, lipstick, and rouge cases, which can be removed and replaced.

VANITY BOX: A fitted traveling cosmetic case.

VANITY POCHETTE: A drawstring powder pouch with a mirror located on the outside base.

VANITY POUCH: A compact with shallow powder pouch.

MINAUDIERE: A rigid metal box-shaped evening bag made of precious metals, some set with precious stones or gemstones, with compartments for powder, lipstick, rouge, mirror, coin holder, comb, cigarettes, and small watch or in any combination of the above.

NECESSAIRE: A smaller version of the minaudiere, cylindrical in shape made in precious metals, base metals, or synthetic materials.

CARRY ALL: A mass-produced, inexpensive version of the minaudiere.

PLI: A make-up tube containing powder at one end and a push puff at the other end.

POWDERETTE: A pencil-shaped powder container that releases powder when the tip is pressed, some times contains lipstick at other end.

PUFF KASE: A tubular powder container with sliding removable puff.

TANGO CHAIN: Lipstick or rouge container attached to a compact or vanity case by a short chain.

FLAP JACK: Slim, flat, round compact resembling a "flap-jack" pancake.

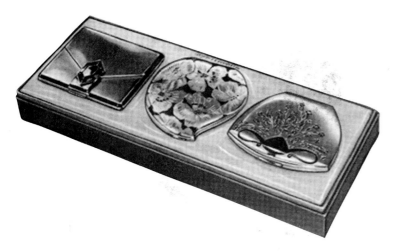

Figure 10 — Triple Compact Ensembles, Elgin American Catalog, 1949.

Portable containers for cosmetics enjoyed immense popularity and became an indispensable fashion accessory. Fashion setters dictated that a woman have a different compact or vanity case for each outfit in her wardrobe. The Elgin-American Co. promoted a popular boxed set of three different compacts, one for daytime, playtime, and nitetime *(Figure 10)*.

Compacts were made to suit every taste and in every price range. The price of compacts varied depending on the manufacturer and on the materials used. The prestigious jewelry houses such as Cartier, Hermes, Boucheron, Tiffany, Van Cleef and Arpels, Aspreys, Maubousson, Chaumet, Faberge, Black, Starr and Frost were often commissioned to manufacture exquisite compacts in precious metals many encrusted with precious gems. Some of these compacts were so elegantly made that they were considered a form of jewelry or dress accessory as well as a portable container for cosmetics *(Figure 11)*.

Figure 11 — Tiffany & Co. owl and pussycat compacts in textured 18-karat gold; cat with diamond, emerald, and sapphire eyes; owl with diamond and emerald eyes. Reproduced with permission from Tiffany & Co.

Cosmetic houses such as Coty, Evening in Paris, Tre-Jur, Charles of the Ritz, Colleen Moore, Dorothy Gray, Helena Rubinstein, Jonteel, Lady Esther, Richard Hudnut, Princess Pat, Ritz, Tangee, Woodbury, Yardley, and Elizabeth Arden jumped on the bandwagon and mass produced affordable compacts in many different styles. Even though these compacts were made of less expensive materials they could equal the beauty of the most expensive compacts. In fact Van Cleef & Arpels, the famous jewelry house, designed affordable compacts for Revlon. These compacts came complete with powder, either pressed or loose, which could be refilled when necessary.

The costume jewelry houses and fashion designers such as Trifari, Eisenberg Original, Coro, Robert, Ciner, Hobé, Hattie Carnegie, Schaparelli, Monet, Lilly Dache, Gloria Vanderbilt, to mention just a few, also featured a selection of beautiful, affordable compacts. These compacts are now eagerly sought after by both compact and costume jewelry collectors.

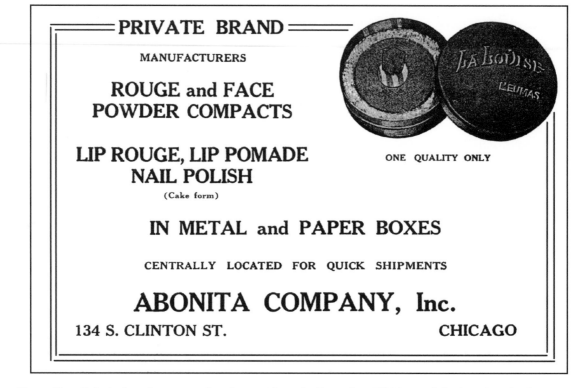

Figure 12 — Private-brand compact advertisement from the December 1920 issue of the American Perfumer.

Many cosmetic houses contracted metal and paper firms to manufacture empty compact cases to be filled with their own cosmetics *(Figure 12)*. The most popular compact manufacturers in the twentieth century were Elgin-American, Volupte, Evans, Whiting & Davis Co., and Stratton of London, Inc. The Elgin National Watch Co., Wadsworth Watch Case Co., and the Illinois Watch Co. were all subsidiaries of Elgin-American in Elgin, Illinois. Elgin-American manufactured compacts, compact/watches, and compact/music boxes, and was the forerunner in the manufacture of the affordable "carry-all."

The Volupte Co. in Elizabeth, New Jersey, was one of the most prolific manufacturers of ladies compacts during the late thirties and forties. Volupte manufactured compacts in every conceivable style, design, and shape.

The Evans Co. in North Attleboro, Massachusetts, manufactured cigarette cases, compacts, vanity pouches, mesh vanity bags, and vanity purses. They were reputed to be the largest manufacturer of vanity accessories.

Stratton of London, Inc. and Whiting and Davis Co. still manufacture compacts today. Stratton of London, Inc. has been manufacturing compacts, mirrors, and lipstick cases for almost fifty years. Today, the company produces several different styles of beautifully painted and decorated compacts, some with matching mirror, comb, and lipstick case.

The Whiting and Davis Co. in Plainville, Massachusetts, has been the leader in the manufacture of mesh bags and vanity bags since the latter part of the nineteenth century. The company's exquisite mesh evening bags and compacts are still being manufactured today.

It is unusual that an article that was essentially utilitarian be produced in such a diversity of materials, styles, shapes, decoration, motif, combinations, and with such painstaking detail. Cosmetic containers were executed in almost every natural and man-made material, from precious metals and gems to paper, damascene, enamel, gemstones, plastics, pewter, fabrics, lacquer, wood, mother-of-pearl, petit point, leather, butterfly wings, and papier-maché.

The kaleidoscope of shapes and motifs used in the manufacture of compacts reflected the mood and spirit of the times. Compacts came in a variety of shapes: square, rectangular, round, triangular, oblong, oval, crescent-shaped, fan-shaped, and hexagonal. Some were shaped as hand mirrors with a lipstick or perfume vial concealed in the handle, round balls, bells (to be used as holiday tree ornaments), hearts, walnuts or acorns, baskets, animals, and birds.

Tutankhamen's tomb, unearthed in 1922, set off

Figure 13 — Silver metal compact with Cleopatra's needle motif; hieroglyphics inscribed on obelisk.

Figure 14 — Volupté Gone With the Wind square silvertone compact; black enamel lids; front lid decorated with the name Scarlett O' Hara and painted enamel Southern scene; insert reads Gone With the Wind Selznick Int. Pictures M.G.M. Release"; interior mirror and powder well; 2⅞" x 2⅞".

an Egyptian revival, with the emergence of many souvenirs. One of them was a Cleopatra's needle compact with hieroglyphics inscribed on the obelisk *(Figure 13)*.

During World Wars I and II, compacts displayed patriotic motifs. Compacts made in the shape of the Army, Navy, and Marine hats were popular. The flag, inscribed messages from loved ones, and emblems of the Armed Forces were also part of the design on the patriotic compacts. The compact was one of the most popular gifts a serviceman could give to his loved ones waiting at home. President Jimmy Carter as an ensign at the Naval Academy in Annapolis gave Rosalynn Smith, his future wife, a beautiful compact for the holidays. The compact was engraved "ILYTG," a Carter family endearment which stands for "I love you the goodest."

Famous fictional and cartoon characters also appeared on the lids of the compacts. Charlie McCarthy, Mickey and Minnie Mouse, Alice in Wonderland, Popeye, and Little Orphan Annie were just a few. One of Candice Bergen's mementos of her ventriloquist father's most famous dummy is a Charlie McCarthy compact! The original movie press book for the epic film *Gone With the Wind* made in 1940, advertised Volupte's "Scarlet O'Hara compact – $2.00 at all department, novelty, etc. stores *(Figure 14)*. Three styles — Southern scenes — inspired by the picture."

There are ingenious three-inch Teddy Bear and Monkey compacts manufactured by Schuco in the

1920s that contain a lipstick tube which is revealed when the head is removed. Their centers open to reveal a powder compartment, puff, and mirror.

In 1940 Volupte manufactured several versions of the hand-shaped compact that were adorned with a black or white lace glove, red manicured nails, a faux engagement ring, a rhinestone tennis bracelet, an unadorned goldtone hand, and various combinations of these versions. In the 1940s Volupte also made several types of "Lucky Purses." Henriette, Kigu, and K & K made several basket-shaped and ball-shaped compacts, some of them are an eight ball, a ball with a pair of dice on the lid, a roulette ball, and floral baskets with handles.

Marhill, one of the leading manufacturers of mother-of-pearl compacts, made mother-of-pearl compacts in a checkerboard design *(Figure 15)*. Mondaine made beautifully tooled leather compacts that resembled miniature books. Exquisite handmade petit point compacts with labels attached to the inner mirror indicating the exact number of stitches per inch were made in Austria by Schildkraut in a variety of shapes and sizes. Although the floral petit point compacts are lovely, the scenic petit point compacts are less plentiful and are considered more desirable.

The designs and decorations of compacts became

Figure 15 — Marhill compact and matching pill box; lids decorated with mother-of-pearl enhanced with goldtone bands and raised painted flowers set with sparkle; 2¾" x 2½", pill box 1¼" square. $50.00–60.00.

more and more ingenious. Some were shaped as musical instruments — drums, guitars, pianos — or as miniature suitcases and cameras, such as the Kamra-Pak. Padlock shaped ones that open when the hasp is pressed *(Figure 16)*. A silver triple-tiered compact was manufactured in the 1920s that swivels open to reveal multiple make-up compartments. Some compacts in the 1930s had an interior windshield

Figure 16 — Zell goldtone compact designed to resemble padlock; picture locket under flower decorated lid; 2½" dia. $75.00–125.00.

wiper to clean the mirror. There were telephone dials made with a goldtone cartouche on the lid that could

Figure 17 — Volupté goldtone compact designed to resemble vanity table; collapsible cabriole legs (silvered metal shown open, goldtone shown closed.)

be personalized with your name or telephone number. And then there were miniature vanity tables and a grand piano with collapsible legs that fold flat on the underside of the compact *(Figure 17)*.

Also in demand were souvenir compacts of the states and foreign countries, scenic spots, historical areas, and commemorative events. College and fraternal organization emblems also appeared on the lids of compacts. Political compacts had candidates names, Wilkie, Stevenson, Eisenhower, or Roosevelt imprinted on the compacts in color combinations of red, white, and blue. The political compact, is another "crossover collectible" — for the compact collector and political memorabilia enthusiasts. Premium compacts were popular during the commercial age and manufacturers had their slogans, logos, or names imprinted on compacts. These premium compacts kept the manufacturer's product in the public eye.

Some of the most stylized, colorful, and desirable compacts were made during the heydays of Art Nouveau and Art Deco. The Art Nouveau style was free flowing with the emphasis on curved lines, natural motifs, and female faces. The Art Deco style was angular with the emphasis on geometric patterns and abstract designs.

These affordable compacts could be purchased over the counter at any novelty, five and dime, drug store, or department store. Women who did not live in an urban area could buy compacts through the mail-order catalogs of Sears Roebuck, Montgomery Ward, Baird-North, Pohlson, and the Boston Shepard Stores.

Many vintage compacts were multipurpose and were combined with other accessories. The combination and gadgetry compacts that include watches, music boxes, barometers, cigarette cases, lighters, canes, hatpins, cameras, mesh bags, and bracelets cross over into other fields of collecting and are very desirable and eagerly sought after by both the compact collector and the secondary accessory collector. Some compacts concealed manicure sets, sewing kits, ivory slates and slim pencils for jotting down notes, dance programs, combs, coin holders for "mad money," compartments for calling cards and pills. The Segal Key Company made a compact with a concealed blank key that slides out by pressing a button. Ladies' fans had a hidden compact on the base so that make-up could be applied discreetly. There were also

compacts that came complete with a flashlight *(Figure 18, 19)*, one version lit up the interior of the compact, another version had an exterior flashlight to help you find your way in a darkened theater. Compacts made for automobiles were incorporated in the visor, steering wheel, and on the gear-shift handle for easy access and an impromptu and hasty touchup *(Figure 20)*.

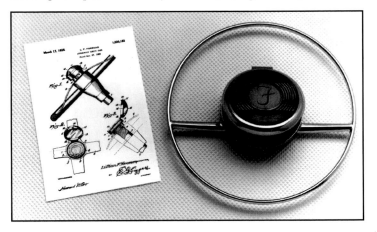

Figure 20 — Automobile steering-wheel compact; compact designed as the horn; silvered metal red and white letter F on compartment lid; interior has mirror and lights (patent shown not necessarily one for compact/wheel shown), 1920s.

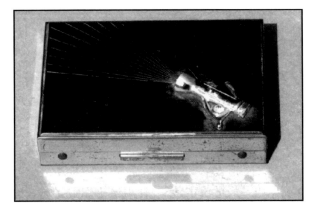

Figures 18 & 19 — Zell "First Nighter" goldtone compact/flashlight combination; brushed goldtone lid decorated with applied wishbone and flashlight; interior reveals mirror, powder compartment with puff, and removable flashlight; insert reads "Easily removed for regular flashlight use to illuminate locks, keyholes, programs, nameplates, maps, etc.; 3¼" x 2¼". $125.00–175.00. (Shown closed.) Photo below shown opened.

The vanity hatpin was popular in 1910 and was considered a dangerous and lethal weapon because of its long steel shank. The ladies compact cane was popular in France and was sold by prestigious jewelry houses such as Hermes, Paris, in the early 1900s.

During probation, many necessaires concealed whiskey flasks and some compacts could even be attached to a woman's garter underneath her dress. There was even a water-proof compact bracelet that could be worn on the beach and into the water. There were several versions of a ladies "pistol" compact, and there were compacts manufactured by Dunhill and by Evans that resemble cigarette lighters.

Today, the pendulum is swinging back to the time when ladies' compacts were all the rage. Present day compact manufacturers are producing lovely affordable compacts, some in limited editions, these compacts should also be considered by compact collectors.

Vintage compacts whose intricate and exacting workmanship, design, and technique made them works of art in themselves, some even worthy of a museum display are still the most desirable. For the vintage compact collector, they are miniature treasures with an elegant history, no less than small jewels of the past.

A Guide for the Collector

THREE LITTLE WORDS

Three terms you should be familiar with when discussing antiques or collectibles are nomenclature, provenance, and attribution.

NOMENCLATURE is the defining word for an article within a category. For example, in the overall category of jewelry, the nomenclature for a specific item of jewelry would be ring, bracelet, brooch, pendant, etc.

PROVENANCE is the history or background of an article. Authenticated proof of the manufacturer, country of origin, date of manufacture, and a receipt showing date and place of purchase would be evidence of provenance. Having the original presentation box or pouch enhances the provenance. Knowing the provenance of an article allows you to command a greater price.

ATTRIBUTION denotes the previous owner of an item, either a family, museum, gallery, or corporation. An item has greater value if a famous — or infamous — person previously owned the object. Items belonging to Andy Warhol and the Duchess of Windsor were recently sold at auctions far above the actual value of the items simply because of their attribution. The attribution of an article is usually included in its provenance.

THE FAMOUS COTY POWDER PUFF

The Coty trademark No. 158,435 was registered in France on September 15, 1914, by Francois Joseph de Spoturno Coty. This trademark is for the Airspun Face Powder and Compact container that is covered with white and gold powder puffs on an orange background. Rene Lalique, the famous French glassmaker, and Leon Bakst, the renowned designer of stage settings and costumes for the Ballet Russe, collaborated on this creation. The powder puff trademark has been used since 1914 on Coty's cosmetic products.

Figure 21 — Coty powder and powder-compact advertisement from a 1926 issue of Theatre Magazine.

WHITING & DAVIS COMPANY MESH BAGS

The Whiting & Davis Co. originally known as Wade Davis, was founded in 1876 in Plainville, Massachussets, and is the oldest ongoing handbag manufacturer in North America. The vanity bags created by Whiting & Davis between 1896 – 1935 have become sought after collectors' items because of their intricate craftsmanship, beautiful colors, and delicate patterns.

The mesh bags were handcrafted from 1892 to 1912 when the first automatic mesh machine was made. Two popular types of mesh ring designs that Whiting & Davis manufactured were the star-shaped mesh (1900 – 1915) and the tiny mesh (1910 – 1925) *(Figure 22)*. Metal tags with the familiar Whiting & Davis Co. trademark were attached to the mesh bags from 1908 until 1925. After 1926 the Whiting & Davis trademark was imprinted on the frame of the mesh bag.

Figure 22 — Whiting & Davis "Elsa" mesh vanity bag with compartments for powder, rouge, and comb (multicolored mesh shown closed, soldered baby mesh shown open).

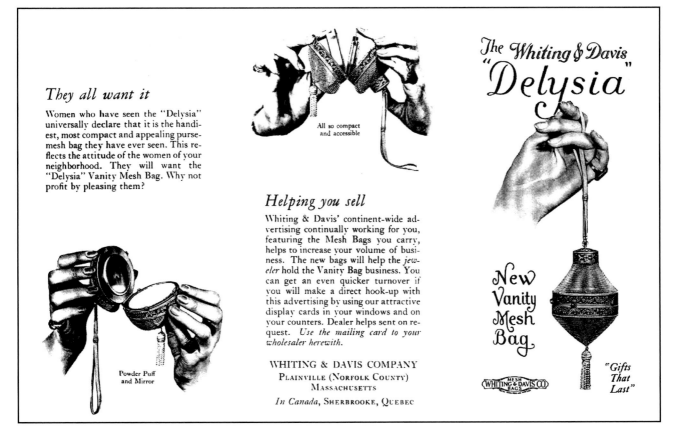

Figures 23 & 24 — The Whiting & Davis "Delysia" mesh vanity bag advertisement, c. 1920s.
Reproduced with permission of the Whiting & Davis Co.

A VANITY BRACELET COMPACT

On November 23, l926, Elijah L. Johnson was granted a patent for a wrist cosmetic holder #1,607,985 *(Figure 25)*. His justification for the need of such a product is as follows:

"Modern usage of cosmetics by the feminine sex demands that certain necessary cosmetics be carried on the person so that they may be conveniently and promptly applied whenever the situation demands it. Cosmetics are usually kept in a vanity case, but places are often frequented by the feminine sex where cases cannot be conveniently carried. One example of this is in a ballroom where a vanity case would be very much in the way. Another example of its utilities is automobile driving where a lady driver's attention is detracted from her driving while searching for cosmetics in a vanity case. With my invention the cosmetics are handy and may be readily applied with little distraction and little danger of accidents which might occur from inattention to driving. It is the object of this invention to provide a cosmetic holder which is adapted to be secured to the wrist. The cosmetic holder of my invention is in the form of a bracelet which will be very convenient for use and will in no manner interfere with a person's activity. It is quite essential to a lady's appearance and particularly to her self-satisfaction that she be able to inspect her countenance at various intervals. A lady, however, is often constrained from such an inspection, since considerable attention might be attracted by opening a vanity case and she might suffer considerable embarrassment. It is another object of my invention to provide a cosmetic holder which is adapted to be secured to the wrist and which has a mirror, by means of which a person's appearance may be very readily inspected without attracting attention."

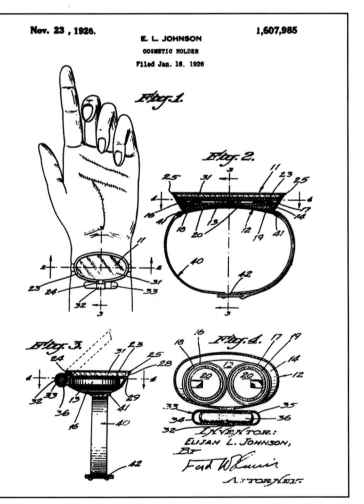

Figure 25— Wrist Cosmetic Holder Patent.

CHATELAINES, CHATELETTES, AND COACH CHATELAINES

In medieval times when the Crusaders were away fighting the wars they entrusted the keys to the many rooms in their castle to their ladies. The ladies carried the keys on chains attached to their belts and became known as chatelaines. Eventually the name chatelaine became associated with an article of jewelry rather than a person.

Chatelaines were popular during the Victorian era as a decorative, utilitarian piece of jewelry. They were made in a variety of shapes, materials, and sizes and consisted of several chains suspended from a hook or clasp that was attached to the belt *(Figure 26)*. The vanity chatelaine usually had a powder compact, lipstick holder, writing slate, slim pencil, coin holder, vinaigrette, or perfume container suspended from these chains.

Chatelettes are chatelaines with shorter and fewer chains *(Figure 26)*.

Coach chatelaines were made with hooks that could be hung inside a coach so the ladies could avail themselves of this portable vanity while they were traveling.

Figure 26 — 1 Antiqued, silvered filigreed coach-chatelette with compact, perfume bottle, and swivel mirror suspended from chain filigree hook, Continental, 19th century.
2 Fluted German silver chatelaine with compact, coin holder, memo book, locket/pin container, and stamp holder.
3 Georg Jensen sterling silver mini chatelette with heart-shaped compact; lipstick container and pin carrier decorated with raised silver orchid.

SALVADOR DALI'S "BIRD-IN HAND" COMPACT

Salvadore Dali, the Spanish surrealist painter, sculptor, and illustrator (May 11, 1904 – January 23, 1989), was born in Figueras, Catalonia, Spain, and studied in Barcelona and Madrid. He became known as the "enfant terrible" of surrealism, as well as its best-known exponent. Since 1932 Dali's works have been shown throughout Europe, the United States, and the Orient.

Dali designed many commercial works of art as well in the 1940s and 1950s. In 1950 he was commissioned to design a compact for Elgin American, which became known as the "Bird-In-Hand" compact.

Figure 28 — Elgin American Dali "Bird-in-Hand" compact opened to reveal lipstick holder, powder, and pillbox compartments.

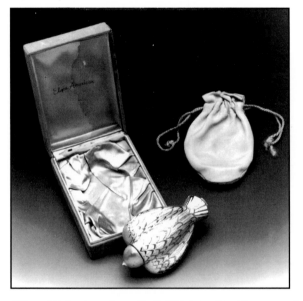

Figure 27 — Elgin American Dali "Bird-in-Hand" compact with turquoise drawstring carrying case and turquoise suede fitted presentation box.

The "Bird-In-Hand" compact is 4½" x 2½" with ruby red eyes and was manufactured in three different finishes — satin bronze, silver, and sterling silver — with a 14k gold overlay effect on the wings. The compact contains a powder compartment, a pillbox, and a lipstick. The bird's head holds the slide-out lipstick and the body contains the powder box, which is revealed when the wings are spread apart *(Figure 28)*. The tailpiece conceals the pillbox. Dali's signature appears on the underside of the bird's head *(Figure 29)*. The compact comes with a turquoise drawstring carrying case and a suede turquoise Elgin American fitted hinged presentation box *(Figure 27)*.

The minimum prices for the "Bird-in-Hand" compact were listed in Elgin American's 1952 – 53 catalog:
Satin bronze finish . Dealer $7.50 . . . . Retail $15.00
Silver finish . . . . Dealer $12.50 . . . Retail $25.00
Sterling silver . . . . . Dealer $50.00 . . . Retail $100.00

Figure 29 — Elgin American Dali "Bird-in-Hand" compact; underside reveals Dali signature.

There has always been a great demand for the works of Salvadore Dali. The Dali "Bird-In-Hand" compact is very desirable because of its beauty, rarity, and uniqueness. It is sought after by compact collectors, collectors of Dali's works, objects d'art, and figural items.

A "Bird-in-Hand" compact is on display in the Salvador Dali Museum, 1000 3rd Avenue South, St. Petersburg, FL 33701.

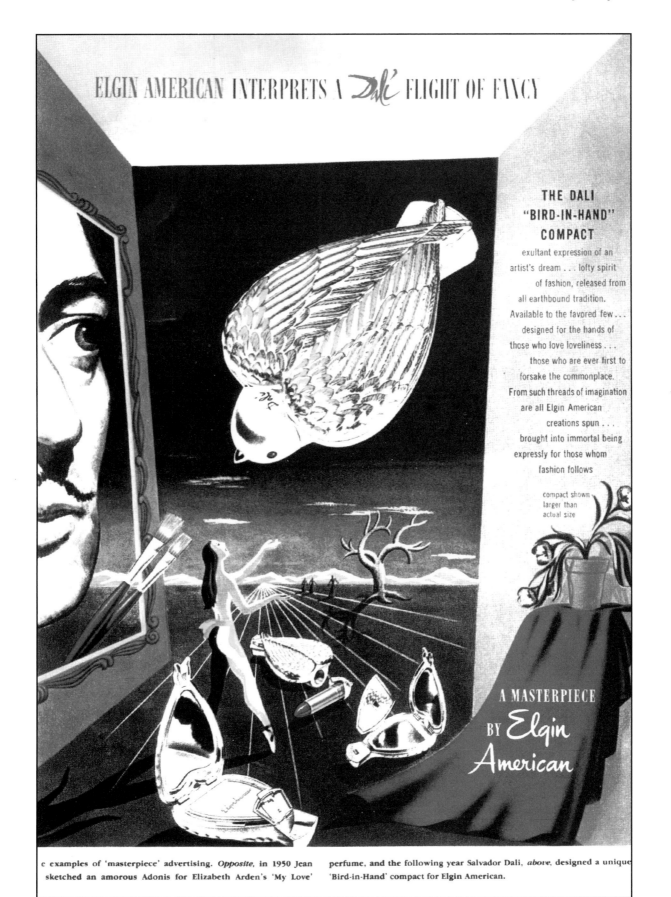

ELGIN AMERICAN INTERPRETS A *Dali* FLIGHT OF FANCY

THE DALI
"BIRD-IN-HAND"
COMPACT

exultant expression of an
artist's dream . . . lofty spirit
of fashion, released from
all earthbound tradition.
Available to the favored few . . .
designed for the hands of
those who love loveliness . . .
those who are ever first to
forsake the commonplace.
From such threads of imagination
are all Elgin American
creations spun . . .
brought into immortal being
expressly for those whom
fashion follows

compact shown
larger than
actual size

A MASTERPIECE
BY *Elgin American*

c examples of 'masterpiece' advertising. *Opposite*, in 1950 Jean
sketched an amorous Adonis for Elizabeth Arden's 'My Love'

perfume, and the following year Salvador Dali, *above*, designed a unique
'Bird-in-Hand' compact for Elgin American.

Vogue ad for "Bird-In-Hand" compact, 1951.

25

MINAUDIÈRES, CARRYALLS, AND NECESSAIRES

In the 1930s women customarily wore evening gowns to dinner parties and the theater. Since women often traveled in the same social circles, the well-dressed woman needed several different gowns with matching bags to wear to these functions. To resolve the problem of changing evening bags to match each costume, Van Cleef & Arpels invented the minaudière *(Figures 30 & 31)*, the one evening bag that could harmonize and complement each dress. The minaudiere is a rigid metal box-shaped evening bag, really a super compact with specific compartments for cosmetic and personal necessities — powder, lipstick, coins, a watch, cigarettes, and comb. It was Estelle Arpels, co-founder with her husband Alfred Cleef of Van Cleef and Arpels, who inspired the name for the firm's jeweled evening bags. Her brothers, Julien, Charles, and Louis, who were also partners, used to say that no one could *minauder*, or charm, in society as their sister Estelle. Thus, the name minaudière. The original minaudieres were sold at fashionable, expensive jewelry houses. They were usually made of gold or silver and sometimes encrusted with precious gems.

The carryall *(Figures 30 & 31)*, an affordable mass-produced version of the minaudière, was manufactured in a variety of beautiful and inexpensive finishes by many popular compact manufacturers.

The Necessaire *(Figures 30 & 31)* is a cylindrical or bolster shaped, smaller version of the minaudière with fewer compartments, made in either precious metals or inexpensive finishes.

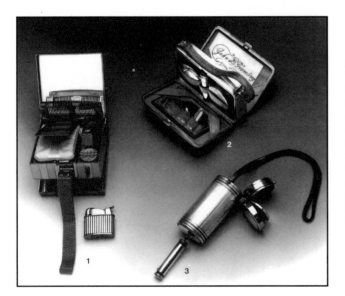

Figure 30 — 1 Evans goldtone swirl-design carryall with mesh wrist chain; dual openings (one side reveals mirror and compartments for powder, lipstick, coins, and comb; the other side has compartments for cigarettes and lighter), c. 1940–50s.
2 Silver minaudière engraved with a lighthouse and sailboat on one side and the monogrammed letter G on the reverse, gray grosgrain interior, dual openings (one with mirror, fitted sleeves with powder, rouge, and lipstick containers; the other with fitted sleeves for calling cards, perfume container, and memo case with slim pencil), probably England, late 19th century.
3 Webster Company sterling silver cylindrical necessaire with lipstick suspended from bottom and gilded interior; mirror separates powder and rouge compartments; second opening reveals cigarette, flask, or money compartment, c. 1920–30s.

Figure 31 — Carryall, minaudière, and necessaire in Figure 30 shown closed.

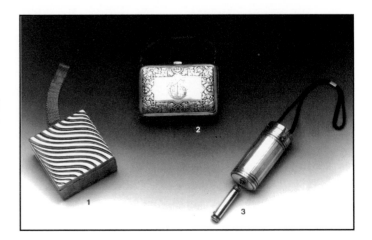

TIPS FROM A COMPACT COLLECTOR

Compacts are found in many different places. Flea markets, tag, and garage sales usually have the best prices but may be time consuming. The best source is still either an antique shop or antique show if you are looking for a specific collectible. The antique dealers have already scouted the garage sales and flea markets and will therefore save you time. Compacts may also be found in thrift stores, vintage clothing stores, and consignments shops. Quality vintage compacts may now be found at many auction houses as well, and many antique papers advertise compacts for sale.

When purchasing a compact by mail, always inquire as to the compact's condition, age, and request a complete description including price. Find out whether you may return the compact if you are not satisfied.

Always request a receipt when making a purchase. The receipt should describe the compact in as much detail as possible. The price, condition, composition, and name and address or phone number of vendor should also be included.

When traveling to different parts of the country, "let your fingers do the walking" check the Antique Section in the Yellow Pages of the local telephone directory for antique shops and the local paper's daily-event section for flea markets, tag sales, and street fairs.

Another source is *Powder Puff* the International Compact Collectors Chronicle, P.O. Box #40 Lynbrook, NY 11563. The newsletter features a Seekers, Sellers, and Swappers column which is offered free to members.

If a compact comes in the original box or pouch, do not destroy or discard it. The value of the compact is increased if it has its original presentation box.

Original parts of a collectible should always be left intact. Missing, broken, or torn parts such as colored stones, tassels, mirrors, or carrying cords may be replaced with parts that will adhere to and not alter the style or original design. Check to see whether there has been a "marriage" between two compacts — one part of a compact attached or inserted in a compact of like design. Lipsticks are sometimes removed from an inexpensive compact and inserted in a more expensive compact. A reputable dealer will tell you if this has been done.

Enameled compacts purchased for investment purposes should be in mint condition. Minor flaws in a compact purchased for your collection and not for resale may be repaired. Repairing chipped or scratched enamels may be costly and decrease the value of the compact.

Only mirrors that are broken should be removed and replaced in a vintage compact. I prefer not to replace a mirror that is discolored, flawed, or in need of resilvering. The original mirror always enhances the value of the compact.

It is adviseable to remove loose powder from your compact before adding it to your collection. Loose powder will inadvertendly spill when the compact is opened. Solid powder, rouge, and lipstick should never be used but may be left in the compact.

Never apply a sticker directly to the surface of a compact. The acids from the glue may discolor or irreparably damage the finish, especially an enamel finish. Apply a price or identification sticker to the metal or mirror inside the compact or on a string-tag attached to the compact.

Parts of a vintage compact may sometimes be very fragile and should be handled as little as possible. The best way to display, share, and enjoy your collection is in a glass enclosed cabinet or case. Compacts may be displayed in a revolving lighted curio cabinet or in a showcase such as those used to display watches. Another way to display compacts is in a viewing table that can also serve as a coffee or cocktail table, or in a 3" to 5" deep shadow box. The compacts can be suspended from hooks or placed on shelves inside the framed box. Several shadow boxes mounted on the wall create an interesting and unusual wall arrangement.

Keep a running inventory of your collection. List the items on index cards and keep them in a file box. Note the date, price, and place of purchase and the name of the seller. Also include any information on the history, previous owner, or background that you can obtain from the seller. Include a full description including size, finish, and condition, and a photograph of the compact.

Photograph or videotape your collection so that you will have a complete and accurate record of your collection for insurance purposes. Don't forget to keep adding pictures as your collection grows. Keep the photos in a safe place in your home and a duplicate set in a friend's home or in a safety deposit box.

Always use a certified appraiser when you have your collection appraised. Your local Society of Appraiser Referral Services will supply you with information about an appraisal specialist in your area. An appraisal should be typewritten, dated, and signed; and contain a complete and accurate description of the collection; (not a "laundry list" type that uses description such as "round," "small," "red," "compact," etc.). It is very important that your appraisal be current. If you should sustain a loss, your insurance company will pay only the latest amount listed by the appraiser.

NEWSWORTHY COMPACTS

Classic vintage and contemporary compacts are making the news. On June 16, 1988, Christie's East Auction House featured a collection of compacts dating from the 1920s and 1930s. The auction catalog described them as "Designed for both function and flash, no bigger than a lady's palm, but large enough for the essentials: a powder puff, loose or pressed powder, and a mirror. Many ingeniously incorporate places for rouge and lipstick. Overall they display a colorful sampling of design applied to the everyday, a glimpse of period style." They were offered in lots of five with the estimated catalog price for each lot $200.00 – $300.00. Souvenir, silver, enameled, tango-chain, plastic, and combination vanities were just a few of the styles offered. Some of the compact manufacturers represented were Elgin, Volupté, Girey, Coty, Mondaine, Houbigant, Evans, La Mode, Yardley, and Richard Hudnut.

A vintage "Charlie McCarthy" compact, manufactured by Evans, sold in 1988 for $400.00 at the "Screen Smart Set" auction. The compact was donated by Mrs. Edgar Bergen, widow of the renowned ventriloquist and voice of Charlie McCarthy. The proceeds from the auction were donated to the Motion Picture Actors' Home.

Nancy Reagan, wife of then-President Reagan, received a Lifetime Achievement Award "for the outstanding contributions she has made to American fashion" from The Council of Fashion Designers of America. This item was reported in the Daily News section of the November 18, 1988, *Chicago Tribune*. The accompanying photograph showed the fashionable Mrs. Reagan using a compact mirror to adjust her makeup.

Raisa Gorbachev and other high-powered guests were invited by Estee Lauder to visit the cosmetic firm in December 1988. The guests received "golden" compacts from Estee Lauder. One of the guests, newswoman Barbara Walters, showed her television audience the compact she received, the "Golden Alligator" compact.

The August 1988 issue of the *Kiplinger Magazine Changing Times* featured "What to Do with a Little Bit of Money" (how to invest $1,000.00 or less), with sensible suggestions that range from savings bonds to undiscovered collectibles. Highlighted is a column on the new collectible — vintage compacts — entitled "Take A Powder." Many collectible vintage compacts were described.

Ten thousand of Andy Warhol's favorite treasures were auctioned off in the spring of 1988 at Sotheby's. Due to the Warhol provenance, the prices averaged about twice the amount that was estimated by Sotheby's. The auction began with the collectibles. There were twenty-four compacts sold singly or along with other items for a total of more than $53,000.00.

Tiffany & Co., Cartier, Van Cleef & Arpels, Boucheron, and Jean Fouquet were some of the prestigious jewelry houses represented. Shagreen, 14 karat, 18 karat, silver, gilt metal, enameled, Art Deco, Art Nouveau, combination compacts, and a silver chatelaine hung with a compact were among the offerings. The highest price was $9,075.00 for a rectangular Jean Fouquet black-and-coral enameled silver vanity case. The lipstick separates two pop-up panels which open to reveal two mirrored cosmetic compartments, c. 1925, France. *The Maine Antique Digest*, June 1988, reported that Paloma Picasso, jewelry designer for Tiffany & Co. bought one lot which consisted of two compacts and one lipstick case, silver and silver gilt with tiny cabochon rubies by Boucheron, Paris, c. 1940 for $1,650.00.

In the July 4, 1993, *New York Times* and in *Vogue*, August 1993, there are ads for "new" vintage compacts. The *New York Times*, "Period Pieces" description "Recalling the glamour of Bacall, Hayworth, Davis...vintage compacts from the 40s and 50s, all imported from England sold at Saks Fifth Avenue- $60.00 – $200.00." *Vogue* describes these compacts as "Collectible Compacts" these 1930s, 1940s, and 1950s compacts sold at Barney's, New York. *Vogue* further states that "...this array of miniature masterpieces were mass-produced for a dressed up generation...these beautiful boxes today are one-of-a-kind, historical collector's items. Lively Art Deco patterns reflect the jazzy spirit of the 1930s and the rare Flying Saucer compact, dated from the late 1950s when UFO spotting became an international craze." (The compacts described are Kigu compacts.)

Antique Week's July 5, 1993, issue had an article written by Mildred Jailer-Chamberlain on celebrity jewelry. In the article she reports that 15 glittering gold objects that once belonged to movie luminaries and other famed personages were purchased from a private California collector by New York antique jewelry dealer Joan Grober. One of these pieces a stunning 14 karat gold compact initialed on the front in amethysts and engraved on the the back "To Ann from George 1940" price, $3,750.00 The compact belonged to Ann Sheridan, rumored to have had a romance with George Raft. Included in the collection were three 18 karat gold Cartier compacts that belonged to singer Kate Smith. These compacts ranged in price from $6,500.00 to $9,500.00.

Beauty Fashion, May 1993 reports a new concept in compacts. The name of the compact is "Powderific." The unique design allows powder to be filled from the bottom of the compact. The powder is released when the puff is pressed on a disc-like center, the disc automatically seals itself when the pressure is released, therfore no powder spillage. (Similiar to the Evans Tap Sift Pat # 1624874 c. 1927.)

Town & Country April 1994 Jewelry Section Compact Dreams by Suzanne Biallot. "A Quintessential Feminine Luxury is Back in Style and out in Public." European women have for centuries been primping publically and use the mirror of their compact to scan the room flirtatiously, in contrast, the American and British women have been taught to be discreet when applying make-up. Peter Martino, jeweler says "Women pared down so much over the past twenty years because of disposable fashion and feminism. But today women are so confident, they can afford to enjoy some of the old symbols of feminity." Ms. Biallot further writes that the cosmetic industry is responsible for the revival of fashionable ladies' compacts. She closes by saying "In the current era of quiet luxuries, nothing could be more appropriate than a precious object that is meant to be flaunted discreetly." Accompanying this article are photos of eight gold and silver compacts, many set with precious stones. The compacts are available from these prestigious jewelry houses, Fred Leighton, NYC; Jewelers Design, Inc., NYC; Tiffany & Co., NYC; Verdura, NYC; and Cartier, Inc., NYC.

Beauty Fashion, October 1993. "Yardley's cosmetics range has got a new face; packaging and presentation have been updated to suit the demands of today's woman. Their compacts are in tactile, rounded shapes and feature push-button closures which make them comfortable to use. Quality puffs and brushes contribute to the up-grading."

Self, March 1994 Global Beauty, The Powder and the Glory: Women and their Compacts by Laurie Drake quotes Janis Altman, psychotherapist specializing in women's issues, "When a woman looks in the mirror it's her way of getting in touch with her self-esteem...". Expensive and gorgeous compacts make you feel special and regardless of whether the compact is an antique, an objet d'art, a status compact, or a disposable plastic compact, the compact we choose is a mirror of our personal style. Here are her comments about the seven compacts that accompany the article. "1. Yves Saint Laurent's faux-jeweled compact is for romantics. 2. The woman who carries Estee Lauder's All-Day, All-Night Compact appreciates elegance and simplicity. 3. For art lovers: sculptor Robert Lee Morris' version for Elizabeth Arden. 4. Chanel is the compact of choice among chic urbanites. 5. Nostalgia buffs will go for this antique compact (blue enamel). 6. Because it's black, Princess Marcella Borghese's case might help those climbing the corporate ladder. 7. No-nonsense nose powderers prefer Cover Girl's Compact."

The *New York Times*, Sunday, April 3, 1994, Cartier Hunts its Own Eggs and Other Old Treasures by Rita Reif. An exhibition "Made by Cartier," shown at Cartier, Fifth Avenue, NY, April 1944. Eighty objects created between 1860 and 1960 were displayed in the show. All of these Cartier objects: compacts, clocks, lighters, boxes, cuff links, cigarette cases, and picture frames are part of the corporate collection. They have been collected over the last decade. The more interesting pieces at the exhibit were crafted between 1910 to 1940. Nearly 80% of these bibelots were exhibited for the first time at Cartier's, NY. After World War II Cartier featured the sunburst motif in these precious articles, compacts, lipstick cases, lighters, and cigarette cases. Every few years they altered this design slightly.

In the February 22, 1994, issue of *Woman's Day*, an excellent article "The New Collectibles: Powder Compacts" by Sheryl Weinstein appears. It features six color photos of compacts and their prices. The text, a brief, interesting overview of compact collecting.

Kovels, April 1993 issue, "Hotline" reports that Le Teint Ricci, a new cosmetic line by Nina Ricci, includes a lipstick case and powder compact designed by two avant-garde French artists. Kovels states that these "organic molded plastic forms in sensual pastels are definitely tomorrow's collectibles."

Vogue, December 1993 "Beauty Clips" by Elizabeth Brous describes purse "jewelry" which is meant to be seen. Lancome's classic tasseled compact and Estee Lauder's new Golden Swirl compact are both mentioned. De rigueur in the forties and fifties were

refillable powder compacts and lipstick cases which make good ecological sense. Powder refills are available from Estee Lauder and Guerlain has lipstick refills.

Vogue, Feb. 1994 "Beauty Clips" by Shirley Lord discusses kohl. Kohl rims the eyes and is the one cosmetic that's meant to be worn smudged. Nina Ricci, Lancome, Princess Marcella Borghese, Elizabeth Arden, and Clarin all have variations of the kohl pen. Several different shades of kohl are available.

The Sunday edition of the *Daily News*, August 14, 1994, has an article "Ancient Egypt's Afterlife at the Met" by Mila Andre. It refers to the Metropolitan Museum of Art (Fifth Ave and 82nd St. New York, NY) exhibit "Pharoh's Gifts: Stone Vessels From Ancient Egypt." One of the vessels included, a cosmetic container of the highest workmanship that dates from approximately 3200 B.C. to 465 B.C. All of the various vessels are a lesson in art and history and are housed in the Lila Acheson Wallace Galleries of Egyptian Art at the Museum. They survived all these years because they were made of stone (a material for eternity).

In *The Echoes Report*, June 1994, there is an article on compacts written by Cynthia Barta. The article "In the Palm of Your Hand, A Short History of Cosmetic Use and Compacts in the 20th Century" includes descriptions of compacts and tips for compact collectors.

In the London newspaper *Daily Mail*, Thursday, July 7, 1994, there is an article "Compact and Bijou" written by Diana Hutchinson. She writes that for nearly 100 years the powder compact was a treasured beauty aid, handcrafted and decorated — often with jewels — to last a lifetime. This ended with the arrival of the disposable plastic compact. In the fifties the compact became important again. Even the Queen was seen using one in public. Presently the traditional vintage compact is a collector's item.

The July 1994 issue of *Antiques and Collecting Magazine* contains an article entitled "Compacts, Objects of Beauty" by Frances Johnson. She states that for decades during the first part of the present century the only acceptable gifts a young man could give his girlfriend were flowers, candy, perfume, or a compact. The compacts being the most acceptable of these gifts. She feels that this probably accounts for the great variety of vintage compacts today.

Beauty Fashion, February 1994, Marc Rosen column "On Design" features objects d'heart. Presently glamorous objects are plentiful in the gift area of the metal compact. Mentioned is the fact that Boucheron, who has made jewelry for over 135 years, produced an exquisite refillable oval compact to match its cabochon ring-shaped perfume bottle. Beautiful compacts have become the new status symbol. Women use them publicly at the theater or restaurant. Estee Lauder and Yves St. Laurent continue to create beautiful new compacts every season.

Wendy Schmid of *Vogue* Magazine, August 1994, has an excellent article "Making Up" in the Beauty Bets section. Pictured are seven beautiful compacts which accompany the article. Her article gives a brief overview of the evolution of the compact since Cleopatra's time. She covers the time when using a compact publically was unacceptable. Presently, she says "Reflecting a return to makeup and all its decorative effects, stylish, meant-to-be-seen compacts are coming out of hiding and giving an age-old beauty ritual fresh allure." With the return of glamour in fashion, women are showing their compacts off more than ever. They are like pieces of jewelry. Cartier has been making compacts since the 1890s and Elizabeth Arden commissioned jewelry designer Robert Lee Morris to create one. Morris says of the beautiful compacts that he designs, "It's a luxurious little toy."

Bevis Hillier's enlightening article, "Powder Compacts On the Thrill of the Chase for the Pressed Powder Case" appeared in the October, 1994 issue of *Country Living*, England. The article is both enjoyable and informative. The article discusses the Compact Collectors Club formation, *Powder Puff* and much more. Excerpts from *Powder Puff* such as Hilda Klyde's recommendations for compact hunting in London and Ruth Wacker's aquisitions in the Seattle Vintage Fashion Show were mentioned. Several photos of compacts accompany this delightful article.

"Open and Shut Cases, The Wonderful World of Ladies' Compacts," an article written by the author of *Ladies' Compacts* and of *Vanity Bags* appears in the Winter 1994/95 issue of *American Country Collectibles*. The history, manufacturers, styles, shapes, composition, and rarity of compacts is discussed in this article. In addition, there are also tips on collecting and on the care and repairing of compacts. Fifteen beautiful photographs of compacts in full color accompany this article.

Mary Gottschalk's delightful, informative article, "Compact Packages" appeared in the Living section of the the *San Jose Mercury News*, December 18, 1994. She quotes Mona Monaghan, vice president of marketing for Estee Lauder, "Using one [compact] is more than simply a matter of putting your best face forward. It's a beauty ritual." Monaghan also says that compacts are "a magical piece of our business and the piece we get the most amount of letters on. They all have stories. This is not an area where the company makes a lot of profit, we do it to give customers elegance, style and additive joy to their daily lives." In addition, there are photos of several new compacts in full color.

VANITY REFLECTIONS

INFLATED FLATO'S

Paul Flato's compacts made in the 40s and 50s are pretty, whimsical, and eagerly sought after by compact collectors. Flato's compacts, either goldtone or silvertone, are decorated with an applied whimisical object usually set with beautiful colored stones. The majority of Flato's compacts also come with a matching lipstick. The matching lipstick has a miniature replica of the theme that decorates the front lid applied to the end of the tube. The set comes complete with a fitted case that holds the compact and lipstick. The cases come in a variety of colors and materials; satin, moire, grosgrain, leather. Flato patented many of his compact designs and also had a patent for the fitted slip case: "Compact and Lipstick Receptacle" Des. 154,670, filed on Feb. 28, 1948 *(Figure 32)*. These vintage compacts were affordable, and could be found priced from $40.00 to $140.00 depending on whether they had original box, puff, lipstick, and case. Now they are going for $300.00 and $400.00 (complete). One of the reasons could possibly be that there have been several articles on jewelry written recently that mention Paul Flato prominently. On October 21, 1991, Christie's American Jewelry Auction catalog had bibliographies on the foremost American jewelers. Paul Flato was one of the jewelers included. Perhaps this write-up, in addition to several other articles on Flato, have made the public again aware of Paul Flato.

Below, reprinted with permission, from Christie's American Jewelry, October 21, 1992, auction catalog is Paul Flato's biography written by Janet Zapatta.

PAUL FLATO

"Paul Flato was born in 1900 in Flatonia, Texas, amid the expectation of a new century, and, in three decades, would become one of the foremost American jewelry designers. Flato's introduction into the jewelry field started in the role of salesman for Edmond E. Frisch. In the late 1920s, he opened his own shop at 1 East Fifty-Seventy Street in New York City, several years before Tiffany & Co. reclocated to their current address just across the street. His design-oriented style, often bordering on the humorous, reached its peak in the 1930s when all the fashionable people of New York gathered at his salon. Adolph Kleaty, George Headley, and Fulco di Verdura were among his designers. Two prominent clients, Mrs. James V. Forrestal and Millicent Rogers Balcom were responsible for his whimsical creations such as the "wiggly clips" and the "puffy heart" series.

In 1937, Flato opened a branch in Beverly Hills, at 8657 Sunset Boulevard, with Fulco di Verdura in charge. He is credited with designing the jewelry Katherine Hepburn wore in *The Philadelphia Story*. This branch remained open for only two years, frequented by such luminaries as Greta Garbo, Joan Crawford, Merle Oberon, and Marlene Dietrich. Later in life, Flato left this country, establishing a shop in Mexico City in the fashionable Zona Rosa district."

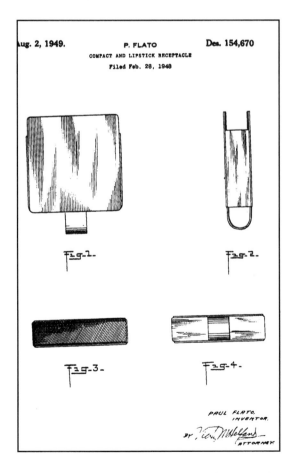

Figure 32 — Paul Flato's Compact and Lipstick Receptacle Patent.

On Tuesday, December 6, 1994, Christie's, NY, had another important jewels auction. Approximately 2,000 original full-color drawings by Paul Flato, one of America's great jewelers was offered *(Figures 34, 35, 36)*. The artwork was in an attic for almost three decades and was sold in group lots. Flato covered every aspect of jewelry design, puffy hearts, animals, telephones, and body parts. In the early 1940s Flato closed his business. In Christie's December 6, 1994, auction, in addition to the drawings, one actual piece of Flato jewelry — a gold telephone dial compact was offered *(Figure 33)*.

AMUSING RETRO GOLD TELEPHONE DIAL COMPACT

Of circular outline in 14K gold, the lid designed as a rotary dial, the finger holes engraved and enameled with the letters "I LOVE YOU" opening to reveal a mirror, in a suede slipcase, circa 1940. Signed by Flato. Estimated auction price $1,500.00 – $2,000.00 — actual price realized was $4,830.00 plus tax.

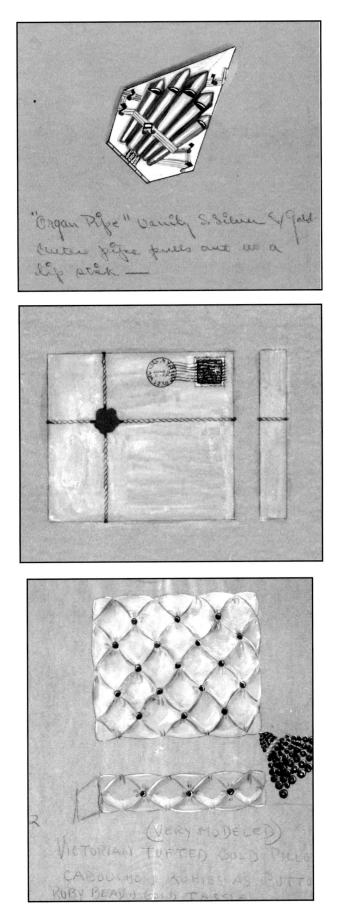

Figures 34, 35, & 36 — Paul Flato's original drawings of ladies' vanities. Photographs reproduced with permission from Christie's, N.Y.

Figure 33 — Paul Flato's 14K gold telephone dial compact. Photograph reproduced with permission from Christie's, NY.

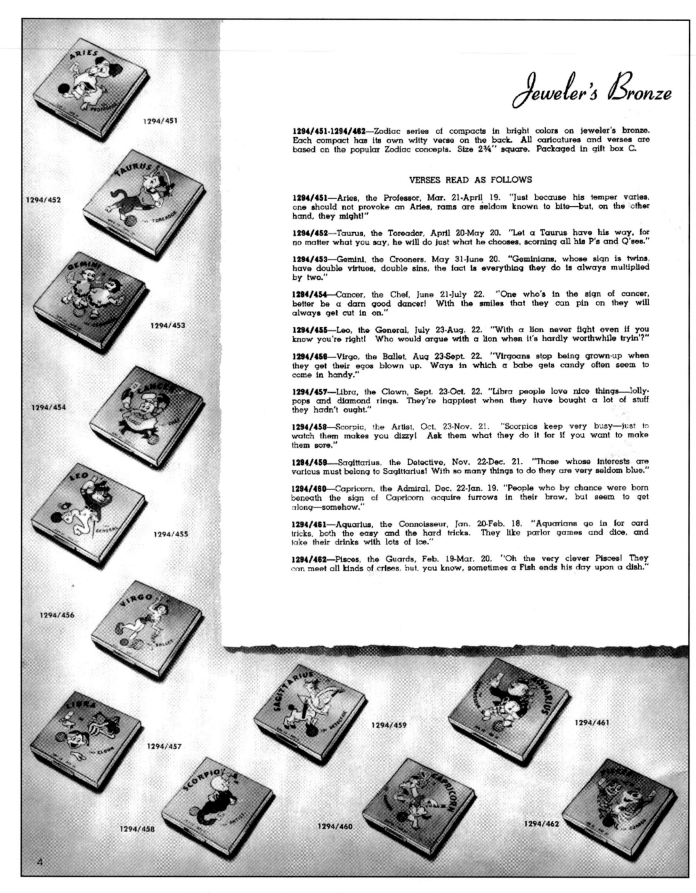

Figure 37 — Elgin American Catalog, 1949; featuring square brushed goldtone Zodiac compacts with interior beveled mirror, puff, and powder well; 2¾" x 2¾". $125.00 – $175.00.

ELGIN AMERICAN ZODIAC SERIES

The Elgin American Zodiac series of compacts come in bright colors on a jeweler's bronze *(Figure 37)*. Each compact has its own witty verse on the reverse side. All caricatures and verses are based on popular Zodiac concepts. Size 2¾" square. Retail price, January 1, 1949, $2.95.

LUCKY PENNY COMPACT

Avon's LUCKY PENNY lip gloss compact was patterned after the rare 1909S V.D.B. Lincoln cent *(Figure 38)*. The Lincoln cent was issued to honor the 100th anniversary of Lincoln's birth and was designed by Victor D. Brenner.

Figure 38 — Avon plastic coppertone Lucky Penny Lip Gloss Compact; round compact designed to resemble 1909 Lincoln penny; screw-off top reveals two compartments for two shades of lip gloss to be applied with fingertip; 2" dia. $40.00 – 60.00.

COPPER COMPACTS

Copper compacts, like all copper surfaces will gradually show tarnish. To restore the shine to a copper compact, rub lightly with a copper cleaner. You will be pleasantly surprised and satisfied with the results.

HANDKERCHIEF VANITY

In the December 1921 issue of *Toilet Requisites* there is an ad for a "Handkerchief Vanity" listed in the column "Clever Novelties for the Hollydays" *(Figure 39)*. "France is never disappointing at the Holiday season, when clever novelties of artistic design are needed to dress up the window and counter displays and to intrigue Madam et Mademoiselle into separating the tired business man at the head of their household from many and sundry shekels for dainty and frivolous acces-

sories to the toilet so dear to the feminine heart. A new vanity which has just arrived is very Frenchy indeed. It is made of a heavy fabric, black silk about a foot across and in the shape of an octagon. A black fringe goes all around the edge attaching the fabric to the lining which is of dainty silk or satin. There are separate pockets; one for the powder puff, another for a mirror, and the other for money and a change purse. A small black ring attached to the exact center of the cloth serves as a handle, and the case drops gracefully and effectively, carried by this ring."

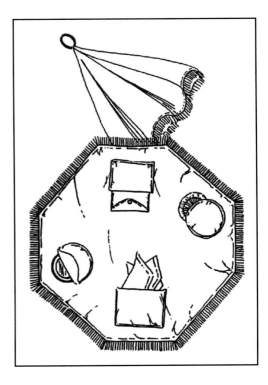

Figure 39 — Toilet Requisites, December 1921.

One of these "Handkerchief Vanities" is on exhibit in The Imperial War Museum in London. The Museum opened an exhibit entitled "Forces Sweetheart" in February 1993. The exhibit covers mementos from World War I to the Gulf War. Included in this display are treasured keepsakes that servicemen sent home to their loved ones. The exhibit features many beautiful, embroidered, souvenir handkerchiefs, manufactured in France that were made specifically for the American and British troops stationed there. One of the most unusual striking hankies on display is a purple "Handkerchief Vanity," a handkerchief with a pocket for a powder puff.

Many times when compact collectors read about rare and unusual compacts featured in *Powder Puff*, they think how wonderful, but feel that they will never find one. One avid compact collector read about the "Handkerchief Vanity," went to an antique show the next day, and found one — and at a "hanky" price! Quite small, 6½" square in two tones of pink silk with a puff enclosed in a drawstring pouch centered on one side of the hanky. Edged with lace that has yellowed but is still in good condition.

Regarding zealous collectors — An ardent compact collector upon returning home after a long antiquing trip discovered that a newly purchased compact was missing. The compact was inadvertently thrown into the town dumpster when passing through a neighboring state. She immediately called the police in that state for assistance. She beseeched them to please retrieve the compact for her. They did and sent it to her the very next day!

SECRET COMPARTMENT

After I completed *Vintage Vanity Bags & Purses* and was repacking or rehanging the bags and purses, I came across a delightful surprise in one of the carryalls. The carryall interior contains a cigarette compartment, swinging mirror, lipstick tube, comb and powder compartment...*and* a secret compartment located underneath the removeable powder well!! A small cardboard inside the powder compartment indicated that this carryall came complete with secret compartment. Many other carryalls with a secret compartment feature passed through my hands while writing the book. Why I chose this particular carryall to examine is beyond me — but I did. I flipped up the powder well and guess what I found? Three bills folded up very neatly. Two One Dollar Silver Certificates, one dated Series 1935 D, the other Series 1935 E and a Five Dollar Silver Certificate dated Series 1934 D. After consulting with our coin/collector friend we learned that if they were brand new (they weren't) and had never been circulated they would be worth quite a bit. As is, they are still worth the grand total of $7.00. The monetary value, unimportant compared to the excitement of discovering bills from 1934 – 1935 concealed in one of my carryalls. The experience was very thrilling!!

MUSICAL COMPACTS REPAIRED

Recently, a musical compact that was wound too tightly was repaired at a very reasonable rate. The man who performed this magic was the "Mechanical Music Man," Emerson E. Whitacre, P.E., of Dayton, OH (513) 898-6044. Here are Mr. Whitacre's suggestions on the care of your music box:

1. When not using your treasure for extended periods, it is a good plan to store a spring wound mechanism in a "wound down" state.

2. Make sure that the mechanism has stopped at the beginning of a tune rather than somewhere in a tune.

3. If you find that a mechanism plays for shorter times with a full winding, it is time to get the unit cleaned and lubricated.

4. Unpleasant squeaking sounds in comb-type music boxes can be the result of improperly adjusted or defective dampers. The enjoyment can be enhanced by having this condition corrected. Oil will not improve this condition.

RED HANDKERCHIEF

This beauty hint first appeared in the November 1931 issue of *Woman & Beauty* magazine, IPC Magazines, England *(Figure 40)*. I came across this clever tip in the enjoyable book, *Compacts* written by Juliette Edwards, 1994, England.

Do you use your handkerchief for removing excess lipstick? If you do, try using a red linen handkerchief instead of a white one. The lipstick doesn't show on red and looks so much daintier than a smeared white handkerchief.

Figure 40 — Women & Beauty, IPC Magazines, November 1931.

NEW COMPACT CHRISTMAS ORNAMENT

Compacts, once again have been recognized by authorities in popular trends, Enesco and Hallmark, both manufacturers of collectible Christmas ornaments that parallel the changing interests and hobbies of the public. Enesco has come out with another beautiful compact/lipstick Christmas ornament, "Happy Holi-date," a mouse sitting on a lipstick tube looking into the mirror of an open compact *(Figure 42)*. This is another one of the Miss Merry Mouse Series by Karen Hahn, the same artist that created the "I Feel Pretty" Christmas ornament, a mouse standing on the puff of an opened goldtone compact, looking into a hand-held mirror *(Figure 43)*. Hallmark's compact Christmas ornament "Sister to Sister" has two mice sitting on the puff of an open compact *(Figure 41)*. If you wish to display your ornaments throughout the year there are also wooden ornament display stands available.

Figure 42 — Enesco 1994 "Happy Holi-date" Christmas ornament designed by Karen Hahn; mouse sitting on lipstick tube that rests on open compact, looking into compact mirror applying make-up.

Figure 41 — Hallmark 1993 "Sister to Sister" Christmas Keepsake ornament; two mice sitting on open compact; "Sisters are forever friends" written on mirror.

Figure 43 — Enesco 1991 "I Feel Pretty" Christmas ornament designed by Karen Hahn; mouse standing on open compact looking into hand mirror.

Figure 44 — GG Woman & Beauty Magazine, IPC, November 1931.

Figure 45 — True Confessions, June 1946.

MAKE-UP PROTECTORS

In the November 1931 issue of *Woman & Beauty Magazine*, IPC Magazines, England, these instructions for a make-up bib appeared *(Figure 44)*. And in the June 1946 issue of *True Confessions* this ad appeared *(Figure 45)*.

AVON POWDER MILL

What goes around comes around! Avon's new plastic compact turns pressed face powder into loose powder. "It is the first do-it-yourself loose powder mill on the market. Directions: simply turn canister top to the right to grind pressed powder to fresh, finely-milled, loose powder. A revolutionary convenience! The neatest, most portable way to enjoy loose powder. Grind only what you need — avoid spills, wasted powder — so innovative, our mill-compact is patent-pending." Avon's disposable compact comes complete with a choice of five different shades of powder. The price, $6.99. This "new" compact is remisicent of many of the vintage "grinder" compacts that we have in our collections. The one that comes most readily to mind is the Elizabeth Arden "grinder" compact.

THE PICCADILLY VANITY BAG

The Piccadilly vanity bag, popular in the 1920s incorporates a compact on the center of the outside frame. Opening the Piccadilly compact can sometimes be very tricky. Immediately underneath the compact there should be an engraved tab. To open the compact, gently pull down on the tab. If the compact resists or the tab is fragile, insert your finger nail between the compact and tab and press down on the tab (should be the same effect as pulling the tab). The compact should then pop open. Remember never use force to open any compact.

KIGU

The Kigu compact was crafted by Gustav Kiashek who was one of the first craftsmen ever to make a powder compact. He was a second generation master silver and goldsmith from Hungary. By the early twenties, he had set up a factory in Budapest to produce small quantities of these beautifully decorated compacts establishing the firm's trade name KI-GU which is derived from KIashek and GUstav. Gustav's son George came to England in 1939 and at the end of the war began to produce the compacts and cigarette cases that made the name of Kigu, as it then became known celebrated worldwide. While he was a goldsmith, George foresaw that powder compacts would become a necessity for every woman. He combined the craftsmanship of the artist with the skill of the engineer to produce compacts of character, and as his slogan put it, at a price which everyone could afford. Many patents, registered designs, and trademarks made Kigu features exclusive. Among these are the patented inner lid catch which makes for easy operation, the built-in mirror frame which guards the glass, and the spill-proof inner lid which prevents powder from escaping. The finish of the compacts is jewel-like and is protected by an invisible coating. Kigu compact shapes and motifs took on a new dimension. Some of these were the "Musical Flying Saucer," "Tennis Ball," "Flower Basket," and assorted "Suitcases." A costume jewelry factory was also acquired which produced decorative adornments for the compacts as well as for other fashion accessories. Kigu stopped making compacts, and manufactured costume jewelry instead when in the latter part of the 1950s and the early part of the 1960s when the au natural look took over and compressed powder in disposable plastic compacts replaced the metal case. The beautifully crafted and figural vintage Kigu compacts are now a much coveted collector item.

"DO-IT-YOURSELF" COMPACT

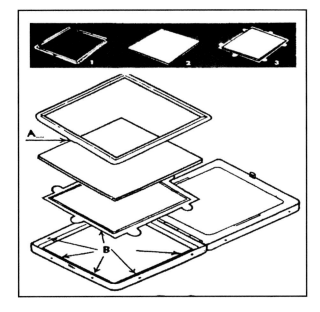

Figure 46 — The Enamelist Compact Assembling Directions

Just when you think you have either seen or heard about every conceivable type of compact e.g. handkerchief, monkey, gun, parasol, fan, etc., surprise, surprise, along comes something new. The "Craftint"

"Do-it-Yourself" break-away Enamelist compact *(Figure 46)*. These vintage compact kits were purchased in craft stores and included an enameling placque. Enamel paints were used to decorate and personalize these placques with scenes, florals, or initials. After this step was completed the compact was assembled and ready for use.

COMPACT ASSEMBLING DIRECTIONS
The ENAMELIST COMPACT comes in 5 parts: (1) Bezel, (2) Mirror, (3) Enameling Placque, (4) Compact Proper, (5) Powder Puff.

NOTE: Only Enamel the Raised Center Square Portion of the Copper Placque. If there is any enamel on the depressed edge it must be removed before assembling the case. In assembling avoid finger prints by using gloves. At all times take precautions against scratching.

1. Place enameled insert in opening of cover.

2. Fasten mirror in bezel seat with two pieces of scotch tape over face of mirror and bezel.

3. Holding mirror and bezel of compact as indicated in drawing (A), tilt one side and insert under side holding pins (B). Insert sufficient crumpled tissue paper between mirror and placque to eliminate any play and to prevent rattling. Then drop other side of bezel and *press at extreme edge exactly at points opposite remaining holding pins. After snapping into place remove scotch tape.

*When pressing into place use a blunt pointed instrument or a small screw driver but cover with tape to avoid scratching.

GUARANTEE: This compact is guaranteed to be of the finest materials and workmanship. This guarantee does not cover damage resulting from abuse, accidental breakage, or improper use.

THE MAGIC MONOGRAM DIAL

The Zell monogram dial compact was one of their most popular designs. Since it could be personalized it was a perfect gift. These compacts have two open panels on their lids and can be personalized by adjusting the moveable dials located on the rim of the compact. Compacts that are engraved "Happy Birthday" or "Congratulations" have two panels, one for the month and the other for the date. The style that comes with letters are used for monogramming the compact *(Figure 47)*.

Figure 47 — Zell "Initially Yours" dial-a-monogram round goldtone compact with complimentary goldtone powder spoon gift; two dials on exterior rim set first and last initials in panels on lid of compact; rhinestones frame panels; lid decorated with incised swirls; interior mirror, puff, and powder well; 3¼" dia. $125.00 – 175.00.

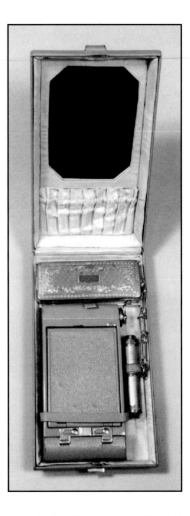

Figure 49 — Kodak Vanity Ensemble; tan leather case contains Kodak camera and a Richard Hudnut Du Barry tango chain goldtone vanity; vanity contains mirror, rouge, and powder compartments; lipstick attached to vanity by link chain; case contains mirror, and small shirred pocket; exterior carrying handle; compact 1⅜" x 3¼", case 3¾" x 7". Shown open. NPA

VANITY KODAK ENSEMBLE

Figure 48 — Eastman Kodak Company Trade Circular, October 1928.

The October 1928 issue of the *Eastman Kodak Trade Circular* introduced the Vanity Kodak Ensemble

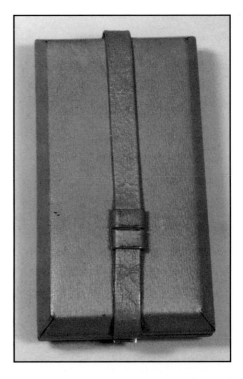

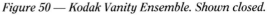

Figure 50 — Kodak Vanity Ensemble. Shown closed.

(Figure 48). In addition to the Kodak camera, the ensemble contained a large mirror, change pocket, a Richard Hudnut combination powder and rouge compact, and lipstick tube. The grained leather strap-style carrying case came in three colors, gray, beige, and green. Production of this vanity ensemble continued through 1929 (for one year only) and the camera to 1933. This ensemble is very rare and is sought after by both vintage camera collectors and compact collectors *(Figures 49, 50)*.

Prior to seeing this ad I wasn't aware that a combination such as this one existed. One day when Alvin and I were out antiquing Alvin spotted the case with the Kodak camera, minus the compact combination, in one of the show cases. He called me over and I remembered that I had the exact Richard Hudnut vanity and lipstick tube at home that would complete the ensemble. Because it was late in the day, and the camera case was not complete, the price of the case with the camera was very affordable. I was thrilled when I came home, found the compact that completed the set. Exactly like the ad! If I had not seen the ad I would have missed out on this great find. This is one of the reasons that vintage ads are very important, they also help determine the date and manufacturer of unmarked compacts. They also illustrate what the original tassel or carrying chain looks like for replacement purposes. For these reasons, the following pages of vintage compact ads have been included. I hope you that you will enjoy them and find them useful.

PAPER PRESERVATIVE

Many compact collectors have newspaper and advertising clipping files of compact articles, advertisements, and related subjects. *KOVELS on Antiques and Collectibles*, Vol. 21 No. 2, recommends a spray that will preserve these paper clippings. The spray is Wei T'o, a deacidifying solution which can be found at art and archival supply firms. The procedure, spray the paper up and down, then from side to side until the paper looks wet.

YOU BET YOUR LIFE

In 1947 – 1948 Elgin American Co. sponsored the first season of the Grouch Marx's radio quiz show, *You Bet Your Life*. The show, in fact, had to go off the air a few weeks earlier than planned, because Elgin American sold out every compact that they had in their warehouse *(Figure 51)*.

Groucho Marx Says:

"I'm here for *Elgin American* to tell you about compacts, and a new way for you to sell more of them. By the way, did you ever hear my radio show for *Elgin American* over the ABC network at 9:30 P. M. Eastern Standard Time, on Wednesday nights? I'd love to have you— Now let's talk compacts. • Back in the days when my big, black cigar was just a little cigarette, most women didn't have special, separate clothes for each type of occasion. One, or maybe two purses were the rule. If the daring young ones had compacts at all they called 'em vanities and they'd never, never use their vanities in front of anyone. And as the use of cosmetics became more widely accepted, the vanity or compact developed into strictly a utility item.

"Not so with purses, though. They were utility items, sure— but they became related to fashion. Now, as you know better than I do, the well-dressed woman needs a different type for each occasion, so that most women today have three or four or five purses • But what about the compact? They used the same one for every occasion— shopping, afternoon parties, dinners, at the theatre, walking the dog. And each time they'd haul that worn-out old compact out of a brand new, fashionable handbag and the contrast was appalling.

"Well, then along came the New Look and that all-purpose compact started to become as out of date as my wife's high-button shoes. Women are beginning to become compact conscious. On my show and in the *Elgin American* full page, four color ads you see in the magazines, we repeatedly ask: "Have you looked at *your* compact lately?" And as women do look at their compacts and notice how shamefully they can ruin an apparel mood, they come in to stores such as yours and buy new compacts. There you have the biggest selling opportunity in years. • Nowadays every woman needs *three* compacts—one for daytime, one for playtime and one for nitetime to be completely fashion-right. Compacts must be keyed to the costume the woman is wearing, just the same as her purse and her hat and her shoes must be in complete fashion harmony with the rest of her costume. In a short time women won't think any more about changing compacts when they change clothes than they do now about changing purses.

"WHAT DOES THIS MEAN TO *YOU?* Well, it means that the demand for compacts is on the increase. Every woman will be buying more compacts, better compacts, and buying them more often. Why—if every woman buys only one compact a year—your sales will double. You'll not only step up the number of your sales but you'll increase the dollars and cents value of each individual sale.

"Every woman needs three. *Elgin American* didn't just dream up that idea (although they've surely provided you with the fashion firsts that'll help you increase your sales). No, this business of 'Every woman Needs Three' is a fashion fact, not a foolish fancy."

Figure 51 — Elgin American Catalog, 1949 #1.

CONVERTIBLE RING VANITIES

In the 1925 *Woman's World* magazine, an ad appeared offering Gift No. 559, a "Convertible Ring Vanity," sent prepaid, for a 2 year subscription — 50 cents for each year — total $1.00. "Useful, Beautiful and Brand New! By far the most convenient and most artistic innovation in the line of vanities which has yet been devised for milady's service and adornment." It was the sensation in the smart Parisian salons this season. These Convertible Vanities Are the Smart Thing Now — Three Combinations in One —

Sautoir, Bracelet or Ring with Mirror, Compact and Puff. It may be worn on the finger as a handsome dinner ring, on a silk ribbon as a modish bracelet, or on a sautoir as an ornate and artistic appendage. But wherever it is worn it is always ready for instant use as a vanity. Open the lid with its beautiful stone setting and, lo! there is revealed a diminutive mirror, a compact and a powder puff large enough to render the full service that is expected of it. The rings are exquisitely etched, filled white gold, mounted with your choice of the following synthetic stones — jade, turquoise, emerald, ruby and onyx *(Figure 52)*. The top of the ring measures one inch long by half inch wide. A handsome piece of workmanship throughout. (A smaller version comes with mirror and filled with lip rouge.)

Figure 52 — Two oval convertible compact/ring combinations; smaller ring is a rouge pot, interior contains rouge and mirror; stone centered on lid of smaller ring; larger ring interior has powder compartment, mirror, and puff; both can be converted to bracelets or worn on a chain as a neck pendant; larger one shown as bracelet with grosgrain wrist band; smaller one shown as ring; larger one ⅝" x 1"; smaller one ¹⁵⁄₁₆" x ⅞".

Woman's World Magazine, 1925.

Exquisite Compacts

$2.25

Vanity Case, made of special **non-tarnishable** metal. Contains loose powder sifter, rouge, two puffs and mirror. Illustration shows actual size. Carrying chain, 3 inches long. Engraved with any letter without extra charge. Mention letter wanted.
4K3600...$2.25

Double Compact, bright gunmetal finish. Contains cake powder, rouge, mirror and two puffs. Illustration shows actual size. Engraved with any name without extra charge. Mention name.
4K3604...,.........$1.85

Unless Otherwise Stated All Illustrations on This Page Show Reduced Size. Shipping Weight of All Compacts and Vanity Cases, 5 Ounces.

Vanity Case, thin model, made of nontarnishable white metal. Solid silver enameled design in center. Loose powder sifter, puff and mirror. To fill box, sift loose powder through perforated top. Measures about 2 inches in diameter. Illustration shows slightly reduced size.
4K3608.....85¢

Vanity Case, nontarnishable metal. Contains loose powder sifter, rouge, two puffs and mirror. Carrying chain. Illustration shows reduced size. Measures about 1¾x2¼ inches.
4K3606.....$1.25

Vanity Case, thin model, white gold plated. Solid silver cloisene enameled center. Contains loose powder sifter, two puffs, rouge and mirror. Carrying chain. Illustration shows reduced size. Measures about 2x2½ inches.
4K3610 ....$3.25

Mesh Bags

High Grade Silver Plated Mesh Bag. Pierced frame. Fish scale mesh, which is practically indestructible. Jeweled catch. Bag about 6 in. deep. Carrying chain. Shg. wt., ¾ lb.
4K3640.....$3.25

Very New and Attractive Mesh Bags. Made of indestructible mesh enameled in colors. Light green background with gold and darker green color design. Enamel guaranteed not to chip. Gold plated frame. Illustrations show reduced sizes. Order by catalog number the size desired. Shpg. wt., ¾ lb.
4K3642 — 3½x6½ inches, including fringe $3.25
4K3644 — 4½ x 7 inches, including fringe $4.50

Mesh Bags made of indestructible mesh enameled in colors. Light blue background with gold and darker blue color design. Enamel guaranteed not to chip. Gold plated frame. Order by catalog number the size desired. Shipping wt., ¾ pound.
4K3646 — 3½x5½ inches $3.50
4K3648 — Pattern similar to above, same color scheme. 4½ x 5 inches $4.75

High Grade Silver Plated Mesh Bag. Piccadilly style. Fine mesh. Jeweled catch. Contains mirror and puff and place for powder as shown in small illustration. Bag, about 7¼ inches deep. Carrying chain. Shipping wt., ¾ pound.
4K3650.....$8.50

Shipping Weight of Compacts and Vanity Cases, 5 Ounces.

Vanity Case, silver plated. A compact attractive as it is useful. Contains loose powder sifter, rouge, two puffs and mirror. Carrying chain. Illustration shows reduced size. Measures about 2 inches square. Any name engraved without extra charge. Mention name wanted.
4K3616 $2.65

Vanity Case silver plated. Beautiful enameled design in center. Contains mirror, loose powder sifter, rouge, two puffs and coin holder. Measures about 2x2 inches. Illustration shows reduced size. Carrying chain.
4K3620 $2.25

Vanity Case, made of nontarnishable white metal, with solid silver enameled center. Contains loose powder sifter, rouge, two puffs and mirror. Carrying chain. Illustration shows reduced size. Measures about 2 inches square.
4K3622 $1.65

Vanity Case. One of our newest compacts that will appeal instantly to the woman of fashion. Made of nontarnishable white metal, with solid silver enameled center. Contains cake powder, rouge, two puffs and mirror. Utility space for cards, etc. Carrying chain. Illustration shows reduced size. Measures about 1¾x2¾ in.
4K3624 $2.50

Vanity Case, silver plated. An unusually beautiful vanity that is sure to gain wide approval this season and is fully as useful as it is attractive. Contains cake powder, rouge, lipstick, two puffs and mirror. Lipstick rises automatically when box is opened. Carrying chain. Illustration shows reduced size. Measures about 2x3 inches.
4K3628 $4.25

Vanity Case, silver plated. A compact that lends a decorative touch as well as being decidedly useful. Contains cake powder, rouge, two puffs, mirror and comb. Carrying chain. Measures about 1¾x3 inches. Illustration shows reduced size.
4K3630 $1.75

Vanity Case, silver plated. Beautiful color design. Contains loose powder sifter, rouge, two puffs and mirror. Carrying chain. Measures about 2 in. in diameter. Illustration shows reduced size.
4K3632 $1.75

Sears, Roebuck and Co., 1927.

— 43 —

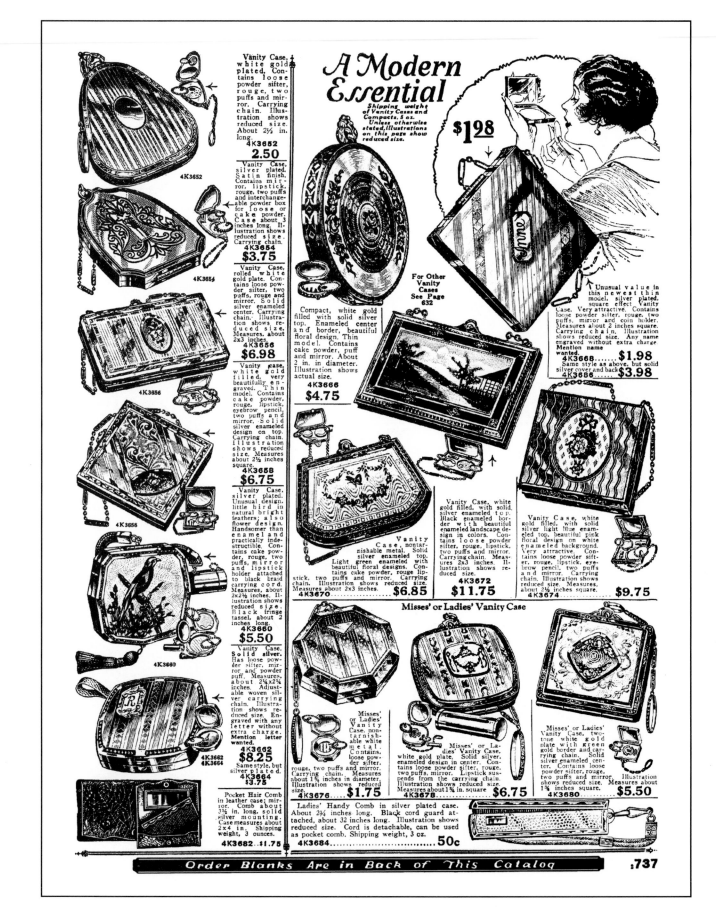

Sears, Roebuck and Co., 1927.

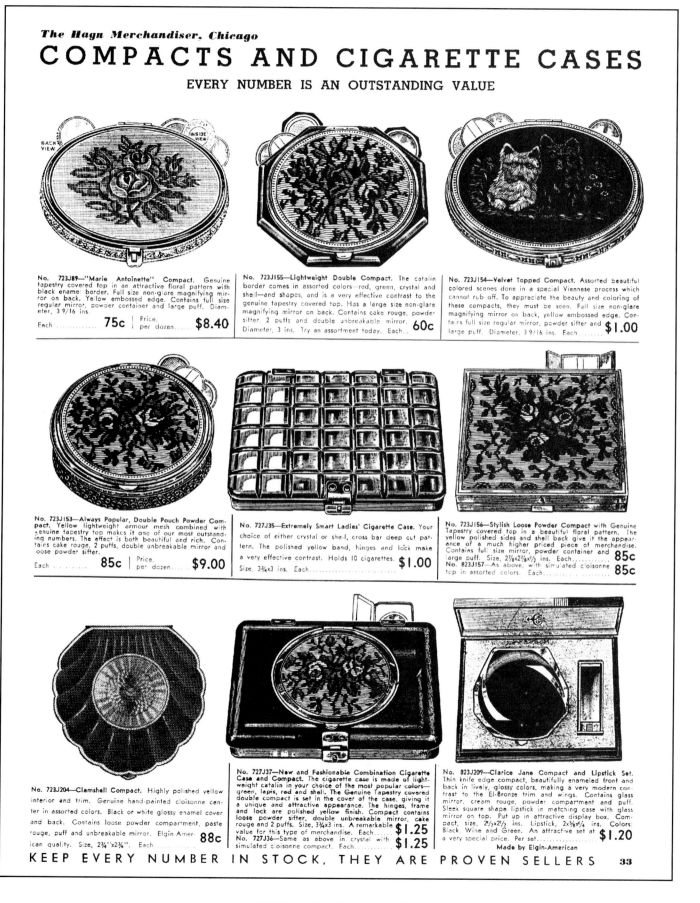

The Hagn Merchandiser, Chicago

COMPACTS AND CIGARETTE CASES

EVERY NUMBER IS AN OUTSTANDING VALUE

No. 723J89—"Marie Antoinette" Compact. Genuine tapestry covered top in an attractive floral pattern with black enamel border. Full size non-glare magnifying mirror on back. Yellow embossed edge. Contains full size regular mirror, powder container and large puff. Diameter, 3 9/16 ins.

Each .... **75c** | Price, per dozen...... **$8.40**

No. 723J155—Lightweight Double Compact. The catalin border comes in assorted colors—red, green, crystal and shell—and shapes, and is a very effective contrast to the genuine tapestry covered top. Has a large size non-glare magnifying mirror on back. Contains cake rouge, powder sifter, 2 puffs and double unbreakable mirror. Diameter, 3 ins. Try an assortment today. Each.. **60c**

No. 723J154—Velvet Topped Compact. Assorted beautiful colored scenes done in a special Viennese process which cannot rub off. To appreciate the beauty and coloring of these compacts, they must be seen. Full size non-glare magnifying mirror on back, yellow embossed edge. Contains full size regular mirror, powder sifter and large puff. Diameter, 3 9/16 ins. Each........ **$1.00**

No. 723J153—Always Popular, Double Pouch Powder Compact. Yellow lightweight armour mesh combined with genuine tapestry top makes it one of our most outstanding numbers. The effect is both beautiful and rich. Contains cake rouge, 2 puffs, double unbreakable mirror and loose powder sifter.

Each .... **85c** | Price, per dozen...... **$9.00**

No. 727J35—Extremely Smart Ladies' Cigarette Case. Your choice of either crystal or shell, cross bar deep cut pattern. The polished yellow band, hinges and lock make a very effective contrast. Holds 10 cigarettes. Size, 3¾x3 ins. Each **$1.00**

No. 723J156—Stylish Loose Powder Compact with Genuine Tapestry covered top in a beautiful floral pattern. The yellow polished sides and shell back give it the appearance of a much higher priced piece of merchandise. Contains full size mirror, powder container and large puff. Size, 2⅞x2⅞x½ ins. Each............ **85c**
No. 823J157—As above, with simulated cloisonne top in assorted colors. Each................. **85c**

No. 723J204—Clamshell Compact. Highly polished yellow interior and trim. Genuine hand-painted cloisonne center in assorted colors. Black or white glossy enamel cover and back. Contains loose powder compartment, paste rouge, puff and unbreakable mirror. Elgin American quality. Size, 2¾"x2¾". Each......... **88c**

No. 727J37—New and Fashionable Combination Cigarette Case and Compact. The cigarette case is made of lightweight catalin in your choice of the most popular colors—green, lapis, red and shell. The Genuine Tapestry covered double compact is set in the cover of the case, giving it a unique and attractive appearance. The hinges, frame and lock are polished yellow finish. Compact contains loose powder sifter, double unbreakable mirror, cake rouge and 2 puffs. Size, 3¾x3 ins. A remarkable value for this type of merchandise. Each...... **$1.25**
No. 727J36—Same as above in crystal with simulated cloisonne compact. Each............ **$1.25**

No. 823J209—Clarice Jane Compact and Lipstick Set. Thin knife edge compact, beautifully enameled front and back in lively, glossy colors, making a very modern contrast to the El-Bronze trim and wings. Contains glass mirror, cream rouge, powder compartment and puff. Sleek square shape lipstick in matching case with glass mirror on top. Put up in attractive display box. Compact, size, 2⅛x2⅛ ins. Lipstick, 2x⅝x¼ ins. Colors: Black, Wine and Green. An attractive set at a very special price. Per set................. **$1.20**
Made by Elgin-American

KEEP EVERY NUMBER IN STOCK, THEY ARE PROVEN SELLERS 33

1938 Hagn Merchandiser Catalog.

45

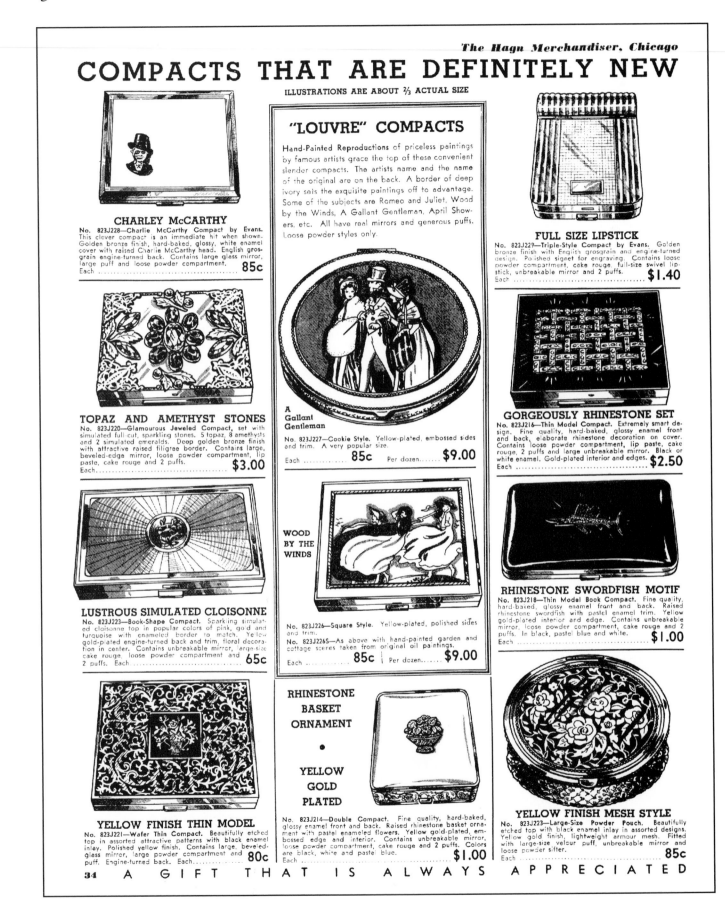

COMPACTS THAT ARE DEFINITELY NEW

ILLUSTRATIONS ARE ABOUT ⅔ ACTUAL SIZE

CHARLEY McCARTHY

No. 823J228—Charlie McCarthy Compact by Evans. This clever compact is an immediate hit when shown. Golden bronze finish, hard-baked, glossy, white enamel cover with raised Charlie McCarthy head. English grosgrain engine-turned back. Contains large glass mirror, large puff and loose powder compartment. **85c**
Each ....

TOPAZ AND AMETHYST STONES

No. 823J220—Glamourous Jeweled Compact, set with simulated full-cut, sparkling stones. 5 topaz, 8 amethysts and 2 simulated emeralds. Deep golden bronze finish with attractive raised filigree border. Contains large, beveled-edge mirror, loose powder compartment, lip paste, cake rouge and 2 puffs. **$3.00**
Each ....

LUSTROUS SIMULATED CLOISONNE

No. 823J223—Book-Shape Compact. Sparkling simulated cloisonne top in popular colors of pink, gold and turquoise with enameled border to match. Yellow gold-plated engine-turned back and trim, floral decoration in center. Contains unbreakable mirror, large-size cake rouge, loose powder compartment and 2 puffs. Each **65c**

YELLOW FINISH THIN MODEL

No. 823J221—Wafer Thin Compact. Beautifully etched top in assorted attractive patterns with black enamel inlay. Polished yellow finish. Contains large, beveled-glass mirror, large powder compartment and puff. Engine-turned back. Each **80c**

"LOUVRE" COMPACTS

Hand-Painted Reproductions of priceless paintings by famous artists grace the top of these convenient slender compacts. The artists name and the name of the original are on the back. A border of deep ivory sets the exquisite paintings off to advantage. Some of the subjects are Romeo and Juliet, Wood by the Winds, A Gallant Gentleman, April Showers, etc. All have real mirrors and generous puffs. Loose powder styles only.

A Gallant Gentleman

No. 823J227—Cookie Style. Yellow-plated, embossed sides and trim. A very popular size.
Each .... **85c** | Per dozen **$9.00**

WOOD BY THE WINDS

No. 823J226—Square Style. Yellow-plated, polished sides and trim.
No. 823J226S—As above with hand-painted garden and cottage scenes taken from original oil paintings.
Each .... **85c** | Per dozen **$9.00**

RHINESTONE BASKET ORNAMENT

•

YELLOW GOLD PLATED

No. 823J214—Double Compact. Fine quality, hard-baked, glossy enamel front and back. Raised rhinestone basket ornament with pastel enameled flowers. Yellow gold-plated, embossed edge and interior. Contains unbreakable mirror, loose powder compartment, cake rouge and 2 puffs. Colors are black, white and pastel blue. **$1.00**
Each ....

FULL SIZE LIPSTICK

No. 823J229—Triple-Style Compact by Evans. Golden bronze finish with English grosgrain and engine-turned design. Polished signet for engraving. Contains loose powder compartment, cake rouge, full-size swivel lipstick, unbreakable mirror and 2 puffs. **$1.40**
Each ....

GORGEOUSLY RHINESTONE SET

No. 823J216—Thin Model Compact. Extremely smart design. Fine quality, hard-baked, glossy enamel front and back, elaborate rhinestone decoration on cover. Contains loose powder compartment, lip paste, cake rouge, 2 puffs and large unbreakable mirror. Black or white enamel. Gold-plated interior and edges. **$2.50**
Each ....

RHINESTONE SWORDFISH MOTIF

No. 823J218—Thin Model Book Compact. Fine quality, hard-baked, glossy enamel front and back. Raised rhinestone swordfish with pastel enamel trim. Yellow gold-plated interior and edge. Contains unbreakable mirror, loose powder compartment, cake rouge and 2 puffs. In black, pastel blue and white. **$1.00**
Each ....

YELLOW FINISH MESH STYLE

No. 823J223—Large-Size Powder Pouch. Beautifully etched top with black enamel inlay in assorted designs. Yellow gold finish, lightweight armour mesh. Fitted with large-size velour puff, unbreakable mirror and loose powder sifter. **85c**
Each ....

34 A GIFT THAT IS ALWAYS APPRECIATED

1938 Hagn Merchandiser Catalog.

another masterpiece

the

Carryall
PAT PENDING

by Elgin American

The *Elgin American* CARRYALL—all her vanity needs in one stunning case —fashion-right in every detail, a conversation piece wherever it is displayed.

Exquisite finish, hairline fittings, and precision workmanship all in one superb package.

In jeweler's bronze, satin silver finish, handset stones, mother-of-pearl, and handsome leather. With black moire carrying case. Special cases and carrying chains available.

Carryall EVENING BAG
THE COMPLETE VANITY HANDBAG

The popular CARRYALL snugly mounted on smart black suede leather evening bag. A true masterpiece in fashion design. Bag available separately. Takes eight different Carryall designs. Fitted with comb.
Order No. 5900.

In engraving *ELGIN AMERICAN* products it is important that the engraver clear the merchandise properly after engraving to prevent tarnishing

—POWDER DOOR
Snug-fitting door for roomy powder tray.

PILLBOX —
Another extra, for pills or keys.

LIPSTICK COMPARTMENT
Equipped with tight-fitting lipstick case.

MONEY HOLDER—
A must—provided for in the Carryall.

— MIRROR
Perfectly backed and finished.

CIGARETTE CASE—
Hinged mirror keeps cigarettes secure.

CARRYING CASE
Each with smart black moire case. (With comb).

CHAIN—
Jeweler's Bronze chain available separately.

1938 Hagn Merchandiser Catalog.

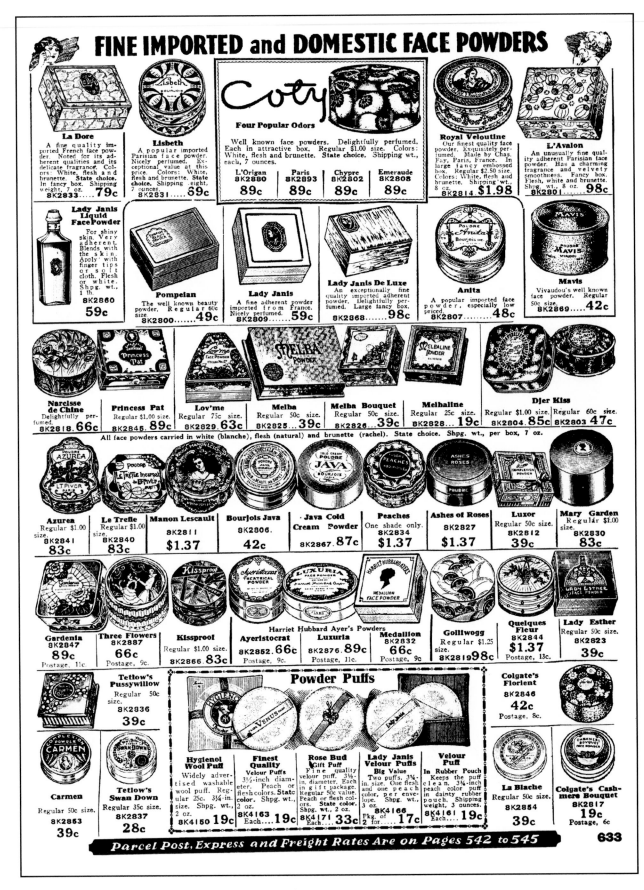

1927 Sears, Roebuck and Co., Catalog.

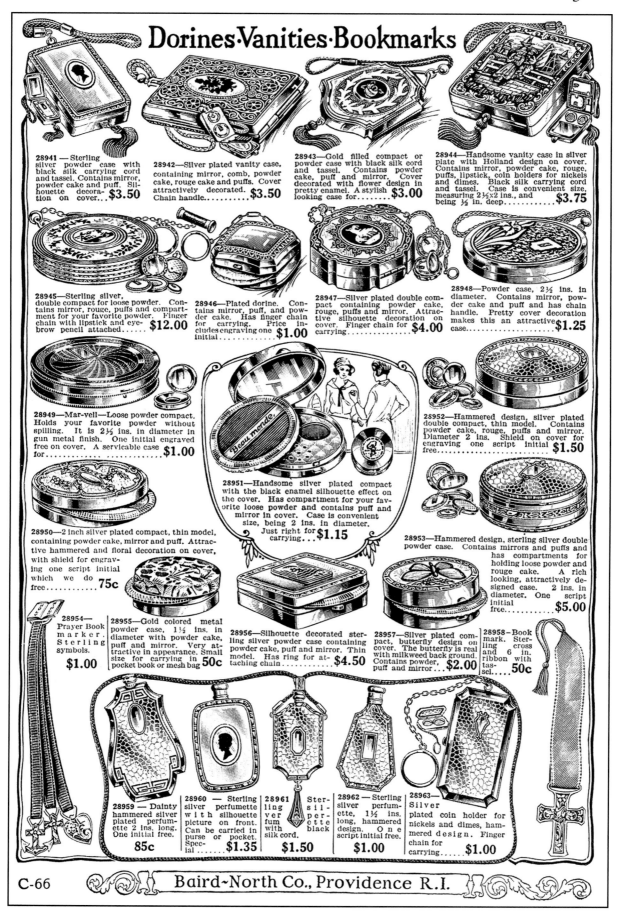

Dorines·Vanities·Bookmarks

28941 — Sterling silver powder case with black silk carrying cord and tassel. Contains mirror, powder cake and puff. Silhouette decoration on cover... **$3.50**

28942—Silver plated vanity case, containing mirror, comb, powder cake, rouge cake and puffs. Cover attractively decorated. Chain handle.......... **$3.50**

28943—Gold filled compact or powder case with black silk cord and tassel. Contains powder cake, puff and mirror. Cover decorated with flower design in pretty enamel. A stylish looking case for.... **$3.00**

28944—Handsome vanity case in silver plate with Holland design on cover. Contains mirror, powder cake, rouge, puffs, lipstick, coin holders for nickels and dimes. Black silk carrying cord and tassel. Case is convenient size, measuring 2½x2 ins., and being ½ in. deep........... **$3.75**

28945—Sterling silver, double compact for loose powder. Contains mirror, rouge, puffs and compartment for your favorite powder. Finger chain with lipstick and eyebrow pencil attached...... **$12.00**

28946—Plated dorine. Contains mirror, puff, and powder cake. Has finger chain for carrying. Price includes engraving one initial.......... **$1.00**

28947—Silver plated double compact containing powder cake, rouge, puffs and mirror. Attractive silhouette decoration on cover. Finger chain for carrying............. **$4.00**

28948—Powder case, 2½ ins. in diameter. Contains mirror, powder cake and puff and has chain handle. Pretty cover decoration makes this an attractive case.................... **$1.25**

28949—Mar-vell—Loose powder compact. Holds your favorite powder without spilling. It is 2½ ins. in diameter in gun metal finish. One initial engraved free on cover. A serviceable case for.............. **$1.00**

28950—2 inch silver plated compact, thin model, containing powder cake, mirror and puff. Attractive hammered and floral decoration on cover, with shield for engraving one script initial which we do free.......... **75c**

28951—Handsome silver plated compact with the black enamel silhouette effect on the cover. Has compartment for your favorite loose powder and contains puff and mirror in cover. Case is convenient size, being 2 ins. in diameter. Just right for carrying... **$1.15**

28952—Hammered design, silver plated double compact, thin model. Contains powder cake, rouge, puffs and mirror. Diameter 2 ins. Shield on cover for engraving one script initial free.................... **$1.50**

28953—Hammered design, sterling silver double powder case. Contains mirrors and puffs and has compartments for holding loose powder and rouge cake. A rich looking, attractively designed case. 2 ins. in diameter. One script initial free........... **$5.00**

28954— Prayer Book marker. Sterling symbols. **$1.00**

28955—Gold colored metal powder case, 1½ ins. in diameter with powder cake, puff and mirror. Very attractive in appearance. Small size for carrying in pocket book or mesh bag **50c**

28956—Silhouette decorated sterling silver powder case containing powder cake, puff and mirror. Thin model. Has ring for attaching chain............ **$4.50**

28957—Silver plated compact, butterfly design on cover. The butterfly is real with milkweed back ground. Contains powder, puff and mirror... **$2.00**

28958—Book mark. Sterling cross and 6 in. ribbon with tassel.... **50c**

28959— Dainty hammered silver plated perfumette 2 ins. long. One initial free. **85c**

28960 — Sterling silver perfumette with silhouette picture on front. Can be carried in purse or pocket. Special...... **$1.35**

28961—Sterling silver perfumette black **$1.50**

28962 — Sterling silver perfumette, 1½ ins. long, hammered design. One script initial free. **$1.00**

28963—Silver plated coin holder for nickels and dimes, hammered design. Finger chain for carrying..... **$1.00**

Baird~North Co., Providence R.I.

Baird-North Co., c. 1925.

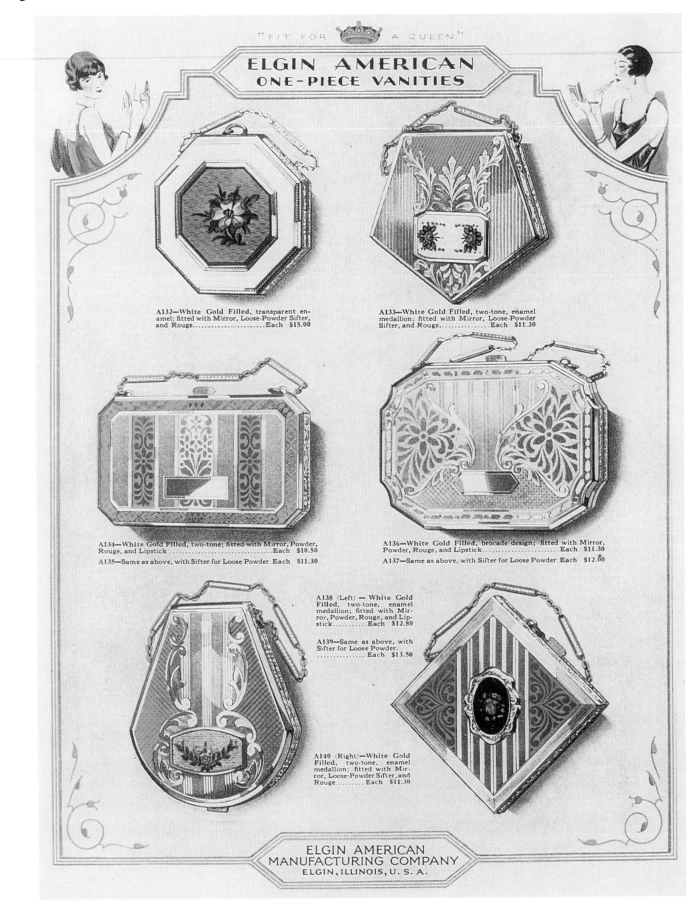

A. C. Becken Company, 1928.

"FIT FOR A QUEEN"

ELGIN AMERICAN
ONE-PIECE VANITIES

A122—White Gold Filled, brocade design; fitted with Mirror, Loose-Powder Sifter, and Rouge.........................Each $9.00

A123—White Gold Filled, transparent enamel; fitted with Mirror, Loose-Powder Sifter, and Rouge.....................Each $15.00

A124—White Gold Filled, transparent enamel; fitted with Mirror, Powder, Rouge and Lipstick.............Each $15.80
A125—Same as above, with Sifter for Loose Powder. Each $16.50

A126—White Gold Filled, two-tone; fitted with Mirror, Powder, Rouge, and Lipstick............................Each $11.30
A127—Same as above, with Sifter for Loose Powder. Each $12.00

A128—White Gold Filled, two-tone; fitted with Mirror, Powder, Rouge, and Lipstick. Each $11.30
A129—Same as above, with Sifter for Loose Powder.............Each $12.00

A130—White Gold Filled, enamel medallion; fitted with Mirror, Powder, Rouge, and Lipstick......................Each $12.80
A131—Same as above, with Sifter for Loose Powder. Each $13.50

ELGIN AMERICAN
MANUFACTURING COMPANY
ELGIN, ILLINOIS, U.S.A.

A. C. Becken Company, 1928.

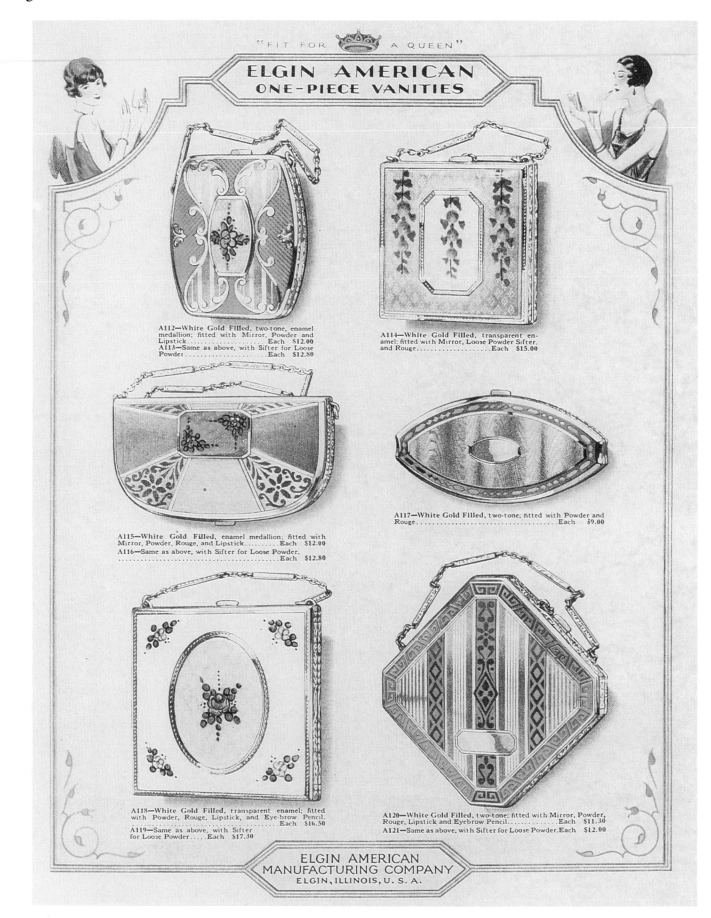

"FIT FOR A QUEEN"

ELGIN AMERICAN
ONE-PIECE VANITIES

A112—White Gold Filled, two-tone, enamel medallion; fitted with Mirror, Powder and Lipstick..................Each $12.00
A113—Same as above, with Sifter for Loose Powder..................Each $12.80

A114—White Gold Filled, transparent enamel; fitted with Mirror, Loose Powder Sifter, and Rouge..................Each $15.00

A115—White Gold Filled, enamel medallion; fitted with Mirror, Powder, Rouge, and Lipstick..........Each $12.00
A116—Same as above, with Sifter for Loose Powder.
..................Each $12.80

A117—White Gold Filled, two-tone; fitted with Powder and Rouge..................Each $9.00

A118—White Gold Filled, transparent enamel; fitted with Powder, Rouge, Lipstick, and Eye-brow Pencil.
..................Each $16.50
A119—Same as above, with Sifter for Loose Powder.....Each $17.30

A120—White Gold Filled, two-tone; fitted with Mirror, Powder, Rouge, Lipstick and Eyebrow Pencil..................Each $11.30
A121—Same as above, with Sifter for Loose Powder.Each $12.00

ELGIN AMERICAN
MANUFACTURING COMPANY
ELGIN, ILLINOIS, U. S. A.

A. C. Becken Company, 1928.

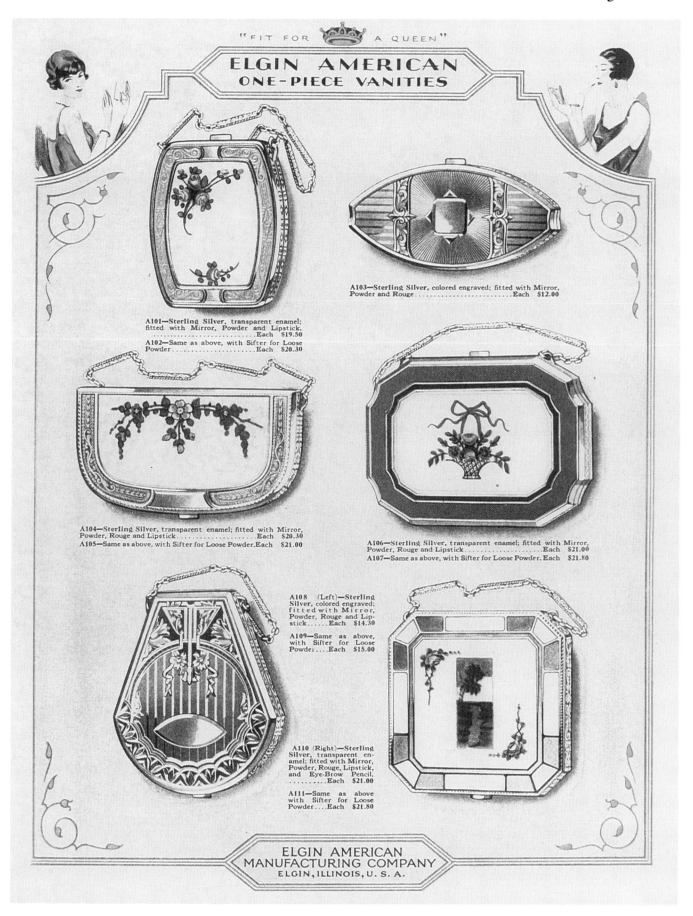

A. C. Becken Company, 1928.

EVANS

No. E1000...........$0.90
Single Compact. Brocade and engine turned design in white gold finish, without chain, containing mirror, loose powder sifter.

No. E1001...........$3.40
Double Compact. White gold finish with hand painted enamel decoration, containing mirror, loose powder sifter and rouge.

No. E1002...........$2.70
Double Compact. White gold finish with hand painted enamel decoration, containing mirror, loose powder sifter and rouge.

No. E1003...........$1.75
Double Compact. Thin watch case model, brocade and engine turned design, white gold finish, containing mirror, loose powder sifter and rouge with finger ring and chain.

No. E1004...........$3.00
Vanity in hammered and engine turned design with chased border, in white gold finish with double chain, containing mirror, powder cake, rouge, and bobbed hair comb.

No. E1005...........$4.25
Double Compact. Cushion shape, brocade and engine turned design with chased border and hand-painted Dresden enamel plaque, in assorted color enamels, white gold finish with finger ring and chain, containing mirror, powder cake and rouge.

No. E1006...........$3.75
Vanity. Brocade and engine turned design, chased border, white gold finish, double chain, containing coin holder, swinging mirror with place for bill back of mirror, powder cake and rouge cake.

No. E1007...........$4.50
Double Compact. Cushion shape, flower basket insert in colors, hand-brocaded border, white gold finish, finger ring and chain, containing mirror, loose powder sifter and rouge.

No. E1008...........$5.75
Double Compact. Pentagon shape, leather covered front and back in assorted colors, applied shield on front, chased border, white gold finish with finger ring and chain, containing mirror, loose powder sifter and rouge.

No. E1009...........$5.75
Double Compact. Square shape, engine turned pattern, chased border, genuine hand-painted, engraved Dresden enamel insert, white gold finish with chain and finger ring, containing mirror, loose powder sifter and rouge.

The LINE with the STERLING TOUCH

A. C. Becken Company, 1928.

54

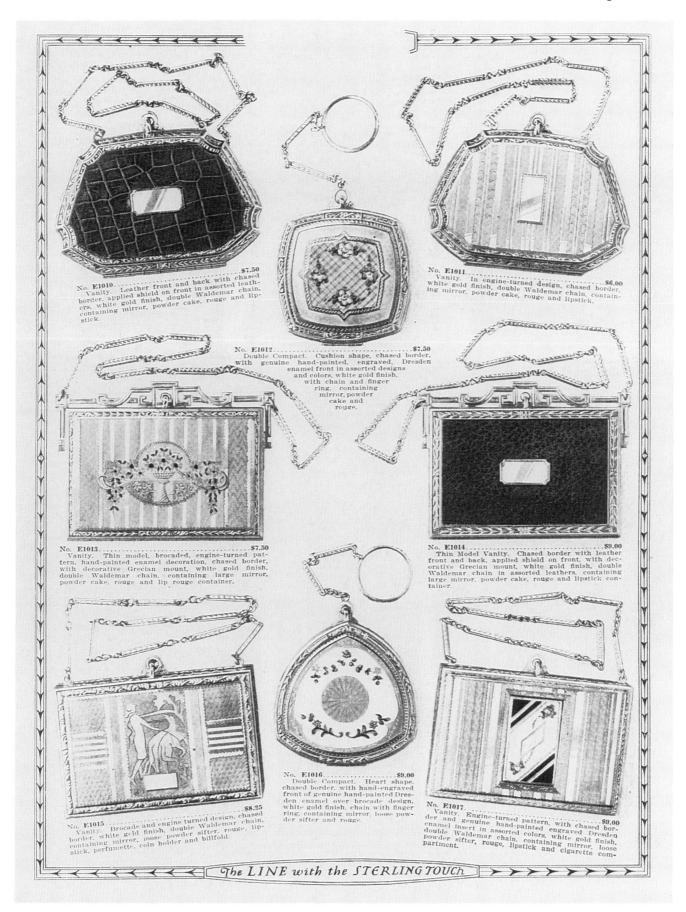

No. E1010..........................$7.50
Vanity. Leather front and back with chased border, applied shield on front in assorted leathers, white gold finish, double Waldemar chain, containing mirror, powder cake, rouge and lipstick.

No. E1011..........................$6.00
Vanity. In engine-turned design, chased border, white gold finish, double Waldemar chain, containing mirror, powder cake, rouge and lipstick.

No. E1012..........................$7.50
Double Compact. Cushion shape, chased border, with genuine hand-painted, engraved, Dresden enamel front in assorted designs and colors, white gold finish, with chain and finger ring, containing mirror, powder cake and rouge.

No. E1013..........................$7.50
Vanity. Thin model, brocaded, engine-turned pattern, hand-painted enamel decoration, chased border, with decorative Grecian mount, white gold finish, double Waldemar chain, containing large mirror, powder cake, rouge and lip rouge container.

No. E1014..........................$9.00
Thin Model Vanity. Chased border with leather front and back, applied shield on front, with decorative Grecian mount, white gold finish, double Waldemar chain in assorted leathers, containing large mirror, powder cake, rouge and lipstick container.

No. E1015..........................$8.25
Vanity. Brocade and engine turned design, chased border, white gold finish, double Waldemar chain, containing mirror, loose powder sifter, rouge, lipstick, perfumette, coin holder and billfold.

No. E1016..........................$9.00
Double Compact. Heart shape, chased border, with hand-engraved front of genuine hand-painted Dresden enamel over brocade design, white gold finish, chain with finger ring, containing mirror, loose powder sifter and rouge.

No. E1017..........................$9.00
Vanity. Engine-turned pattern, with chased border and genuine hand-painted engraved Dresden enamel insert in assorted colors, white gold finish, double Waldemar chain, containing mirror, loose powder sifter, rouge, lipstick and cigarette compartment.

The LINE with the STERLING TOUCH

A. C. Becken Company, 1928.

55

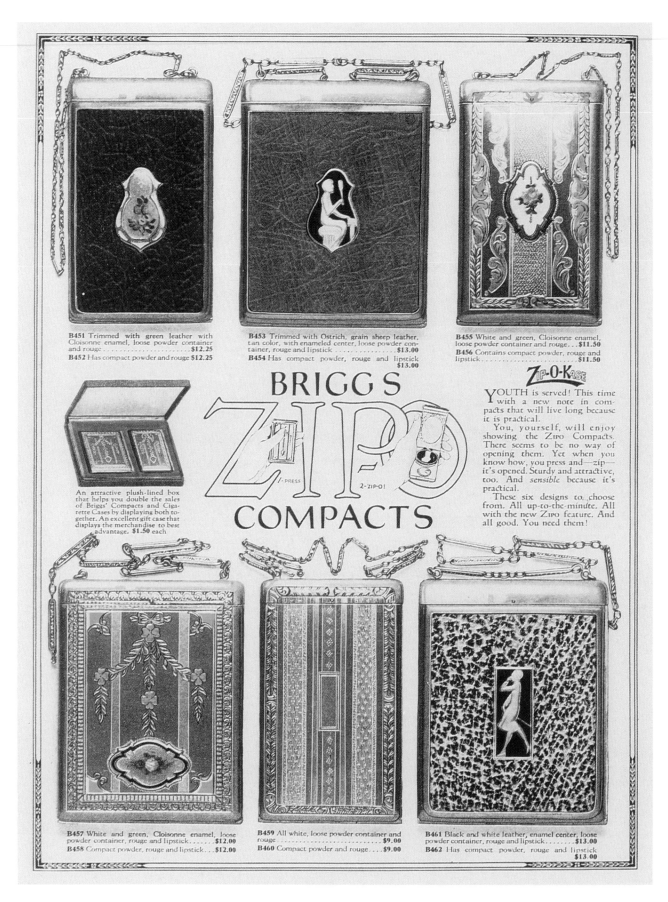

B451 Trimmed with green leather with Cloisonne enamel, loose powder container and rouge $12.25
B452 Has compact powder and rouge $12.25

B453 Trimmed with Ostrich, grain sheep leather, tan color, with enameled center, loose powder container, rouge and lipstick $13.00
B454 Has compact powder, rouge and lipstick $13.00

B455 White and green, Cloisonne enamel, loose powder container and rouge. . . $11.50
B456 Contains compact powder, rouge and lipstick $11.50

ZIP-O-KASE

BRIGGS ZIPO COMPACTS

An attractive plush-lined box that helps you double the sales of Briggs' Compacts and Cigarette Cases by displaying both together. An excellent gift case that displays the merchandise to best advantage. $1.50 each

1 - PRESS   2 - ZIP-O!

YOUTH is served! This time with a new note in compacts that will live long because it is practical.

You, yourself, will enjoy showing the Zipo Compacts. There seems to be no way of opening them. Yet when you know how, you press and—zip—it's opened. Sturdy and attractive, too. And *sensible* because it's practical.

These six designs to choose from. All up-to-the-minute. All with the new Zipo feature. And all good. You need them!

B457 White and green, Cloisonne enamel, loose powder container, rouge and lipstick. $12.00
B458 Compact powder, rouge and lipstick. . . $12.00

B459 All white, loose powder container and rouge $9.00
B460 Compact powder and rouge $9.00

B461 Black and white leather, enamel center, loose powder container, rouge and lipstick. $13.00
B462 Has compact powder, rouge and lipstick $13.00

A. C. Becken Company, 1928.

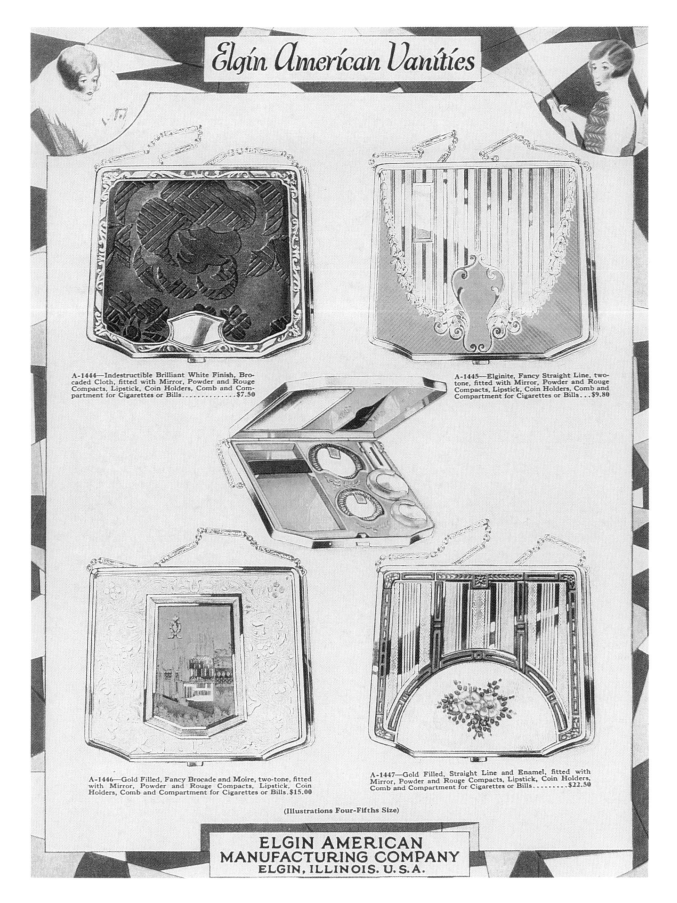

A-1444—Indestructible Brilliant White Finish, Brocaded Cloth, fitted with Mirror, Powder and Rouge Compacts, Lipstick, Coin Holders, Comb and Compartment for Cigarettes or Bills.............$7.50

A-1445—Elginite, Fancy Straight Line, two-tone, fitted with Mirror, Powder and Rouge Compacts, Lipstick, Coin Holders, Comb and Compartment for Cigarettes or Bills...$9.80

A-1446—Gold Filled, Fancy Brocade and Moire, two-tone, fitted with Mirror, Powder and Rouge Compacts, Lipstick, Coin Holders, Comb and Compartment for Cigarettes or Bills.$15.00

A-1447—Gold Filled, Straight Line and Enamel, fitted with Mirror, Powder and Rouge Compacts, Lipstick, Coin Holders, Comb and Compartment for Cigarettes or Bills.........$22.50

(Illustrations Four-Fifths Size)

ELGIN AMERICAN MANUFACTURING COMPANY
ELGIN, ILLINOIS. U.S.A.

Morgan and Allen Company, 1929.

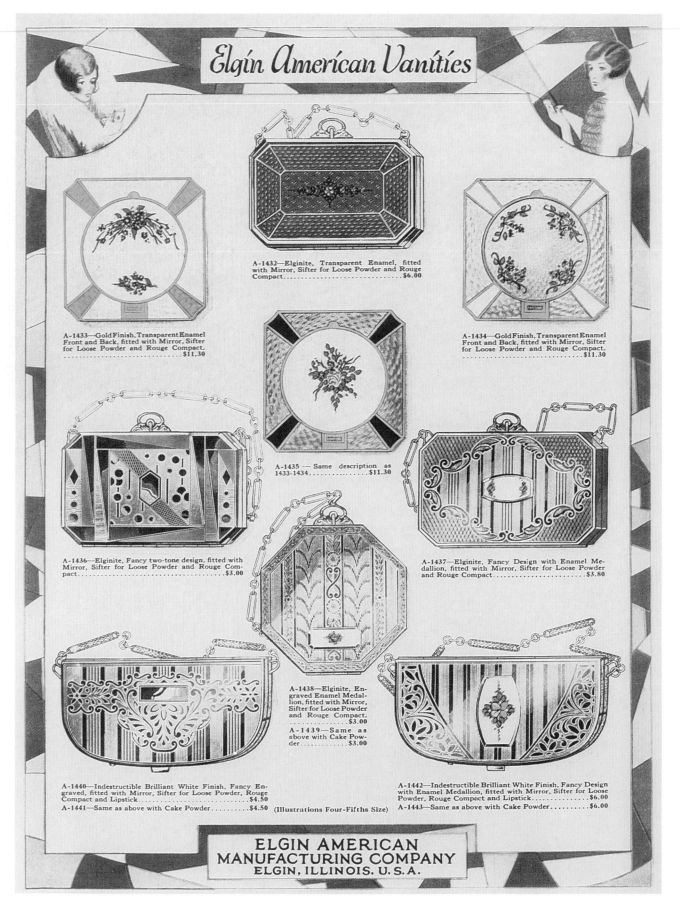

Elgin American Vanities

A-1432—Elginite, Transparent Enamel, fitted with Mirror, Sifter for Loose Powder and Rouge Compact.................................$6.00

A-1433—Gold Finish, Transparent Enamel Front and Back, fitted with Mirror, Sifter for Loose Powder and Rouge Compact. $11.30

A-1434—Gold Finish, Transparent Enamel Front and Back, fitted with Mirror, Sifter for Loose Powder and Rouge Compact. $11.30

A-1435 — Same description as 1433-1434................$11.30

A-1436—Elginite, Fancy two-tone design, fitted with Mirror, Sifter for Loose Powder and Rouge Compact...$3.00

A-1437—Elginite, Fancy Design with Enamel Medallion, fitted with Mirror, Sifter for Loose Powder and Rouge Compact.......................$3.80

A-1438—Elginite, Engraved Enamel Medallion, fitted with Mirror, Sifter for Loose Powder and Rouge Compact. $3.00
A-1439—Same as above with Cake Powder............$3.00

A-1440—Indestructible Brilliant White Finish, Fancy Engraved, fitted with Mirror, Sifter for Loose Powder, Rouge Compact and Lipstick........................$4.50
A-1441—Same as above with Cake Powder.........$4.50

(Illustrations Four-Fifths Size)

A-1442—Indestructible Brilliant White Finish, Fancy Design with Enamel Medallion, fitted with Mirror, Sifter for Loose Powder, Rouge Compact and Lipstick...............$6.00
A-1443—Same as above with Cake Powder.........$6.00

ELGIN AMERICAN MANUFACTURING COMPANY
ELGIN, ILLINOIS. U.S.A.

Morgan and Allen Company, 1929.

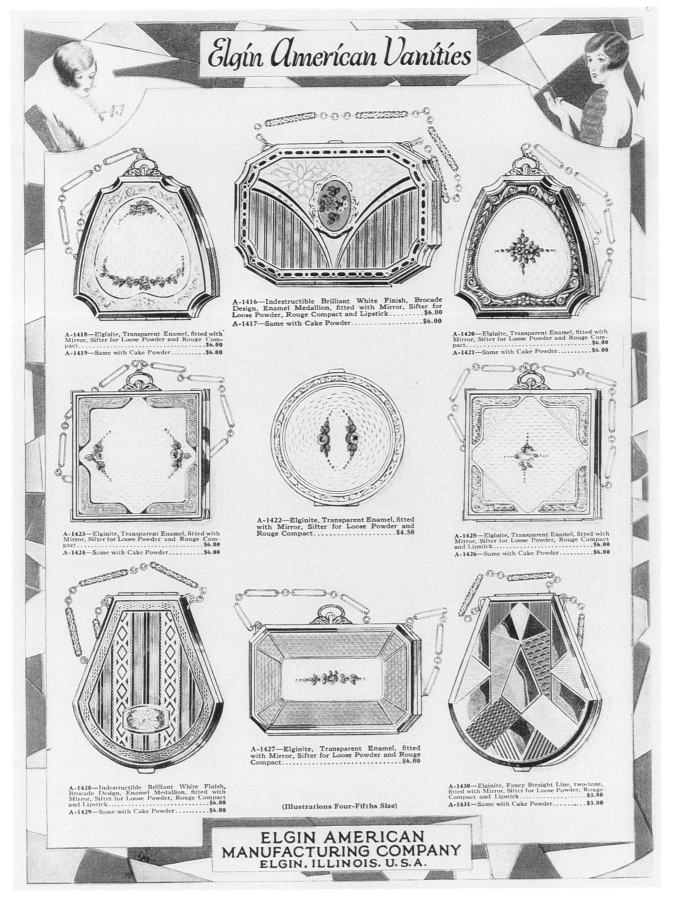

Morgan and Allen Company, 1929.

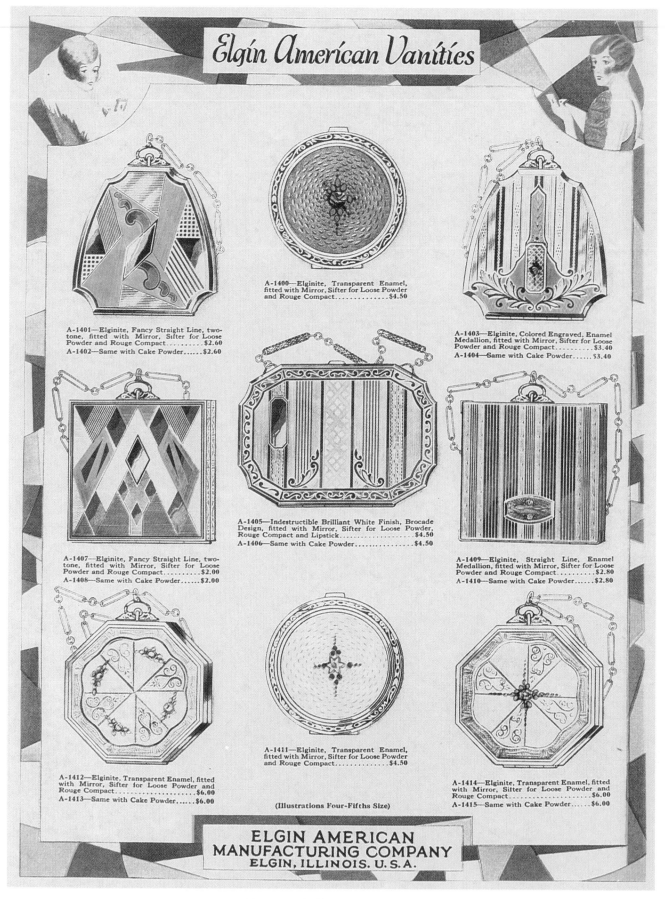

Elgin American Vanities

A-1401—Elginite, Fancy Straight Line, two-tone, fitted with Mirror, Sifter for Loose Powder and Rouge Compact..........$2.60
A-1402—Same with Cake Powder......$2.60

A-1400—Elginite, Transparent Enamel, fitted with Mirror, Sifter for Loose Powder and Rouge Compact.............$4.50

A-1403—Elginite, Colored Engraved, Enamel Medallion, fitted with Mirror, Sifter for Loose Powder and Rouge Compact..........$3.40
A-1404—Same with Cake Powder......$3.40

A-1407—Elginite, Fancy Straight Line, two-tone, fitted with Mirror, Sifter for Loose Powder and Rouge Compact..........$2.00
A-1408—Same with Cake Powder......$2.00

A-1405—Indestructible Brilliant White Finish, Brocade Design, fitted with Mirror, Sifter for Loose Powder, Rouge Compact and Lipstick...................$4.50
A-1406—Same with Cake Powder...............$4.50

A-1409—Elginite, Straight Line, Enamel Medallion, fitted with Mirror, Sifter for Loose Powder and Rouge Compact..........$2.80
A-1410—Same with Cake Powder......$2.80

A-1412—Elginite, Transparent Enamel, fitted with Mirror, Sifter for Loose Powder and Rouge Compact......................$6.00
A-1413—Same with Cake Powder......$6.00

A-1411—Elginite, Transparent Enamel, fitted with Mirror, Sifter for Loose Powder and Rouge Compact.............$4.50

(Illustrations Four-Fifths Size)

A-1414—Elginite, Transparent Enamel, fitted with Mirror, Sifter for Loose Powder and Rouge Compact......................$6.00
A-1415—Same with Cake Powder......$6.00

ELGIN AMERICAN MANUFACTURING COMPANY
ELGIN, ILLINOIS. U.S.A.

Morgan and Allen Company, 1929.

EWANS

E1562—White finish, French enamel front, contrasting colors, fitted with mirror, loose powder container, rouge and coin holders. $4.50 ea.

E1563—White finish, French enamel front, contrasting colors, fitted with large mirror, loose powder sifter, rouge and lipstick. $4.50 ea.

E1564—White finish, French enamel front, contrasting colors, fitted with mirror loose powder container, rouge and coin holders. $4.50 ea.

E1565—White finish, thin model, engine turned design with French enamel decoration in contrasting colors, fitted with large mirror, loose powder container, rouge and lip rouge container. $5.25 ea.

E1566—White finish, thin model French enamel decoration in contrasting colors, ultra-modern design, fitted with mirror, loose powder container, rouge and lip rouge container. $9.00 ea.

E1567—White finish, thin model French enamel front, modernistic design with flexible handle, fitted with large mirror, loose powder container, rouge and lip rouge container. $6.75 ea.

E1568—White finish, thin model, French enamel front with signet shield, fitted with large mirror, loose powder sifter, rouge and lipstick. $6.00 ea.

E1569—White finish, thin model combination vanity and cigarette case, French enamel front in contrasting colors, fitted with large mirror, loose powder container, rouge, lip rouge container and cigarette compartment. $7.50 ea.

E1570—White finish, French enamel front in contrasting colors, fitted with mirror, loose powder sifter, rouge, lip rouge container, perfumette, coin holders and bill fold. $8.25 ea.

Illustrations four-fifth size.

The LINE with the STERLING TOUCH

E. L. Rice, 1930.

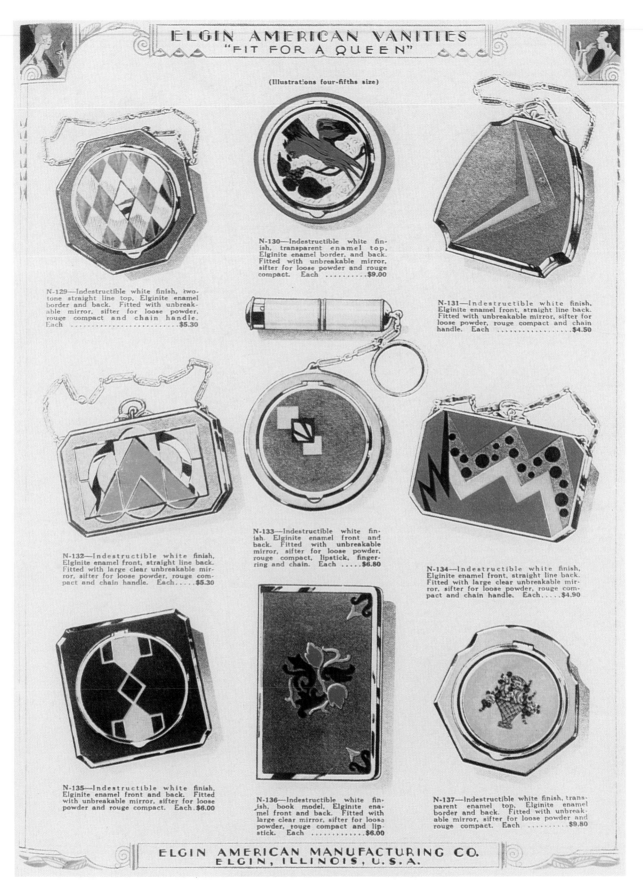

ELGIN AMERICAN VANITIES
"FIT FOR A QUEEN"

(Illustrations four-fifths size)

N-130—Indestructible white finish, transparent enamel top, Elginite enamel border, and back. Fitted with unbreakable mirror, sifter for loose powder and rouge compact. Each $9.00

N-129—Indestructible white finish, two-tone straight line top, Elginite enamel border and back. Fitted with unbreakable mirror, sifter for loose powder, rouge compact and chain handle. Each $5.30

N-131—Indestructible white finish, Elginite enamel front, straight line back. Fitted with unbreakable mirror, sifter for loose powder, rouge compact and chain handle. Each $4.50

N-133—Indestructible white finish. Elginite enamel front and back. Fitted with unbreakable mirror, sifter for loose powder, rouge compact, lipstick, finger-ring and chain. Each $6.80

N-132—Indestructible white finish, Elginite enamel front, straight line back. Fitted with large clear unbreakable mirror, sifter for loose powder, rouge compact and chain handle. Each.....$5.30

N-134—Indestructible white finish, Elginite enamel front, straight line back. Fitted with large clear unbreakable mirror, sifter for loose powder, rouge compact and chain handle. Each.....$4.90

N-135—Indestructible white finish, Elginite enamel front and back. Fitted with unbreakable mirror, sifter for loose powder and rouge compact. Each.$6.00

N-136—Indestructible white finish, book model. Elginite enamel front and back. Fitted with large clear mirror, sifter for loose powder, rouge compact and lipstick. Each $6.00

N-137—Indestructible white finish, transparent enamel top, Elginite enamel border and back. Fitted with unbreakable mirror, sifter for loose powder and rouge compact. Each $9.80

ELGIN AMERICAN MANUFACTURING CO.
ELGIN, ILLINOIS, U.S.A.

E. L. Rice, 1930.

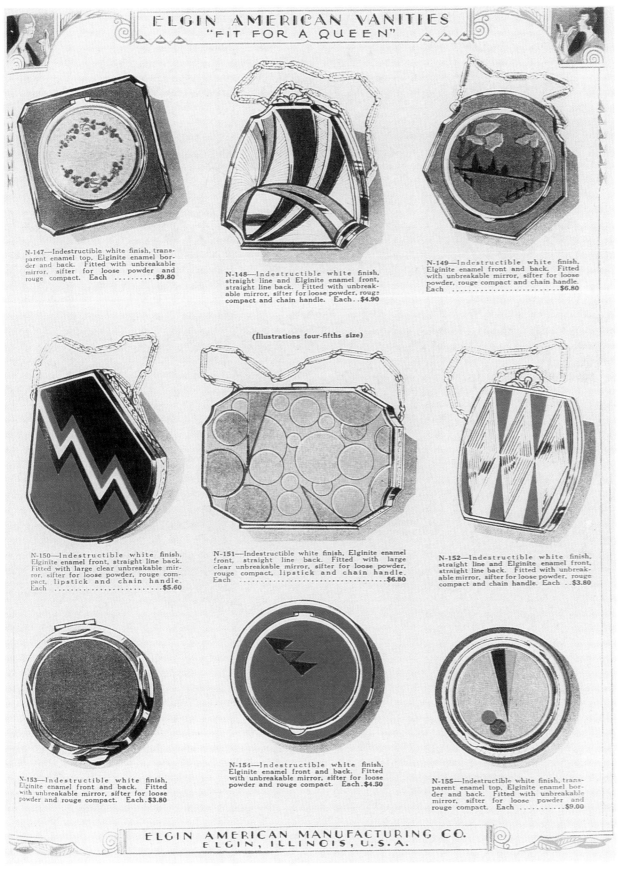

ELGIN AMERICAN VANITIES
"FIT FOR A QUEEN"

N-147—Indestructible white finish, transparent enamel top, Elginite enamel border and back. Fitted with unbreakable mirror, sifter for loose powder and rouge compact. Each $9.80

N-148—Indestructible white finish, straight line and Elginite enamel front, straight line back. Fitted with unbreakable mirror, sifter for loose powder, rouge compact and chain handle. Each ..$4.90

N-149—Indestructible white finish, Elginite enamel front and back. Fitted with unbreakable mirror, sifter for loose powder, rouge compact and chain handle. Each $6.80

(Illustrations four-fifths size)

N-150—Indestructible white finish, Elginite enamel front, straight line back. Fitted with large clear unbreakable mirror, sifter for loose powder, rouge compact, lipstick and chain handle. Each $5.60

N-151—Indestructible white finish, Elginite enamel front, straight line back. Fitted with large clear unbreakable mirror, sifter for loose powder, rouge compact, lipstick and chain handle. Each $6.80

N-152—Indestructible white finish, straight line and Elginite enamel front, straight line back. Fitted with unbreakable mirror, sifter for loose powder, rouge compact and chain handle. Each ...$3.80

N-153—Indestructible white finish, Elginite enamel front and back. Fitted with unbreakable mirror, sifter for loose powder and rouge compact. Each.$3.80

N-154—Indestructible white finish, Elginite enamel front and back. Fitted with unbreakable mirror, sifter for loose powder and rouge compact. Each.$4.50

N-155—Indestructible white finish, transparent enamel top, Elginite enamel border and back. Fitted with unbreakable mirror, sifter for loose powder and rouge compact. Each $9.00

ELGIN AMERICAN MANUFACTURING CO.
ELGIN, ILLINOIS, U.S.A.

E. L. Rice, 1930.

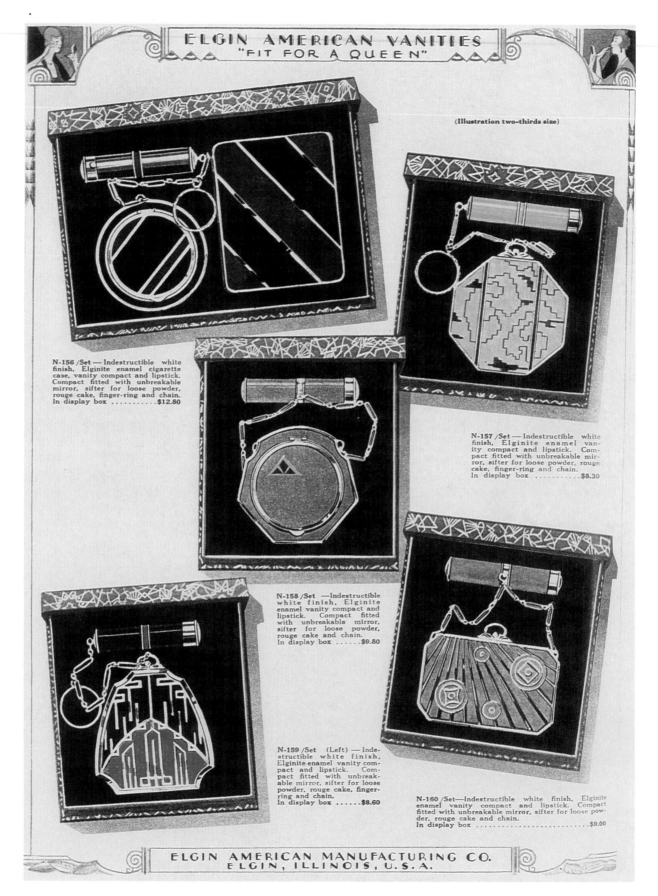

ELGIN AMERICAN VANITIES
"FIT FOR A QUEEN"

(Illustration two-thirds size)

N-156 /Set — Indestructible white finish, Elginite enamel cigarette case, vanity compact and lipstick. Compact fitted with unbreakable mirror, sifter for loose powder, rouge cake, finger-ring and chain. In display box $12.80

N-157 /Set — Indestructible white finish, Elginite enamel vanity compact and lipstick. Compact fitted with unbreakable mirror, sifter for loose powder, rouge cake, finger-ring and chain. In display box $8.30

N-158 /Set —Indestructible white finish, Elginite enamel vanity compact and lipstick. Compact fitted with unbreakable mirror, sifter for loose powder, rouge cake and chain. In display box $9.80

N-159 /Set (Left) — Indestructible white finish, Elginite enamel vanity compact and lipstick. Compact fitted with unbreakable mirror, sifter for loose powder, rouge cake, finger-ring and chain. In display box $8.60

N-160 /Set—Indestructible white finish, Elginite enamel vanity compact and lipstick. Compact fitted with unbreakable mirror, sifter for loose powder, rouge cake and chain. In display box $9.00

ELGIN AMERICAN MANUFACTURING CO.
ELGIN, ILLINOIS, U.S.A.

E. L. Rice, 1930.

ELGIN AMERICAN VANITIES
"FIT FOR A QUEEN"

N-139—Indestructible white finish, Elginite enamel front and back. Fitted with unbreakable mirror, sifter for loose powder and rouge compact. Each $5.30

N-138—Indestructible white finish, Elginite enamel front, straight line back. Fitted with unbreakable mirror, sifter for loose powder, rouge compact and chain handle. Each $3.90

(Illustrations four-fifths size)

N-140—Indestructible white finish, straight line and Elginite enamel front, straight line back. Fitted with unbreakable mirror, sifter for loose powder, rouge compact and chain handle. Each $4.50

N-141—Indestructible white finish, Elginite enamel and brocade top, enamel border and back. Fitted with unbreakable mirror, sifter for loose powder, rouge compact and chain handle. Each ..$6.80

N-142—Indestructible white finish, Elginite enamel front, straight line back. Fitted with large clear mirror, sifter for loose powder, rouge compact, comb and chain handle. Each $4.90

N-143—Indestructible white finish, Elginite enamel front and back. Fitted with unbreakable mirror, sifter for loose powder and rouge compact. Each.$6.00

N-144—Indestructible white finish, transparent enamel top, Elginite enamel border and back. Fitted with unbreakable mirror, sifter for loose powder and rouge compact. Each $8.30

N-145—Indestructible white finish, straight line and Elginite enamel front, straight line back. Fitted with large clear unbreakable mirror, sifter for loose powder, rouge compact, lipstick and chain handle. Each $6.00

N-146—Indestructible white finish, transparent enamel top, Elginite enamel border and back. Fitted with unbreakable mirror, sifter for loose powder, rouge compact and chain handle. Each.$10.50

ELGIN AMERICAN MANUFACTURING CO.
ELGIN, ILLINOIS, U.S.A.

E. L. Rice, 1930.

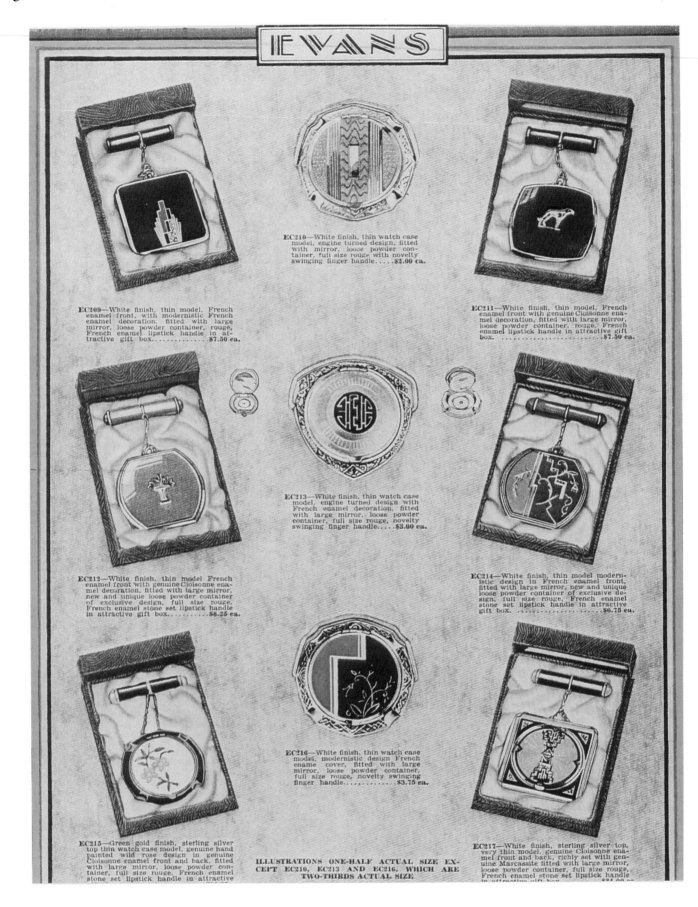

EC209—White finish, thin model, French enamel front, with modernistic French enamel decoration, fitted with large mirror, loose powder container, rouge, French enamel lipstick handle in attractive gift box.............$7.50 ea.

EC210—White finish, thin watch case model, engine turned design, fitted with mirror, loose powder container, full size rouge with novelty swinging finger handle.....$2.00 ea.

EC211—White finish, thin model, French enamel front with genuine Cloisonne enamel decoration, fitted with large mirror, loose powder container, rouge, French enamel lipstick handle in attractive gift box. ....$7.50 ea.

EC212—White finish, thin model French enamel front with genuine Cloisonne enamel decoration, fitted with large mirror, new and unique loose powder container of exclusive design, full size rouge, French enamel stone set lipstick handle in attractive gift box..........$8.25 ea.

EC213—White finish, thin watch case model, engine turned design with French enamel decoration, fitted with large mirror, loose powder container, full size rouge, novelty swinging finger handle.....$3.00 ea.

EC214—White finish, thin model modernistic design in French enamel front, fitted with large mirror, new and unique loose powder container of exclusive design, full size rouge, French enamel stone set lipstick handle in attractive gift box. ....$6.75 ea.

EC215—Green gold finish, sterling silver top thin watch case model, genuine hand painted wild rose design in genuine Cloisonne enamel front and back, fitted with large mirror, loose powder container, full size rouge, French enamel stone set lipstick handle in attractive

EC216—White finish, thin watch case model, modernistic design French ename cover, fitted with large mirror, loose powder container, full size rouge, novelty swinging finger handle.............$3.75 ea.

ILLUSTRATIONS ONE-HALF ACTUAL SIZE EXCEPT EC210, EC213 AND EC216, WHICH ARE TWO-THIRDS ACTUAL SIZE

EC217—White finish, sterling silver top, very thin model, genuine Cloisonne enamel front and back, richly set with genuine Marcassite fitted with large mirror, loose powder container, full size rouge, French enamel stone set lipstick handle in attractive gift box..........$24.00 ea.

Evans, The Jewelry Sales Guide, 1931.

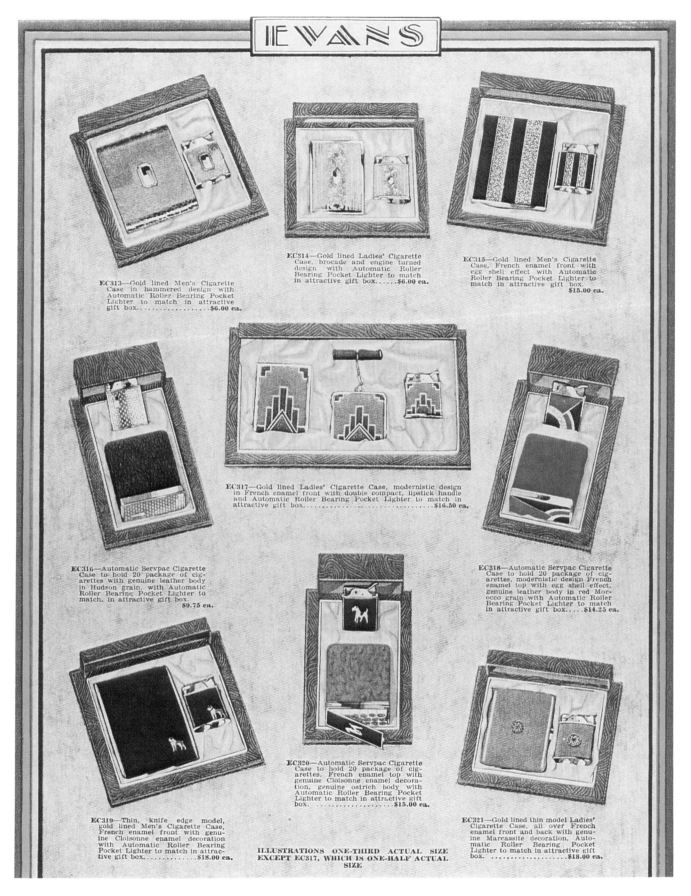

EC313—Gold lined Men's Cigarette Case in hammered design with Automatic Roller Bearing Pocket Lighter to match in attractive gift box................$6.00 ea.

EC314—Gold lined Ladies' Cigarette Case, brocade and engine turned design with Automatic Roller Bearing Pocket Lighter to match in attractive gift box......$6.00 ea.

EC315—Gold lined Men's Cigarette Case, French enamel front with egg shell effect with Automatic Roller Bearing Pocket Lighter to match in attractive gift box. $15.00 ea.

EC317—Gold lined Ladies' Cigarette Case, modernistic design in French enamel front with double compact, lipstick handle and Automatic Roller Bearing Pocket Lighter to match in attractive gift box................$16.50 ea.

EC316—Automatic Servpac Cigarette Case to hold 20 package of cigarettes with genuine leather body in Hudson grain, with Automatic Roller Bearing Pocket Lighter to match, in attractive gift box. $9.75 ea.

EC318—Automatic Servpac Cigarette Case to hold 20 package of cigarettes, modernistic design French enamel top with egg shell effect, genuine leather body in red Morocco grain with Automatic Roller Bearing Pocket Lighter to match in attractive gift box.....$14.25 ea.

EC320—Automatic Servpac Cigarette Case to hold 20 package of cigarettes, French enamel top with genuine Cloisonne enamel decoration, genuine ostrich body with Automatic Roller Bearing Pocket Lighter to match in attractive gift box. ....$15.00 ea.

EC319—Thin, knife edge model, gold lined Men's Cigarette Case, French enamel front with genuine Cloisonne enamel decoration with Automatic Roller Bearing Pocket Lighter to match in attractive gift box.............$18.00 ea.

ILLUSTRATIONS ONE-THIRD ACTUAL SIZE EXCEPT EC317, WHICH IS ONE-HALF ACTUAL SIZE

EC321—Gold lined thin model Ladies' Cigarette Case, all over French enamel front and back with genuine Marcassite decoration, Automatic Roller Bearing Pocket Lighter to match in attractive gift box. ....$18.00 ea.

Evans, The Jewelry Sales Guide, 1931.

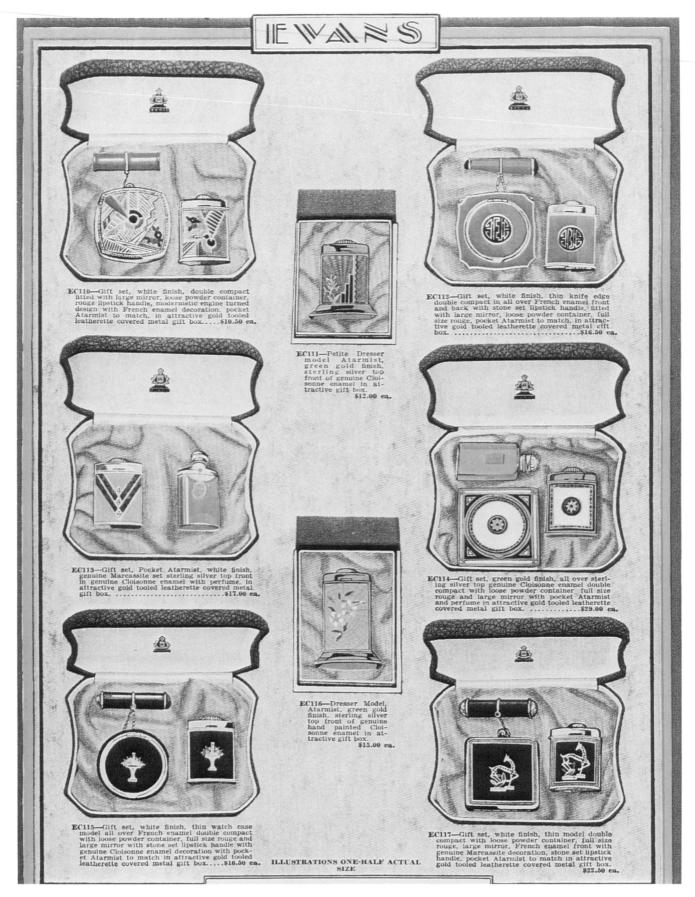

EC110—Gift set, white finish, double compact fitted with large mirror, loose powder container, rouge lipstick handle, modernistic engine turned design with French enamel decoration, pocket Atarmist to match, in attractive gold tooled leatherette covered metal gift box.....$16.50 ea.

EC111—Petite Dresser model Atarmist, green gold finish, sterling silver top front of genuine Cloisonne enamel in attractive gift box. $12.00 ea.

EC112—Gift set, white finish, thin knife edge double compact in all over French enamel front and back with stone set lipstick handle, fitted with large mirror, loose powder container, full size rouge, pocket Atarmist to match, in attractive gold tooled leatherette covered metal gift box. ....$16.50 ea.

EC113—Gift set, Pocket Atarmist, white finish, genuine Marcassite set sterling silver top front in genuine Cloisonne enamel with perfume, in attractive gold tooled leatherette covered metal gift box. ....$17.00 ea.

EC114—Gift set, green gold finish, all over sterling silver top genuine Cloisonne enamel double compact with loose powder container full size rouge and large mirror with pocket Atarmist and perfume in attractive gold tooled leatherette covered metal gift box. ....$29.00 ea.

EC115—Gift set, white finish, thin watch case model all over French enamel double compact with loose powder container, full size rouge and large mirror with stone set lipstick handle with genuine Cloisonne enamel decoration with pocket Atarmist to match in attractive gold tooled leatherette covered metal gift box.....$16.50 ea.

EC116—Dresser Model Atarmist, green gold finish, sterling silver top front of genuine hand painted Cloisonne enamel in attractive gift box. $15.00 ea.

EC117—Gift set, white finish, thin model double compact with loose powder container, full size rouge, large mirror, French enamel front with genuine Marcassite decoration, stone set lipstick handle, pocket Atarmist to match in attractive gold tooled leatherette covered metal gift box. $22.50 ea.

ILLUSTRATIONS ONE-HALF ACTUAL SIZE

Evans, The Jewelry Sales Guide, 1931.

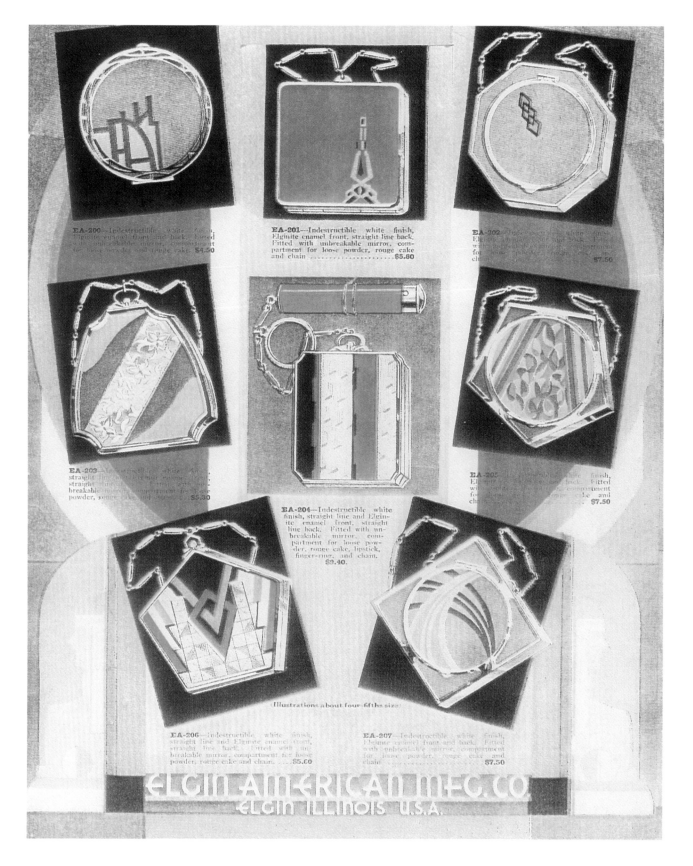

Evans, The Jewelry Sales Guide, 1931.

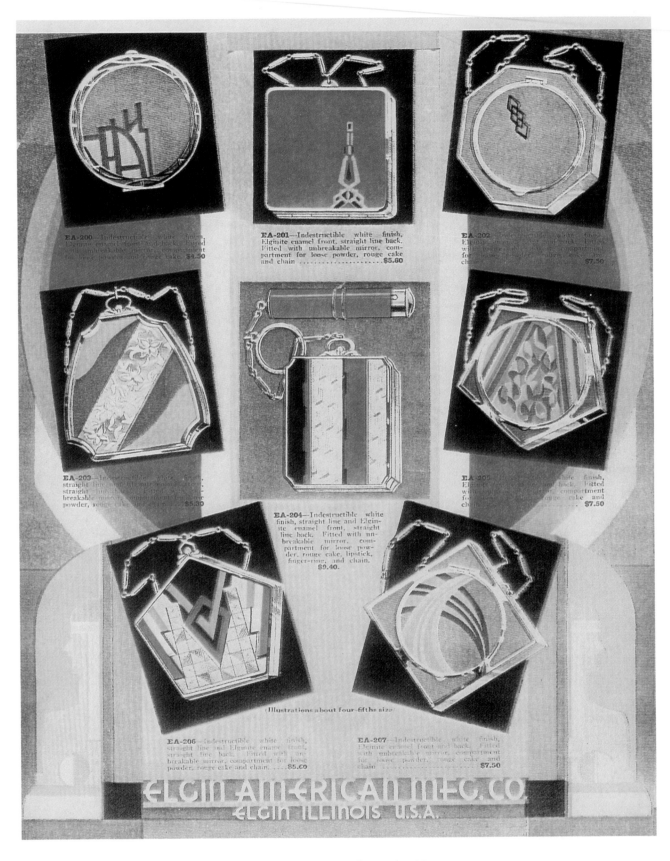

Evans, The Jewelry Sales Guide, 1931.

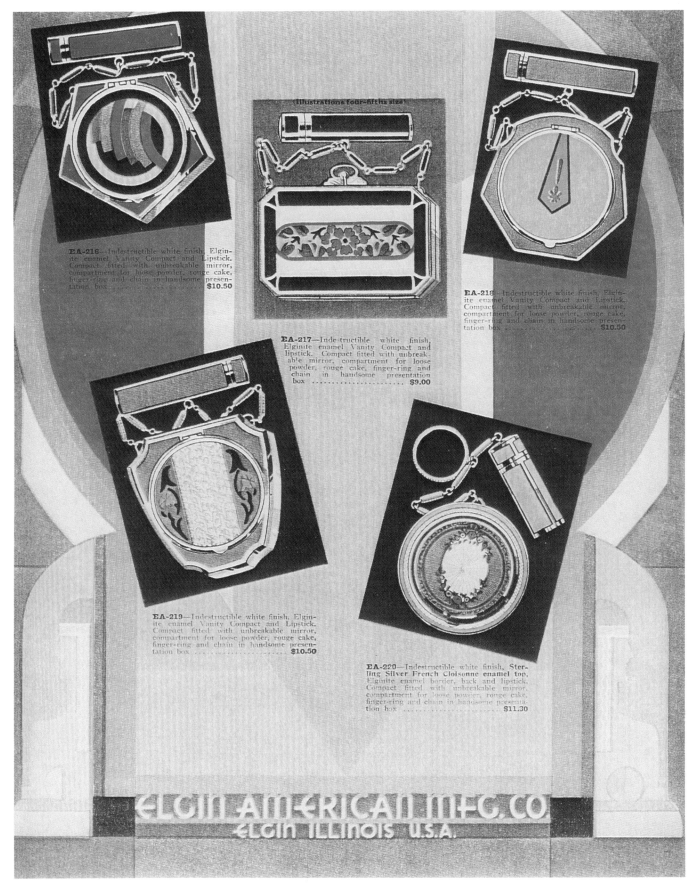

EA-216—Indestructible white finish, Elginite enamel Vanity Compact and Lipstick. Compact fitted with unbreakable mirror, compartment for loose powder, rouge cake, finger-ring and chain in handsome presentation box $10.50

(Illustrations four-fifths size)

EA-217—Indestructible white finish, Elginite enamel Vanity Compact and lipstick. Compact fitted with unbreakable mirror, compartment for loose powder, rouge cake, finger-ring and chain in handsome presentation box $9.00

EA-218—Indestructible white finish, Elginite enamel Vanity Compact and Lipstick. Compact fitted with unbreakable mirror, compartment for loose powder, rouge cake, finger-ring and chain in handsome presentation box $10.50

EA-219—Indestructible white finish, Elginite enamel Vanity Compact and Lipstick. Compact fitted with unbreakable mirror, compartment for loose powder, rouge cake, finger-ring and chain in handsome presentation box $10.50

EA-220—Indestructible white finish, Sterling Silver French Cloisonne enamel top, Elginite enamel border, back and lipstick. Compact fitted with unbreakable mirror, compartment for loose powder, rouge cake, finger-ring and chain in handsome presentation box $11.30

ELGIN AMERICAN MFG. CO.
ELGIN ILLINOIS U.S.A.

Evans, The Jewelry Sales Guide, 1931.

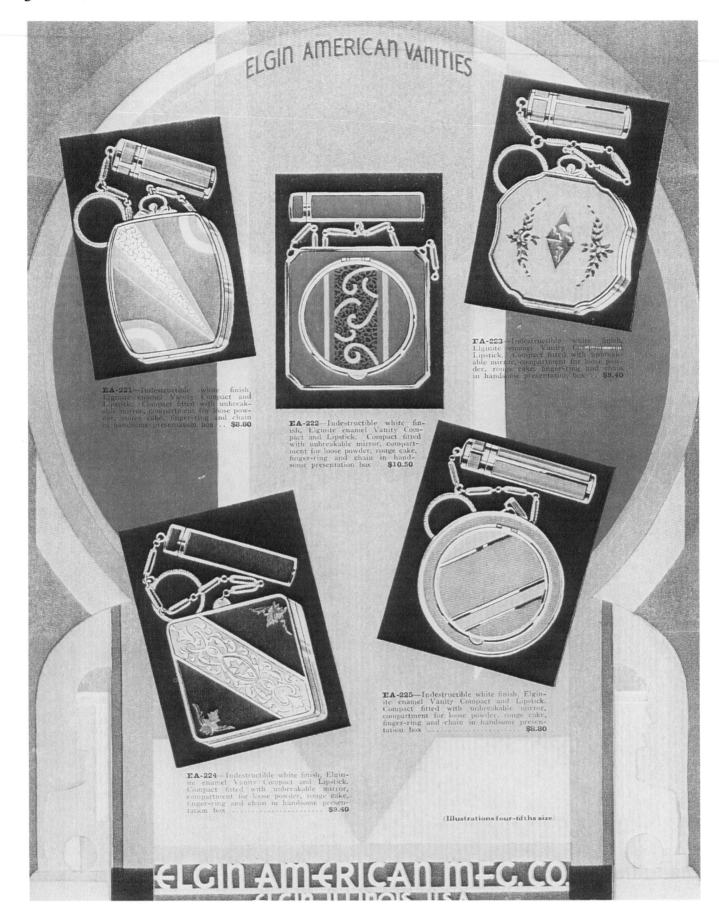

ELGIN AMERICAN VANITIES

EA-221—Indestructible white finish, Elginite enamel Vanity Compact and Lipstick. Compact fitted with unbreakable mirror, compartment for loose powder, rouge cake, finger-ring and chain in handsome presentation box . . **$8.80**

EA-222—Indestructible white finish, Elginite enamel Vanity Compact and Lipstick. Compact fitted with unbreakable mirror, compartment for loose powder, rouge cake, finger-ring and chain in handsome presentation box . **$10.50**

EA-223—Indestructible white finish, Elginite enamel Vanity Compact and Lipstick. Compact fitted with unbreakable mirror, compartment for loose powder, rouge cake, finger-ring and chain in handsome presentation box . . **$9.40**

EA-224—Indestructible white finish, Elginite enamel Vanity Compact and Lipstick. Compact fitted with unbreakable mirror, compartment for loose powder, rouge cake, finger-ring and chain in handsome presentation box **$9.40**

EA-225—Indestructible white finish, Elginite enamel Vanity Compact and Lipstick. Compact fitted with unbreakable mirror, compartment for loose powder, rouge cake, finger-ring and chain in handsome presentation box **$8.80**

(Illustrations four-fifths size)

ELGIN AMERICAN MFC. CO.

Evans, The Jewelry Sales Guide, 1931.

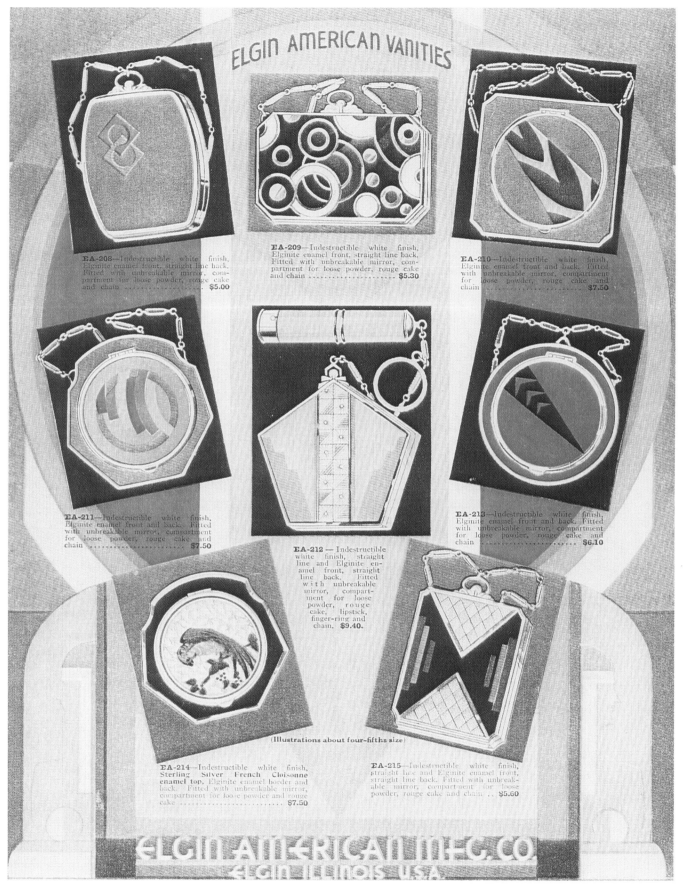

ELGIN AMERICAN VANITIES

EA-208—Indestructible white finish, Elginite enamel front, straight line back. Fitted with unbreakable mirror, compartment for loose powder, rouge cake and chain **$5.00**

EA-209—Indestructible white finish, Elginite enamel front, straight line back. Fitted with unbreakable mirror, compartment for loose powder, rouge cake and chain **$5.30**

EA-210—Indestructible white finish, Elginite enamel front and back. Fitted with unbreakable mirror, compartment for loose powder, rouge cake and chain **$7.50**

EA-211—Indestructible white finish, Elginite enamel front and back. Fitted with unbreakable mirror, compartment for loose powder, rouge cake and chain **$7.50**

EA-212 — Indestructible white finish, straight line and Elginite enamel front, straight line back. Fitted with unbreakable mirror, compartment for loose powder, rouge cake, lipstick, finger-ring and chain, **$9.40.**

EA-213—Indestructible white finish, Elginite enamel front and back. Fitted with unbreakable mirror, compartment for loose powder, rouge cake and chain **$6.10**

(Illustrations about four-fifths size)

EA-214—Indestructible white finish, Sterling Silver French Cloisonne enamel top, Elginite enamel border and back. Fitted with unbreakable mirror, compartment for loose powder and rouge cake **$7.50**

EA-215—Indestructible white finish, straight line and Elginite enamel front, straight line back. Fitted with unbreakable mirror, compartment for loose powder, rouge cake and chain .. **$5.60**

ELGIN AMERICAN MFG. CO.
ELGIN ILLINOIS U.S.A.

Evans, The Jewelry Sales Guide, 1931.

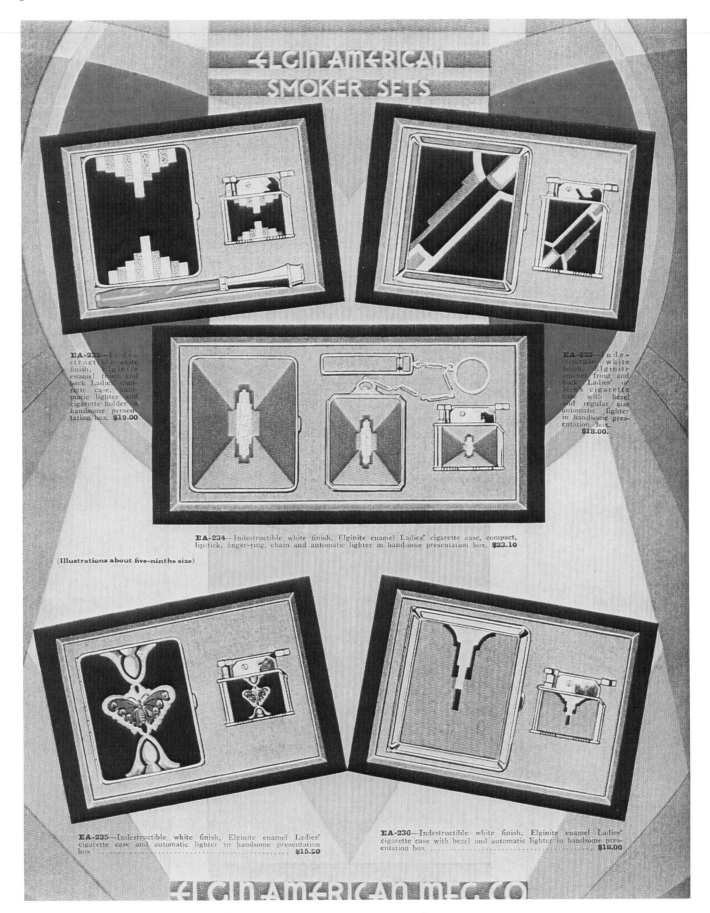

Evans, The Jewelry Sales Guide, 1931.

Evans, The Jewelry Sales Guide, 1931.

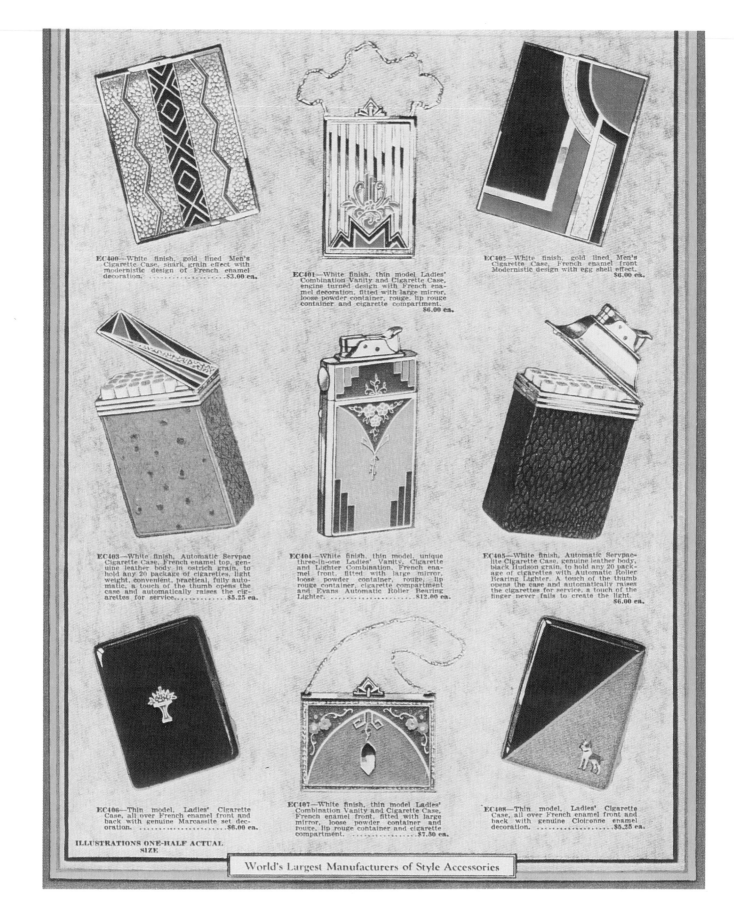

EC400—White finish, gold lined Men's Cigarette Case, snark grain effect with modernistic design of French enamel decoration. ....$3.00 ea.

EC401—White finish, thin model Ladies' Combination Vanity and Cigarette Case, engine turned design with French enamel decoration, fitted with large mirror, loose powder container, rouge, lip rouge container and cigarette compartment. $6.00 ea.

EC402—White finish, gold lined Men's Cigarette Case, French enamel front Modernistic design with egg shell effect. $6.00 ea.

EC403—White finish, Automatic Servpac Cigarette Case, French enamel top, genuine leather body in ostrich grain, to hold any 20 package of cigarettes, light weight, convenient, practical, fully automatic, a touch of the thumb opens the case and automatically raises the cigarettes for service............$5.25 ea.

EC404—White finish, thin model, unique three-in-one Ladies' Vanity, Cigarette and Lighter Combination, French enamel front, fitted with large mirror, loose powder container, rouge, lip rouge container, cigarette compartment and Evans Automatic Roller Bearing Lighter. ....$12.00 ea.

EC405—White finish, Automatic Servpaclite Cigarette Case, genuine leather body, black Hudson grain, to hold any 20 package of cigarettes with Automatic Roller Bearing Lighter. A touch of the thumb opens the case and automatically raises the cigarettes for service, a touch of the finger never fails to create the light. $6.00 ea.

EC406—Thin model, Ladies' Cigarette Case, all over French enamel front and back with genuine Marcassite set decoration. ....$6.00 ea.

EC407—White finish, thin model Ladies' Combination Vanity and Cigarette Case, French enamel front, fitted with large mirror, loose powder container and rouge, lip rouge container and cigarette compartment. ....$7.50 ea.

EC408—Thin model, Ladies' Cigarette Case, all over French enamel front and back with genuine Cloironne enamel decoration. ....$5.25 ea.

ILLUSTRATIONS ONE-HALF ACTUAL SIZE

World's Largest Manufacturers of Style Accessories

Evans, The Jewelry Sales Guide, 1931.

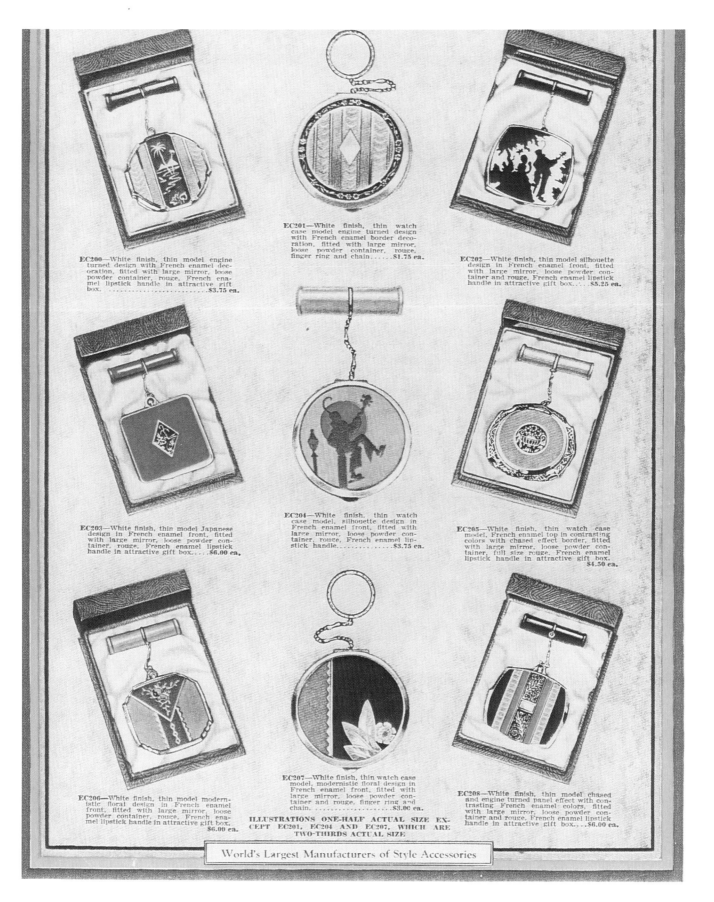

EC201—White finish, thin watch case model engine turned design with French enamel border decoration, fitted with large mirror, loose powder container, rouge, finger ring and chain......$1.75 ea.

EC200—White finish, thin model engine turned design with French enamel decoration, fitted with large mirror, loose powder container, rouge, French enamel lipstick handle in attractive gift box. ....$3.75 ea.

EC202—White finish, thin model silhouette design in French enamel front, fitted with large mirror, loose powder container and rouge, French enamel lipstick handle in attractive gift box....$5.25 ea.

EC203—White finish, thin model Japanese design in French enamel front, fitted with large mirror, loose powder container, rouge, French enamel lipstick handle in attractive gift box.....$6.00 ea.

EC204—White finish, thin watch case model, silhouette design in French enamel front, fitted with large mirror, loose powder container, rouge, French enamel lipstick handle.............$3.75 ea.

EC205—White finish, thin watch case model, French enamel top in contrasting colors with chased effect border, fitted with large mirror, loose powder container, full size rouge, French enamel lipstick handle in attractive gift box. $4.50 ea.

EC206—White finish, thin model modernistic floral design in French enamel front, fitted with large mirror, loose powder container, rouge, French enamel lipstick handle in attractive gift box. $6.00 ea.

EC207—White finish, thin watch case model, modernistic floral design in French enamel front, fitted with large mirror, loose powder container and rouge, finger ring and chain. ....$3.00 ea.

ILLUSTRATIONS ONE-HALF ACTUAL SIZE EXCEPT EC201, EC204 AND EC207, WHICH ARE TWO-THIRDS ACTUAL SIZE

EC208—White finish, thin model chased and engine turned panel effect with contrasting French enamel colors, fitted with large mirror, loose powder container and rouge, French enamel lipstick handle in attractive gift box....$6.00 ea.

World's Largest Manufacturers of Style Accessories

Evans, The Jewelry Sales Guide, 1931.

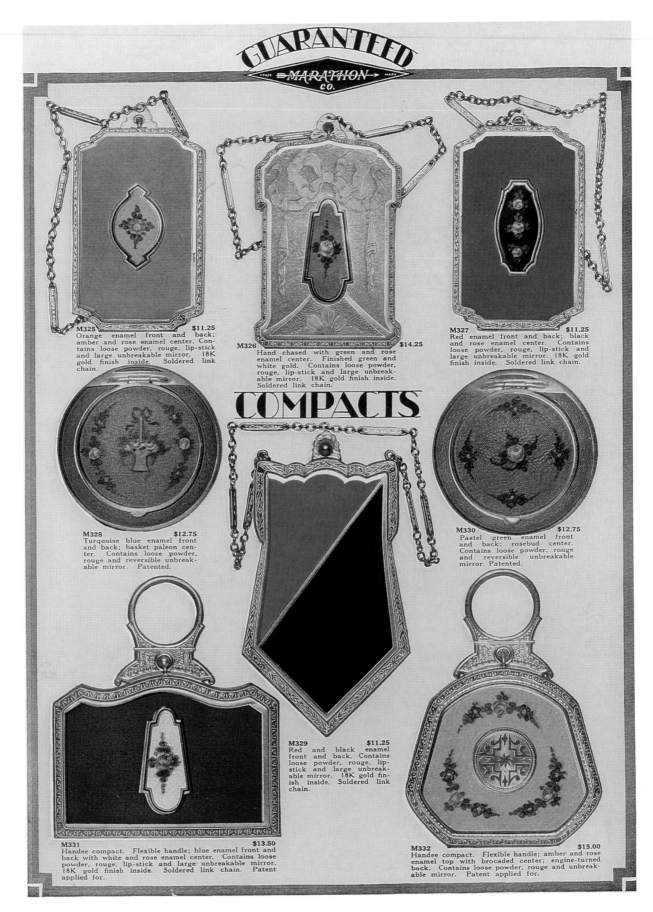

GUARANTEED

Marathon CO.

COMPACTS

M325   **$11.25**
Orange enamel front and back;
amber and rose enamel center. Contains loose powder, rouge, lip-stick
and large unbreakable mirror. 18K
gold finish inside. Soldered link
chain.

M326   **$14.25**
Hand chased with green and rose
enamel center. Finished green and
white gold. Contains loose powder,
rouge, lip-stick and large unbreakable mirror. 18K gold finish inside.
Soldered link chain.

M327   **$11.25**
Red enamel front and back; black
and rose enamel center. Contains
loose powder, rouge, lip-stick and
large unbreakable mirror. 18K gold
finish inside. Soldered link chain.

M328   **$12.75**
Turquoise blue enamel front
and back; basket paleon center. Contains loose powder,
rouge and reversible unbreakable mirror. Patented.

M330   **$12.75**
Pastel green enamel front
and back; rosebud center.
Contains loose powder, rouge
and reversible unbreakable
mirror. Patented.

M329   **$11.25**
Red and black enamel
front and back. Contains
loose powder, rouge, lip-
stick and large unbreak-
able mirror. 18K gold finish inside. Soldered link
chain.

M331   **$13.50**
Handee compact. Flexible handle; blue enamel front and
back with white and rose enamel center. Contains loose
powder, rouge, lip-stick and large unbreakable mirror.
18K gold finish inside. Soldered link chain. Patent
applied for.

M332   **$15.00**
Handee compact. Flexible handle; amber and rose
enamel top with brocaded center; engine-turned
back. Contains loose powder, rouge and unbreakable mirror. Patent applied for.

Marathon Co., 1930s.

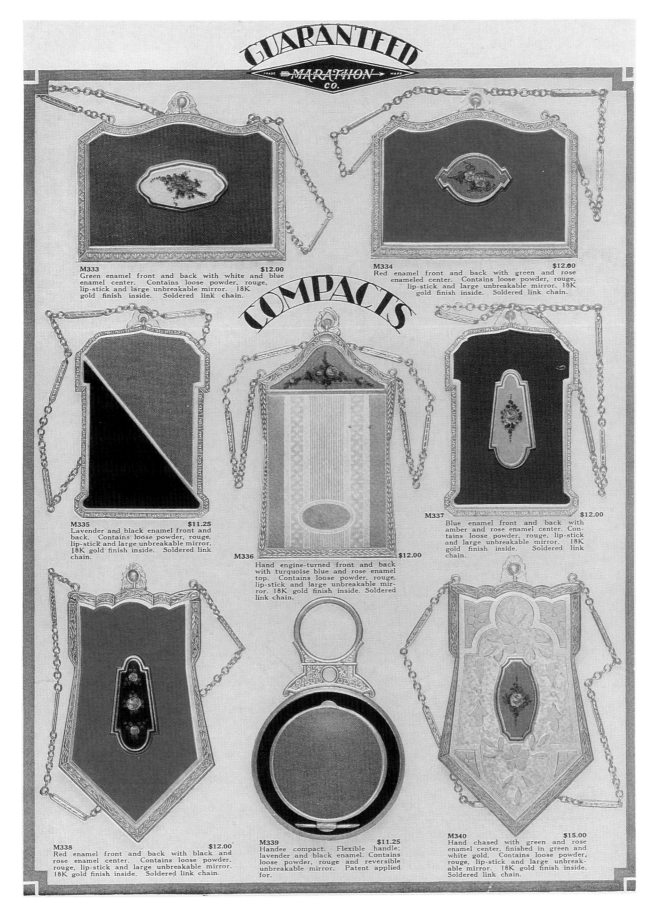

GUARANTEED Marathon Co.

COMPACTS

M333 $12.00
Green enamel front and back with white and blue enamel center. Contains loose powder, rouge, lip-stick and large unbreakable mirror. 18K gold finish inside. Soldered link chain.

M334 $12.00
Red enamel front and back with green and rose enameled center. Contains loose powder, rouge, lip-stick and large unbreakable mirror. 18K gold finish inside. Soldered link chain.

M335 $11.25
Lavender and black enamel front and back. Contains loose powder, rouge, lip-stick and large unbreakable mirror. 18K gold finish inside. Soldered link chain.

M336 $12.00
Hand engine-turned front and back with turquoise blue and rose enamel top. Contains loose powder, rouge, lip-stick and large unbreakable mirror. 18K gold finish inside. Soldered link chain.

M337 $12.00
Blue enamel front and back with amber and rose enamel center. Contains loose powder, rouge, lip-stick and large unbreakable mirror. 18K gold finish inside. Soldered link chain.

M338 $12.00
Red enamel front and back with black and rose enamel center. Contains loose powder, rouge, lip-stick and large unbreakable mirror. 18K gold finish inside. Soldered link chain.

M339 $11.25
Handee compact. Flexible handle; lavender and black enamel. Contains loose powder, rouge and reversible unbreakable mirror. Patent applied for.

M340 $15.00
Hand chased with green and rose enamel center, finished in green and white gold. Contains loose powder, rouge, lip-stick and large unbreakable mirror. 18K gold finish inside. Soldered link chain.

Marathon Co., 1930s.

79

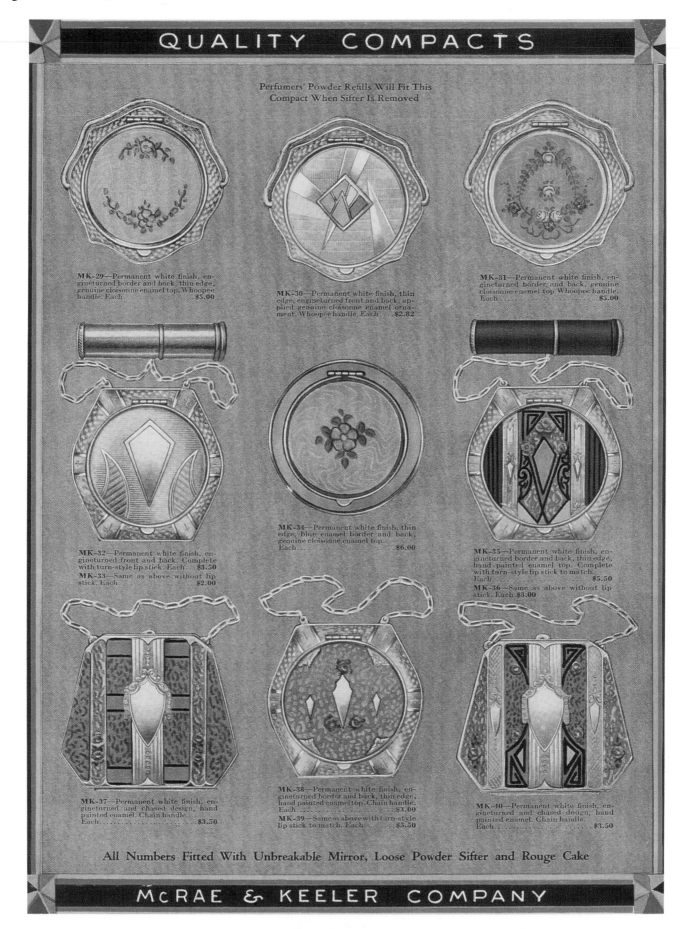

QUALITY COMPACTS

Perfumers' Powder Refills Will Fit This
Compact When Sifter Is Removed

MK-29—Permanent white finish, engineturned border and back, thin edge, genuine cloisonne enamel top. Whoopee handle. Each $5.00

MK-30—Permanent white finish, thin edge, engineturned front and back, applied genuine cloisonne enamel ornament. Whoopee handle. Each $2.82

MK-31—Permanent white finish, engineturned border and back, genuine cloisonne enamel top. Whoopee handle. Each $5.00

MK-32—Permanent white finish, engineturned front and back. Complete with turn-style lip stick. Each $3.50
MK-33—Same as above without lip stick. Each $2.00

MK-34—Permanent white finish, thin edge, blue enamel border and back, genuine cloisonne enamel top. Each $6.00

MK-35—Permanent white finish, engineturned border and back, thin edge, hand painted enamel top. Complete with turn-style lip stick to match. Each $5.50
MK-36—Same as above without lip stick. Each $3.00

MK-37—Permanent white finish, engineturned and chased design, hand painted enamel. Chain handle. Each $3.50

MK-38—Permanent white finish, engineturned border and back, thin edge, hand painted enamel top. Chain handle. Each $3.00
MK-39—Same as above with turn-style lip stick to match. Each $5.50

MK-40—Permanent white finish, engineturned and chased design, hand painted enamel. Chain handle. Each $3.50

All Numbers Fitted With Unbreakable Mirror, Loose Powder Sifter and Rouge Cake

McRAE & KEELER COMPANY

McRae & Keeler Co., 1930s.

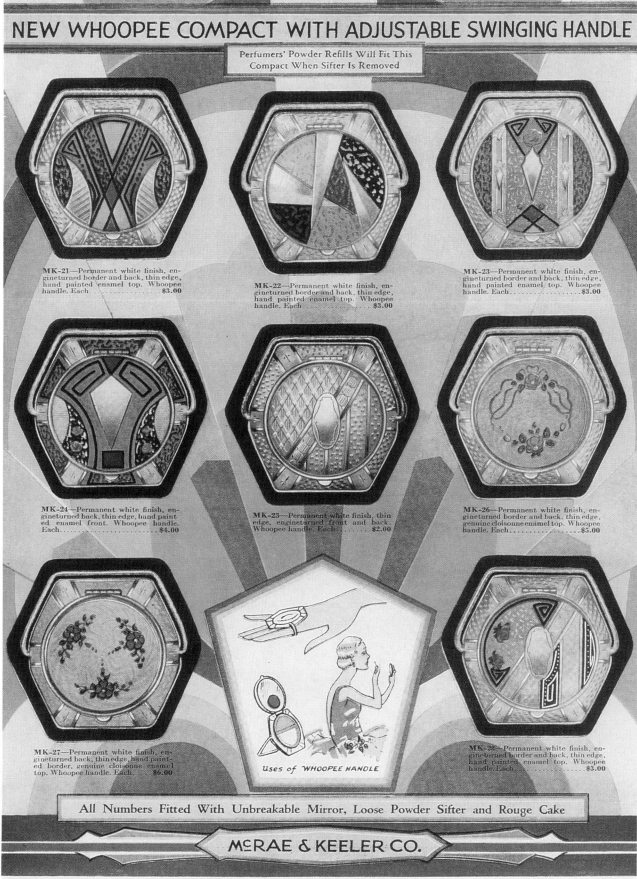

NEW WHOOPEE COMPACT WITH ADJUSTABLE SWINGING HANDLE

Perfumers' Powder Refills Will Fit This
Compact When Sifter Is Removed

MK-21—Permanent white finish, engineturned border and back, thin edge, hand painted enamel top. Whoopee handle. Each.................$3.00

MK-22—Permanent white finish, engineturned border and back, thin edge, hand painted enamel top. Whoopee handle. Each.................$3.00

MK-23—Permanent white finish, engineturned border and back, thin edge, hand painted enamel top. Whoopee handle. Each.................$3.00

MK-24—Permanent white finish, engineturned back, thin edge, hand painted enamel front. Whoopee handle. Each.................$4.00

MK-25—Permanent white finish, thin edge, engineturned front and back. Whoopee handle. Each........$2.00

MK-26—Permanent white finish, engineturned border and back, thin edge, genuine cloisonne enamel top. Whoopee handle. Each.................$5.00

MK-27—Permanent white finish, engineturned back, thin edge, hand painted border, genuine cloisonne enamel top. Whoopee handle. Each. $6.00

Uses of WHOOPEE HANDLE

MK-28—Permanent white finish, engineturned border and back, thin edge, hand painted enamel top. Whoopee handle. Each.................$3.00

All Numbers Fitted With Unbreakable Mirror, Loose Powder Sifter and Rouge Cake

McRAE & KEELER CO.

Illustrations are about 4/5 actual size

McRae & Keeler Co., 1930s.

Gallery of Compacts

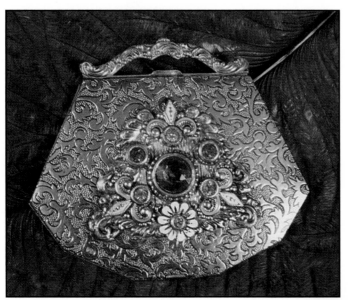

Prinzess goldtone compact designed to resemble purse; over-all engraved design; push-back handle reveals powder compartment; lid centered with colored stones and raised enamel flowers; Czechoslovakia; 3½" x 3". $150.00 – 200.00.

Goldtone Trinity Plate two sided vanity; lids and rim decorated with filigree overlay enhanced with cabachon and faceted blue and green colored stones; one side opens to reveal mirror and powder well; other side reveals pocket with pull-string powder puff; black tassel and carrying cord; 2½" dia x 1¼". $325.00 – 500.00.

Antique goldtone filigree vanity case with multicolored stones on lid; opens on either side; two sliding lipsticks at sides; one side opens for powder compartment, other side for rouge; screw perfume knob at top conceals metal perfume wand; black tassel and carrying cord; 2" x 1¼". $350.00 – 450.00.

Small round goldtone vanity; applied raised star design enhanced with blue stones decorates top lid; goldtone filigree and blue stones encircle second lid opening; top opens to reveals lip rouge; second opening reveals mirror separating powder and rouge compartment; 2" dia x 1¼". $175.00 – 250.00.

Left – Gilded-metal embossed vanity case; multicolored intaglio decorated lid; cameo disc centered on lid; metal tassel; carryng chain; velvet interior with compartment for powder, rouge, and lipstick tube; deeply beveled mirror framed with metal scallop; France; 3" x 2½". $300.00 – 400.00.

Top – Oblong gilded-metal embossed compact; multicolored intaglio decorated lid; prong set with red stones and painted cloisonne inserts; carrying chain; deeply beveled mirror framed with metal scallop; France; 1½" x 2½". $150.00 – 200.00.

Right – Gilded-metal embossed vanity case; multicolored intaglio decorated lid; prong set with pale pink stones; turquoise stones surround painted cloisonne centered disc; velvet interior with compartment for powder and lipstick tube; deeply beveled mirror framed with metal scallop; tassel; carrying chain; France; 2¾" x 2¾". $300.00 – 400.00.

Bottom – Gilded-metal embossed vanity case; multicolored intaglio decorated lid; prong set with blue stones; velvet interior with compartments for powder and two lipstick tubes; deeply beveled mirror framed with metal scallop; tassel; carrying chain; France; 2" x 2¾". $250.00 – 300.00.

Left – Brushed goldtone purse-motif vanity case; lid decorated with colored stones set on filigree plaque; interior reveals powder sifter, rouge compartment, and mirror; carrying chain; 3" x 2". $100.00 – 175.00.

Top – Antique goldtone vanity; lid set with colored stones; interior reveals compartments for powder, rouge, and lipstick tube; mesh carrying chain; 2¼" x 2½". $100.00 – 175.00.

Right – Purse-motif dark grained goldtone compact; interior reveals powder compartment, mirror, and coin and bill holders; blue stone centered on lid; carrying chain; 2¾" x 1¾". $75.00 – 100.00.

Bottom – Morss oblong brass compact; deeply engraved lid centered with pavé set rhinestones and green colored stones; 2⅞" x 2⅛". $100.00–125.00.

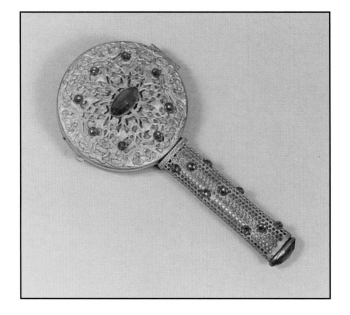

Goldtone vanity shaped as hand mirror; filigree lid and lipstick tube enhanced with red stones; interior opens to reveal mirror and powder and rouge compartments; lipstick slides out of handle; large faceted marquis red stone centered on lid and end of lipstick tube; 2" dia x 4". $200.00 – 250.00.

Top – Gilded-metal compact; filigree lid decorated with prong set red and green cabachon stones and prong set pearls; dome-shaped painted enamel disc centered on lid; interior reveals mirror and powder compartment; France; 2¼" x 2¼". $175.00 – 225.00.

Top Center – Horseshoe-shaped gilded-metal embossed compact; lid decorated with prong set red and green cabachon stones; blue disc with fleur-de-lis centered on lid; interior reveals beveled mirror and powder well; France; 1⅜" x 1¾". $125.00 – 150.00.

Bottom Center – Round embossed gilded-metal compact; lid set with dome-shaped painted enamel disc; interior contains mirror and powder well; France; 1½" dia. $40.00 – 60.00.

Bottom – Gilded-metal engraved comb case with comb; case decorated with enamel flower and bezel set colored stones; 4" x 1". $35.00 – 50.00.

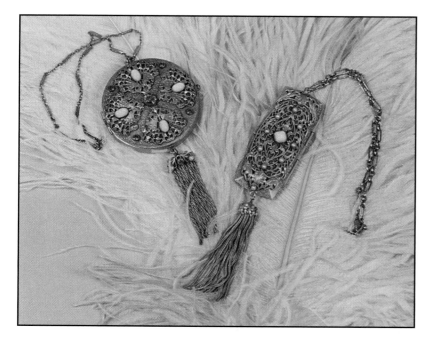

Left – Round antique goldtone compact; filigree lid set with pearls and yellow stones; interior reveals mirror and powder well; metal tassel and carrying chain; 2½" dia. $200.00–250.00.

Right – Oblong antique goldtone coin holder; filigree lid set with pearls; metal tassel and carrying chain; 1½" x 3¾". $175.00 – 225.00.

Left – Antique goldtone oblong filigree vanity; filigree lids set with pearls and yellow stones; interior reveals powder and rouge compartments and mirror; metal tassel and carrying chain; 1½" x 3". $300.00 – 350.00.

Right – Round antique goldtone filigree compact; filigree lids set with pearls; interior reveals mirror and powder compartment; metal tassel and carrying chain; 2" dia. $275.00 – 325.00.

Antique goldtone filigree vanity case; outer rims set with pearls and blue stones; openings on either side; one side powder compartment and mirror; other side rouge compartment and mirror; metal tassel and carrying chain; 2¾" dia. $300.00 – 400.00.

Antique goldtone vanity bag; filigree goldtone lid decorated with blue stones; moonstone centered on front lid of vanity; front lid opens to reveal framed mirror and compartments for rouge and powder; interior of bag silk lined with pockets on either side; silk back; jeweled carrying chain and tassel; Trinity Plate; 2" x 3½" x 1". NPA.

Left – Hallmarked sterling round compact; lavender cloisonne lid decorated with flowers; finger ring chain; 2" dia. $225.00 – 275.00.

Top – Silvertone and yellow enamel vanity; enamel lid decorated with flowers; interior reveals mirror and compartments for rouge and powder; finger ring chain; 2" x 2". $125.00 – 150.00.

Right – Green, off-white, and silvertone champleve vanity; interior reveals mirror and compartments for rouge and powder; finger ring chain; 2¼" dia. $100.00–125.00.

Bottom – E.A.M. blue cloisonne enamel vanity; lid decorated with flowers; interior reveals metal mirror, powder, and rouge compartments; wrist chain; 2½" x 1½". $125.00–150.00.

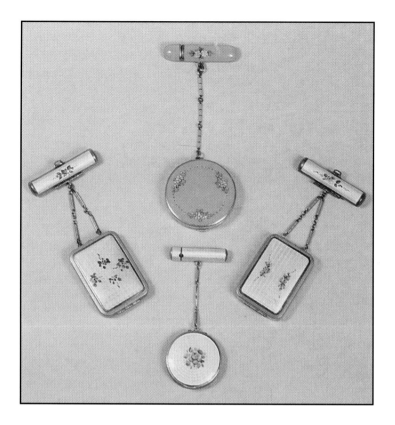

Left – Green enamel tango chain vanity; lid of vanity and lipstick holder decorated with flowers; lipstick holder suspended by two chains; interior of vanity reveals metal mirror separating powder and rouge compartments; lipstick holder opens up to accept slim lipstick tube; 1 ½" x 2" x 4 ½". $125.00 – 150.00.

Top – Hallmarked sterling green enamel tango chain vanity; enamel lid and lipstick holder decorated with flowers; lipstick suspended green enamel link chain; interior of vanity reveals mirror and compartments for powder and rouge; engraved next to hallmark is date 3–4–15; 2" dia x 5 ½". $250.00 – 300.00.

Right – Blue same as compact on left.

Bottom – Round yellow enamel mini-tango chain vanity; enamel lid and lipstick decorated with flowers; lipstick suspended by link chain; interior of vanity reveals metal mirror separating powder and rouge compartments; $100.00 – 125.00.

Left – D.F.B. Co. blue enamel vanity case with painted windmill scene; wrist carrying chain with key; powder sifter and rouge compartment; "Pat'd Feb. 9, 1926"; 3" x 2". $150.00 – 250.00.

Right – Same as left compact except for unusual feature, carrying finger ring on underside of compact.

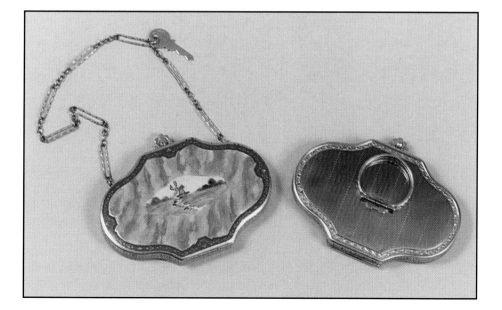

Lower Left – Lavender enamel vanity; enamel lid decorated with flowers; interior reveals metal mirror separating powder and rouge compartments; 2" x 1 ½". $40.00 – 60.00.

Top Left – RAC octagon-shaped green enamel tango chain compact; center of lid decorated with transfer decal of man and woman; lipstick tube decorated with flowers; 2" x 2" x 5". $150.00 – 175.00.

Top Center – Blue enamel octagon-shaped vanity; enamel lid decorated with flowers; finger chain; interior reveals powder well, metal mirror, and rouge compartmemt; 1 ¾" x 1 ¾". $60.00 – 75.00.

Top Right – White enamel octagon-shaped tango chain vanity; enamel lid decorated with flowers; lipstick tube suspended by two chains; interior reveals metal mirror, powder, and rouge compartments; 2" x 2" x 5". $150.00 – 175.00.

Lower Right – Blue, same as lower left compact.

Bottom Center – Yellow enamel vanity; enamel lid decorated with flowers; interior reveals metal mirror separating rouge and powder compartments; 1 ¾" x 2 ¼". $50.00 – 75.00.

Center – Round green enamel mini compact; enamel lid decorated with goldtone star design; 1 ½" dia. $75.00 – 100.00.

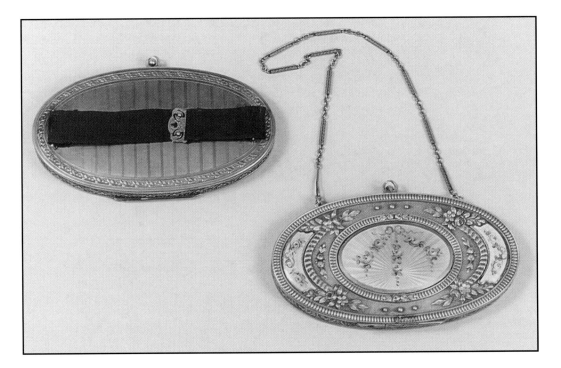

Left – Antiqued goldtone oval embossed vanity case; cloisonne lid decorated with flowers; compartments for powder sifter, rouge, lipstick, and coins; unusual grosgrain carrying handle on back lid; 4 ¾" x 2 ½". $350.00 – 500.00.
Right – Same as compact on the left except comes with carrying chain.

Foster & Bailey sterling silver green cloisonne vanity case suspended from enameled perfume container; powder and rouge compartments; lipstick attched at base; tassel and black enameled finger ring chain; 2" dia. x 8". $800.00 – 1,250.00.

Gilded turquoise enamel compact; turquoise lid decorated with a gold foliate overlay design; centered on lid is a hand-painted portrait on enamel; interior reveals beveled mirror; 2¾" x 2¼". $250.00 – 300.00.

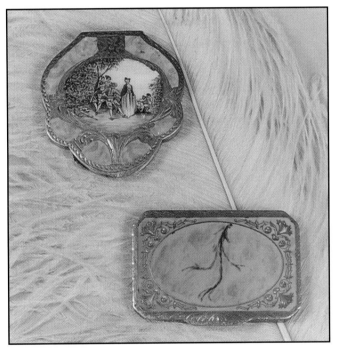

Top – Semi-scalloped blue enamel and gilded compact; hand-painted pastoral scene centered on lid; engraved back lid; interior reveals deeply beveled mirror and powder well; 2¾" x 2¾". $175.00 – 250.00.

Bottom – Gilded oblong blue enamel compact; enamel lid framed by deeply etched design; engraved back lid; interior reveals deeply beveled mirror and powder well; 2" x 3⅛". $150.00 – 175.00.

Gilded silver blue enamel compact; front lid decorated with exquisite hand-painted scene; back lid engraved; interior reveals deeply beveled mirror and powder well; carrying pouch reads "David Webb, Inc. New York"; 4" x 3". $350.00 – 400.00.

Left – Round gilt and enamel neck pendant compact with chain; colorful enameled lid decorated with Egyptian motif; interior reveals wire framed mirror, powder puff, and powder compartment; 1⅜" dia. $100.00 – 150.00.

Right – Round gilt and enamel neck pendant compact with chain; blue enameled lid decorated with green leaves; interior reveals wire framed mirror, powder puff, and powder compartment; 1⅜" dia. $100.00 – 150.00.

Shown open.

Shown closed.

Sterling and enamel round miniaudière; lid centered with stunning hand-painted pastoral scene; blue enamel dots encircle painting; interior reveals deeply beveled mirror; comb holder and comb swing down from mirror frame; lower center part for small necessities; flanked on either side by powder well and removeable lipstick tube and holder; interior lids, exterior back lid, and outer rim heavily engraved; decorative metal link chain; ornate clasp designed as bow; 3½" x 1". NPA.

Cobalt blue enamel coppertone compact designed to resemble an acorn; interior reveals mirror and powder well; matching enamel lipstick case concealed in tassel; carrying cord; Austria; 1½" x 2¾". $350.00 – 450.00.

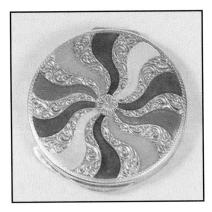

Round sterling compact; lid decorated with red, yellow, green, and blue enamel swirls; interior reveals beveled mirror and powder well; 2¾". $250.00 – 350.00.

Robert dresser vanity set; polished armchair-shaped compact; legs, arms, and back heavily engraved; filigree on back and skirt of chair elaborately decorated with pink flowers, rhinestones, and pink stones; lid of chair opens to reveal mirror, puff, and powder compartment; matching clock, perfume bottles, double sided hand mirror, mirrored tray, and picture frame; label affixed to compact mirror reads "Original by Robert"; compact 2½" dia x 5", clock 4½" x 3", perfume bottle holder 3" x 2½" x 2¾", hand mirror 4" dia x 9", tray 6" dia x 1½", frame 2¾" 3½". NPA.

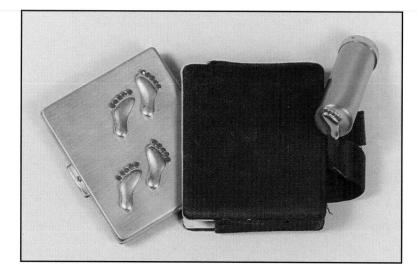

Flato goldtone compact, two sets of feet enhanced with red stones applied to lid; lipstick top has foot and red stones; complete with black satin case, 2½" x 2". NPA. Courtesy of Joan Orlen.

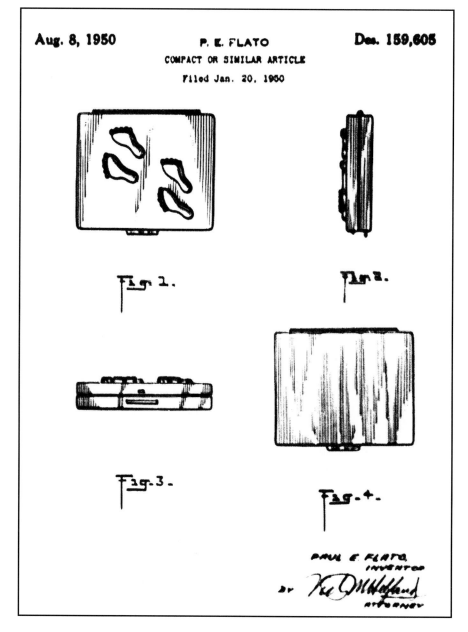

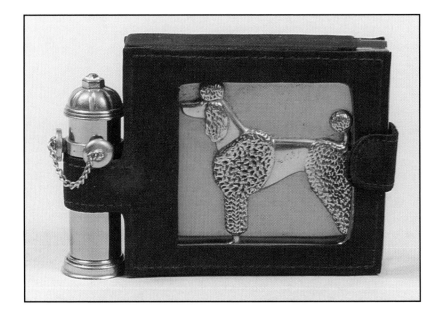

Robert square goldtone compact with large poodle applied to lid; lipstick takes the form of a fire hydrant; top of hydrant decorated with clear rhinestone; complete with black moire carrying case; Original by Robert logo imprinted on red carrying case lining and puff, 2¾" x 2¾". NPA. Courtesy of Joan Orlen.

Tokalon "Petalia" powder box; lid decorated with picture of Pierrot, collar design decorates sides of box; 2¼" dia. NPA.

Left – Flato goldtone compact with blue leather case; lid of compact and lipstick tube engraved with good luck symbols; goldtone horseshoe affixed to lid; attached sleeve for lipstick; 2½" x 3 ". $175.00 – 250.00.

Top Center – K & K brushed goldtone cigarette case; lid enhanced with band of turquoise and red stones; 3½" x 1½". $60.00 – 80.00.

Center – K & K brushed goldtone compact; compact opens when attached lipstick is pressed back; lid enhanced with band of turquoise and red stones; beveled mirror; Patent # 1802795; 2¼" x 3 ". $100.00 – $150.00.

Right – Flato goldtone compact; lid enhanced with raised circles centered with rhinestones; pink silk case with sleeve for lipstick; 2" x 2¾". $100.00 – 125.00.

Bottom Center – Rex round brushed silver tango chain compact; lid decorated with polished goldtone flowers; lipstick attached by chain; 3½" dia x 8". $175.00 – 200.00.

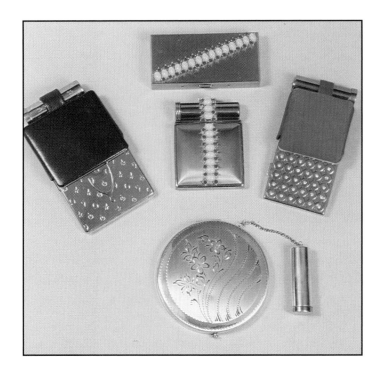

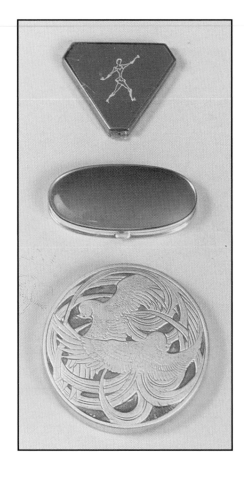

Top – *Schiaparelli triangular goldtone rouge compact; dark pink lid decorated with goldtone feminine figure; interior reveals mirror, heart shaped puff and rouge compartment; case signed; 2" x ⅜".*
$60.00 – 100.00.

Center – *Tiffany & Co. sterling oval compact; interior mirror and powder well; case signed; 2¾" x 1¼". $100.00 – 125.00.*

Bottom – *Roger & Gallet "Lalique" designed round aluminum compact; lid decorated with embossed cut-out birds on a light orange background; interior mirror, powder compartment, sifter, and "Roger & Gallet" powder puff; inner rim signed; France; 3" dia x ½". $200.00 – 250.00.*

Schiaparelli Rouge Compact Ad,
September, 1939.

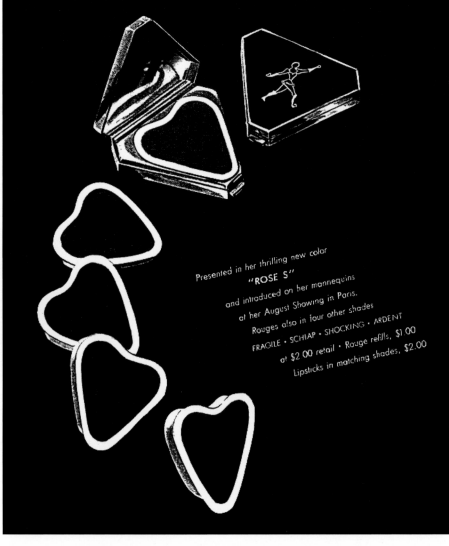

Presented in her thrilling new color
"ROSE S"
and introduced on her mannequins
at her August Showing in Paris.
Rouges also in four other shades
FRAGILE • SCHIAP • SHOCKING • ARDENT
at $2.00 retail • Rouge refills, $1.00
Lipsticks in matching shades, $2.00

Left – Ciner square goldtone compact with matching lipstick; compact lid and lipstick top decorated with faux pearls; interior mirror and powder well; gold threads decorate black fitted case; powder lid signed; 2¾" square. $175.00 – 200.00.

Center – Ciner square goldtone mini compact with matching lipstick; compact lid and lipstick tube covered in brown alligator leather; interior mirror and powder well; goldtone alligator applied to the top of lipstick tube and centered on compact lid; brown corduroy fitted case; powder lid signed; 2" x 2". $175.00 – 200.00.

Right – Ciner square goldtone compact with matching lipstick; compact lid and lipstick top decorated with pale orange cabachon stones; interior mirror and powder well; gold threads decorated black fitted case; powder lid signed; 2¾" square. $150.00 – 175.00.

Paloma Piccaso silver and goldtone round compact; dome shaped lid; interior mirror set at angle; red faceted stone and signature on inside gilded lid; 2½" x ¾". $125.00 – 175.00.

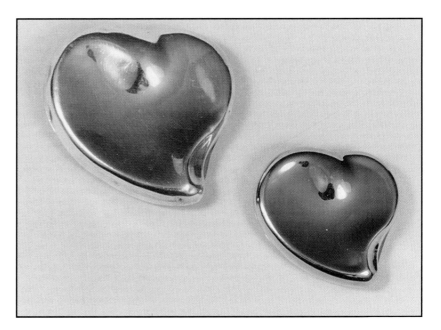

Left – Halston Elsa Peretti-designed silver-plated heart-shaped compact; #56620 incised on bottom of powder well; interior mirror; 3" x ¾". $150.00 – 200.00.

Right – Halston Elsa Peretti-designed goldtone heart-shaped compact; label on reverse side reads "Not for individual sale," sold boxed in conjunction with Halston fragrance; interior mirror, pressed powder, and puff; 2" x ½". $125.00 – 175.00.

Left – Eisenberg Original brushed goldtone square compact; large emerald-colored stoned applied to outer lid; interior mirror and powder well; powder lid signed; 3" x 3". $125.00 – 200.00.

Right – Eisenberg Original brushed goldtone square compact; lid set with multicolored marquis and round faceted stones; interior mirror and powder well; powder lid signed; 3" x 3". $125.00 – 200.00.

Gloria Vanderbilt square goldtone compact; lid decorated with painted raindrops, umbrellas, and figures holding umbrellas; "Apres la pluie, le beau temps" painted on front lid; interior mirror and powder well; case signed; 3¾" x 3¾". $150.00 – 225.00.

Left – Hattie Carnegie round goldtone compact with matching lipstick; outer rim of compact and lipstick tube set with green pronged faceted stones; interior reveals mirror and powder well; compact lid and inner lipstick tube signed; 2" dia. $150.00 – 180.00.

Right – Hattie Carnegie goldtone compact with matching lipstick; polished strip with small applied goldtone knots set with colored stones decorate deeply incised compact lid; interior mirror and powder well; powder lid and lipstick tube signed; 3¾" x 2¼". $175.00 – 225.00.

Left – Estee Lauder round silvertone compact; lid decorated with light blue, gray, and white Art Deco design; interior reveals mirror and powder well; signed interior rim; beautiful blue suede fitted presentation box with tassel; 4" dia. $175.00 – 225.00.

Right – Estee Lauder round polished silvertone compact; lid decorated with repousse leaf and ball design; interior reveals mirror and powder well; signed interior rim; beautiful blue suede fitted presentation box with tassel; 4" dia. $175.00 – 225.00.

Roger & Gallet Lucite compact; sunburst medallion molded and painted separately; hand applied to lid; two hinged closures on either side of front lid; interior reveals mirror and powder compartment; 4" x 4". $125.00 – 225.00.

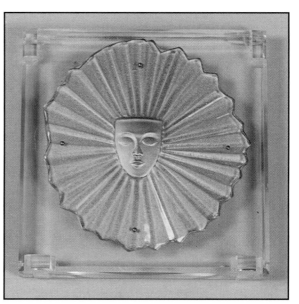

A Find: hand-pressed powder compact to eliminate siftings and the pfouff! of flying powder when you snap shut the lid. It's Roger & Gallet's, made of clear lucite, with a golden sunburst lifted from an Egyptian coin. Bonwit Teller.

Vogue, 1945.

Top – Trifari "lip-lock" brushed goldtone compact; lid decorated with applied framed disc of colored stones; pull-out lipstick opens compact; interior reveals signed powder well and mirror; 3¼" x 2¼" x 1". $225.00 – 275.00.

Bottom – Trifari square brushed goldtone compact; center of lid decorated with applied colored stones; interior reveals signed powder well and mirror; 3" x 3". $150.00 – 200.00.

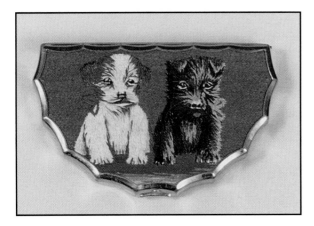

Scalloped half moon-shaped goldtone compact with two hand-stitched puppies on lid; scalloped interior mirror; reverse side engraved with wedding date of Tzeepa and Lenny 5/7/5; 3¾" x 2" x ½". $125.00 – 175.00. Courtesy of Joan Orlen.

Lilly Daché "Loving Touch" ivorene matching compact, lipstick, and rouge case; carved figures on a swing and foliage decorate round plastic compact lid, goldtone lipstick tube, and rouge case; compact interior reveals mirror and powder compartment; initials L.D. imprinted on compact and rouge lid; compact comes in hat box presentation box; compact 2¾" dia., rouge 4½" x 2½" x ⅞". NPA.

98

Round goldtone compact; plastic textured dog with moveable head applied to pearlized plastic lid; head moves right and left; Great Britain; 3" diam. $80.00 – 150.00.

Lower Left – Round pink enameled silvertone compact; three enameled dogs applied to center of lid; finger ring; 2⅛". $50.00 – 70.00.

Upper Left – Coppertone compact with black enamel cat decorated with blue stars on lid; 2¾" x 2⅜". $40.00 – 60.00.

Top Center – Square chrome vanity with cut corners; lid decorated with a three-dimensional blue elephant balancing on blue faceted ball; interior contains powder and rouge compartments; 2½" x 2½". $60.00 – 100.00.

Upper Right – Shields, Inc. square compact; light yellow enameled lid decorated with brown wash tub and two three-dimensional dogs; 2½" x 2½". $100.00 – 125.00.

Lower Right – Round coppertone compact with embossed black enamel cat centered on lid; finger ring chain; 1½" dia x ½". $75.00 – 125.00.

Bottom Center – Astor-Pak round plastic compact; silvertone Scottie dog centered on top of ivorene lid; bottom lid black; 3½" dia. $100.00 – 125.00.

Center – Round white enamel compact with mesh bottom; black poodle with raised fur centered on lid; 2½" dia. $60.00 – $80.00.

Shown closed.

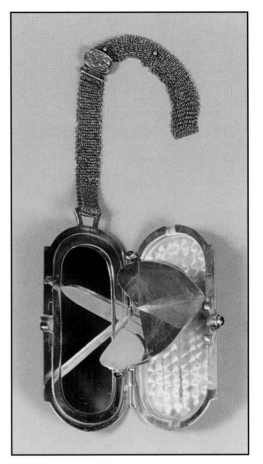

Tiffany & Co. sterling vanity case; exterior of case beautifully embossed; cartouche centered on both lids; interior reveals framed mirror, powder, and rouge covered compartments; sapphire thumb-pieces; wide mesh adjustable wrist carrying chain; 1¾" x 3¾" NPA.

Shown open.

Round dark green marbelized Bakelite compact; lid decorated with pink carved Bakelite roses and painted green leaves; interior reveals beveled mirror and powder compartment; plastic link carrying chain with finger ring; 2½" round. $125.00 – 200.00.

Oval coral Bakelite vanity; lid decorated with painted flowers set with clear and blue rhinestones; interior reveals mirror and compartments for powder and rouge; carrying cord; tassel conceals lipstick tube; 2" x 3⅓".
$225.00 – 300.00.

Round brown Bakelite compact; lids decorated with carved flowers; front lid further decorated with rhinestones; interior reveals mirror and powder compartment; carrying cord and tassel; 2" dia.
$125.00 – 200.00.

Round yellow Bakelite compact; lid decorated with pink flowers; Bakelite tube (lipstick or perfume) concealed in tassel; carrying cord; interior reveals mirror and powder well; 1¾" dia., tube 2½".
$150.00 – 190.00.

Chatain round red Bakelite vanity; lids decorated with carved goldtone highlights; interior reveals mirror, compartment for powder, and two Tokalon lipsticks, carrying cord and two tassels (replaced); Paris; 3¾" x 4". $250.00 – 350.00.

Round Bakelite rouge pot; screw-off top lid decorated with goldtone Buddah framed with black Bakelite; bottom lid butterscotch colored; interior reveals mirror, rouge, and decorated puff with same design as front lid; marked Germany; carryng cord centered on bottom lid; 1¾" dia x ½". NPA.

Left – Octagonal celluloid green marbelized compact; black compact lid decorated with rhinestones; interior reveals mirror and powder well; tassel; unusually long carrying cord; 2¼" x 2¼". $175.00 – 225.00.

Right – Black Bakelite compact; white engraved flowers on lid highlighted with colored stones; interior reveals mirror and powder compartment; tassel; unusually long carry cord; 2¼" x 2¼". $125.00 – 175.00.

Left – Octagonal celluloid compact; sides ivorene colored; lids decorated with multicolored sparkle; interior reveals mirror and powder compartment; carrying chain and tassel; 2½" x 2½". $150.00 – 200.00.

Right – Oblong coral colored Bakelite compact; sides ivorene; front lid decorated with black enamel designs and red colored stones; interior contains mirror and powder compartment; carrying cord and tassel; 2" x 2½" x ¾". $175.00 – 225.00.

Brown plastic composition compact; lids decorated with embossed textured flying cranes; interior reveals mirror and powder well; carrying cord; tassel (replaced); 3" x 4". NPA.

Black and ivorene Bakelite necessaire; front lid decorated with rhinestones; front opening reveals mirror and compartments for rouge and powder; back opening reveals fabric pocket for change, keys, etc.; carrying cord and tassel; 1¾" dia x 4". $350.00 – 450.00.

Black triangle-shaped Bakelite vanity; lid decorated with painted silver leaves enhanced with rhinestones; interior reveals powder well and lipstick compartment; ivorene rim; carrying cord and tassel; $175.00 – 225.00.

Tan plastic vanity case; lid decorated with maroon flowers; interior reveals mirror, powder and rouge compartments, two lipsticks, noir and vif, and pocket for puff; carrying cord and two tassels (replaced); 3¾" x 5". $350.00 – 450.00.

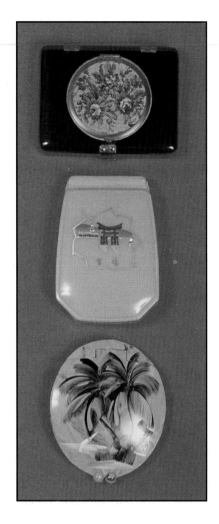

Top – Black Bakelite and tapestry vanity/cigarette case combination; black cigarette case lid incorporates tapestry-covered round vanity; interior of vanity reveals powder well, metal mirror, and rouge compartment in lid; Patent # 2055389; vanity case, 2¼" dia.; cigarette case, 3¾" x 3".
$150.00 – 175.00.

Center – Light green celluloid vanity case; lid decorated with hand painted Oriental scene; interior reveals compartments with removeable covered lip and cheek rouge containers, mirror, and powder compartment; 2¾" x 4".
$125.00 – 175.00.

Bottom – Yellow marbelized oval shaped plastic souvenir compact; Miami, Fla. and painted palm trees decorate lid; interior contains mirror and powder well; 3" x 3½". $40.00 – 80.00.

Green marbelized Bakelite stylized acorn-shaped compact; interior reveals mirror and large powder cavity; front decorated with silver etched designs enhanced with green colored stones; carrying cord; tassel (replaced); 2" dia x 4½". $250.00 – 350.00.

Black oblong Bakelite vanity; exterior beautifully decorated with clear
and green colored rhinestones; interior reveals mirror,
covered removeable powder and rouge containers and lipstick
compartment; carrying cord; tassel (replaced); 2¼" x 4".
$350.00 – 475.00.

Beautiful ivory, coral, and green colored plastic compact;
lid decorated with a Bohidsattva in a lotus blossom;
interior reveals mirror and powder well; carrying cord
and tassel; 2½" x 3¾". NPA.

Bone colored octagon plastic compact; textured front lid decorated with carved red flowers and green leaves; green marbelized back lid; compact centered on front lid, interior reveals mirror and powder well; plastic carrying chain; tassel (replaced); 3" x 3¾". $250.00 – 350.00.

Round avocado colored plastic compact; lid decorated with silver metal beads and rhinestones; interior reveals mirror and powder compartment; carrying cord and tassel; 3½" x 4¼". $300.00 – 375.00.

Bone colored plastic compact; detailed figures of male and female carved on front lid; interior of compact reveals mirror and powder well; fancy braided carrying cord; two lipsticks and one perfume bottle concealed in tassels; glass perfume bottle decorated with blue enamel stripes, perfume label reads "Rose-Calderara-Bankmann-Vienne"; 2" dia. NPA.

Black Bakelite compact; front lid decorated with rhinestones; interior of compact reveals mirror and powder well; carrying cord; two lipsticks marked Paris and one Bakelite tube containing perfume bottle concealed in fancy tassels; 2" dia. NPA.

Exquisite brown plastic vanity; exterior decorated with hand carved designs; top opening unscrews and reveals cheek rouge; second opening reveals mirror and powder well; third opening reveals cavity for change, keys, etc; lipstick tube concealed in silk embroidered tassel; rope carrying cord; 2¼" x 5". NPA.

Shown closed.

Black oblong Bakelite vanity and watch combination; front lid decorated with beautiful engraved silver roses enhanced with rhinestones; side closure rhinestone filigree clasp; removeable wrist watch; watch face shows through front lid; interior reveals mirror, powder compartment, two lipstick compartments, and watch compartment; Bakelite tube with perfume bottle concealed in silk tassel; fancy braided carrying cord;
2½" x 4". NPA.

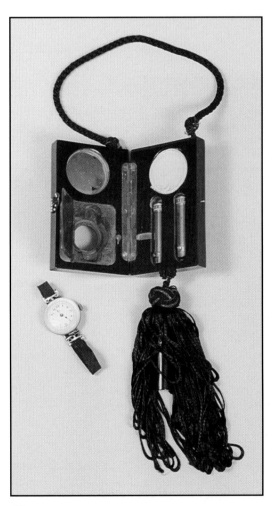

Shown open.

Left – Black shield-shaped Bakelite compact; lid enhanced with silver and gold metal beading and rhinestones; interior reveals beveled mirror, powder well, and second compartment; carrying cord and tassel (replaced); 3¼" x 5¼". $350.00 – 500.00.

Right – Green and black shield-shaped Bakelite compact; front and back lids green; lid decorated with metal beading and rhinestones; interior reveals beveled mirror, powder well, and second compartment; carrying cord and tassel (replaced); 3¼" x 5¼". $350.00 – 500.00.

Top – Fillkwik Co. Art Deco silvertone step pyramid-shaped black and red striped vanity; interior reveals metal mirror which separates powder and rouge compartments; small triangular fraternal emblem applied to lid; 1½" x 1¾". $75.00 – 100.00.

Top Center – Round silvertone compact; orange, black, and silver Art Deco design on lid; 2" dia. $50.00 – 75.00.

Bottom Center – Goldtone oblong vanity; lid decorated with blue and goldtone Art Deco design; interior reveals mirror and side by side rouge and powder compartments; 2¾" x 1½". $75.00 – 100.00.

Bottom – Zanadu goldtone vanity; beautiful orange, black, and goldtone Art Deco/Art Moderne design on lid; interior reveals mirror, powder and rouge compartments, and separate lipstick compartment with mini goldtone lipstick tube; 3½" x 1½". $100.00 – 125.00.

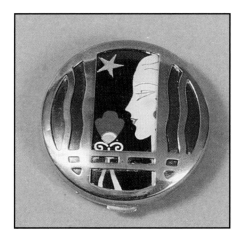

Karess round compact; goldtone top lid decorated with profile of woman, a rose, and a star on a dark blue and black background framed with goldtone bars; silvertone bottom lid; 1¾" dia. $80.00 – 150.00.

111

Silvertone octagon powder grinder "Flapper" compact; lid beautifully decorated with dancing couple and saxaphone player and drummer in black and silvertone; U.S. Patent # 1674525; 2" x 2". $120.00 – 200.00.

Round compact designed to resemble picture hat; lid covered with fabric resembling beads; lid further enhanced with colorful beads and mother-of-pearl petals; trimmed in pink velvet; reverse side black silk; 3" dia. NPA.

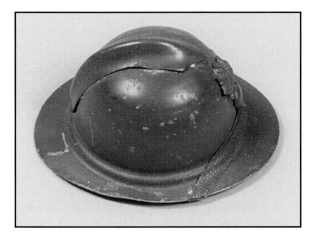

World War I miniature compact formed in the style of helmet; strap on front of olive green helmet; Cherbourg written on side; bottom opens to reveal interior mirror; 1 ¾" x 2 ¼". NPA.

Miref goldtone compact designed to resemble five star general's cap; visor decorated with five green stones centered on five engraved stars; interior beveled mirror; France; 2 " dia x 2 ¾". NPA.

Polished goldtone jockey cap; black visor decorated with red plastic bow; interior mirror and puff; 2" dia x 2¾". NPA.

Dorothy Gray round silvertone compact fashioned as picture hat; raised dome centered on lid; decorated with with bow and flowers; 3⅞" dia. $125.00 – 175.00.

Lower Left – Elgin American brushed goldtone compact; thermometer centered on lid; incised polished goldtone figures of women playing tennis, golf, ice skating, and horse back riding decorate the four corners of lid; 2¾" x 2¾". $120.00 – 150.00.

Upper Left – Round goldtone compass compact combination; working compass on lid protected by beveled glass dome; glass bottom lid; interior reveals deeply beveled mirror and powder compartment; 2¾" dia. $120.00 – 150.00.

Upper Right – Agme "dial-a-scene" gold and silvertone compact; silvertone lid framed by goldtone border; centered on lid are two openings which reveal scenes of Paris; moveable dials on either side; Switzerland; 2" x 3¼". $125.00 – 175.00.

Lower Right – Hingeco Vanities, Inc. "sardine can" compact; white enameled lid decorated with colorful scenes of Paris, London, New York, Swiss Alps, and Morocco; key on bottom of lid pulls out and turns to open compact; 2½" x 3". $150.00 – 200.00.

Bottom Center – Le Rage goldtone "dial-a-date" compact lid decorated with colorful activities; two moveable dials, one to indicate activity and the second one indicates time; England; 4" dia. $225.00 – 250.00.

Left – Goldtone "dial-a-date" compact with appointment reminders printed on lid protected by clear plastic; two moveable dials, one to set time, one to indicate appointment destination; beveled mirror, France, 2½" x 3". $150.00 – 175.00.

Right – Schildkraut goldtone "dial-a-date" compact with two moveable clock hands centered on round raised dome which indicates different activities and times, 3" x 2½". $150.00 – 175.00. Courtesy of Joan Orlen.

Lower Left – Volupte brushed goldtone compact; lid decorated with red, white, and blue enamel stripes and red, white, and blue stones; 3" x 3". $60.00 – 80.00.

Top Left – Plastic U.S. Navy hat compact; blue and black; lid decorated with goldtone navy insignia; 3" x 1¼". $75.00–90.00.

Top Center – Photo cigarette and compact combination; light blue enameled lid with American flag and "God Bless America" and "Liberty" in goldtone; hinged mirror separates powder and cigarette compartment; photo slides into back of mirror; 2¾" x 2½" x ¾". $125.00 – 150.00.

Upper Right – Sterling U.S. Army hat compact; lid decorated with embossed insiginia; interior lid of hat acts as mirror; 3" dia x 1¼". $125.00 – 175.00.

Lower Right – Elgin American goldtone compact; lid decorated with red, white, and blue enamel stripes; 2¾" x 2¾". $50.00 – 70.00.

Bottom Center – White enameled vanity; U.S. Marine insignia centered on lid; interior reveals metal mirror which separates powder and rouge compartments; 2¼" x 2¼". $40.00 – 60.00.

Center – Volupte round white enameled compact; lid decorated with a red anchor and a blue rope; 2½" dia. $50.00 – 70.00.

Round brushed silvertone compact; lid decorated with applied goldtone sailor and heart inscribed with the word "Taken"; matching silvertone sailor pin; pin was a gift from Alvin to me when he was in the U.S. Navy in 1945. Set $150.00 – 200.00.

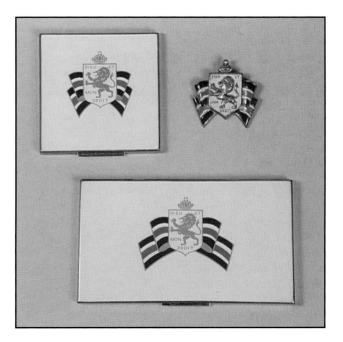

Henriette white enameled compact and matching cigarette case; matching pin by Accesscraft; lids decorated with goldtone lion centered on blue, white, and red ribbon; label affixed to compact mirror reads "Sole Authentic Case for Benefit of British War Relief Society and Bundles For Britain"; reverse side of pin reads "Official BWRS and BB"; compact 3" x 3", cigarette case 5 ¼" x 3". $175.00 – 225.00.

Silver compact designed to resemble drum; applied drum sticks on top lid; snares applied on bottom lid; tension wires encircle rims of drum; interior reveals metal mirror and powder well; 1 ½ dia x 1". NPA.

Black plastic compact designed to resemble guitar; plastic struts; interior reveals mirror, powder compartment, puff, and sifter; 2" x 5½". NPA. Courtesy of Barbara Schwerin.

Lower Left – Atomette goldtone suitcase compact; tan leather covers both front and back lids; metal handle, 3" x 2⅛" x ¾". $80.00 – $120.00.

Upper Left – Marbeized tortoise colored suitcase compact with goldtone hardware, 3" x 2½" x ½". $150.00 – 175.00.

Top Center – Mini black enameled suitcase vanity with goldtone hardware; decorated with gold travel stickers; interior has metal mirror separating rouge and powder compartments, 2" x 2". $80.00 – 120.00.

Upper Right – Kigu Compact of Character goldtone suitcase compact with lipstick encased in lid cover; marquesite horse and carriage decorate lid; interior mirror sticker reads "The inner lid opens automatically if outer lid is eased back fully; To close, return outer lid to vertical position and then press down inner lid," 3" x 2½" x ½". $175.00 – 225.00.

Lower Right – Goldtone suitcase compact decorated with B.O.A.C. travel stickers; push-back ridged handle, 3" x 2½" x ½". $160.00 – 180.00.

Center – Brown leather suitcase compact decorated with colorful travel stickers, double leather handles, 2¾" x 2½" x¾". $150.00 – 175.00.

*Lower Left – Blue enameled suitcase compact with goldtone snap opening, 3" x 2¼" x ¾".
$80.00 – $120.00.*

*Upper Left – Kigu goldtone suitcase compact; incised goldtone hardware; cartouche centered on lid;
"Bon Voyage" and Kigu logo inscribed on inner powder lid; push-back handle; 3¼" x 2¼" x ½".
$150.00 – 175.00.*

*Top Center – Wadsworth two-sided tan leather mini hatbox vanity; polished goldtone lids on either side;
powder/mirror compartment one side, rouge/locket compartment other side; leather finger carrying
handle, 1½" dia. x 1". $50.00 – 75.00.*

*Upper Right – Red marbelized suitcase vanity; goldtone hardware; colorful sticker scenes of New York
applied to both lids; interior reveals powder and rouge compartments; patent # 1883793 U.S.A.; 3" x
2½". $125.00 – 150.00.*

*Lower Right – Brushed goldtone suitcase compact with blue and red straps and corners, U.S.A.;
3" x 2¼". $150.00 – 175.00.*

*Bottom Center – Hingeco Vanities Inc. black enameled suitcase vanity; goldtone hardware; interior
reveals compartment for rouge, powder, and beveled mirror; 2¾" x 1¾". $175.00 – 225.00.*

*Middle – Zell round maroon hatbox compact; goldtone hardware; anchor and U.S.N. emblem centered
on lid; 3" dia. $150.00 – 175.00.*

Bottom – *Green leather photo compact popular during the war years; beveled mirror; open slot on lid to insert picture; picture protected by clear plastic; goldtone frame around picture; 1940s; 3" x 3". $80.00–120.00.*

Center – *Round goldtone photo vanity; interior reveals powder well, mirror, and rouge compartment; interior compartment can be removed to insert photo which is protected by clear plastic; 1920s; 2" diam x ½". $75.00 – 100.00.*

Top – *Red leather photo compact popular durng the war years; beveled mirror; open slot on lid to insert picture; picture protected by clear plastic; goldtone frame around picture; 1940; 3" x 3". $80.00–120.00.*

Left – *Abarbanel Original lucite photo compact; interior mirror slides out to permit insertion of picture; 3¾" x 3¾". $80.00–120.00.*

Top – *Lucite photo compact; picture placed behind removeable mirror; 3¼" x 3¼". $60.00–90.00.*

Right – *Ziegfeld Creation lucite photo compact with scalloped edges; photo slides into slot behind interior mirrror; 1940s; 4" x 4". $80.00–120.00.*

Lower Left – Elgin American round goldtone compact; lid decorated with a multi-colored enamel Eastern Star emblem; 3". $40.00 – 60.00.

Center Left – Parisian Nov. Co.; round promotional compact for Marksons Furniture; colored birthstones printed around outer lid; Pat. 11-2-15, 6-26-17; 2¼" dia. $80.00 – 100.00.

Upper Left – Parisian Nov.Co.; round promotional compact for Christo Cola; green background; Pat. 11-2-15, 6-26-17; 2¼" dia. $80.00 – 100.00.

Top Center – Brushed goldtone oblong compact; three transfers of cigarette packages on lid; 2⅜" x 3½". $100.00 – 125.00.

Upper Right – Cruver Manufcturing Co. round souvenir compact with picture of "House In Which Jenny Wade Was Shot," Gettysburg, PA; 2¼" x ½". $80.00 – 100.00.

Center Right – Parisian Nov. Co. round promotional compact for The Golden Pumpkin; Pat. 11-2-15, 6-26-17; 2¼" dia. $80.00 – 100.00.

Lower Right – Stratton round blue enameled compact; multicolored enameled Eastern Star decorates lid; England; 2¾" dia. $60.00 – 80.00.

Center – Vashe round silvertone vanity green enameled promotional vanity for Howard's; lid decorated with palm trees; interior has powder and rouge compartments; puff reads "Dine and Dance"; 2¾" dia. $80.00 – $100.00.

Lower Left – Ritz goldtone souvenir compact of Hawaii; brushed goldtone lid decorated with polished goldtone map of the Hawiian Islands; side clip for lipstick tube; 3½" x 2½". $60.00 – 100.00.

Top Left – Stratton souvenir compact from England; Queen Elizabeth and Prince Philip pictured on lid under clear plastic protector; England; 3" dia. $150.00 – 175.00.

Upper Right – Volupte goldtone souvenir compact of Brooklyn; silvertone compact lid decorated with polished goldtone famous Brooklyn sites; 3" x 3". $80.00 – 125.00.

Lower Right – Gwenda silvertone souvenir compact of Scotland; plaid lid decorated with stitched heather; back lid black enamel, matching plaid powder puff; England; 3" dia. $125.00 – 150.00.

Center – Black enameled souvenir compact of Paris; front lid decorated with goldtone Paris sites; France; 3½" x 2¾". $125.00 – $175.00.

Left – Round silvertone souvenir compact of Disneyland; polished goldtone Disneyland scene centered on brushed silvertone lid; 3½" dia. $60.00 – 100.00.

Top – Chrome octagonal-shaped souvenir of Canada; lid decorated with colorful flags; 2½" x 2½". $80.00– 120.00.

Right – Rosenfeld blue round leather souvenir compact of Israel; zipper closure; gold colored disc with dancing man and woman centered on lid; 3" dia. $60.00 – 100.00.

Bottom – Heart-shaped silvertone souvenir compact of Washington, D.C.; polished goldtone D.C. attractions on lid; 2¾" x 3 ". $40.00 – 60.00.

Center – Round green enameled souvenir compact with goldtone "U.S. Zone Germany" map and army insignia on lid; polished goldtone scalloped edges frame lid; reverse side goldtone; 4" dia. $250.00 – 300.00.

Round ball-shaped pink suede compact with goldtone trim around decorative closure; three bands of Austrian crystals encircle suede ball; pink suede finger holder; metal interior; beveled mirror; France; 2" dia. NPA.

Left – Henriette round ball-shaped gold-tone "Loves Me Loves Me Not" compact; Yes-No-Maybe printed around daisy petals; rolling ball selector; all enclosed under plastic dome; metal interior; Patent # 2138514; 2" dia. $150.00 – 225.00.

Center – Wadsworth goldtone "Ball & Chain" compact; goldtone lipstick tube attached by chain to round goldtone compact; plastic interior; 2" dia. $150.00 – 175.00.

Green iridescent ball-shaped Christmas ball compact; exterior highlighted with red and white stripes; plastic interior; also comes in solid iridescent colors of red or green and in a striped red iridescent color; 2" dia. $100.00 – 150.00.

Left – Kigu goldtone ball-shaped world globe compact; plastic interior; 1940s – 1950s; England; 1⅛" dia. $150.00 – 200.00.

Center – Kigu goldtone and silvertone ball-shaped world globe compact; continents in goldtone; oceans in silvertone; plastic interior; 1940s – 1950s; England; 2⅛" dia. $200.00 – 250.00.

Right – Pygmalion goldtone ball-shaped compact; exterior engraved with beautiful floral design; plastic interior; 2⅛" dia. $150.00 – 200.00.

Left – Rust colored leather mini ball-shaped compact with goldtone bands around fip-over closure; leather lined swinging beveled mirror; France; 1⅞".
$150.00 – 250.00.

Center – Majestic goldtone egg-shaped compact; metal interior; 2" x 3".
$80.00 – 100.00.

Right – Multicolored fabric mini ball-shaped compact with goldtone bands around flip-over closure; leather lined; interior mirror; 1¾".
$150.00 – 250.00.

Sterling silver mini ball-shaped pendant compact; engraved exterior; 1" dia. $200.00 – 250.00.

Left – K & K brass-colored basket-shaped compact; engine tooled; satin-finish lid; embossed swinging handle; metal interior; 2⅛" dia x 1¼". $80.00 – 120.00.

Center – Henriette black enamel basket-shaped compact without handle; goldtone trim; metal interior; Patent # 2138514; 2" dia x 1¼". $80.00 – 100.00.

Right – Kigu "Bouquet" goldtone basket-shaped compact; embossed with swing handle; plastic interior; England; 2" dia x 1⅛". $100.00 – 150.00.

Round red plastic compact with the embossed white "Stork Club" logo applied to lid; surrounded by two white plastic lipsticks with a black Stork Club logo and the names Jacqueline and Shermaine imprinted on them; Stork Club match book and postcards; many of these items were given away as promotional gifts by Sherman Billingsley, 4½" dia x ¾". NPA.

Left – Goldtone mother-of-pearl vanity designed to resemble book; lipstick tube slides out from spine; interior reveals beveled mirror, powder, and rouge compartments; 2" x 2½" x ½". $60.00 – 100.00.

Right – Mother-of-pearl compact with swing-out lipstick on back lid; interior mirror; exterior mirror on back lid beveled; 2" x 2" x ½". $60.00 – 80.00.

Center – Elgin American mother-of-pearl vanity; rouge compartment with mother-of-pearl lid centered on compact lid; 2¾" x 2¾". $60.00 – 100.00.

Left – Polished goldtone compact with lock motif; 2½" dia. $80.00 – 100.00.

Top – Zell goldtone heart-shaped compact; embossed key with red enamaling applied to lid; slit on top of applied key comes complete with cardboard key and red tassel; the cardboard key is meant to be replaced with an actual key; 2¾" x 2¾" x ½". $125.00 – 200.00.

Right – Zell Fifth Avenue goldtone compact with lock motif; outer lid decorated with ring of rhinestones; inner circle has clock face centered with a rotating dial; 2½" dia. NPA

Bottom – Hingeco sterling silver heart-shaped compact; interior reveals heart-shaped puff, screen, and mirror; cartouche on lid monogrammed with initials R.G.; 2½" x 2½". $125.00 – 175.00.

Back shown.

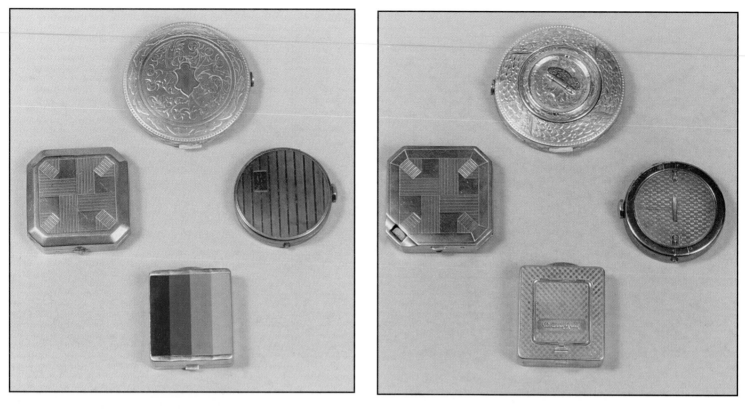

Left – S.G.D.G. silvertone powder-grinder vanity; interior reveals metal mirror which separates powder and rouge compartments; interior powder well lifts up to reveal solid powder grinder; France; 2" x 2". $70.00 – 90.00.

Top – Elizabeth Arden engraved silvertone powder sifter compact; top unscrews to reveal powder sifter; Switzerland; 2½" dia. $60.00 – 100.00.

Right – Montre A Poudre round goldtone powder-grider; back unscrews to reveal powder grinder; France; 2" dia. $60.00 – 100.00.

Bottom – Dorothy Gray silvertone vanity powder-grinder; lid decorated with four shades of blue enamel; interior reveals metal mirror which separates powder and rouge and lipstick compartments; back lid lifts off to reveal powder grinder; 1¾" x 2". $45.00 – 65.00.

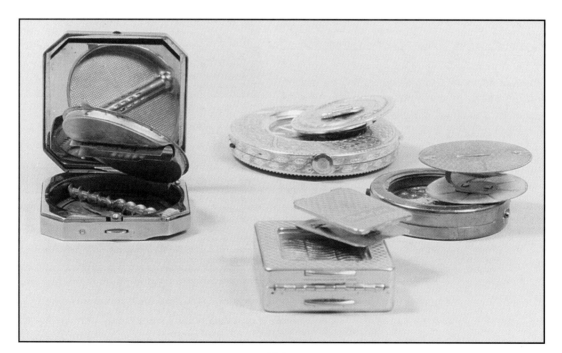

Shown open.

Left – Petit-point compact/cigarette case combination with lip-lock lipstick; front lid decorated with floral petit-point; opens to reveal powder compartment; back lid brushed goldtone opens to reveal cigarette compartment; Patent # 2060466; 3½" x 2½" x ¾". $125.00 – 175.00.

Center – Petit-point compact in fitted B. Altman Co. presentation box; front lid decorated with scene of man and woman walking hand-in-hand; back lid of compact black faille; 3¼" x 3¼" x ⅜". $175.00 – 225.00.

Right – Elgin American petit-point compact; lid decorated with petit-point city scene bordered by floral petit-point; back lid brushed goldtone; 3½" x 3". $80.00 – 120.00.

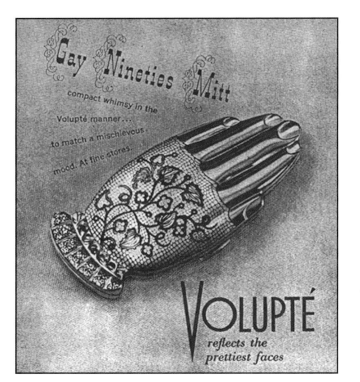

Volupté Gay Nineties Mitt, 1948.

Left – Volupte goldtone hand-shaped compact; lid decorated with enameled white lace mitt; multicolored enamel bracelet; Des. Patent # 120,347; 4½" x 2". $200.00 – 250.00.

Center – Volupte goldtone hand-shaped compact; lid decorated with enameled black lace mitt; faux "diamond" engagement ring; faux "diamond" bracelet; 4½" x 2". NPA.

Right – Volupte goldtone hand-shaped compact; front and back lids personalized with engraved bracelet and monograms; 4½" x 2". NPA.

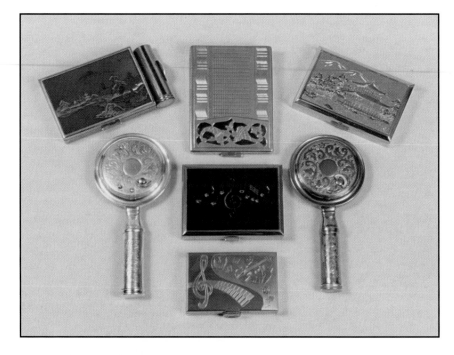

Lower Left – German silver engraved compact/music box combination designed to resemble hand mirror; interior beveled mirror; lipstick in handle; Germany; 2½" dia x 5¼". $150.00 – 225.00.

Upper Left – Wan damacene compact/music box combination with side clip for lipstick; interior beveled mirror; 2" x 3¾". $125.00 – 175.00.

Top Center – Marquis wedge-shaped engraved goldtone compact/music box combination; lid decorated with two cornucopias set on black disc; 2¾" x 3½". $125.00 – 175.00.

Upper Right – Clover goldtone compact/music box combination; lid decorated with Asian scene; 3½" x 2¼". $125.00 – 175.00.

Lower Right – Goldtone same as lower left.

Lower Center – Elgin American brushed goldtone compact/music box combination; lid engraved with polished goldtone instruments; lyre-shaped closure; 2¾" x 1¾". $125.00 – 150.00.

Center – Black enamel and goldtone compact/music box combination; enamel lid decorated with music notes set with green stones and G cleff; 3¼" x 2½". $150.00 – 175.00.

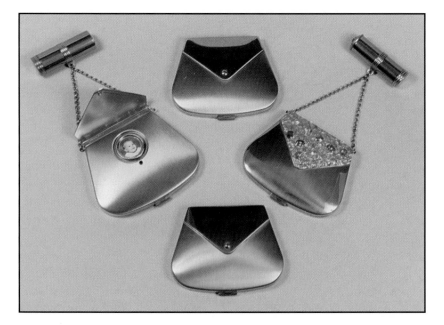

Left – Volupte brushed goldtone "Lucky Purse" compact "With Captive Lipstick"; polished goldtone flap opens to reveal opening for picture or rouge; tango chain lipstick tube suspended by two chains; sticker on mirror reads "Genuine Collectors Item by Volupte"; 3½" x 2¾". $135.00 – 160.00.

Top – Volupte brushed silvertone "Lucky Purse" compact; polished silvertone flap; sticker on mirror reads "Genuine Collectors Item by Volupte"; 3½" x 2¾". $80.00 – 100.00.

Right – Volupte polished goldtone "Lucky Purse" compact "With Captive Lipstick"; hammered goldtone flap decorated with multicolored stones; tango chain lipstick tube suspended by two chains; sticker on mirror reads "Genuine Collectors Item by Volupte"; 3½" x 2¾". $150.00 – 175.00.

Bottom – Volupte brushed goldtone "Lucky Purse" compact; polished goldtone flap; sticker on mirror reads "Genuine Collectors Item by Volupte"; 3½" x 2¾". $80.00 – 100.00.

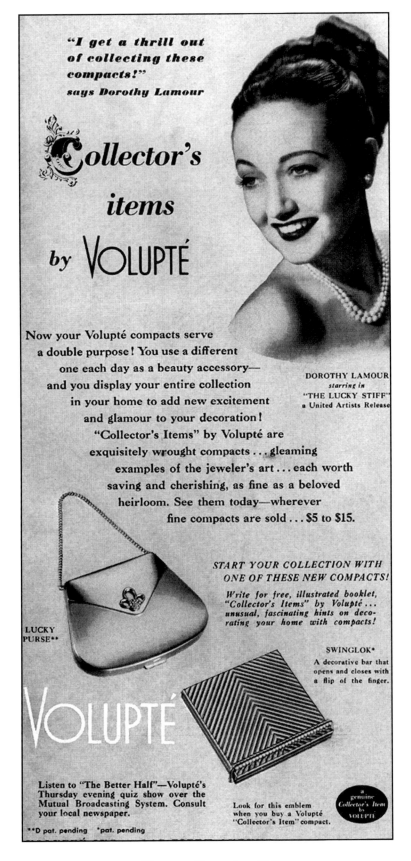

Glamour, November 1948.

Left – Pygmalion goldtone compact designed to resemble grand piano; interior puff reads "Sonato"; cartouch on embossed lid; collapsible legs; 2¼" x 2¾" x 1½". $350.00 – 450.00.

Center – Pygmalion goldtone compact designed to resemble grand piano; interior puff reads "Sonato"; mother-of-pearl lid; sticker on interior mirror reads "Marhill Genuine Mother-of-Pearl"; collapsible legs; 2¼" x 2¾" x 1½". NPA.

Right – Pygmalion goldtone compact/music box combination designed to resemble grand piano; interior puff reads "Sonato"; starburst design on lid; music box wind-up key located underneath compact; collapsible legs; 2¼" x 2¾" x 1½". NPA.

719,710
3 SHEETS
COMPLETE SPECIFICATION
This drawing is a reproduction of the Original on a reduced scale.
SHEET 1

Fig.1.

Fig.2.

Top – Volupte silvertone compact designed to resemble vanity table; collapsible cabriole legs; exterior and interior metal mirrors; presentation box reads "Petit Boudoir" "Miniature replica of Maria Antoinette's carved golden dressing table"; 3" x 2¼". $150.00 – 275.00.

Bottom – Wadsworth goldtone compact designed to resemble vanity table; collapsible cabriole legs; interior and exterior mirrors; 3" x 2". $150.00 – 275.00.

Patent By Salo David Rand, England, filed September 30, 1952.

128

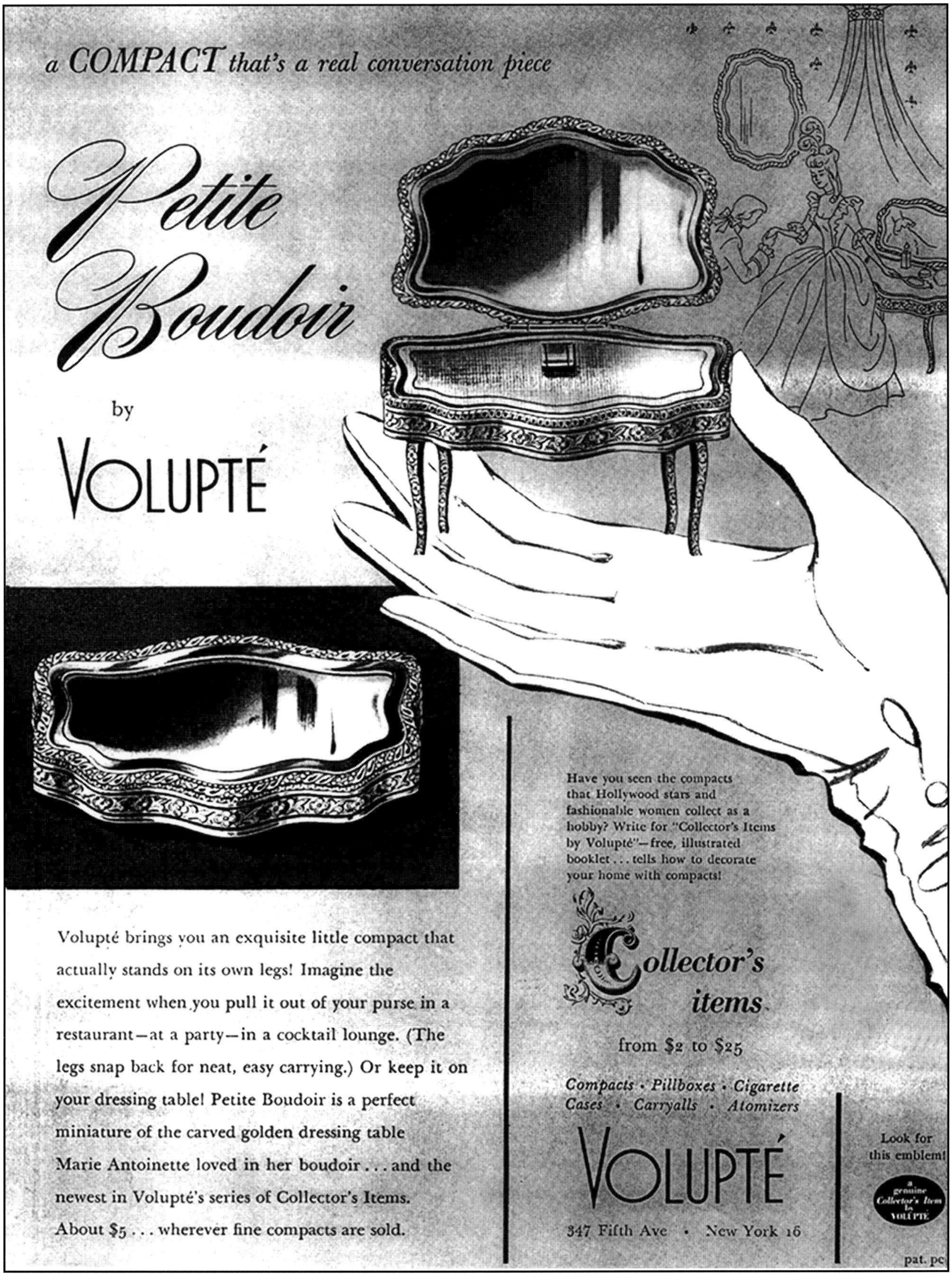

a COMPACT that's a real conversation piece

Petite Boudoir

by

VOLUPTÉ

Volupté brings you an exquisite little compact that actually stands on its own legs! Imagine the excitement when you pull it out of your purse in a restaurant—at a party—in a cocktail lounge. (The legs snap back for neat, easy carrying.) Or keep it on your dressing table! Petite Boudoir is a perfect miniature of the carved golden dressing table Marie Antoinette loved in her boudoir . . . and the newest in Volupté's series of Collector's Items. About $5 . . . wherever fine compacts are sold.

Have you seen the compacts that Hollywood stars and fashionable women collect as a hobby? Write for "Collector's Items by Volupté"—free, illustrated booklet . . . tells how to decorate your home with compacts!

Collector's items

from $2 to $25

Compacts · Pillboxes · Cigarette Cases · Carryalls · Atomizers

VOLUPTÉ

347 Fifth Ave · New York 16

Look for this emblem!

a genuine Collector's Item by VOLUPTÉ

pat. pe

Vogue, 1950.

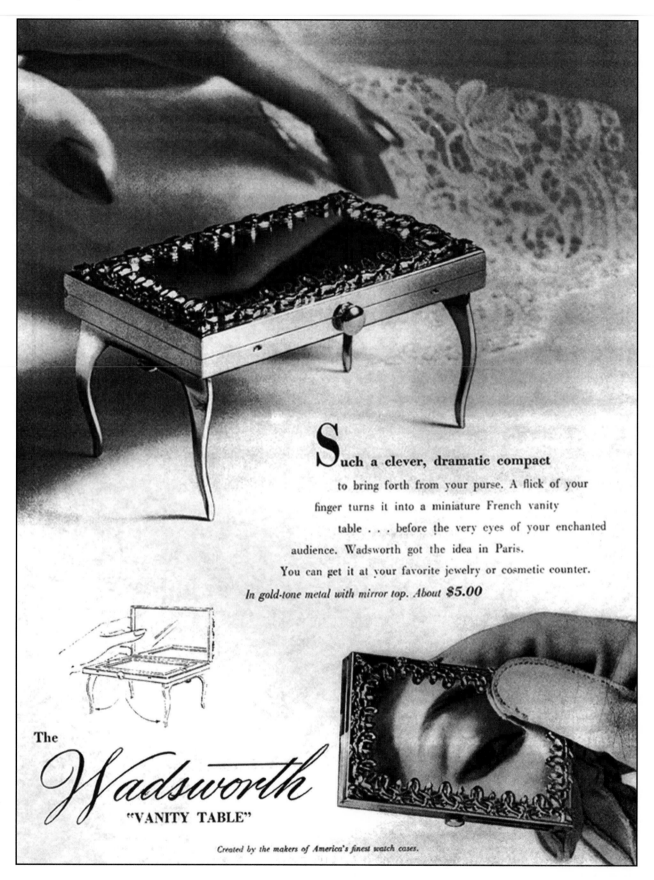

Such a clever, dramatic compact to bring forth from your purse. A flick of your finger turns it into a miniature French vanity table . . . before the very eyes of your enchanted audience. Wadsworth got the idea in Paris.

You can get it at your favorite jewelry or cosmetic counter.

In gold-tone metal with mirror top. About $5.00

The

Wadsworth

"VANITY TABLE"

Created by the makers of America's finest watch cases.

Vogue, 1950.

Sterling Siamese octagon compact belt buckle combination; three silver elephants decorate black compact lid; reverse side reveals belt loop and hook; 2¾" x 2¾". NPA.

Underside of compact revealing belt loop and hook.

Shown open.

Shown closed.

Silver compact designed as hand gun; complete exterior beautifully hand engraved; back end of barrel of gun contains lipstick tube which slides out; front end of barrel of gun contains perfume atomizer which releases perfume when trigger is pulled; front lid opens to reveal powder well and beveled mirror; bottom of powder well reads "Weihnachten 1928"; 3" x 2½". NPA.

*Gilt-inlaid vanity case; lid decorated with Asian scene; interior reveals compartments for powder, rouge, framed mirror, and cigarettes; carrying chain with finger ring; 3½" x 2¾".
$225.00 – 275.00.*

Winnie Winkle silvertone mini bolster-shaped vanity; beautiful engine turned case; mirror on outside of bottom cap; bottom cap contains rouge compartment and puff; upper compartment contains puff and powder compartment; wrist chain attached to top lid; 1920s; 1" dia x 1¾". NPA.

Shown closed.

Shown open.

Left – Red, white, and blue round compact designed to resemble telephone dial with campaign slogan "We Need Stevenson" imprinted on lid; red map of the United States centered on lid; 3½" dia. $200.00 – 225.00.

Top Right – Red, white, and blue round compact with campaign slogan "We Want Willkie" imprinted on lid; 2¾" dia. $175.00 – 225.00.

Bottom Right – Copper compact/coin holder combination; front lid decorated with raised elephant; slots for coins on front lid; back lid contains exterior mirror; interior reveals metal powder sifter and puff; 2⅛". $150.00 – 200.00.

compact
convenient

Winnie Winkle VANITIE

This New Vanitie Is Taking the Market By Storm

Featured in Fifth Avenue's finest shops

HERE is a new wrinkle—a bit of feminine embellishment that contains a collapsible powder puff, powder compartment, rouge case, rouge pad and diminishing mirror—all in one.

Swings from a dainty wrist chain—opened and closed in a jiffy. Made and finished like a piece of jewelry in white gold plate, green gold plate and 14-Kt. gold plate, richly engine turned. RETAILS from $3.00 up.

Write for sample or order a sample dozen.

C. Wolfson & Co., Inc.

JEWELRY & NOVELTIES
295 Fifth Avenue
New York

10/26

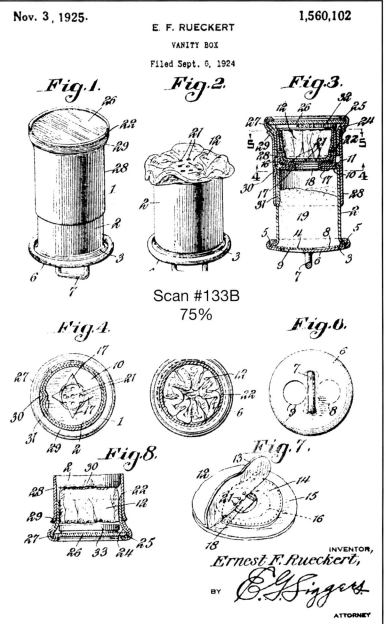

Nov. 3, 1925.

E. F. RUECKERT

VANITY BOX

Filed Sept. 6, 1924

1,560,102

Scan #133B
75%

Winnie Winkle Vanitie Ad, October 1926.

Shown closed.

Silver vanity designed to resemble bottle; exterior bottom lid contains mirror; bottom lid opens to reveal powder compartment; upper lid decorated with cabochon turquoise stone which pulls out to reveal rouge compartment with lipstick tube underneath; second tube under top tube unscrews to reveal perfume container; 2" x 3". NPA.

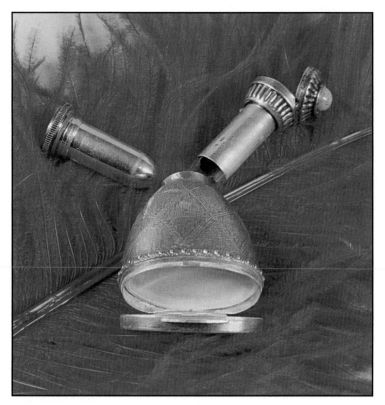

Shown open.

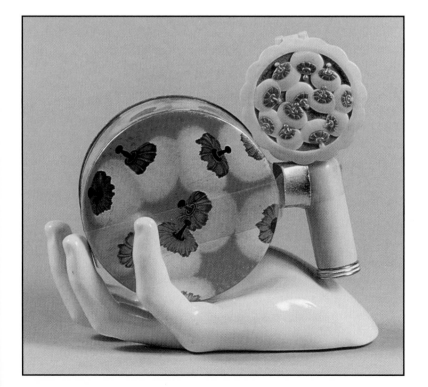

Coty "Air-Spun" box of powder with plastic Coty "Parisienne Vanity" attached by plastic band; vanity insert reads "Cream Powder Patty" and "Sub-Deb" lipstick sold only attached to "Air-Spun Face Powder" "NOT FOR SALE SEPARATELY"; 2¼" x 4½" box 3½" dia. $60.00 – 100.00.

Frosted milk glass compact designed as clam shell; goldtone interior; hallmarked with a hammer and sicle; Russia; 2½" x 3". NPA.

Top – Schildkraut round cloisonne enamel goldtone compact; lid decorated with French scene; 2½" dia. $50.00 – 70.00.

Bottom – Schildkraut oblong cloisonne enamel goldtone compact; lid decorated with French scene; 2¾" x 2½". $50.00 – 70.00.

Left – Textured goldtone compact formed in the shape of an owl; faux emerald and diamond eyes; beveled interior mirror; Italy; 2¾" x 2". $250.00 – 350.00.

Right – Textured goldtone compact formed in the shape of a fox; faux diamond eyes; framed interior mirror; Italy; 2¾" x 2". $250.00 – $350.00.

Center – Textured goldtone compact formed in the shape of a cat; faux sapphire, emerald, and diamond eyes; interior beveled framed mirror; Italy; $250.00 – 350.00.

Shown closed.

Shown open.

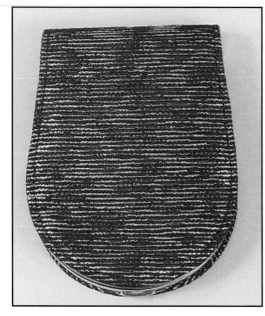

*Purple and black saddle bag-shaped lamé
fabric vanity case; opens to reveal attached
compact, sleeve with lipstick tube, and pocket
with comb; closed 3¼" x 4"; open 3¼" x 8¾".
$125.00 – 175.00.*

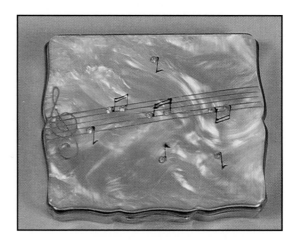

*Top – Hand-painted enamel compact; lid decorated
with Japanese scene; 2¾" x 2½". $50.00 – 75.00.*

*Bottom – Hand-painted enamel compact; lid
decorated with Japanese scene; 2½" x 2".
$50.00 – 75.00.*

*Stratton compact/music box combination;
mother-of-pearl lid decorated with notes and G
clef; 3¼" x 2¾" x ¾". $150.00 – 175.00.*

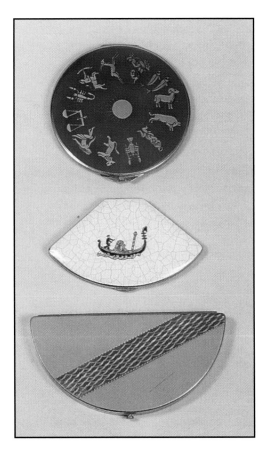

Top – Round blue enamel compact; border of lid decorated with goldtone astrological signs; 3¾" dia. $80.00 – 125.00.

Center – Melissa inverted fan shaped compact; enamel gondola centered on white cracked eggshell lid; England; 4¼" x 2½". $80.00 – 125.00.

Bottom – Rex half moon-shaped compact; blue enamel lid decorated with goldtone band; 5¼" x 2½". $60.00 – 100.00.

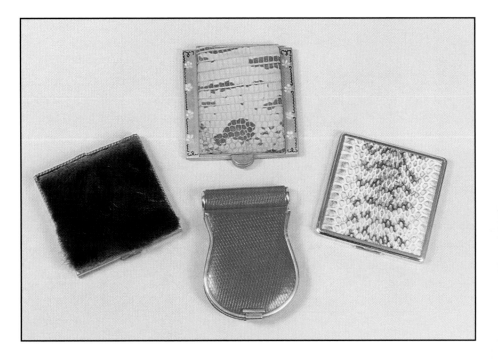

Left – Volupté mink covered compact; 3" x 3". $75.00 – 100.00.

Top – Tan snakeskin compact; enamel decorated strips flank compact on two sides; 3" x 3". $75.00 – 100.00.

Right – Crystal gray snakeskin compact; back lid brushed goldtone; 3" x 3". $40.00 – 60.00.

Bottom – Red lizard saddle bag-shaped vanity; interior contains beveled mirror; pull-out lipstick tube on one side of top; perfume container on other side of top; 2½" x 3½". $100.00 – 125.00.

Top – Dorset round brushed goldtone compact; lid decorated with polished goldtone heart and arrow and "I Love You" printed around lid; 2½" dia. $60.00 – 80.00.

Center – Schildkraut goldtone compact; lids decorated with "I love you" hand painted in different languages and colors; applied pen point; 2¾" x 2¼" x ½". $60.00 – 100.00.

Bottom – Elgin American brushed goldtone stylized heart-shaped compact; lid decorated with polished goldtone cupid, hearts, and "I love you" in several languages; 3¼" x 3¼". $60.00 – 100.00.

Left – Dunhill "Clearview" blue leather compact; interior reveals mirror windshield wiper; attached sleeve for lipstick; 2½" x 3½". $150.00 – 175.00.

Top – Majestic unique green leather compact/note pad combination; first opening reveals mirror and powder compartment; second opening reveals blue paper note pad; sleeve for pencil on outer lid; 2¾" x 2¾". $175,00 – 225.00.

Right – Red leather compact; attached sleeve for lipstick; pull-out mirror; 3" x 3½". $125.00 – 150.00.

Bottom – Lampl black enamel vanity; top lid has slide out comb; interior has mirror, rouge, lipstick, powder sifter, and powder compartments; 3" x 3". $150.00 - $175.00.

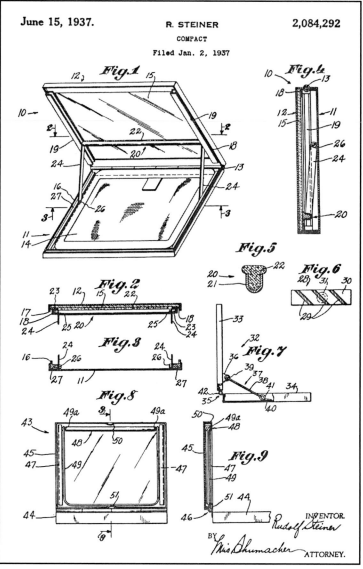

Sterling hallmarked pendant compact; black onyx lid with silver cartouche center; silver tassel; 1½" dia x 3". $250.00 – 350.00.

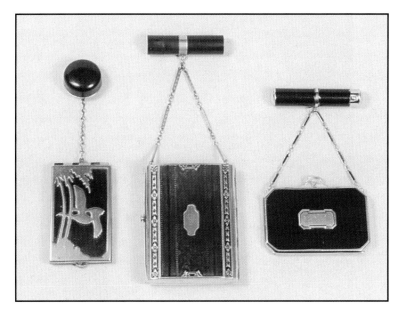

Left – Vashe black and silvertone fob compact; lid decorated with silvertone scene; fob cream lip and cheek rouge attached by chain; 1½" x 2½", fob 1" dia. $80.00 – 125.00.

Center – Terri black and silvertone tango chain vanity; silvertone cartouche centered on lid; lipstick tube attached by two chains; interior reveals mirror which separates powder and rouge compartments from cigarette compartment; 2½" x 3" x 6½". $125.00 – 175.00.

Right – E.A.M. black enamel and silvertone tango chain vanity; monogrammed silver cartouche centered on lid; interior reveals mirror, powder, and rouge compartments; lipstick attached by enamel link chain; 2½" x 1¾" x 4½". $125.00 – 175.00.

Toilet Requisites, September, 1927.

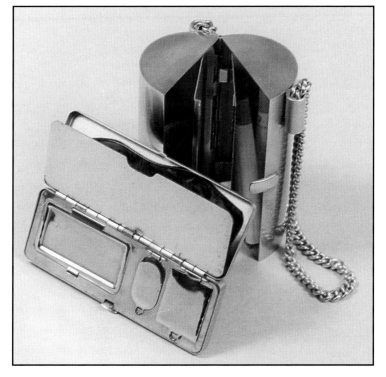

Volupté brushed silvertone necessaire; interior reveals metal mirror which encloses cigarette compartment; center panel conceals slim removeable vanity case; compartment on other side of vanity for small necessities; removeable silvertone vanity has compartments for powder, lip and cheek rouge, metal mirror, and compartment for comb; metal carrying chain; 2" dia x 4¼". NPA.

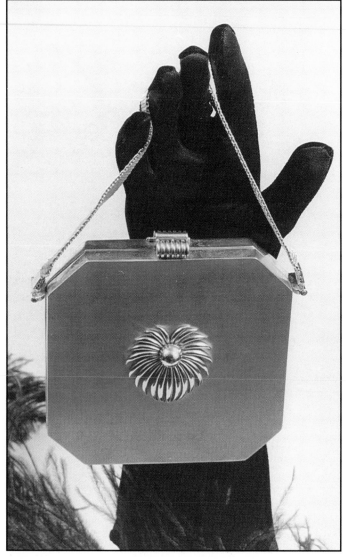

Shown closed.

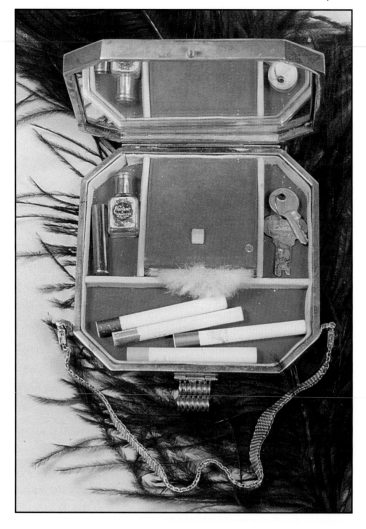

Square brushed goldtone minaudiere with cut off corners; brown suede interior reveals mirror, compartments for powder and other small necessities; lid centered with polished goldtone stylized flower; mesh carrying handle; 5" x 5". $200.00 – 250.00.

Goldtone pearl and rhinestone compact/perfume/lipstick combination; lipstick tube attached to side of mini-compact and mini-perfume holder; compact and perfume holder are attached back-to-back; mirror on exterior of perfume holder; exterior decorated with pearls and rhinestones; 2" x 2½" x 1¼". $100.00 – 150.00.

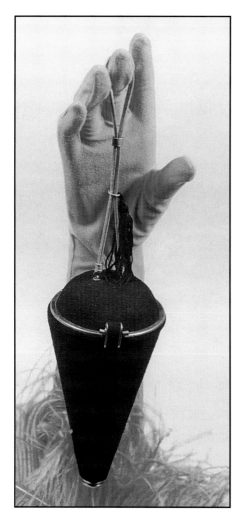

Black suede and brass cone-shaped vanity purse; opens to reveal compact; second opening reveals purse; pull-out lipstick on bottom of bag; carrying chain; France; 3½" dia x 6½". $300.00 – 400.00.

Black suede and brass heart-shaped vanity purse decorated with brass bow; top opens to reveal compact; front opens to reveal purse; carrying chain; France; 3½" x 5½" x 2¼". $300.00 – 400.00.

Shown closed.

Shown open.

Oval compact/cameo pendant combination; shell cameo bezel set in sterling Art Nouveau ribbon filligree frame; female profile carved in relief, mounted on lid; interior reveals mirror on one side, fitted metal powder sifter and fitted puff on other side; sterling filligree neck chain; 1½" x 2". NPA.

Vanuette round lavender enamel sterling silver compact/vinagrette pendant combination; first opening reveals convex mirror and powder lid covering powder well; second opening reveals vinagrette compartment; perforations around rim of vinagrette section; sterling longnette neck chain; 1" dia. $275.00 – 375.00.

Left – Elgin American hammered goldtone square compact; lid centered with rhinestone Christmas bell; red stone moveable clapper; 2¾" x 2¾". $60.00 – 100.00.

Top – Faberge gold-and silver-plated basket weave design triangle compact; one side silvertone other side goldtone; packet of powder refill; 3" each side of triangle. $65.00 – 80.00.

Right – Henriette copper colored "Jack-in-the-Box" compact; lid decorated with rhinestone and green colored stones; center rhinestone motif, hearts, diamonds, spades, and clubs; bellow sides allows for expansion when filled with powder; 3" x 3". $125.00 – 175.00.

Bottom – Elgin American brushed goldtone compact; the endearement "Mother" and leaves in polished goldtone decorate lid; 3" x 2¼". $60.00 – 100.00.

Center – Volupte brushed goldtone square compact with dime centered on lid; 2½" x 2½". $40.00 – 60.00.

Left – Round silvertone compact with large pink cabachon stone centered on lid; plastic interior; mirror; 3" dia. Contemporary compact from Poland. NPA.

Right – White plastic compact with black etched balcony scene on lid; interior mirror and sponge powder puff; 2¾" x 2¾". Contemporary compact from Poland. NPA.

Center – Woven green, brown, and gold fabric compact; zippered closing; plastic interior; mirror; 2½" dia. Contemporary compact from Poland. NPA.

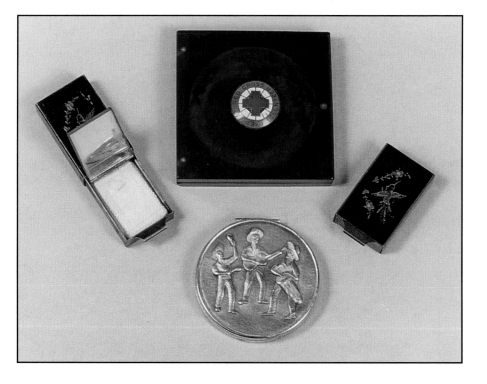

Left – Beauty Mate mini black enamel compact; lid decorated with enameled hummingbird and flowers; pull-out compact with pop-up mirror and powder compartment; 1" x 1¾". $25.00 – 50.00.

Top Center – Green plastic compact; enameled disc with "American Red Cross Volunteer" encircling the Red Cross insignia centered on lid; 2¾" x 2¾". $60.00 – 80.00.

Right – Same as compact on left. (Shown closed.)

Bottom Center – Round silvertone compact with plastic discs on either side; discs depict musicians in relief playing instruments 2¼" dia; $50.00 – 75.00.

Shown closed.

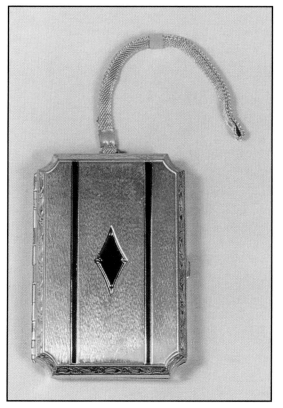

Shown open.

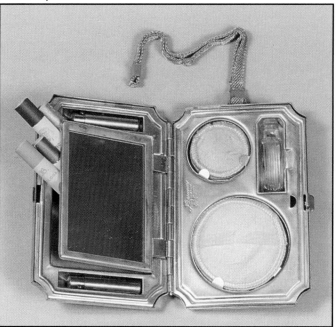

Dermay gold-plate mini-carryall; textured polished goldtone lid decorated with bands of black enamel and black cartouch; gilded interior reveals powder and rouge compartments and well with mini-perfume bottle; center mirror flanked by two lipstick tubes; cigarette compartment behind mirror; mesh carrying chain; 2¾" x 4". $175.00 – 250.00.

Three sterling silver charms. Left: hammered silver compact charm; interior mirror and powder well; ⅝" dia. Center: engine turned silver vanity tango chain charm; interior reveals mirror, rouge, and powder compartments; lipstick attached to compact by chain; ⁷⁄₁₆" dia; lipstick ¾". Right: basket weave silver compact charm; interior mirror and powder well; ½". $25.00 – 50.00.

Round celluloid compact; lid decorated with a painted three-dimensional face of Pierrot, a French pantomime; interior contains mirror and puff; Austria; 2¼" dia. NPA.

Round plastic compact; Lucite lid encloses painted picture of lady on a swing; marbelized iridescent background; France; 2½" dia. $150.00 – 225.00.

Plate "Trio-ettes;" green, tortoise, white, pink, and blue plastic vanities shaped like hand mirrors; opens on both sides; one side, mirror and powder compartment with puff; other side contains rouge compartment with puff; exterior mirror on rouge lid; lipstick slides out of handle; also available in other colors; 2¾" dia x 4¼". $125.00 – 250.00 all things being equal, prices vary according to color — blue, pink, and green command higher prices.

House & Garden, June, 1946.

145

Left – Green enameled compact; lid designed to resemble telephone dial; red numbers and black letters imprinted on white enameled goldtone framed circles; center goldtone cartouche engraved with the name "Helen"; 3½" dia. $150.00 – 200.00.

Center – Pink enameled goldtone compact; lid designed to resemble telephone dial; numbers and letters around lid; 2¾" dia.
$100.00 – 125.00.

Right – Black enameled compact; same as compact on left; logo "Telephone Pioneers of America" centered on cartouche. $150.00–200.00.

TELEPHONE DIAL COMPACT
The Right Number for Your Gift List!
Clever black and gold compact is 3½" across, with dial in natural colors! Engraved with phone number up to 10 letters and spaces, or 3 initials! Ideal for gifts! Sorry, no C.O.D.'s. **$2.00** postpaid. Ask for Free Gift Catalog!

MEREDITH'S EVANSTON 32 ILLINOIS

Lest you forget your telephone number (we must admit we do), this clever compact acts as a reminder. Black enamel cover, a facsimile of an actual phone dial, is engraved with your name and number. 3½" in diameter, with powder sifter, velour puff and full mirror, $2.25

Redbook, 1954.

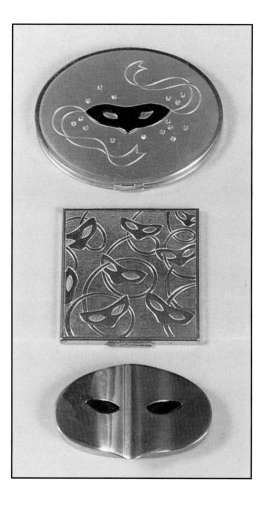

Top – Dorothy Gray oval brushed goldtone Savoir Faire compact; black raised enameled harlequin mask centered on lid; lid enhanced with rhinestones and incised ribbons; 3¾" x 3". $100.00 – 125.00.

Center – Elgin American goldtone compact; textured lid decorated with polished goldtone harlequin masks; 2¾" x ¾". $40.00 – 60.00.

Bottom – Elizabeth Arden polished goldtone harlequin-shaped compact; 3" x 1⅝". $125.00 – 175.00.

Vogue, 1949.

THE DOROTHY GRAY GALLERY OF FASCINATING WOMEN – ONE OF A SERIES

"Savoir Faire"

unique beauty creams...
fragrance...make-up...
sumptuously presented

"Savoir Faire"—*know-how*. So very expressive of these beautiful new cosmetics. *Know-how* in that the fine creams contain protective ingredients exclusive with "Savoir Faire." *Know-how* in that the Eau de Parfum possesses a fragrance of great style and originality. *Know-how* in that the make-up accessories are so decorative as to be conversation pieces!

Illustrated: Dusting Powder, $5; Compact, $10; Night Cream, $5; Eau de Parfum, $12 ... Also available: Perfume, $25 and $5; Cleansing Cream and Face Powder, each $5; Lipstick, $3. *(Plus tax.)*

Mrs. John J. Astor of New York City, the former Gertrude Gretsch.
Portrait by the celebrated painter, Walter Klett.

Dorothy Gray

THE DOROTHY GRAY SALON • 445 PARK AVE., NEW YORK

147

Left – Red reptile skin Kamra-Pak compact/music-box/cigarette case combination; top front lid incorpoartes music box; lower portion contains powder compartment; sliding lipstick; back contains cigarette case; 2" x 3⅞". $175.00 – 225.00.

Center top and bottom – Multicolored Persian design embossed leather Kamra-Pak compact/cigarette case combination; powder compartment on front lid; sliding lipstick; cigarette case on reverse side; matching cigarette lighter; 2" x 3⅞". $125.00 – 175.00.

Right – Marbelized tortoise shell colored Kamra-Pak compact/cigarette case combination; front lid decorated with petit point; powder compartment; sliding lipstick; reverse side reveals cigarette compartment; Germany; 2" x 3⅞". $150.00 – 175.00.

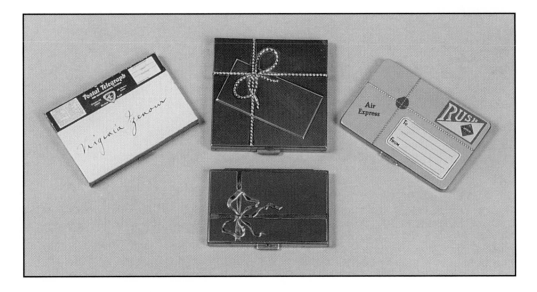

Left – Goldtone compact designed to resemble a Postal Telegraph message; white lid decorated with Postal Telegraph heading and the name "Virginia Zenour"; interior powder well inscribed with the name "Andre Duval"; 3¼" x 2". $125.00 – 200.00.

Top Center – Volupté goldtone compact; lid designed to resemble gift package; raised gift card and bow decorate lid; 3" x 3". $50.00 – 75.00.

Right – Goldtone vanity designed to resemble Air Express delivery; blue lid decorated with "Air Express, RUSH Railway Express Agency" and destination labels; raised goldtone cord; interior reveals mirror, powder, and rouge compartments; Patent #1883793; 3⅛" x 2⅛". $125.00 – 200.00.

Bottom Center – Coty goldtone and green enamel vanity designed to resemble gift package; lid decorated with raised goldtone bow; interior reveals mirror, powder, and rouge compartments; 3" x 1⅞". $80.00 – 120.00.

Bottom Left – Stratton goldtone compact with lipstick incorporated in lid; front lid decorated with troubadour transfer scene; Stratton hand logo on interior powder well; label on mirror reads "To open inner door: press mirror-lid gently back; door springs open—To shut bring mirror lid forward and press door down"; England; 3¼" x 2¾". $60.00 – 80.00.

Upper Left – Stratton round goldtone compact; lid decorated with drinking toasts in different languages; Stratton hand logo on interior powder well; inner powder door release; England; 3" dia. $40.00 – 60.00.

Top Center – Kigu round goldtone compact; white enameled lid decorated with simulated clock, pictures, and suggestions not to waste time; England; 3¼" dia. $40.00 – 60.00.

Upper Right – Stratton round goldtone compact; white lid decorated with windmill scene; Stratton written on inner powder lid; England; 2¾". $30.00 – 50.00.

Lower Right – same as compact to the left, lid decorated with all-over black and gold design.

Center – Round black plastic commemorative compact; lid decorated with coronation picture of King George VI and Queen Elizabeth, 1937; 3" dia. $60.00 – 100.00.

Left – Silvertone framed black silk vanity bag; oval frame heavily embossed; silver carrying chain; pink silk interior contains mirror, pocket for puff, and second pocket with change purse; 3¾" x 5½". $175.00 – 250.00.

Right – Trinity Plate goldtone vanity bag; petit point front lid opens to reveal beautifully framed beveled mirror and green silk pocket for puff; second opening reveals green silk lining with shirred pockets on either side; top of frame enhanced with red enameled flowers and colored stones; carrying chain interspersed with red beads; metal tassel; 2¾" x 5". $225.00– 325.00.

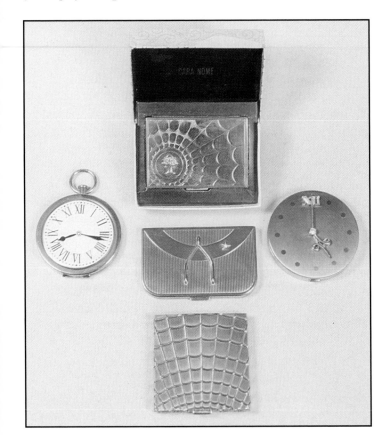

Left – Wadsworth round goldtone compact designed to resemble train conductor's pocket watch; lid decorated with paper transfer of watch face with Roman numerals; back lid decorated with old-fashioned steam locomotive; 2¾" dia. $40.00 – 60.00.

Top Center – Cara Noma, Langlois goldtone vanity; lid decorated with flower basket centered in incised web; interior reveals mirror, powder, and rouge compartments; 3¼" x 2¼". $60.00 – 85.00.

Right – Round brushed goldtone compact; lid decorated as watch; hands decorated with rhinestones; 3" dia. $40.00 – 60.00.

Bottom Center – Volupté goldtone compact designed to resemble spider web; lid decorated with raised web; 3" x 3". $50.00 – 75.00.

Center – Coty goldtone vanity; lid decorated with wishbone and star set with rhinestone; interior reveals rouge and powder compartments; 3¾" x 2¼". $80.00 – 100.00.

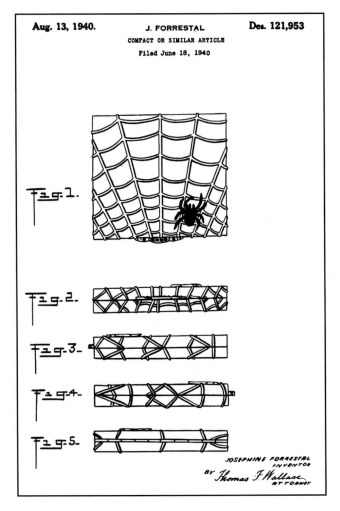

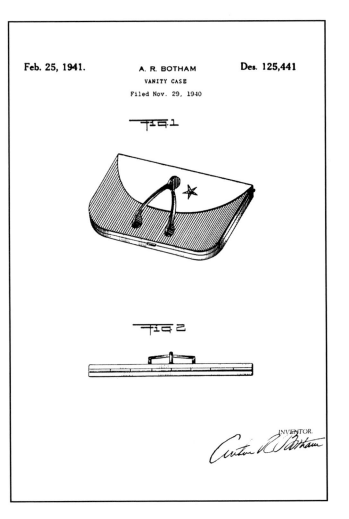

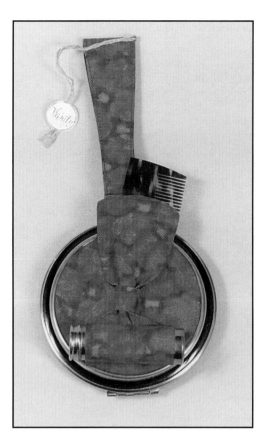

Vanity, round red floral fabric and metal compact;
interior reveals powder well; outer rim of compact
black enamel and goldtone; front and back lids fabric;
bow on front lid contains sleeve for lipstick tube;
comb slides in behind top of bow; carrying handle;
3¼" dia x 7" long. $100.00 – 150.00.

Left – Triangle-shaped red velvet cardboard compact; interior
reveals mirror and powder compartment; exterior red velvet
lid decorated with miniature applied raised Egyptian face
framed by black rings; two additional white rings decorate lid;
metal tassel; carrying cord with wooden handle; 2½" x 2⅛".
$120.00 – 200.00.

Right – Blue silk cardboard vanity case; interior reveals mirror, powder, rouge, and lipstick compartments; blue silk lid
decorated with metallic cord and miniature fabric flowers;
wooden tassel; metallic carrying cord; 3" x 4".
$150.00 – 250.00.

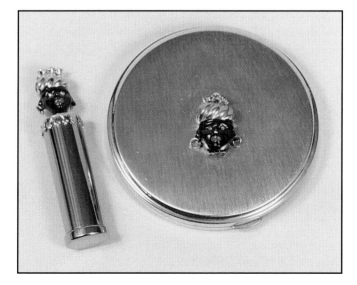

Round brushed goldtone compact with matching lipstick;
compact lid and lipstick tube decorated with a raised
applied blackamoor head; head decorated with a pearl and
rhinestone turban, green stone eyes, red enamel lips, and
moveable goldtone hoop ear rings; 3½" dia.
NPA.

Lower Left – Raquel embossed leather vanity designed to resemble book; multicolored leather lids; interior reveals metal-framed mirror, powder, and rouge compartments; 2" x 3". $80.00 – 125.00.

Upper Left – same as lower left compact — lid green and gold embossed leather.

Top Center – same as lower left compact — lid red and gold embossed leather (shown open).

Upper Right – same as lower left compact — lid tan and gold embossed leather.

Lower Right - exactly the same as lower left compact.

Center – Mondaine embossed multicolored leather vanity; interior reveals beveled mirror; compartments for powder and rouge; 1⅞" x 2¾". $80.00 – 125.00.

Shown closed.

Shown open.

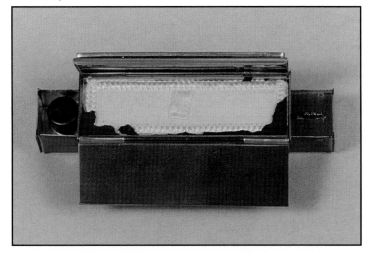

Quinto goldtone vanity; raised squares enhanced with rhinestones applied to lid; interior reveals powder well, and puff; sides contain slide out lipstick and perfume bottle; 3" x 1¼" x 1". $75.00 – 125.00.

Even the Hard-Boiled Get a thrill –

NO MATTER how hard-boiled and calloused you may be from looking at new offerings, if you haven't yet seen this new Vanity Book by Raquel, then there's a thrill awaiting you.

Done in **luxurious leather** — as befits a book for the replenishment of beauty.

Please let your mind grasp the full significance of that.

Not merely book **shape**, but **bound** like a costly book — a De Luxe edition in the softest and richest of fine leather.

Because encased in luxurious leather, the Raquel Vanity Book is truly a joy to behold—and likewise a joy to hold in the hand. Book compacts of metal or composition simply can't be compared with it.

As aristocratic inside as out.

Stores of the highest calibre are stocking it at sight—and selling it at sight.

By all means see it. Set your expectations high — our guess is that the reality will exceed anything you can visualize in advance.

Raquel Vanity Book

Bound in

De Luxe Leather

In three colors:

Black Calf	Red Morocco	Green Morocco

Each color offered in three cover designs, of Spanish motif, tooled on in Gold.

Each book contains Rouge and Powder Compacts (Refill form) in all standard shades, and in a choice of the three Raquel odeurs.

Raquel

INCORPORATED

475 Fifth Avenue   New York

Creators of

Orange Blossom Fragrancia   *L'Endcley*   *Olor de la Noche (Fragrance of the Night)*

Each in parfum and toiletries.

Toilet Requisites, September, 1927.

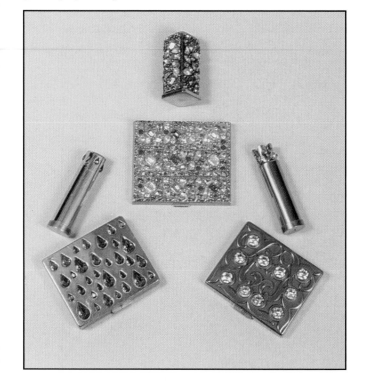

Left – Flato goldtone compact with matching lipstick; compact lid and lipstick tube decorated with green pear shaped stones; interior reveals powder well, puff, and mirror; 2½" x 2⅛". $150.00 – 200.00.

Center – Schildkraut goldtone compact with matching lipstick; compact lid and lipstick tube decorated with beautiful bezel set multi-colored, various shaped stones; 2¾" x 2½". $125.00 – 175.00.

Right – Flato goldtone compact with matching lipstick; compact lid has applied cut-out design enhanced with bezel set turquoise stones; lipstick tube decorated with turquoise stones; 2½" x 2¼". $150.00 – 225.00.

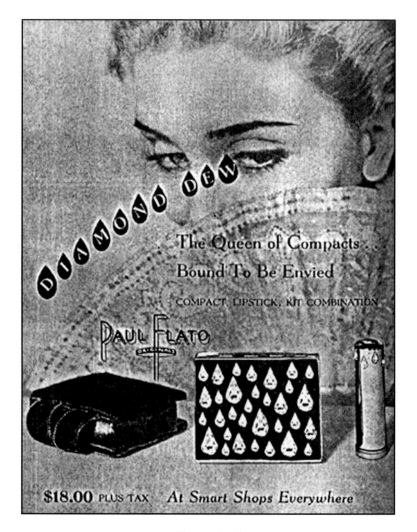

Vogue, 1950.

Brass compact on black velvet display stand; exterior mirror framed with beautiful cut-out brass design; deeply beveled interior mirror; France; 3¼" x 4". $150.00 – 200.00.

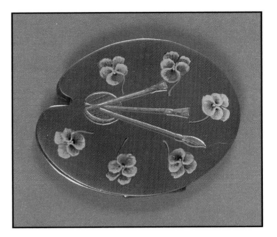

Henry A La Pensee handmade coppertone compact designed to resemble an artist's palette; lid decorated with engraved brushes and colorful enamel flowers; Paris; 3" x 2¼". NPA.

Plate silver bullet-shaped vanity; engine turned exterior; cartouche on side; interior reveals framed mirror that separates powder compartment from second compartment; finger ring carrying chain; 1" dia x 3½". $150.00 – 250.00.

Houpalix black fabric compact designed to resemble bellows; front lid decorated with gold design enhanced with orange and gun metal beads; France; 3" x 4½". NPA.

155

Shown closed.

Goldtone compact designed to resemble beach umbrella; lid decorated with brightly colored green, yellow, blue, and red panels; interior reveals mirror; handle folds flat against back of compact, pulls away, and acts as handle while using compact; 2¾" closed, 3½" upright. NPA.

Shown open.

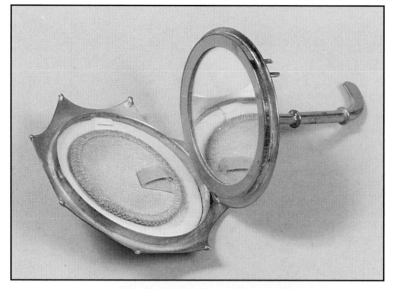

"Merry-Go-Round" goldtone compact designed to resemble carousel; colorful red, white, and blue horses decorate the outer rim; goldtone and white carousel lid top; 2½" dia. NPA.

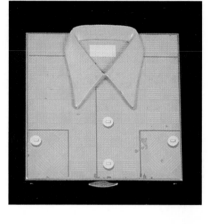

Wadsworth compact designed to resemble shirt; raised gray collar extends above lid; interior mirror reads "A Madison Creation"; 3" x 3¼". NPA.

Miref "Mirador" round goldtone compact; incised rings around compact; slide-out lipstick; top and bottom exterior beveled mirrors; interior reveals beveled mirror and powder compartment; Paris; 2" dia. $125.00 – 175.00.

Left – Round fabric powder case; top lid decorated with flapper girl; black lace around exterior rim; ribbon on front lid lifts to reveal puff attached to lid and powder compartment; exterior mirror on reverse side; 4" dia. NPA.

Top and Bottom – two black silk paddles on black sticks; composition female faces decorated with string of pearls and blonde hair applied to lid; maribou feathers around outer rims of paddles; reverse side of one reveals puff, other reveals mirror; 3" dia. x 9".
$35.00 – 70.00.

Right – Miniature puff concealed in yellow dress of doll; flapper doll wears lace and silk hat; yellow skirt snaps open to reveal puff; 3" x 2¾". NPA.

Round goldtone compact; lid has picture of a female flamenco dancer with an applied lace skirt protected by beveled glass dome; beveled glass bottom lid; 2¾" dia. $80.00 – 100.00.

Red faux leather compact designed to resemble hat box; snaps open and shut; faux zipper; interior reveals mirror and puff; carrying handle; 3" x 2¾".
$75.00 – 125.00.

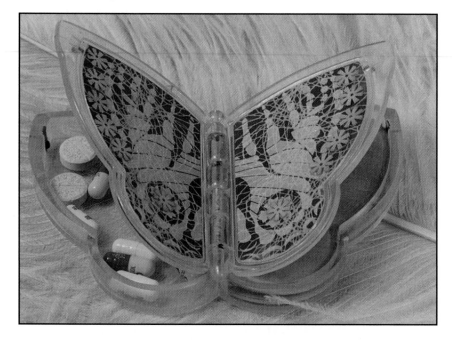

Wadsworth "Crystelle" butterfly compact; black, blue, and silver design on lid; mirrors on interiors of both wings; puff and powder compartment on one side; other side for pills; 4¼" x 2¾". $150.00 – 225.00.

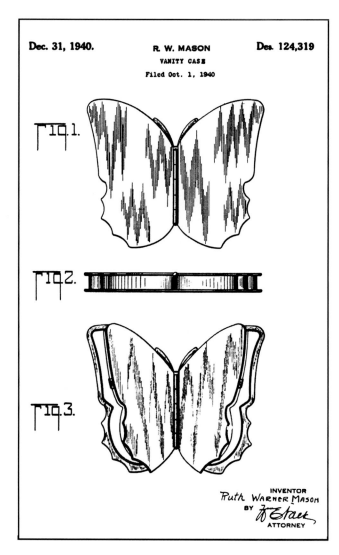

Dec. 31, 1940.

R. W. MASON
VANITY CASE
Filed Oct. 1, 1940

Des. 124,319

Fig. 1.

Fig. 2.

Fig. 3.

INVENTOR
Ruth Warner Mason
BY
ATTORNEY

Wadsworth Compact Ad, 1952.

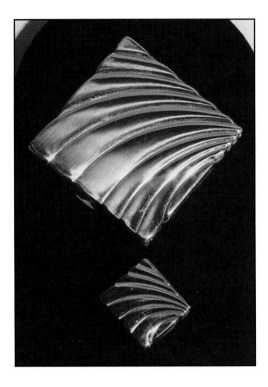

Volupté matching "Mother-Daughter" gold-tone compacts; lids decorated with raised swirls; interiors reveal mirror and puff; daughter's, 1 ¼" x 1 ⅛"; mother's 3" square. $175.00 – 200.00.

Ladies' Home Journal, December 1947.

Left – Evans round blue enamel mesh vanity pouch; light blue mesh bottom; interior reveals powder well; metal mirror opens to reveal rouge compartment; 2 ¼" dia. $40.00 – 60.00.

Right – Large round blue enamel mesh vanity pouch; silvertone mesh bottom; interior reveals mirror and powder compartment; 4" dia. $60.00 – 80.00.

Shown closed.

Hallmarked silver compact/brush combination; compact centered on elegently engine turned top of hair brush; side pull-out comb; interior of compact reveals mirror and puff; 3¾" x 2¾". NPA.

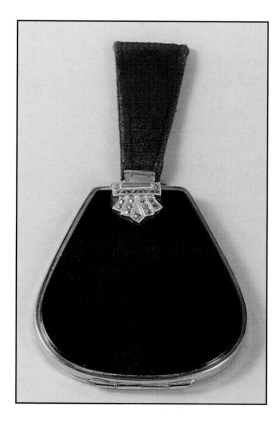

Black enamel and goldtone saddle bag-shaped compact; lid decorated with marcasites; interior reveals powder compartment and beveled mirror; suede finger carrying handle; West Germany; 2¾" x 5". $150.00 – 225.00.

Simone peach and blue colored garters with matching wrist compact; garters decorated with peach colored maribou feathers and blue silk flowers; wrist compact decorated with blue silk flower and blue maribou feathers; reverse side reveals wrist band and purse; purse interior has attached mirror and drawstring puff; France. NPA.

Top – Richard Hudnut "le Début" octagon-shaped light blue enameled tango chain finger ring vanity; fitted presentation box; light blue and white enamel decorate lid and lipstick tube; interior reveals powder and rouge compartments separated by mirror; 2" dia. $175.00 – 250.00.

Bottom – Richard Hudnut "le Début" octagon-shaped light blue vanity case; interior reveals powder and rouge compartments separated by mirror; 2" dia. $50.00 – 75.00.

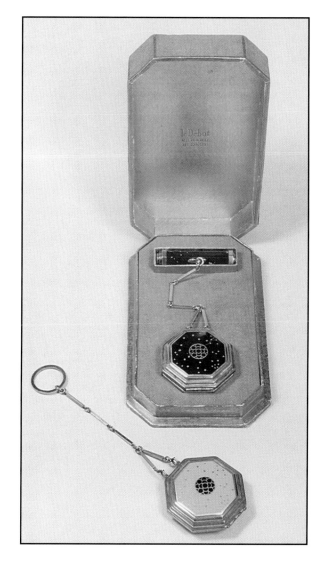

Left – Marbelized metal compact; lid decorated with transfer of period portrait; interior reveals mirror and powder well; 2¾" x 2¾". $40.00 – 60.00.

Center – Round goldtone compact; lid decorated with painted silhouette; interior reveals mirror and powder well; 2½" dia. $40.00 – 60.00.

Right – Square black enamel vanity with rounded sides; lid decorated with signed hand-painted period portrait; interior reveals powder compartment; metal mirror concealing rouge compartment, powder puffs; 2" x 2". $60.00 – 90.00.

Top – Richard Hudnut "le Début" octagon-shaped dark blue enameled tango chain vanity; fitted presentation box; dark blue and gold enamel decorate lid and lipstick tube; interior reveals powder and rouge compartments separated by mirror; 2" dia. $175.00 – 250.00.

Bottom – Richard Hudnut "le Début" octagon-shaped green enameled finger ring vanity; green and gold enamel decorate lid; interior reveals powder and rouge compartments separated by mirror; 2" dia. $150.00 – 225.00.

161

Top – Zell tan leather oval compact designed to resemble football; impressed simulated laces on front lid; coppertone interior reveals mirror and powder compartment; 4½" x 3½". $60.00 – 100.00. Courtesy of Barbara Schwerin.

Center – Round white enamel compact designed to resemble baseball; team name "Giants" centered on front lid; lid also decorated with blue and white painted stitching; interior reveals mirror and powder compartment; 3" dia. $60.00 – 100.00.

Bottom – De Corday "Silver Queen" round white compact designed to resemble golf ball; textured lids slightly domed; interior reveals mirror and powder well; 2" dia. $25.00 – 50.00. Courtesy of Barbara Schwerin.

Silver Queen Golf Ball Compact Ad
May, 1928.

"Right on the Nose!"

The New Sports Compact "Silver Queen"

The golf ball is the inspiration for this newest of toilet accessories.
Very thin, very smart, very practical.

Single or Double. Poudre: 4 shades (Naturelle, Rachel, Blanche, Tan). Rouge: 2 shades.

Perfumed with "Blanchette" an enticing odor by

CORDAY, 15 Rue de la Paix. Paris

Left – Dual opening goldtone carryall; lids beautifully inlaid with fluted lavender and purple shaded mother-of-pearl; mesh carrying chain; one opening reveals lipstick tube, mirror, money clip, and powder compartment; second opening, cigarette case; 3¼" x 5½". $250.00 – 300.00.

Top – Black silk and goldtone vanity bag; lid lavishly decorated with beads, pearls, mother-of-pearl, and embroidery; top closure decorated with rhinestones; interior contains beveled mirror, powder, and rouge sleeves; link carrying chain; imprinted in gold on interior lining "Made in France for The French Bazaar, Colon-Panama"; 5½" x 3¾". $225.00 – 275.00.

Right – Evans dual opening goldtone carryall; watch centered on embossed sunburst lid; interior contains powder compartment, mirror and coin, lipstick, comb holders; cigarette case on other side; mesh carrying chain; 3¼" x 5½". $250.00 – 325.00.

Bottom – Mini-goldtone carryall; lid enhanced with bezel set Aurora Borealis rhinestones; interior contains powder compartment, lipstick tube, comb pouch, swinging mirror concealing cigarette compartment; snake carrying chain; 4¼" x 3". $175.00 – 225.00.

Ciner black enamel and gilt egg-shaped minaudiere; stripes of black enamel and gilt decorate exterior; interior reveals center framed mirror separating powder compartment from second compartment; black enameled finger ring carrying chain; 2" dia x 3". $250.00 – 350.00.

1⅝" round compact/dress clip combinations; riding crop applied to brown enameled compact; navy insignia applied to blue compact; flag applied to black compact; Scottie dog transfer applied to silvertone compact; compact with carved orange Bakelite lid; compact with marcasite lid; and lower center, 1½" x 2" brown compact has transfer portrait on lid; upper center compact shown open. $75.00 – 150.00.
Scottie dog and marcasite compact courtesy of Barbara Schwerin.

Silvertone vanity; lids beautifully engine turned; enamel flowered disc centered on lid interior reveals mirror, powder, rouge, and lipstick compartments; metal carrying chain; 2⅞" x 1¾". This compact was the start of my collection, purchased on July 4, 1976. $125.00 – 200.00.

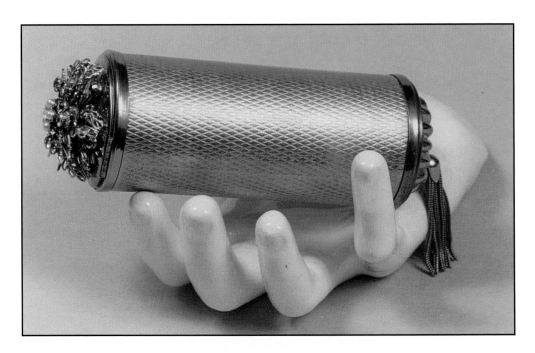

Wadsworth "Bon Bon" textured goldtone necessaire with goldtone tassel; top lid decorated with filigree leaves, pearls, rhinestones, and colored stones; top opens to reveal mirror and powder well; bottom pulls out to reveal tube for cigarettes or other small items; 1¾" x 4¾". $150.00 – 175.00.

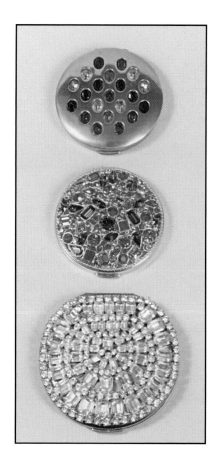

Black enamel egg-shaped compact with sterling chain; rhinestones encircle circumference of compact, top and lower portion of compact decorated with onyx stones and rhinestones; compact opens to reveal beveled mirror and powder well; 1¾" dia x 2¼". NPA.

Top – Calvaire round brass compact; lid decorated with faceted oval shaped colored stones; interior mirror and powder compartment; 2½" dia. $75.00 – 150.00.

Center – Round goldtone compact; lid set with multi-shaped, multicolored stones; interior powder well and mirror; 2½" dia. $50.00 – 80.00.

Bottom – Pilcher round goldtone compact; prong set emerald cut and round rhinestones decorate lid; interior mirror and powder well; 3½" dia. $75.00 – 150.00.

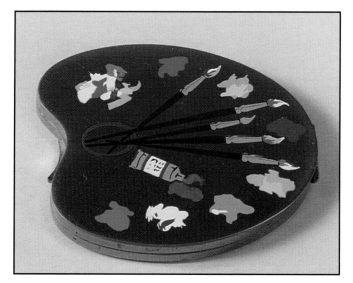

Volupté brushed goldtone compact designed to resemble artist's palette; lid decorated with paint tube, paint brushes, and colors; interior mirror and powder compartment; 3" x 2¾". $125.00 – 175.00.

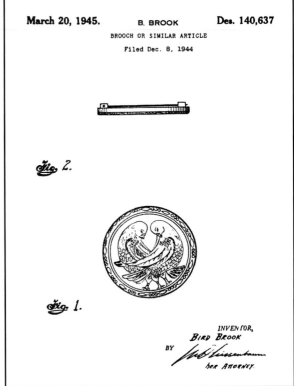

March 20, 1945.   B. BROOK   Des. 140,637

BROOCH OR SIMILAR ARTICLE

Filed Dec. 8, 1944

Fig. 2.

Fig. 1.

INVENTOR,

BIRD BROOK

BY

her ATTORNEY.

Left – Round polished goldtone compact; two repousse doves centered on lid; interior reveals mirror and powder compartment; 2⅞" dia. $80.00 – 120.00.

Right – Clear square Lucite compact; sterling repousse medallion of two doves centered on lid; 2⅞" x 2⅞". $150.00 – 175.00.

J.M. Fisher silvertone vanity; lid decorated with colorful enamel scene of Robin Hood in Sherwood Forest; interior contains mirror, two lipstick tubes, powder, and rouge compartments; link carrying chain; 3" x 2¼". $150.00 – 250.00.

Wadsworth square goldtone compact; colorful enameled picture of Madam DuBarry centered on lid; outer rim of lid reads "QUITE A GAL WAS MADAM DUBARRY — WAS SHE A LADY? — WELL NOT VERY"; interior mirror and powder compartment; 3" x 3". $125.00 – 150.00.

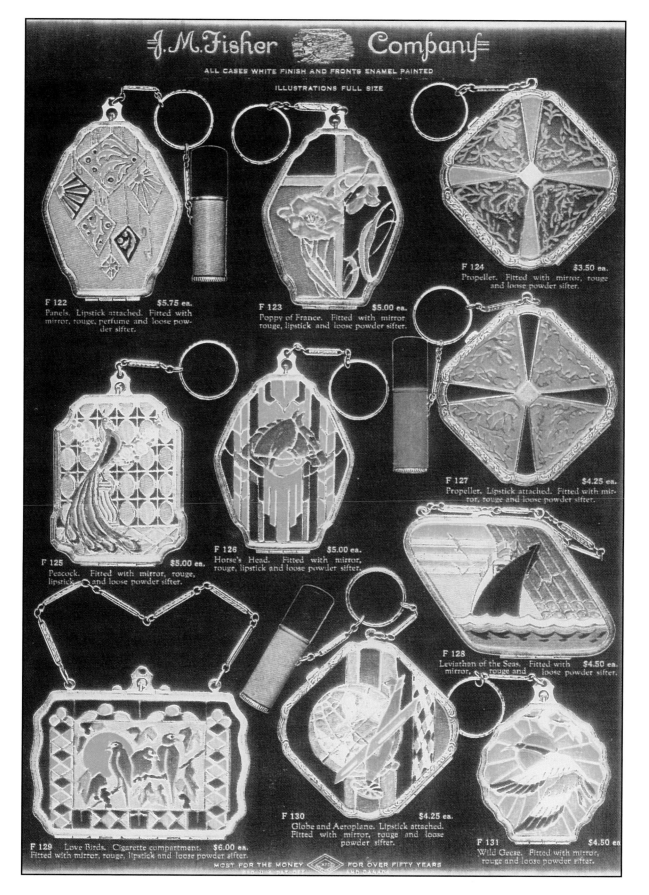

Jewelry Sales Guide, 1931.

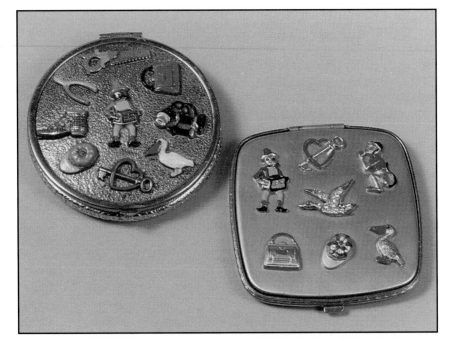

Left – Round goldtone compact; textured silvertone lid decorated with applied enameled charms, heart, cap, wishbone, etc.; black enameled reverse lid; interior mirror and powder compartment; 2" dia. $150.00 – 175.00.

Right – Square brushed goldtone compact; lid decorated with applied enameled charms, suitcase, monkey organ grinder, duck, etc.; interior mirror and powder compartment; 2¼" x 2¼". $150.00 – 175.00.

Stratton Wedgwood Jasperware convertible goldtone compact; lid inset with cameo of the "Three Graces" Aglair, Euprosyne, and Thalia, Greek mythological companions of Venus who endow mortals with beauty, wisdom, and charm; blue label on interior beveled mirror reads, "The cameo on this STRATTON PRODUCT is made by Josiah Wedgwood & Sons, Ltd."; 3¼" dia. $50.00 – 75.00.

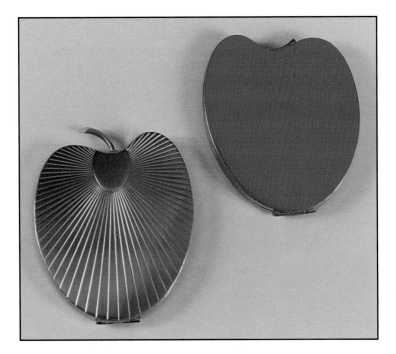

Left – Volupté polished goldtone compact designed to resemble apple; engraved lines radiate from top; stem opens compact; interior mirror and powder well; 3" x 3". $125.00 – 185.00.

Right – Volupté red enameled compact designed to resemble apple minus stem; interior mirror and powder well; 3" x 3". $150.00 – 225.00.

Super-sized round bi-colored goldtone compact; polished goldtone lid decorated with raised polished pink goldtone leaping gazelles; pink goldtone scalloped design at top and bottom of front lid; deeply beveled interior mirror, puff, and powder compartment; 5⅞" dia x ⅝". 300.00 – 350.00.

Elgin American polished goldtone compact; lid decorated with crown set with five red stones, lady sitting on chair, banner underneath chair reads "Queen for a Day"; beveled mirror and powder compartment; 3½" x 2¾".
$100.00 – 150.00.

Coty "Memo" goldtone compact with matching lipstick/ perfume combination; compact designed to resemble book; embossed basketweave design on lid; cartouche on polished goldtone spine; lipstick/perfume combination designed to resemble pencil; one side of tube contains creamy lipstick, other side contains small bottle of Chypre perfume; 3½ x 2¼"; lipstick, 3½". $175.00 – 225.00.

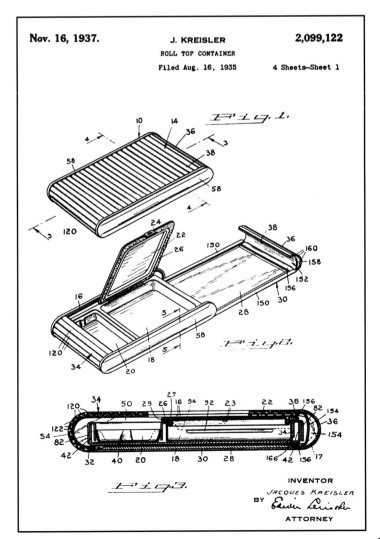

Mini roll-top vanity; coppertone roll-top, red enameled side pieces; interior mirror, powder, and rouge compartments; 2" x 3".
$75.00 – 125.00.

Left – Volupté square goldtone compact in black moire "Whisk-er Brush" slip-case containing outside sleeve for lipstick tube; 3" x 4". $50.00 – 100.00.

Right – Volupté square goldtone compact in black moire "Whisk-er Brush" slip-case; 3" x 4". $25.00 – 75.00.

Square ivorene compact/easel; centered on lid of compact is round picture of man and woman in goldtone embossed frame; easel is made in same design as outer rim of compact; back of picture reads "La Musette" (Boucher); 3⅛" x 1¾". NPA.

Mini round compact/key chain combination; snakeskin lids; interior metal mirror, swansdown puff, and powder compartment; key chain attached to side rim of compact; Italy; 1½" dia. $80.00 – 100.00.

Schuco miniature Teddy Bear compact; opens to reveal powder compartment; head lifts off to reveal lipstick tube; Patent #1,693,563; 3¾". $600.00 – 800.00.

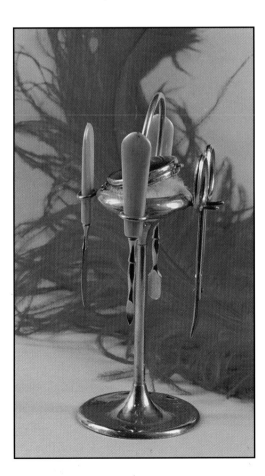

Dresser vanity/manicure combination; round compact centered on top of silvertone stand; blue butterfly wings under glass decorate compact lid; rings around outer rim secure manicure implements; carrying handle; Germany; 2¼" x 6¼". NPA.

Red leather-rimmed compact designed as tambourine; red and yellow chenille ball fringe; hand-painted scene of bull-fighter on front lid; "Mallorca" written on top of front lid; interior mirror and powder compartment; 4" dia x ⅞". NPA.

Shari "Langlois" round goldtone vanity; lid decorated with beautiful Oriental scene; unusual fitted silk octagonal presentation box has identical scene executed in color on the lid; interior of compact reveals metal mirror separating rouge and powder compartments; compact 2¼" dia.; box 3". $150.00 – 225.00.

Left – Evans silvertone vanity case; lid decorated with purple, lavender, and silvertone designs; interior reveals mirror, powder and rouge compartments, and two coin holders; carrying chain. 2" x 3½". $175.00 – 225.00.

Right – Evans silvertone vanity case; lid decorated with purple, lavender, and silvertone designs; interior reveals mirror, powder, and rouge compartments; finger ring chain; 2" x 2". $125.00 – 150.00.

Mini-goldtone compact designed to resemble fan; exterior lid decorated with yellow, pink, silvertone, and goldtone flowers; pearl twist lock; interior mirror and powder well; 2½" x 1½". $40.00 – 60.00.

Left - Evans silvertone vanity with through handle; black enamel disc with scene of bird and flowers centered on engine-turned vanity lid; interior reveals mirror, powder, rouge, and lipstick compartments; 3" x 3½". $125.00 – 175.00.

Right - Evans silvertone vanity with through handle; black enamel disc with scene of bird and flowers centered on engine-turned vanity lid; interior reveals mirror, powder, and rouge compartments; 2" x 3¼". $75.00 – 100.00.

Shown open.

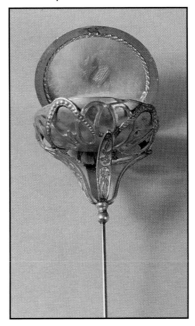

Shown closed.

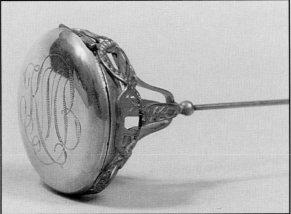

Goldtone compact/hatpin combination; silvertone compact lid monogrammed; interior reveals mirror and puff; decorative Art Nouveau goldtone mounting; 12" shank; compact 1½" dia. $800.00 – 1,200.00.

Wooden egg-shaped compact; carved design on exterior of compact; interior contains unusual puff with plastic dog's head on top; no mirror; lipstick tube concealed in tassel; carrying cord; 1¾" dia x 3". NPA. Courtesy of Barbara Schwerin.

Shown open.

Round bone colored plastic compact/perfume combination; screw off bottom lid decorated with black painted ruffles; man with pilgrim hat centered on top lid; hat screws off to reveal perfume bottle; interior reveals powder well and puff, mirror missing; 1½" dia x 3". NPA. *Courtesy of Barbara Schwerin.*

Shown closed.

Ivory celluloid compact designed as hand mirror; exterior mirror; top lid opens to reveal powder compartment; 2¾" dia x 5". $100.00 – 125.00.

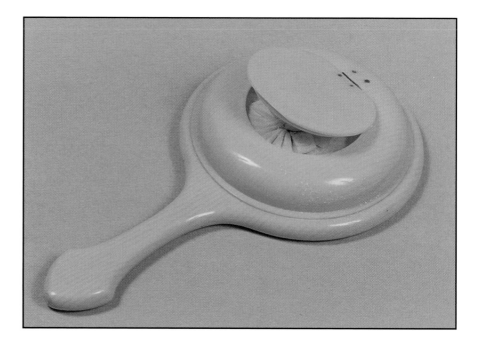

Round silvertone vanity; painted flapper celluloid domed disc applied to lid; eyes inset with blue faceted stones; rhinestones decorate hair; interior mirror, rouge, and powder compartments; 1⅞" x ½". NPA.

Front Shown.

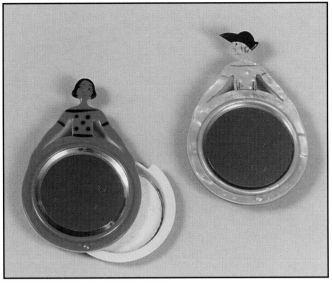

Two celluloid compacts designed to resemble females; exterior swinging beveled mirrors incorporated as part of skirt; left – front of dress orange accented with black dots; interior powder well showing; right – front of dress marbelized pink, black hat, shown with mirror in closed position; imprinted above mirrors "Pat'd Apr 28 – 25." $100.00 – 200.00.

Reverse side shown; left – back of dress carmel colored, black hat; right – back of dress white with red and black decorations.

Enamel and sterling dresser vanity designed as period piece lady in a ball gown; ivorene female figure dressed in light blue and lavender cloisonne enameled ball gown; gilded lower interior section reveals mirror and powder well; exterior bottom lid reads "Depose"; inner rim of compact reads "Sterling" and "Germany"; 2½" dia x 3". NPA.

Jacqueline Cochran make-up kit; red and white plastic tubular container with compartments for cleansing cream, blended foundation cream, night cream, cream rouge, face powder section, face powder sifter; plastic cream applicator; 1" dia x 4". $60.00 – 80.00.

Left 1 – Green plastic pli painted to resemble doll; tri-cornered hat; France; 4¼". $150.00 – 200.00.

Left 2 – S.G.D.G. green plastic pli; powder well in bottom; puff pushes out on top; France; $60.00 – 100.00.

Top 1 – Red enamel and silvertone cannister-type powder container; outside bottom lid contains mirror; bottom lid reveals powder puff; top unscrews to reveal powder scoop; France 1" dia x 2¼". $75.00 – 125.00. (Shown closed.)

Top 2 - Blue same as red. (Shown open.)

Bottom Right – Princess Pat goldtone powderette lipstick; lipstick concealed under upper lid; ¾" dia x 2½". $75.00 – 125.00.

Bottom Center – Luxor cream colored enamel powderette; powder releases when top is pushed down; Luxor logo on lid; premium gift "Compliments of Luxor" written on bottom lid; Patent # 1872836; ⅝" x 2½". $40.00 – 60.00.

Bottom Left – Princess Pat silvertone powderette lipstick; lipstick concealed under upper lid; ½" dia x 3". $50.00 – 75.00.

- Princess Pat rouge and puff in handy, roomy compartment.

- To release powder, press the Vaniteen point on puff. Lift it and it closes automatically, spill-proof.

ACTUAL SIZE

PRINCESS PAT

"*Vaniteen*"

COMBINATION ROUGE COMPACT AND AUTO-MATIC LOOSE POWDER HOLDER—**RETAIL $1**

This Princess Pat Vaniteen solves that knotty problem—the low-price gift that makes an instant hit. Vaniteen has class and distinction, yet its price of one dollar makes it a fast, easy seller. Very handsomely finished in the color of gold and richly embossed, the Vaniteen looks right at home in the proudest purse. If ever an idea held allure for the gift-seeking eye, this one is well-nigh irresistible. It's the kind of item each Christmas shopper will buy *several* of and it's just the thing all the year round for that adorable bridge prize, hostess gift or birthday token. It supplies that search for something really different and clever.

Real Holiday Helps—You can have Vaniteens on the handsome silver-crystal display tree, each vanity in a transparent package (see illustration at left) or, if preferred, we will package them individually in beautiful Christmas holly-and-snowflake boxes, satin lined, as pictured above. Please indicate your choice when ordering. Minimum fair trade retail price of this Vaniteen is $1 subject to regular trade discount.

FREE
beautiful display ↓

:illiant silvery display tree, mounted in crystal-cut glass base.

A sales-inspiring decoration in your holiday scheme—exceptionally attractive and very, very smart. 20 inches high, displays a dozen Vaniteens and is pilfer-proof.

Princess Pat ad, September 1940.

Instructions for use of "Pli."

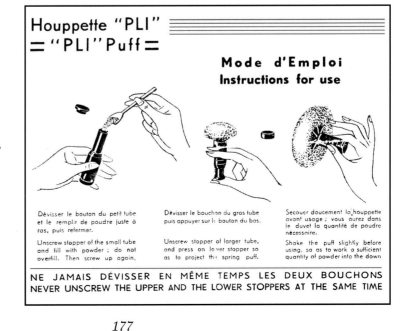

Houppette "PLI"
= "PLI" Puff =

**Mode d'Emploi
Instructions for use**

Dévisser le bouton du petit tube et le remplir de poudre juste à ras, puis refermer.

Unscrew stopper of the small tube and fill with powder; do not overfill. Then screw up again.

Dévisser le bouchon du gros tube puis appuyer sur le bouton du bas.

Unscrew stopper of larger tube, and press on lower stopper so as to project the spring puff.

Secouer doucement la houppette avant usage; vous aurez dans le duvet la quantité de poudre nécessaire.

Shake the puff slightly before using, so as to work a sufficient quantity of powder into the down

NE JAMAIS DÉVISSER EN MÊME TEMPS LES DEUX BOUCHONS
NEVER UNSCREW THE UPPER AND THE LOWER STOPPERS AT THE SAME TIME

Hallmarked sterling compact/cane combination; cane handle is a compact; interior contains framed mirror and powder compartment; compact lid decorated with black island scene; "Erica" engraved on the collar of the cane; dark brown wood shaft designed to resemble bamboo; metal ferrule protector at end of stick; wrist cord under compact handle; 1¾" dia x ½". $375.00 – 500.00.

Hallmarked sterling compact/cane combination; cane handle is a compact; gilded interior contains framed mirror and powder compartment; textured lid and collar; slightly domed lid centered with round polished cartouche; tan wood shaft designed to resemble bamboo; metal ferrule protector at end of stick; 2" dia x ⅜". $250.00 – 325.00.

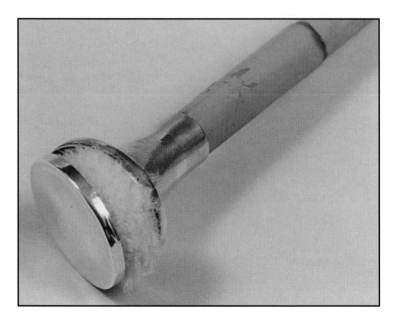

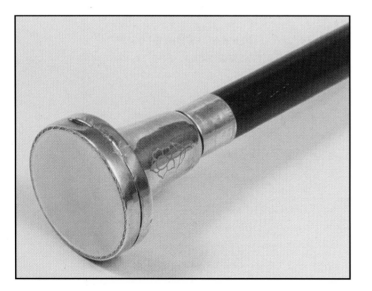

Hallmarked sterling compact/cane combination; cane handle is a compact; gilded interior contains framed mirror and powder compartment; blue cloisonne enameled lid; incised flower on collar; black wood shaft; metal ferrule protector at end of stick; 1⅞" dia x ½". $350.00 – 450.00.

Hallmarked sterling compact/cane combination; cane handle is a compact; gilded interior contains framed mirror and powder compartment; lid decorated with black Siamese scene; mahogany wood shaft; metal ferrule protector at end of stick; 2⅛" dia x ½". $350.00 – 450.00.

Ivorene lipstick tube holder/cane combination; disc with painted cat's head on lid of handle; handle unscrews to reveal well with removeable sterling lipstick tube; brown wood shaft; metal ferrule protector at end of stick; 1½" dia x 2¾". $275.00 – 375.00.

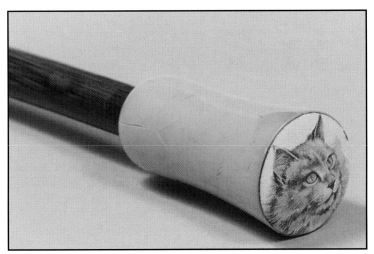

Shown closed.

Shown open.

Shown closed.

Shown open.

Lucille Buhl "Vaniti-Bank" square compact/bank combination; textured goldtone lid highlighted with blue enamel acorns; logo "The Broadway National Bank of Paterson" imprinted on dime bank; reverse side reads "A.R. Martine Co. Inc., 2 Wall St., New York"; interior reveals mirror, bank, and powder compartment; 2¼" x 2¼" x ¾". NPA.

Silver compact/parasol combination; knob shaped handle contains compact; elaborate engravings and repousse work decorate knob compact and collar; gilded interior contains framed mirror, puff, and powder well; braided wrist cord under compact; black silk ruffled parasol (replaced); black wooden shaft; metal ferrule protector at end of parasol; 1½" dia. NPA.

Flamand-Fladium Oar goldtone compact cuff bracelet; medallions on compact lid and side pieces decorated with a griffin; red enameled flowers applied to lattice work on side pieces; beveled mirror and puff; Paris; 2¼" round x 1¾". $250.00 – $350.00. Courtesy of Joan Orlen.

Shown closed.

Shown open.

Round goldtone compact/bank combination; textured lid slightly dome shaped; opening for coin near top hinge on back lid: bank on back lid opens with key for removal of coins; interior mirror and powder compartment; 1⅞" dia. NPA.

Left – Le Rage goldtone compact/bracelet designed to resemble wrist watch; hours on the lid of compact set with green and clear stones; moveable hands; bubble link chain; interior reveals mirror and puff; England; 1½" dia., 7" long. $350.00 – 400.00.

Right – Round goldtone compact/bracelet combination; multicolored stones centered on lid of compact; interior reveals mirror and puff; 1½" dia., 7" long. $250.00 – 300.00.

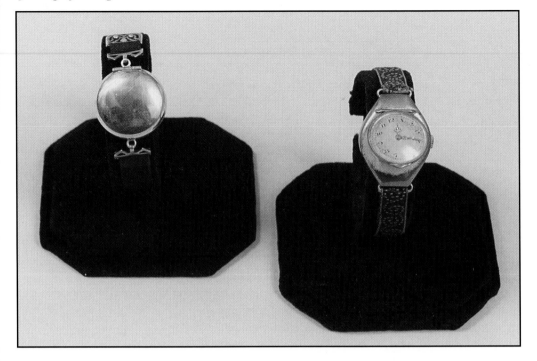

Left – Round polished silvertone compact/bracelet; grosgrain band with silver buckle closure; reverse side of compact reads "Junior Prom, 1923"; interior reveals convex mirror; 1" dia. $100.00 – 125.00.

Right – Goldtone compact/bracelet designed to resemble wrist watch; watch face under glass crystal on lid; faux winder; interior reveals convex mirror; black and gold grosgrain band; 1" x 1¼". NPA.

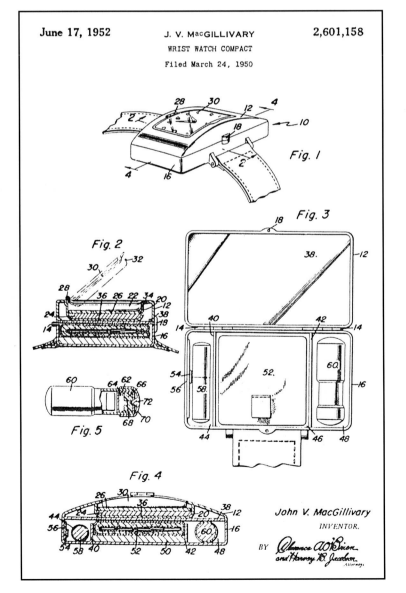

Left – K & K polished satin-finish compact/bracelet combination; hinged bracelet; shown opened; 2" x 1½". $200.00 – 250.00.

Right – K & K polished satin finish compact/bracelet combination; lid of compact set with red and clear crystal stones; 2" x 1½". $250.00 – 300.00.

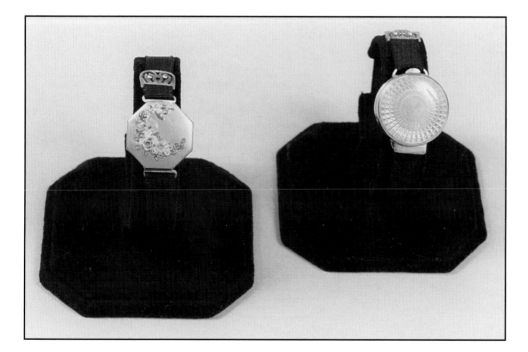

Left – Octagon-shaped enamel compact/bracelet combination; pearlized pink enamel lid decorated with raised flowers; interior reveals mirror and puff; grosgrain band with silver catches; 1" x 1". $200.00 – 250.00.

Right – Round sterling silver compact/bracelet combination; pink cloisione enamel lid; interior reveals mirror; grosgrain band with silver catches; 1" dia. $250.00 – 300.00.

Flamand-Fladium goldtone compact/bracelet combination; compact lid decorated with goldtone stars on an onyx disc; cutouts of stars surround cuff bracelet; signed by Claudine Cereola; France; 1½" dia. NPA.

Left – F.J. Co. antique gold-tone compact bracelet combination; lid set with black onyx; marquesite flowers centered on onyx; flowers on hinged band; 1 7/8" dia. $225.00 – 300.00.

Right – F.J. Co. antique goldtone compact bracelet combination; compact lid decorated with filigree; flowers on hinged band; 1 7/8" dia. $300.00 – 350.00.

Shown closed.

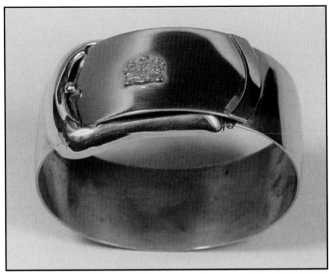

Silvertone compact/bracelet combination; bracelet designed to resemble buckle; applied goldtone insignia; bracelet opens to reveal powder well, metal mirror, puff, and powder well cover; 2 1/4" dia. NPA.

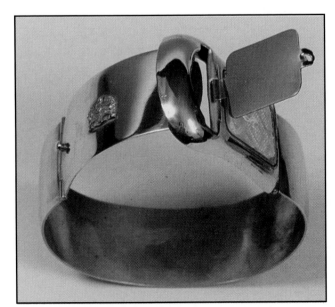

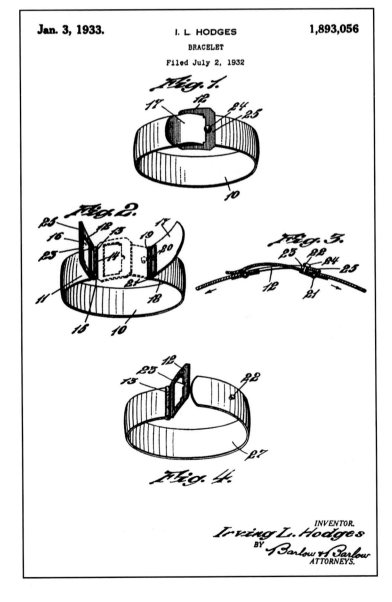

Shown open.

184

Shown closed.

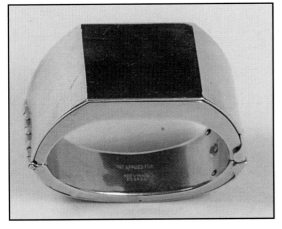

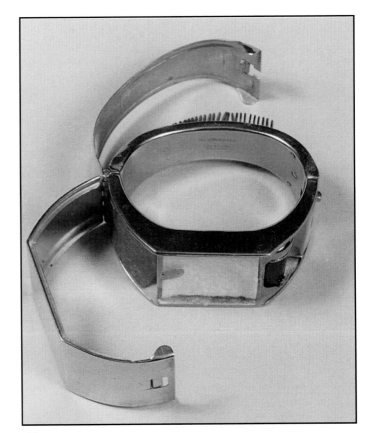

Zama polished goldtone compact/bracelet combination; one side of hinged cuff bracelet opens to reveal mirror, powder and rouge compartments, and compartment with lipstick tube; other side of hinged cuff bracelet opens to reveal comb; France; 1½" x 2¾ dia. NPA.

Shown open.

Flamand gold and silvertone compact/bracelet combination; lipstick separates the two Bakelite discs on the cuff bracelet; one side has compact centered on disc, other side has mirror centered on disc; goldtone bands decorate discs; rumor has it that that this was one of the compact bracelets that Josephine Baker commissioned to be made for her to give as gifts to her friends; 1¾" x 2¼" dia. NPA.

Princess Eve goldtone cosmetic bracelet combination; four cosmetic tubes suspended from link chain; tubes contain eye make-up, lipstick, wick (possibly for scent), collapsible plastic cigarette holder; bracelet 7"; tubes 1¼".
$60.00 – 90.00.

Three Marlowe Co. "Parisienne" plastic compact/bracelet combinations; decorative metal band slides to reveal two mirrors and five cosmetic compartments; green and butterscotch shown closed; burgandy shown open; also available in other colors; ¾" deep. $175.00 – 325.00.

Antique silvertone dresser powder box; exterior heavily embossed; interior reveals mirror; Greece; 5" x 5". $75.00 – 125.00.

Town & Country, September 1942.

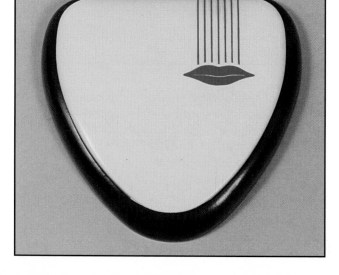

Tangee dresser/vanity; white enameled top lid decorated with stylized red lips; blue bottom lid; interior reveals wells for lipstick, powder, and rouge cases; Patent # D-128-188; 5" x 5". $75.00 – 125.00.

W.B. Manufacturing Co. stylized silvertone triangular dresser vanity; lid decorated with elephant; interior reveals fitted wells for powder, rouge, and lipstick cases; Pat. 7-22-30; 4½" x 3½" x 3½". $125.00 – 175.00.

Dresser Vanity ad, 1931.

187

Shown closed.

Shown open.

White metal baseball dresser
vanity; raised stitches on seams;
set on goldtone pedestal; goldtone interior reveals beveled
mirror, puff, and powder well;
Germany; 2½" dia.
$150.00 – 250.00.

"Victory Vanity" amber glass army hat dresser vanity; exterior
beveled mirror; raised army insignia on crown; interior reveals powder compartment; 4¾" dia x 2". $50.00 – 125.00.

Evans gray suede fitted presentation boxed set;
lipstick tube, cigarette case, compact, and cigarette
lighter; white enamel decorated with hand-painted
roses; 9½ " x 4" x 1½".
$125.00 – 175.00.

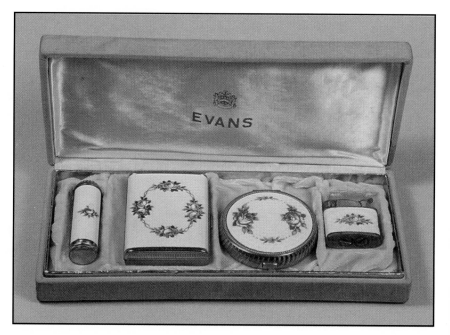

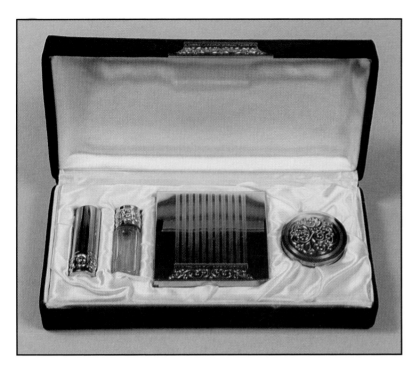

*Avon black faille fitted presentation boxed set;
matching goldtone lipstick tube, perfume bottle,
compact and rouge case; interior white satin;
enclosed card reads "In addition to the pleasure
and satisfaction the lovely contents of this Avon Set
will give you, the box itself can be used as a jewel
case for your Dressing Table. Just remove the puffed
satin platform and you will have a lovely, smooth
satin lined case for this purpose."
compact 2¾" x 2¾"; box 8" x 4" x 1¾".
$100.00 – 125.00.*

*Left – Kreisler brown suede fitted presentation boxed set; brushed goldtone with silvertone
flap envelope style vanity; matching cigarette lighter; compact interior contains mirror
and powder and rouge compartments; Patent # 1987533; compact 3" x 2",
box 6" x 4¼" x ¾". $100.00 – 125.00.*

*Center – Evans tan suede fitted presentation boxed set; matching goldtone compact and
cigarette lighter; compact and lighter decorated with scenic transfer; compact tap-sift
model; compact 2" dia., box 5" x 3" x 1½". $60.00 – 100.00.*

*Right – Lentheric holiday wrapped presentation boxed set; black and goldtone
matching vanity and lipstick; interior reveals metal mirror that separates powder and
rouge compartments; Patent # 1987533, Des Patent # 96680; compact 2¾" x 2¼";
box 4¼" x 4". $50.00 – 75.00.*

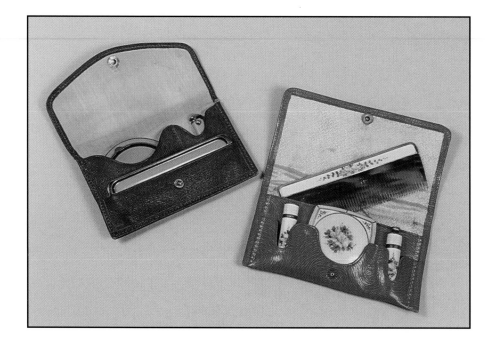

Left – Green leather envelope-style presentation case; interior includes matching green and black compact, lipstick tube, and comb all in designated fitted slots; compact 2½" dia., case 5" x 3". $125.00 – 150.00.

Right – B.B. & Co. red leather envelope-style presentation case; interior contains matching sterling silver compact, lipstick tube, perfume flacon, and comb; all pieces are green cloisonne decorated with hand-painted pink flowers; compact 2" x 2", case 5½" x 3". $275.00 – 300.00.

Left – La Mode red velvet fitted presentation boxed set; contains matching mother-of-pearl vanity and locket with chain; interior of compact reveals metal mirror that separates powder and rouge compartments; compact 2¼" dia, box 4¾" x 3¾" x 1". $100.00 – 125.00.

Right – La Mode matching compact and locket set; green enamel compact and matching locket decorated with hearts; interior of compact reveals metal mirror that separates powder and rouge compartments; 2¼" x 2¼". $200.00 – 250.00.

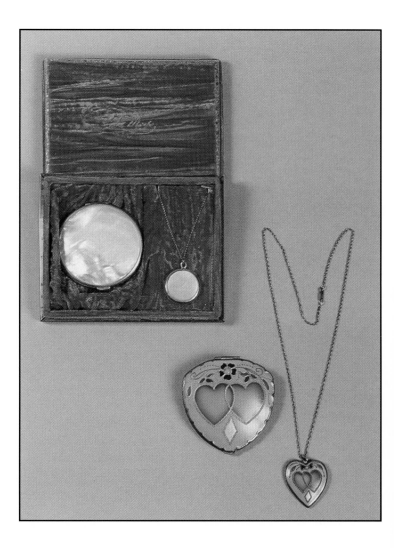

Left – La Mode fitted red suede presentation boxed set; goldtone heart-shaped compact with matching heart-shaped expansion bracelet; heart-shaped cartouche on pink and yellow goldtone decorates lid of compact and bracelet; compact 2½" x 2¼", box 7" x 3¾" x 1½". $175.00 – 250.00.

Right – Henriette maroon velvet fitted presentation boxed set; brushed and satin goldtone decorated compact with Air Force insignia centered on lid and on matching bracelet; braided goldtone mesh bracelet band with tassel; gift boxed by Hilborn-Hamburger, Inc, Military Jewelers, N.Y.; compact 2½" x 2½", box 7" x 4" x 1". $175.00 – 225.00.

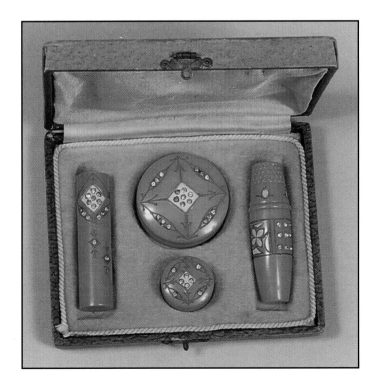

Coral, green, and white Bakelite compact, rouge pot, perfume container, and sewing container in original fitted presentation box; rouge pot ⅞"; compact has mirror and puff, 1½" dia; perfume bottle in Bakelite tube, 2¼"; sewing tube contains needles, thread, and pins, top is a thimble, 2½"; all have green and white engraved decorations enhanced with rhinestones. $175.00 – 225.00.

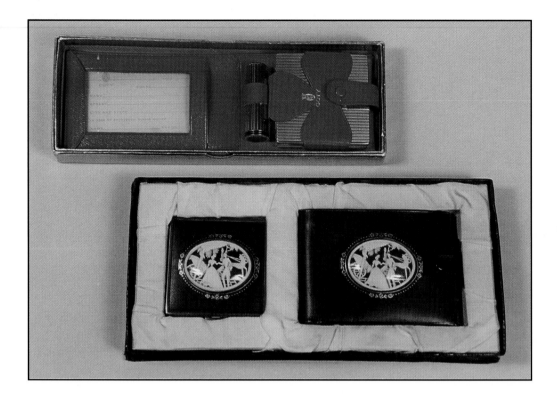

Top – Coty red leather billfold; interior of billfold contains sleeves with matching Coty compact and lipstick tube; 2¾" x 2¾". $80.00 – 100.00.

Bottom – Daniel black leather compact with matching billfold; centered on compact lid and billfold is an ivorene three-dimensional cut-out scene of a man and woman encased under a plastic dome; 2¾" x 2¾". $150.00 – 175.00.

Sterling round blue enamel compact/ perfume combination; lid of compact decorated with goldtone decoration; top cap unscrews to reveal perfume well; Austria; 2½" dia. $450.00 – 500.00.

Turquoise enamel and goldtone clover-shaped purse-motif compact; interior reveals framed beveled mirror and powder compartment; matching brooch and clip on earrings; Italy; 2¾" x 2½". $250.00 – 300.00.

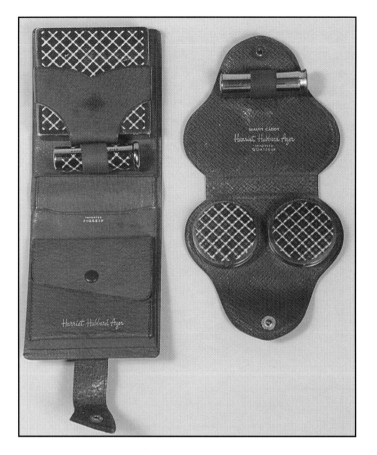

Left – Harriet Hubbard Ayer green pigskin compact/billfold combination; opened billfold has sleeves for H.H.A. compact and matching lipstick tube; closed 4" x 3", opened 8½" long. $100.00 – 125.00.

Right – Harriet Hubbard Ayer clover-shaped red goatskin "Beauty Caddy"; opened caddy reveals sleeve for lipstick holder and permanent powder and rouge cases; 3¾" x 3¾", opened 7½" long. $125.00 – 150.00.

Harriet Hubbard Ayer ad, 1951.

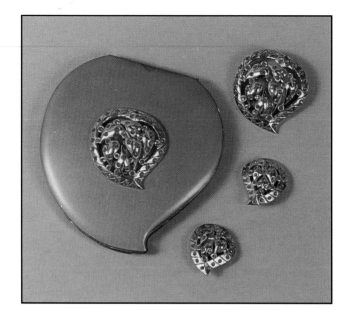

Elgin American polished goldtone compact, earrings, and pin suite; stylized heart shape; center of compact set with applied heart enhanced with red stones; matching earrings and pin; 3¼" x 3¼". $150.00 – 225.00.

Vanity-Kid silvertone engine-turned vanity front lid opens to reveal compact; lipstick tube on right side of compact; perfume tube on left side of compact; France; 2¼" x 2¼". $150.00 – 175.00.

Elgin American Catalog, 1949.

6062/037—Set consists of compact, brooch and matching earrings. Compact has an applied heart-shaped ornament set with imitation rubies on a gold Roman finish. Brooch matches compact ornament. Set is supplied with a heart-shaped red velvet covered, satin lined display and gift box. Subject to federal excise tax.

600/001—Set consists of heart-shaped brooch set with imitation rubies, matching earrings. Gift box 42. Subject to federal excise tax.

Gift Box No. 40. Special book style box, covered with red velvet and trimmed with white satin. Sold individually to dealer for $1.00.

Shown closed.

Shown open.

Blue enamel compact centered on multi-sided cut crystal perfume bottle; etched flowers on perfume bottle surround compact;
blue enamel perfume cap; 2½" dia. NPA.

Black enamel oval compact/perfume combination;
compact suspended by two ornate filigree chains to a finger ring;
lid centered with oval floral silver cut-out disc; silver perfume
screw top; gilt interior with powder compartment; mirror framed
in gilt braid; Austria; 1½" x 2½". $350.00 – 450.00.

Square silvertone compact/perfume combination; lid
decorated with painted scene on enamel; shown with
perfume wand extended; wrist carrying chain;
2¾" x 2¾". $250.00 – 300.00.

Shown open.

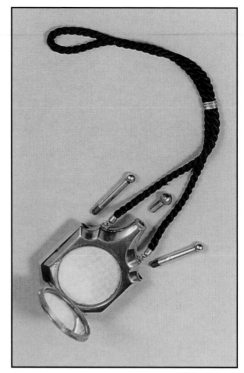

Shown closed.

Dual opening brass vanity; powder compartment and mirror on one side; rouge compartment and mirror on other side; two pull-out lip rouge sticks; top center unscrews to reveal perfume compartment; silk braid carrying cord; 2" x 2¾". NPA.

Light blue oval hallmarked sterling cloisonne enamel compact/perfume combination; gilded interior reveals mirror and powder well; perfume knob unscrews to reveal perfume compartment; carrying chain; 1½" x 2½". $250.00 – 350.00.

R.& G. Co. gold and silvertone compact/perfume combination; screw top perfume closure on top complete with perfume wand; engine-turned lid decorated with blue flag with the letter M; front lid opens to reveal powder well and mirror; 1¾" x 2". $100.00 – 150.00.

Front shown.

Back shown.

H.W.K. Co. round silvertone compact/bridge indicator combination; enameled blue and white front lid; reverse side reveals center dial indicating raised numbers 1, 2, 3, 4, 5, or 6; spinning selector displays heart, diamond, spade, club, or NT; suits in black or red enamel; interior reveals mirror and powder well; 1¾" dia. NPA.

Coty black and white enamel goldtone vanity designed as domino; lid divided into two sections, one white enamel and one black enamel; white enamel has two round black indentations, black enamel has five round white indentations; interior reveals mirror, powder and rouge compartments, and puffs; 3¾" x 2¼". $150.00 – 250.00.

*Left – Illinois Watch Case Co. brushed goldtone vanity watch combination;
interior reveals powder and rouge compartments; 2¾" x 2¾". $100.00 – 125.00.*

*Right – Evans compact-watch-music box combination; watch centered on embossed
sunburst design lid; interior reveals powder well and music box; 3" x 2 ". $175.00 – 250.00.*

*Bottom – Evans compact watch combination; beautiful white cloisione enhanced
with hand-painted roses decorate lid; interior metal swinging mirror conceals watch;
2½" x 2½". $150.00 – 200.00.*

Shown open revealing powder compartment.

Shown open revealing watch.

*Sterling red enamel side-by-side compact/watch combination; one side opens to reveal powder compart-
ment, puff, and mirror; other side reveals watch; pull out lipstick; Germany; 1" x 3 ". NPA.*

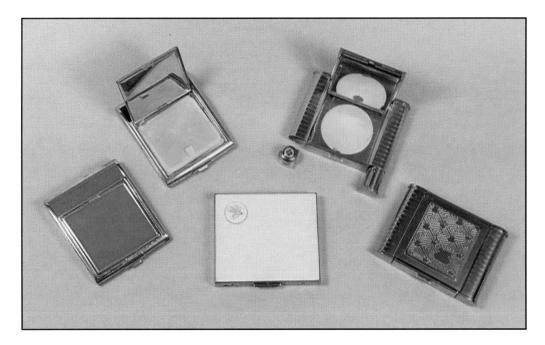

*Lower Left – Green enamel goldtone compact with interior light; wedge shaped;
2¾" x 3¼". Shown closed. $80.00 – 100.00.*

Upper Left – Black enamel. Shown open.

*Upper Right – Venus-Ray goldtone compact with interior light; engraved compact lid; one
side of compact contains lipstick tube; small perfume container and opening for battery on
other side; 3½" x 2¾". Shown open. $125.00 – 175.00.*

Lower Right – Shown closed.

*Bottom Center – White enamel compact/flashlight combination; lid decorated with a
firefly; exterior flashlight activated when button is pushed on outer lid; 3½" x 3".
$125.00 – 150.00.*

*Plastic Art Deco compact/flashlight
combination; interior contains metal mirror which
conceals battery; flashlight above mirror; powder
compartment; black and white shown open;
purple shown closed; 1⅜" x 3¼". $80.00 – 150.00.
Black and white courtesy of Barbara Schwerin.*

Shown with powder pli and lipstick tube removed.

Case and binoculars shown.

Black plastic faux vanity/binoculars complete with fitted black silk case; lipstick tube and powder pli slide out from top eye pieces; mirrors on bottom lens; case lined with interior mirror on lid; 3" x 2½". NPA.

Shown open.

Shown closed.

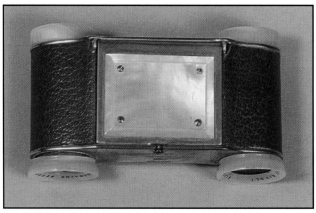

Colmont "Pomponnette" opera glasses/compact; goldtone opera glasses covered in green leather, white pearlized lens dial rims; compact set in center; white pearlized lid which opens to reveal beveled mirror and powder; puff attached to powder well lid; Paris; 3½" x 2" x1". NPA
Courtesy of Joan Orlen.

THE OPERETTA— *a "let me see" bit of whimsy. With lipstick holder, powder room and a fluffy, twist-out swansdown puff. Encased in rich, black satin. About $10.00.*

Expect to turn heads...
and conversation your way

Such a clever way to capture your audience completely.

Imagine! A carryall, looking for all the world like a camera.

A powder-lipstick case, masquerading as opera glasses.

Most intriguing ideas—for imaginative you . . . for an imaginative gift!

Wadsworth "CONVERSATION PIECES"

For over 60 years the makers of America's finest watch cases

THE COMPAKIT—*focus for widening eyes. With powder compartment, lipstick holder, lighter, cigarette section, comb, keys-hanky-money pocket. In a smart black faille case. About $12.50 tax included.*

Other beautiful Wadsworth Powder Cases $2.00 to $65.00

Vogue, 1950.

Lower Left – Evans compact/cigarette case/lighter combination; black enamel case has white enamel compact enhanced with Art Deco motif on lid; Patent #1624874 and 1869983; 3¼" x 6¾". $175.00 – 200.00.

Upper Left – Brushed goldtone vanity cigarette case combination; lid decorated with black enamel design; white enamel vanity decorated with white flower cloisonne disk on lid; interior vanity reveals powder and rouge compartments; Licensed Patent #1869983; 3" x 5". $150.00 – 175.00.

Upper Right – Brushed goldtone vanity cigarette case combination; lid decorated with black enamel design; black enamel vanity decorated with mother-of-pearl disc on lid; interior vanity reveals powder and rouge compartments; Licensed Patent #1869983; 3" x 5". $150.00 – 175.00.

Lower Right – La Mode black enamel vanity cigarette case combination; white enamel vanity on lid; interior vanity reveals metal mirror with powder and rouge compartments; 3" x 7". $150.00 – 175.00.

Lower Center – Marathon white enamel goldtone combination compact/lighter/cigarette case; white enamel lid of compact decorated with enamel flowers; Patent #2053455 and 2071601; 2½" x 4¼". $150.00 – 175.00.

Center – La Mode green enamel vanity cigarette combination; green enamel lid of vanity decorated with flowers; vanity reveals powder and rouge compartments; 2½" x 2¾". $50.00 – 75.00.

Left – Black enamel vanity cigarette case combination; white enamel disc with pink flowers centered on vanity lid; Army Air Force insignia applied to center of cigarette case; Licensed Patent # 1869983; 3" x 4". $100.00 – $125.00.

Top – Lampl goldtone compact/cigarette case/watch combination; compact in center flanked by compartment for cigarettes; watch set on front lid; Patent # 2085502; 5½" x 3". $175.00 – 250.00.

Right – Richard Hudnut goldtone vanity cigarette case combination; white enamel lids decorated with purple enamel orchids; vanity interior reveals compartments for powder, rouge, and lipstick tube; 3" x 4½". $150.00 – 175.00.

Bottom – Brushed goldtone side-by-side bolster compact cigarette combination; 5" x 1¾". $60.00 – 80.00.

Center – Girey red enamel vanity cigarette combination case; black enamel vanity lid; interior contains rouge and powder compartments; 3¼" x 3½. $100.00 – 125.00.

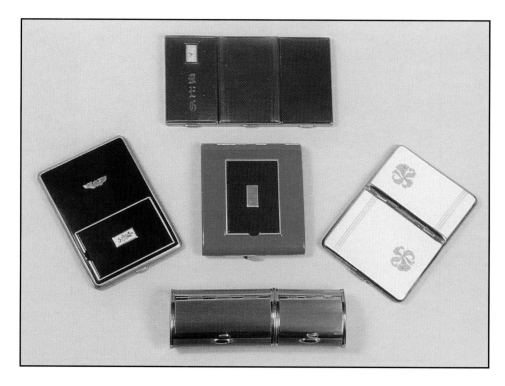

Shown closed.

Left – Alfred Dunhill sterling engine-turned vanity designed to resemble cigarette lighter; front opens to beveled mirror, powder, and rouge compartments; top lifts to reveal sliding lipstick; Patent No. 1639628; 1⅞" x 1⅞". $225.00 – 300.00.

Right – Alfred Dunhill goldtone vanity designed to resemble cigarette lighter; front lifts up and reveals beveled mirror, powder, and rouge compartments; sliding lipstick on one side of vanity; phial for perfume on other side of vanity; pencil on top behind vanity; Reg. No. 737179; 2¼" x 2¼". Similar item (enameled) sold at auction, Phillips, London, March 8, 1990, for $510.00. NPA.

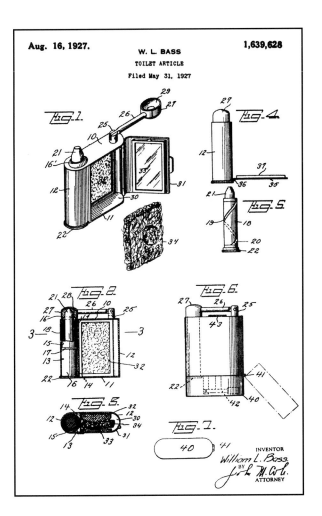

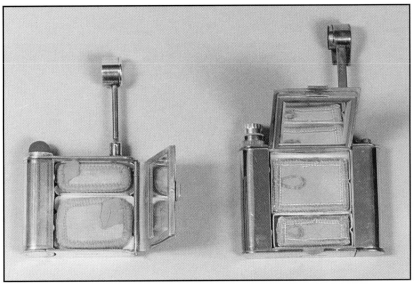

Shown open.

La Brise tortoise shell compact/fan combination; exterior mirror on compact lid; lid opens to reveal powder compartment and puff; reverse side has three blades; pressure of thumb on metal plunger activates blades which creates a breeze; England; Patent: # 21777-13; blade span 5¼", compact 1¾" dia. NPA.

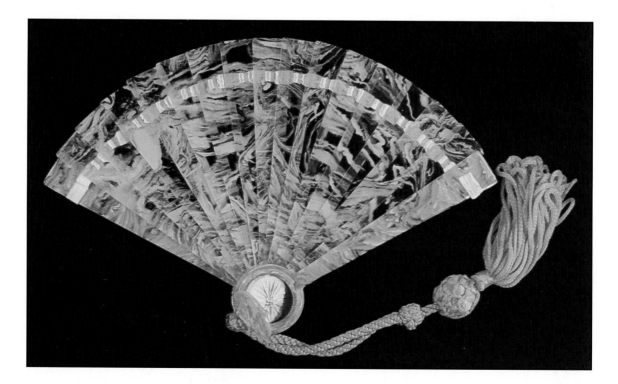

Tortoise shell compact/fan combination; compact located at bottom of fan; one side opens to reveal compartment for powder and puff; reverse side of compact has exterior mirror; matching silk braided carrying cord; span of fan when opened 6½" x 6½". NPA.
Courtesy Ruth and Herman Wacker.

Lower Left – White enamel compact shaped like hand mirror; hand-painted flowers on lid; 2" x 5". $100.00 – 125.00.

Center Left – Volupté goldtone "Demitasee" compact formed as hand mirror; black enamel lid decorated with goldtone dots; lipstick in handle; 2" x 4½". $75.00 – 125.00.

Upper Left – Petit-point goldtone compact shaped as hand mirror; filigree handle; Austria; 2¾" dia x 4". $60.00 – 80.00.

Top – Art Deco style miniature compact shaped as hand mirror; lid decorated with rhinestones and purple and lavender colored stones; interior mirror and exterior mirror on back lid; 2" x 3½". $75.00 – 100.00.

Upper Right – Round black enamel compact shaped as hand mirror; lid decorated with floral disc; interior and exterior mirrors; 1½" dia x 3½". $60.00 – 80.00.

Center Right – Miref "Mirador" gilt compact formed as hand mirror; lipstick in handle; interior and exterior beveled mirrors on both outer lids; 2" dia x 4¼". $125.00 – 150.00.

Lower Right – Black and goldtone compact shaped as hand mirror; lid decorated in black and gold swirls; lipstick in handle; interior and exterior beveled mirrors; 2½" x 5¼". $150.00 – 175.00.

Lower Left – Silver mini compact shaped as hand mirror; brushed silver lid decorated with scattered engraved flowers; lipstick in handle; Italy; 1¼" x 3¾". $125.00 – 175.00.

Upper Left – Sterling compact formed as hand mirror; exterior beveled mirror; interior ivory writing slate; 1½ x 2" x 4½". NPA.

Top – Silver compact shaped as hand mirror; exterior of lid engraved; lipstick in handle; interior and exterior mirrors; scalloped frame around exterior mirror; 2" x 5". $200.00 – 250.00.

Upper Right – D.R.G.M. silvertone vanity shaped as hand mirror; compartments on both sides, one for powder, one for rouge; both lids engraved; interior mirrors; top cap opens for perfume; German; 1½" x 3½". $150.00 – 175.00.

Lower Right – Silver mini compact shaped as hand mirror; heavily engraved; lipstick in handle; blue cabachon thumbpiece; Italy; 1½" x 3¾". $150.00 – 200.00.

Bottom – International Sterling octagon vanity with handle; cartouche on lid; interior reveals rouge and powder compartments; 2" x 3". $80.00 – 100.00.

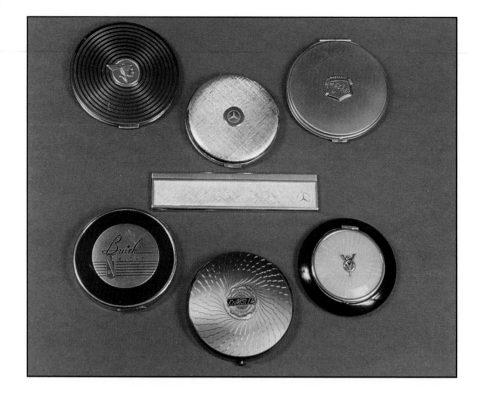

Lower Left – Round silvertone and maroon compact with "Buick Eight" logo applied to lid; 3" dia. $70.00 – 85.00.

Upper Left – Round goldtone compact with "Pontiac" logo applied to lid; 3¼" dia. $50.00 – 65.00.

Upper Right – Round brushed goldtone compact with "Buick" logo applied to lid; 3" dia. $50.00 – 65.00.

Lower Right – Round black plastic compact with "Ford" logo centered on pearlized plastic; framed by silvertone rim; 3" diam. $70.00 – 85.00.

Lower Center – Round goldtone compact with "Chrysler" logo applied to lid; 3" dia. $50.00 – 65.00.

Center – Brushed silver compact and matching comb/case with "Mercedes Benz" logo; Germany; 2¾" dia. $75.00 – 150.00.

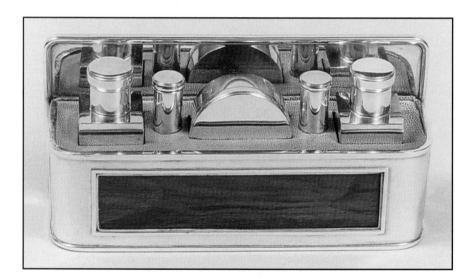

Chrome and leather car vanity/bar accessory; bar contains chrome compact, two chrome lipstick tubes, and two chrome metal containers; vanity bar affixed either to dashboard or side panel of luxury car; 6½" x 3¼". $250.00 – 350.00.

Elgin Vanity silvertone car/vanity and Elgin Smoker cigarette/match stick caddy vanity contains removeable Elgin American vanity case; interior reveals covered powder and rouge cases, covered cold cream case, two lipstick tubes, and mirror; mesh carrying chain; smoker contains removeable match stick holder flanked by two removeable cigarette holders on either side; vanity and smoker affixed to side panels of luxury car; 5½" x 3¾". $350.00 – 500.00.

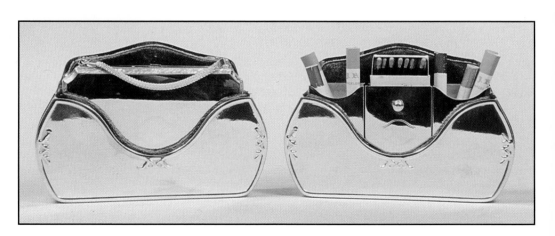

ℋew Ensemble Sets

Now, Ternstedt provides sets of vanity and smoking cases, *especially designed for each particular car.* Look for these Ensemble Sets on the finer cars—and note how exactly they harmonize with the interior. ¶ Not only is the "theme" design wrought into the metal but the exterior panelling of the cases is in perfect harmony with the car's interior color scheme and appointments. ¶ Ternstedt designers and silversmiths are keenly aware of the public's ever growing appreciation of quality and beauty, in automobile fittings. The new Ensemble Sets are certain to further increase that appreciation, for they surpass even the rich and beautiful craftsmanship which has won for Ternstedt recognition as the leader in its field. ¶ The significance of "Fittings by Ternstedt" in a motor car—the fact that they actually are indicative of a higher degree of quality—is at once made evident to anyone who contrasts the Ternstedt-equipped car in any given price field with any other car in that field which lacks the advantage of Ternstedt equipment.

FITTINGS BY

TERNSTEDT

UNIT OF FISHER BODY CORPORATION

The Saturday Evening Post, September 28, 1929.

Evans engine-turned silvertone miniature vanity designed to resemble cigarette lighter; top opens to reveal powder compartment; lipstick tube slides out of bottom; 1 ½" x 1 ⅞". $125.00 – 150.00.

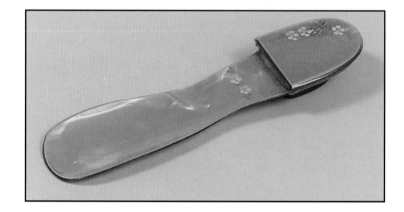

Green marbelized celluloid compact/shoe horn combination; top of shoe horn decorated with painted flowers; reverse side butterscotch colored; heel lifts to reveal framed mirror, puff, and deep powder compartment; 1 ¾" x 6" x 1". NPA.

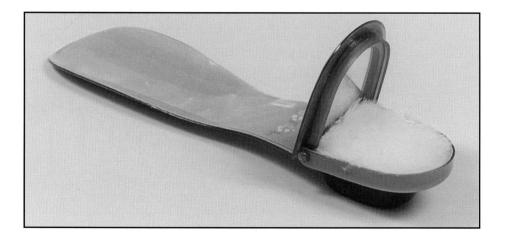

The following section photographed by Arthur Field.

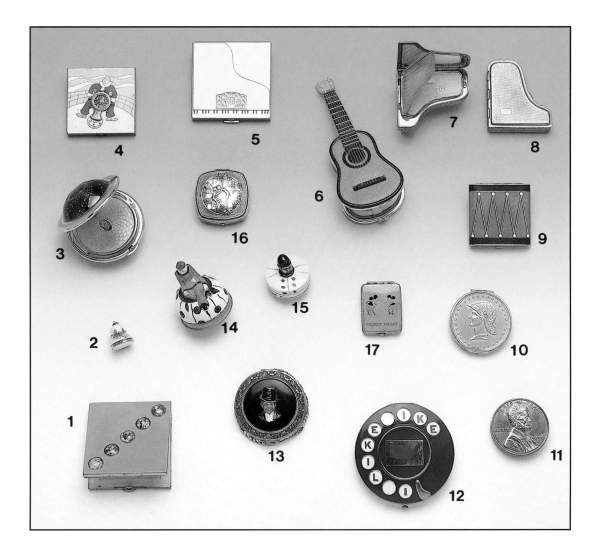

1 Lampl light blue enamel compact with five colorful three-dimensional scenes from "Alice in Wonderland" encased in plastic domes on lid. $150.00 – 250.00.

2 Sterling silver white cloisonné mini bell-shaped compact decorated with painted holly; diminishing mirror and loop for chain. NPA.

3 Kigu "Flying Saucer" metal compact with blue celestial scene on both sides (shown open). $350.00 – 400.00.

4 Square goldtone compact with sailor steering ship and copper steering wheel mounted on lid. $80.00 – 120.00.

5 Volupté "Collector's Item" metal compact with grand piano on lid and raised keys on keyboard. $150.00 – 200.00.

6 Samaral brown leather and brass compact designed to resemble guitar with strings; Spain. NPA.

7, 8 Pygmalion textured-brass compact designed to resemble grand piano; collapsible legs; England (7 shown open, 8 shown closed). $350.00 – 450.00.

9 Charbert red, white, and blue enamel "Drumstick" compact, c. 1930s. $150.00 – 200.00.

10 Elgin American silvered-metal compact designed to resemble coin. $150.00 – 200.00.

11 Avon copper-colored lip gloss container designed to resemble Lincoln penny. $40.00 – 60.00.

12 Red, white, and blue compact designed to resemble telephone dial with slogan "I Like Ike" imprinted on lid; red map of the United States on lid. $200.00 – 250.00.

13 Evans "Charlie McCarthy" mesh vanity pouch with raised Charlie McCarthy head on black enamel lid. $250.00 – 350.00.

14 Orange, blue, and white lusterware compact with colorful Oriental figure mounted upright on screw-top lid. NPA.

15 French ivory mini compact with raised Bobby's head mounted upright on screw-top lid. NPA.

16 Djer-Kiss silvered-metal vanity case with raised nymphs on lid; powder and rouge compartments c. 1920s. $150.00 – 200.00.

17 Orange enamel mini compact with painted intaglio figures of Mickey and Minnie Mouse; powder sifter. $300.00 – 350.00.

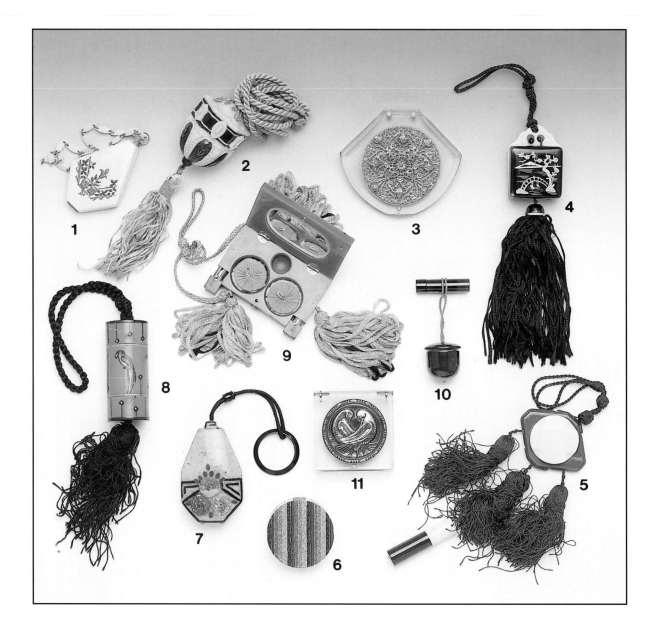

1 *French ivory compact with painted red and green flowers; carrying chain made of plastic links; c. 1920s. $175.00 – 225.00.*
2 *French ivory and green molded plastic dual-opening vanity case with carrying chain and tassel; powder and rouge compartments; c. 1920s. $300.00 – 350.00.*
3 *Yellow Lucite compact with filigree metal lid, c. 1920s. $150.00 – 200.00.*
4 *Ebony and French ivory dual-opening vanity case with Oriental scene on lid; powder and rouge compartments; carrying cord with lipstick concealed in tassel; c. 1920s. $250.00 – 300.00.*
5 *Blue and ivory plastic screw-top compact; carrying cord with lipstick concealed in tassel; c. 1920s. $250.00 – 350.00.*
6 *Multicolor striped glitter plastic compact, c. 1920s. $50.00 – 75.00.*

7 *Marbleized yellow plastic vanity case with raised multi-colored flower on lid; ring carrying cord with ojime button; c. 1920s. $250.00 – 350.00.*
8 *Pink bolster-shaped vanity case decorated with painted parrot; carrying cord with lipstick concealed in tassel; c. 1920s. $250.00 – 300.00.*
9 *Oblong green plastic vanity case striped with ebony; compartments for powder, rouge, and slide-out lipsticks; tassel and tasseled carrying cord; c. 1920s (shown open). $300.00 – 350.00.*
10 *Brown plastic tango chain screw-top compact designed as an acorn; lipstick attached by gold cord. $125.00 – 200.00.*
11 *Blue Lucite compact with sterling repoussé medallion of two doves on lid. $150.00 – 175.00.*

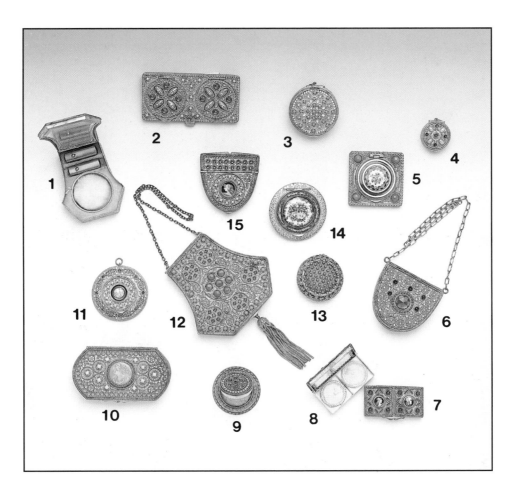

1 Gilded-metal embossed vanity case with multicolored intaglio decoration; prong set with red stones and pearls; compartments for powder and lipsticks; France, turn of the century (shown open). $200.00 – 275.00.

2 Oblong gilded-metal embossed vanity case with multicolored intaglio decoration; prong set with red stones and painted cloisonné inserts; powder and rouge compartments and sliding lipstic; France, turn of the century. $200.00 – 275.00.

3 Goldtone embossed compact with multicolored intaglio decoration; prong set with green stones; loop for chain; France, turn of the century. $100.00 – 150.00.

4 Gilded-metal embossed mini compact with multicolored intaglio decoration and lid set with blue stones and pearls; France, turn of the century. $100.00 – 150.00.

5 Gilded-metal embossed compact with multicolored intaglio decoration and enameled painted lid set with blue cabochon stones; France, turn of the century. $150.00 – 250.00.

6 Horseshoe-shaped gilded-metal embossed vanity case with multicolored intaglio decoration; prong set with purple stones; carrying chain and compartments for powder and lipsticks; France, turn of the century. $200.00 – 300.00.

7, 8 Oblong gilded-metal embossed vanity case with multicolored intaglio decoration; prong set with blue stones and painted disk; powder and rouge compartments; France, turn of the century. (7 shown closed, 8 shown open). $150.00 – 225.00.

9 Goldtone mini compact with multicolored intaglio decoration; prong set with purple stones; France, turn of the century. $125.00 – 175.00.

10 Gilded-metal embossed vanity case with multicolored intaglio decoration with cameo-like disk on lid; prong set with pink stones; France, turn of the century. $200.00 – 250.00.

11 Gilded-metal compact with multicolored intaglio decoration; prong set with blue stones and pearls; loop for chain; France, turn of the century. $150.00 – 200.00.

12 Goldtone embossed vanity case with multicolored intaglio decoration; prong set with red and turquoise stones; tassel and carrying chain; France, turn of the century. $300.00 – 400.00.

13 Goldtone filigree miniature compact; prong set with turquoise stones; Continental, 19th century. $150.00 – 225.00.

14 Goldtone enameled compact with red, green, and goldtone enamel back and painted enamel scene on lid; Continental, turn of the century. $150.00 – 200.00.

15 Horseshoe-shaped gilded-metal embossed vanity case with multicolored intaglio decoration; openings for powder and rouge; prong set with blue stones, pearls, and painted disk; France, turn of the century. $200.00 – 275.00.

1 Ebony wooden compact shaped as castanets with metal Paris ensignia on lid and orange tasseled carrying cord; France. $200.00 – 250.00.

2 Yellow bolster-shaped vanity case with silhouette and black polka dots; carrying cord with lipstick concealed in tassel; c. 1920s. $250.00 – 300.00.

3 Platé "Trio-ette" rose cameo molded-plastic vanity case shaped as hand mirror; powder on one side, rouge on the other; lipstick concealed in handle; c. 1940s. $125.00 – 250.00.

4 Crystal Lucite compact with polished metal cutout of man taking siesta next to cactus plant, c. 1940s. $60.00 – 80.00.

5 Ebony plastic rhinestone-studded compact with screw top, c. 1920s. $60.00 – 80.00.

6 Red beetle-shaped novelty plastic compact. $80.00 – 125.00.

7 Oval red plastic compact set with rhinestones; carrying cord and tassel; c. 1920s. $250.00 – 350.00.

8 Pink Lucite-rimmed sterling silver compact with sterling hinge and catch. $150.00 – 200.00.

9 Venine blue plastic vanity case with goldtone filigree lid; compartments for powder and rouge. $60.00 – 80.00.

10 A. Bourjois & Co. "Novita" ebony plastic compact with canal scene painted on lid; fancy braided carrying cord with two lipsticks and perfume containers concealed in tassels; France. NPA.

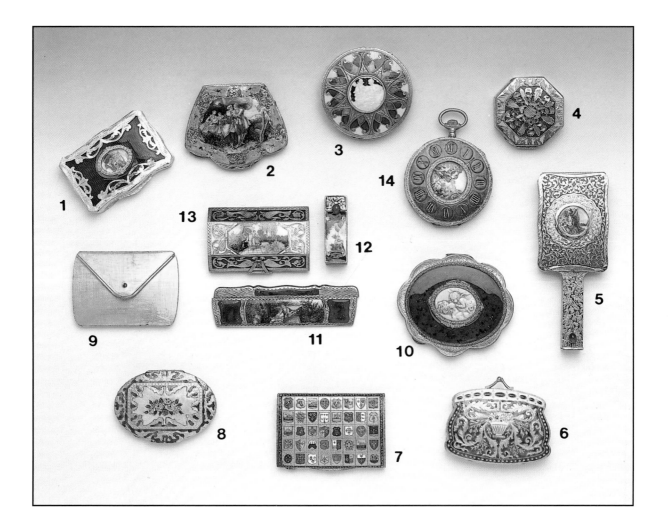

1 *Green and goldtone embossed oblong compact with painting of two girls in disk on lid; Italy, turn of the century. $125.00 – 175.00.*

2 *Vermeil etched silver and blue enamel compact, Italy, turn of the century. $250.00 – 400.00.*

3 *Silver etched compact with colorful enamel design on lid and French ivory cutout; Continental, turn of the century. $250.00 – 350.00.*

4 *Octagonal champlevé, gilded and embossed compact with two shades of blue; Italy, turn of the century. $125.00 – 150.00.*

5 *Red and goldtone champlevé compact shaped as hand mirror; lipstick concealed in handle; red cabochon lipstick thumbpiece; Italy, turn of the century. $300.00 – 400.00.*

6 *Shaded red and green enamel goldtone compact designed to resemble purse; Italy, turn of the century. $150.00 – 250.00.*

7 *Gilded embossed compact with colorful enameled coats-of-arms on lid; Italy, turn of the century. $150.00 – 250.00.*

8 *Shaded red enamel goldtone compact with painted flowers on lid; Italy, turn of the century. $100.00 – 125.00.*

9 *Antiqued goldtone envelope compact with blue stone thumbpiece; Italy. $125.00 – 175.00.*

10 *Scalloped antique goldtone compact with blue enamel encircling French ivory miniature on lid; Italy, turn of the century. $150.00 – 225.00.*

11, 12, 13 *Vermeil engraved silver compact, lipstick, and comb set decorated with blue enamel and multicolored painted scenes; red cabochon lipstick thumbpiece; Italy, turn of the century. $600.00 – 700.00.*

14 *Goldtone embossed compact designed to resemble pocket watch; lid with Roman numerals and painted country scene; Italy, turn of the century. $200.00 – 250.00.*

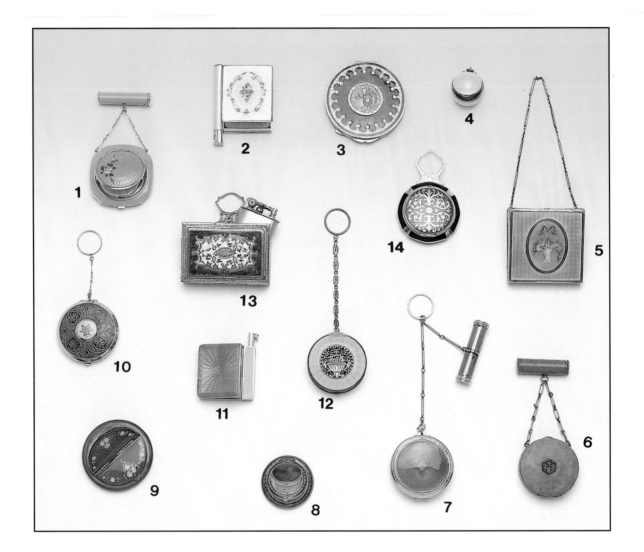

1 Evans blue enamel tango chain vanity with painted cloisonné lid; powder and rouge compartments (shown open). $150.00 – 200.00.

2 La Mode gilded metal cloisonné compact with painted flowers on lid; sliding lipstick. $100.00 – 150.00.

3 Gilded-metal engraved compact with blue enamel lid and rhinestones on outer edge; metal "Saint Genesius, Guide My Destiny" medallion on lid; Continental. $200.00 – 250.00.

4 Sterling silver hallmarked light blue cloisonné ball-shaped compact; loop for chain, Germany. $200.00 – 300.00.

5 Square, embossed silver, lavender cloisonné vanity case with painted basket of flowers on lid; goldtone interior with compartments for powder, rouge, and lipsticks; carrying chain. $250.00 – 350.00.

6 Shagreen tango chain compact with initial set with marcasites, c. 1930s. $250.00 – 300.00.

7 Richard Hudnut "Deauville" blue cloisonné tango chain vanity; metal mirror and powder and rouge compartments; lipstick attached to finger ring chain; c. 1920s. $200.00 – 250.00.

8 Green cloisonné goldtone vanity case with openings for powder and rouge; Austria, 19th century (shown open). NPA

9 Sterling silver hallmarked blue enamel vanity case with painted roses; adjacent openings for powder and rouge. $200.00 – 250.00.

10 Round nickel-silver red and black enamel compact; metal mirror and compartments for powder sifter and rouge; finger ring carrying chain; c. 1920s. $125.00 – 150.00.

11 Sterling silver hallmarked green cloisonné compact; lipstick in upper section; Germany. $250.00 – 300.00.

12 Sterling silver hallmarked yellow cloisonné compact with cutout silver medallion on lid; finger ring chain; Austria. $150.00 – 225.00.

13 Engine-turned nickel-silver compact/cigarette case/lighter combination with green enamel lid. $200.00 – 300.00.

14 Red and black champlevé and gilded vanity case with powder and rouge compartments and through handle. $150.00 – 200.00.

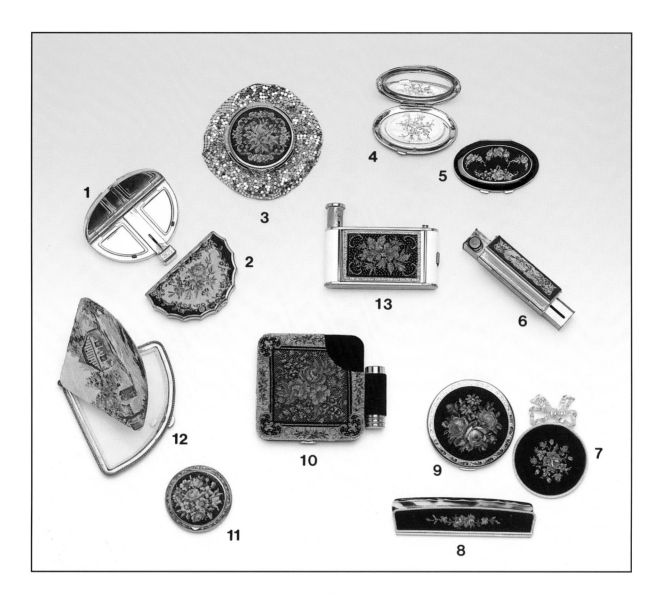

1 *Petit point half-moon-shaped goldtone vanity case with powder and rouge compartments and sliding lipstick, c. 1930s (shown open). $100.00 –150.00.*
2 *Petit point scalloped half-moon-shaped goldtone vanity case, c. 1930s. $80.00 –125.00.*
3 *Evans petit point goldtone mesh vanity bag with metal mirror and powder and rouge compartments in lid, c. 1940–50s. $150.00 –175.00.*
4, 5 *Rowenta oval enameled petit point compacts (4, brown enamel, shown opened; 5, black enamel, shown closed). $30.00 – 50.00.*
6 *Quinto petit point compact with sliding lipstick and perfume container (shown open). $125.00 – 175.00.*

7, 8, 9 *Petit point gilt mirror, comb, and compact set, Austria. $75.00 – 100.00.*
10 *Petit point goldtone compact backed in black faille with tandem lipstick. $150.00 – 225.00.*
11 *Petit point lid, rim, and back of round compact with powder sifter. $80.00 – 120.00.*
12 *Triangular petit point compact with swivel mirror. $150.00 – 175.00.*
13 *White enamel metal petit point compact with petit point lid designed to resemble camera; lipstick at top, cigarette case in back; West Germany. $125.00 – 150.00.*

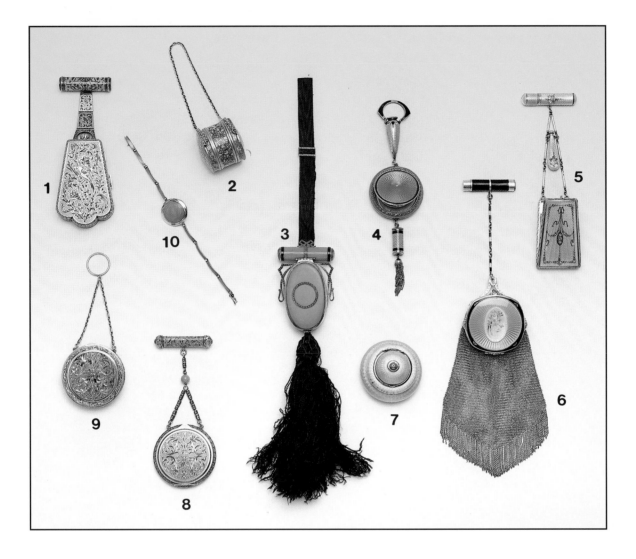

1 Sterling silver hallmarked green enamel vanity case with goldtone interior; lipstick attached to vanity by enameled links; embossed perfume knob at base of links; partitions for powder, rouge, and cigarettes; Austria, turn of the century. $550.00 – 700.00.

2 Blue flowered enamel two-sided vanity case with powder on one side and rouge on the other; wrist chain; Continental, turn of the century. $250.00 – 350.00.

3 Sterling silver hallmarked salmon-colored plastic vanity case with marcasite trim; tandem lipstick and powder and rouge compartments; tassel and marcasite-decorated carrying cord; Continental. NPA.

4 Foster & Bailey blue cloisonné vanity case suspended from enameled perfume container; powder and rouge compartments; lipstick attached at base; tassel and black enameled finger ring chain. $800.00 – 1,250.00.

5 Green cloisonné silver tango chain vanity with pink roses; powder and rouge compartments; lipstick attached by two enameled link chains with perfume suspended between the two chains. $500.00 – 700.00.

6 Foster & Bailey sterling silver mesh tango chain vanity bag with light blue cloisonné lid with painted flowers; powder and rouge compartments; lipstick attached by enamel chain; turn of the century. $500.00 – 700.00.

7 Peach copper and cloisonné vanity case with two-tier openings for powder and rouge; Germany, 19th century. NPA.

8 Sterling silver hallmarked green champlevé tango chain with bar-brooch lipstick; Austria, turn of the century. $300.00 – 400.00.

9 Sterling silver hallmarked green champlevé compact with finger ring chain; Austria, turn of the century. $200.00 – 300.00.

10 Sterling silver hallmarked blue cloisonné compact/bracelet with enameled links; Germany, 19th century. NPA.

1 *Coty goldtone compact with Coty trademark (stylized white puffs on an orange background) on lid. $60.00 – 80.00.*

2 *Elgin American goldtone compact with colorful enamel swirls and "G.E. Color T.V." logo on lid. $125.00 – 175.00.*

3 *Segal red enamel nickel-silver compact with sliding key blank in lid, c. 1930s. $150.00 – 225.00.*

4 *Turquoise plastic screw-top perfume container with lipstick and eye makeup containers suspended from gold cord. $100.00. – 150.00.*

5 *Brown lizard zippered compact designed to resemble suitcase with carrying handles. $125.00 – 175.00.*

6 *Vantine's blue silk compact decorated with embroidery and gold thread; beaded tassel and carrying cord with ojime bead; c. 1920s. $100.00 – 175.00.*

7, 8 *Molded orange plastic round clip-on compact (7 shown closed, 8 shown open). $100.00 – 125.00.*

9 *Yellow marbleized plastic ball compact decorated with faux pearls; tassel and carrying cord. $200.00 – 350.00.*

10 *Wadsworth compact with "Simplicity Printed Pattern 25 cents" on lid. $125.00 – 175.00.*

11 *Pink satin vanity case with gold braid; powder and rouge compartments; carrying cord with ojime bead and beaded tassel; c. 1920s. $100.00 – 175.00.*

12 *Volupté black enamel goldtone compact designed to resemble artist's palette with raised paint tube, brushes, and colors on lid. $175.00 – 275.00.*

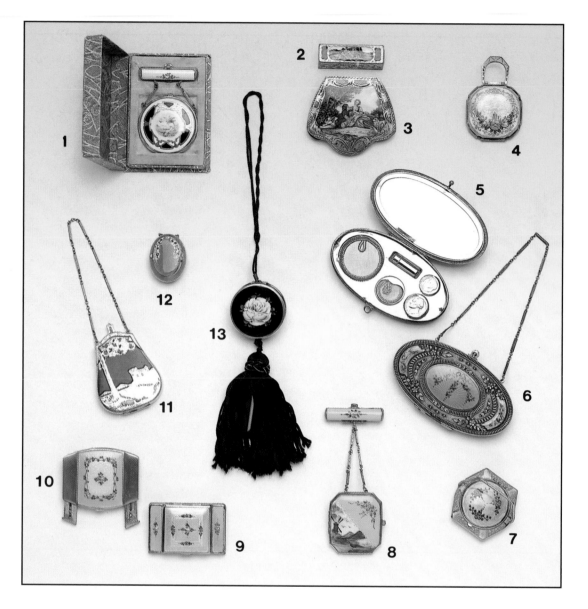

1 White enamel tango chain vanity case with country scene on lid; lipstick attached by two link chains; powder sifter and rouge compartments; original fitted presentation box. $300.00 – 400.00.

2, 3 Embossed vermeil compact and lipstick set with enameled country scene on lid; Italy, turn of the century. $125.00 – 150.00; $350.00 – 450.00.

4 Octagonal silvered-metal blue cloisonné vanity case with roses; powder sifter and rouge compartment and through handle; c. 1920s. $200.00 – 225.00.

5, 6 Antiqued goldtone oval embossed vanity case with cloisonné lid, carrying chain, and compartments for powder sifter, rouge, lipstick, and coins (5 shown open, 6 shown closed). $350.00 – 500.00.

7 Lavender cloisonné silvered-metal vanity case with blue flowers; powder sifter and rouge compartment; swivel handle. $100.00 – 150.00.

8 Green enamel tango chain vanity case with flowers on lid and lipstick; powder sifter and rouge compartment; double-link chain; c. 1920s. $200.00 – 250.00.

9 La Mode blue cloisonné goldtone vanity case with metal mirror; compartments for powder and rouge, and two sliding lipsticks, one on either side. $100.00 – 150.00.

10 La Mode green cloisonné goldtone vanity case with picture locket in lid; and metal mirror, compartment for powder, and two sliding lipsticks, one on either side (shown open). $100.00 – 150.00.

11 Silvered-metal and enameled vanity case with painted raised tree and house on lid; engine-turned link chain; compartments for powder, rouge, and lipsticks; c. 1930s. $150.00 – 250.00.

12 Sterling silver blue cloisonné vanity case with pink flowers; openings on either side for powder and rouge; two loops for chain. $175.00 – 275.00.

13 Black enamel goldtone vanity case with pink rose; two sides open (one for powder, the other for rouge); carrying cord with lipstick concealed in tassel. $125.00 – 150.00.

1, 2 Richard Hudnut "Deauville" vanity case with red and black enamel profiles on lid; powder and rouge compartments; lipstick holder attached to compact and finger ring; c. 1920s (1 shown open, 2 shown closed). $250.00 – 300.00.

3 Richard Hudnut "Deauville" vanity case with white and green enamel profiles on lid; powder and rouge compartments; original fitted presentation box; c. 1920s. $200.00 – 300.00.

4 Evans "Tap Sift" white cloisonné vanity case with black stylized "skyscraper" motif and key pattern around rim; powder sifter and rouge compartment; c. 1920s. $125.00 – 150.00.

5 Evans "Tap Sift" green cloisonné tango chain vanity case with black stylized "skyscraper" motif; powder sifter and rouge compartment; lipstick attached by double chain; c. 1920s. $150.00 – 250.00.

6 Richard Hudnut "le Debut" silvered-metal vanity case with powder and rouge compartments; lipstick attached to compact and finger ring; c. 1920s. $150.00 – 250.00.

7 Art Deco abstract cloisonné vanity case with link carrying chain; compartments for powder, rouge, and lipstick. $200.00 – 300.00.

8 Silvaray Art Nouveau red enamel metal compact. $80.00 – 100.00.

9 Bree green enamel vanity case with metal profile on lid; powder slide and compartments for rouge and lipstick; c. 1930s. $100.00 – 125.00.

10 Art Nouveau silvered half-moon-shaped enameled vanity case with multicolored swirls; goldtone interior, link carrying chain, and compartments for powder, rouge, and lipstick. $150.00 – 250.00.

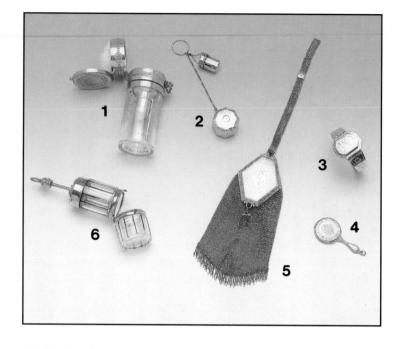

1 Cylindrical etched-glass compact/perfume container with gold-tone compact on top; probably France (shown open). NPA.
2 Tiffany & Co. gold octagonal two-sided tango-chain mini compact with floral design around rim; turn of the century. $800.00 – 1,000.00.
3 Octagonal gold compact/bracelet with engraved lid and band. $500.00 – 600.00.
4 Gold engraved mini compact shaped as hand mirror; loop for chain. $300.00 – 400.00.
5 Gold mesh vanity bag with sapphire cabochon thumbpieces and fringes set with pearls; carrying chain; c. 1920s. $2,500.00 – 3,500.00.
6 Etched-glass compact/perfume container with goldtone lids, glass striped with blue enamel; carrying ring (shown open). NPA.

Compact with three enameled shields on screw-top lid, suspended from dance-program book; "Bal Kolejowy, Stanislawowie, 8 lutego, 1908" in gold-tone on cover; white velvet fringed belt hook; Poland. NPA.

Embossed brass vanity/hatpin; 1½" round, with raised fleur-de-lis on lid; 11½" steel pin. $400.00 – 500.00.

1, 2, 3 Enameled compact shaped as hand mirror; interior and exterior mirrors and matching comb (1 shown closed, 2 shown open, 3 matching comb). $200.00 – 250.00 set; $150.00 – 200.00 compact.
4 Sterling-silver hallmarked white cloisonné miniature oval compact shaped as hand mirror with painted roses on lid; loop for chain; Continental. $300.00 – 350.00.
5 Sterling-silver hallmarked pink cloisonné enameled miniature compact shaped as hand mirror with painted flowers on lid; loop for chain; Continental. $300.00 – 350.00.
6 Brass miniature compact shaped as hand mirror with painted flowers on lid; loop for chain; Continental. $200.00 – 250.00.
7 Sterling-silver blue cloisonné miniature oval compact shaped as hand mirror; interior and exterior mirrors and loop for chain; Continental. $300.00 – 350.00.
8 Sterling-silver hallmarked yellow cloisonné miniature compact shaped as hand mirror; loop for chain; Continental. $300.00 – 350.00.
(Continued on next page.)

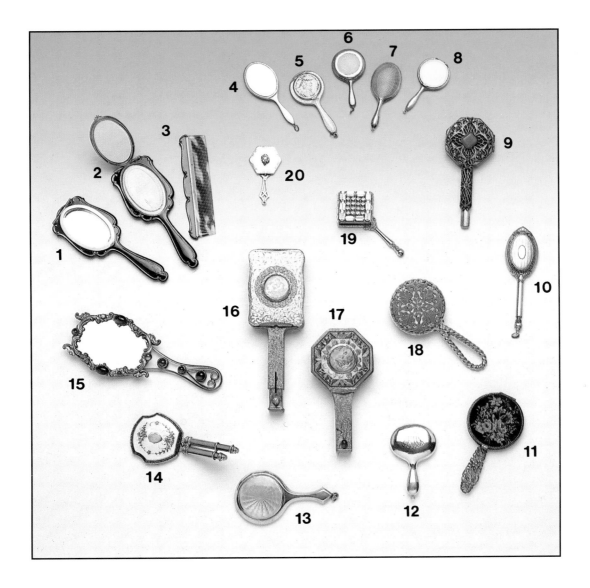

9 *Octagonal silvered-filigree metal vanity case shaped as hand mirror; interior reveals powder sifter; two-sided mirror and rouge compartment decorated with red stones; lipstick in handle. $175.00 – 225.00.*

10 *Sterling silver oval miniature compact shaped as hand mirror; handle unscrews to reveal lipstick and perfume containers; loop for chain; Continental. $300.00 – 350.00.*

11 *Petit point compact shaped as hand mirror; filigree handle and interior and exterior mirrors; Austria. $60.00 – 80.00.*

12 *Sterling silver miniature oval compact shaped as hand mirror; exterior diminishing mirror and loop for chain; Continental. $250.00 – 300.00.*

13 *Vermeil sterling silver hallmarked compact shaped as hand mirror with pink cloisonné lid and exterior mirror; interior lid incorporates writing slate; loop for chain. $350.00 – 400.00.*

14 *White cloisonné compact shaped as hand mirror with painted flowers on lid; fold-over handle contains compartments for lipstick and eye makeup; interior and exterior mirrors. $350.00 – 450.00.*

15 *Goldtone compact shaped as hand mirror decorated with colored cabochon stones; interior and exterior mirrors; France. $225.00 – 300.00.*

16 *Blue and white champlevé goldtone compact shaped as hand mirror with painting of man and woman on lid; lipstick in handle and blue cabochon thumbpiece; Italy. $300.00 – 400.00.*

17 *Red and white champlevé octagonal goldtone compact shaped as hand mirror with painting of girl on swing on lid; lipstick in handle and red cabochon thumbpiece; Italy. $300.00 – 400.00.*

18 *Goldtone compact shaped as hand mirror with green enamel-decorated lid; interior and exterior mirrors; France. $100.00 – 125.00.*

19 *Art Deco miniature compact shaped as hand mirror with rhinestones on lid; interior and exterior mirrors. $75.00 – 100.00.*

20 *Sterling silver, hexagonal mini compact shaped as hand mirror with coat-of-arms on lid; loop for chain; Continental. $150.00 – 175.00.*

1 Antique goldtone vanity case with faux baroque pearls and blue stones on filigree lids; opening on either side for powder and rouge; pearl-decorated tassel and braided finger-ring chain. $250.00 – 300.00.

2 Antique goldtone chatelette; compact with lipstick case, coin holder, and belt hanger decorated on both sides with filigree overlay set with aquamarine-colored stones; Continental. NPA.

3 Pierced silvered-metal bolster-shaped necessaire with onyx filigree disk set with blue stones and marcasites on lid; tassel and carrying chain (shown open). NPA.

4 Pattie Duette "Vivaudou" antique goldtone-filigree vanity bag set with blue stones; vanity case on inside hinge; lined interior; carrying chain with lipstick concealed in tassel; Continental, turn of the century (shown open). NPA.

5 Antique goldtone-filigree vanity case with multicolored stones on lid; opening on either side for powder and rouge, slid-ing lipsticks at sides, and perfume vial at top; tassel and carrying cord; Continental, turn of the century. $350.00 – 450.00.

6 Antique goldtone filigree oval vanity case with stones and center cabochon stone; braid carrying chain with lipstick concealed in tassel; Austria, turn of the century. $275.00 – 350.00.

7 Antique goldtone vanity bag with blue stones and pearls; cover incorporates compact with onyx disk set with blue stones; tassel and carrying chain; silk back; Continental, turn of the century. $350.00 – 450.00.

8 Antique goldtone tango-chain vanity bag compact with green stones; tassel and filigree lipstick holder; silk back; Continental, turn of the century. $350.00 – 450.00.

9 Gilded filigree compact with turquoise stones; butterflies suspended from neck chain. NPA.

1 *Stratton goldtone compact with scenic transfer on lid, c. 1950s. $40.00 – 60.00.*
2 *Rex Fifth Avenue painted, enameled compact with two pink flamingoes on a turquoise background. $75.00 – 100.00.*
3 *Schildkraut goldtone cloisonné compact with two blue peacocks on a white background. $30.00 – 50.00.*
4 *Marhill mother-of-pearl carryall with painted peacock and glitter on lid. $150.00 – 200.00.*
5 *Gwenda goldtone enameled painted foil compact, England. $80.00 – 100.00.*

6 *Goldtone compact with two pink and gray simulated feathered birds enclosed in a plastic dome. $100.00 – 150.00.*
7 *Blue enameled silvertone mini-flapjack compact, c. 1930s. $50.00 – 70.00.*
8 *Goldtone triangular enameled compact with two green birds in flight on a light blue background and finger ring chain. $80.00 – 120.00.*
9 *Wadsworth goldtone hand-painted yellow enamel fan-shaped compact, c. 1940s. $80.00 – 100.00.*

1 Volupté goldtone hand-shaped compact, c. 1940s.
$100.00 – 125.00.
2 Volupté goldtone "faux diamond engagement ring"
hand-shaped compact, c. 1940s. $200.00– 250.00.
3 Volupté goldtone "manicured" hand-shaped compact,
c. 1940s. $150.00 – 175.00.

4 Volupté goldtone "lace gloved" hand-shaped compact,
c. 1940s. $200.00 – 250.00.
5 Volupté goldtone hand-shaped compact, c. 1940s
(shown open).

1 *Kigu "Cherie" goldtone heart-shaped compact with jeweled crown on lid; England, c. 1940–50s. $50.00 – 80.00.*
2 *Elgin American stylized heart-shaped enameled compact with "Give me your answer do!" on lid, c. 1940–50s. $80.00 – 120.00.*
3 *Kigu goldtone blue enamel compact with heart-shaped enameled flower on lid; England, c. 1940–50s. $50.00 – 75.00.*

4 *Marathon goldtone compact with heart on lid; lid opens to reveal a locket; compact opens by pressing the plastic side panels. $60.00 – 80.00.*
5 *Evans pink and yellow goldtone basketweave compact, c. 1946. $150.00 – 225.00.*

1 *Goldtone heart-shaped compact with brocade lid, c. 1930s. $40.00 – 60.00.*

2 *American Maid goldtone heart-shaped compact with engraved lid (shown open). $40.00 – 60.00.*

3 *La Mode silver-plated heart-shaped compact. $50.00 – 75.00.*

4 *Enameled goldtone heart-shaped lock-motif compact. $120.00 – 150.00.*

5 *Engraved silver-plated heart-shaped compact with carrying chain. $75.00 – 100.00.*

6 *Matte goldtone mini compact. $30.00 – 60.00.*

7 *Goldtone heart-shaped compact with purple orchid inlaid in black plastic on lid. $60.00 – 90.00.*

8 *Evans goldtone heart-shaped compact with lipstick concealed in black tassel and black carrying cord, c. 1940s. $200.00 – 300.00.*

1 Amita damascene compact inlaid with gold and silver view of Mt. Fuji capped in silver on black matte-finish lid; Japan, c. 1920s. $100.00 – 150.00.

2 Gilt inlaid vanity case with carrying-chain mirror, coin holder, and powder compartment; Japan, c. 1920s (shown open). $225.00 – 275.00.

3 Damascene compact inlaid with gold and silver view of Mt. Fuji capped in silver on black matte-finish lid; complete with hinged, fitted presentation box; K24. $150.00 – 200.00.

4 Damascene compact black matte-finish inlaid with gilt Egyptian scene. $75.00 – 100.00.

5 Damascene vanity case, with gold and silver view of Mt. Fuji capped in silver on black matte-finish lid; carrying chain and compartments for powder, lipstick, and rouge; K24. $150.00 – 200.00.

6 Damascene compact with elaborate gold inlaid pagoda scene on front lid, bamboo inlaid on back lid; loop for chain; c. 1920s. $250.00 – 300.00.

7 Amita damascene compact with gold and silver floral motif on black matte-finish lid; Japan, c. 1920s. $100.00 – 150.00.

8 Damascene-style gilt compact with scene of man and horse on lid, c. 1930s. $40.00 – 60.00.

1 *Silver-plated vanity case with white pearlized miniature of woman walking a dog on black background mounted on the front lid; carrying chain; compartments for powder, lipstick, rouge, and compartment that "May be used for either Cigarettes, Money, Calling Card or Rosary"; c. 1920s. $150.00 – 225.00.*

2 *Black enamel silvered-metal tango-chain vanity case with silvered Scottie dogs; compartment for powder, metal mirror opens to reveal rouge; lipstick attached with a chain; c. 1920–30s. $150.00 – 225.00.*

3 *Sabor gilt and plastic compact with Lucite dome enclosing two kissing poodles made of thread; France, c. 1930s. $60.00 – 80.00.*

4 *Small blue enamel vanity case with Scottie dog transfer; powder compartment and metal mirror opens to reveal rouge compartment; c. 1920–30s. $30.00 – 50.00.*

5 *Zell Fifth Avenue goldtone compact with poodle motif set with red cabochon stones; lipstick in a fitted black grosgrain case, c. 1940–50s. $125.00 – 175.00.*

6 *Sterling ¾" square compact with chain attached to a ring mounted with a hunting dog, c. 1920s. $200.00 – 250.00.*

7 *Sterling black enamel compact with small plastic dome enclosing a three-dimensional head of a Scottie; Germany, c. 1920–30s. $150.00 – 200.00.*

8 *Black enamel compact with painted poodle on a white enamel disk on lid, c. 1930s. $40.00 – 60.00.*

9 *Black enamel gilt vanity case with gilt Scottie on lid; powder compartment; metal mirror lifts to reveal rouge compartment; c. 1920–30s. $50.00 – 75.00.*

10 *Plastic cigarette/compact combination with metal cutout Scottie on lid, c. 1940s. $80.00 – 110.00.*

11 *Tooled leather bulldog-motif compact with beaded eyes and bell at base. NPA.*

1 *Girey "Kamra-Pak" sparkling confetti plastic vanity case resembling camera; mirror, powder and rouge compartments, and slide-out lipstick; c. 1930–40s. $50.00 – 80.00.*

2 *Wadsworth "Compakit" black plastic vanity case resembling camera with carrying case; powder compartment in front of case, lipstick and cigarette lighter on top, opening for cigarettes at bottom of case; c. 1940s (shown open). $150.00 – 225.00.*

3 *Same as 2 (shown in carrying case). $150.00 – 225.00.*

4 *Kamra-Pak-style blue checkerboard enamel vanity case with compartments for powder and lipstick; reverse side opens to reveal manicure kit; c. 1940. $150.00 – 200.00.*

5 *Kamra-Pak-style lizard vanity case for powder and lipstick; reverse side opens to sewing kit; c. 1940s (shown open). $150.00 – 200.00.*

6 *Snakeskin Kamra-Pak-style vanity purse with carrying handle; compartments for lipstick, powder, rouge, comb, and coins; other side reveals manicure kit; c. 1940–50s (shown open). $200.00 – 250.00.*

7 *Black suede Kamra-Pak-style vanity purse with carrying handle; compartments for lipstick, powder, rouge, comb, and coins; other side has cigarette compartment and lighter; c. 1940–50s. $200.00 – 250.00.*

8 *Kamra-Pak-style black enamel vanity case with powder compartment, lipstick, and perfume bottle. $100.00 – 175.00.*

9 *Girey "Kamra-Pak" vanity case in blue leather with pink plastic top resembling camera; mirror, powder and rouge compartments, and slide-out lipstick; c. 1930–40s. $50.00 – 75.00.*

10 *Multicolored tooled leather-covered Persian-design compact. $125.00 – 175.00.*

11 *Kamra-Pak-style blue painted enamel vanity case with girl leaning against lamp post mounted on front lid; compartments for powder, lipstick, and cigarettes; c. 1940s. $125.00 – 175.00.*

12 *Mireve black enamel vanity case with powder compartment, sliding lipstick, and perfume bottle; France. $125.00 – 175.00.*

13 *Kamra-Pak-style green painted enamel vanity case with Oriental scene on front lid; compartments for powder, lipstick, and cigarettes; c. 1940s. $100.00 – 150.00.*

1 Black and white mother-of-pearl vanity case with attached lipstick, c. 1930s. $50.00 – 75.00.

2 Mother-of-pearl fan-shaped miniature compact with rhinestones, Japan. $40.00 – 60.00.

3 Miniature 1"-round mother-of-pearl compact with faux ruby surrounded by rhinestones. $30.00 – 40.00.

4 Volupté mother-of-pearl "Swinglok" carry-all, c. 1940–50s. $150.00 – 200.00.

5, 6, 7 Marhill mother-of-pearl set with compact, comb, and lipstick/mirror. $75.00 – 100.00.

8 Stylized mother-of-pearl checkerboard compact designed as a book. $50.00 – 75.00.

9 Petit-point-bordered mother-of-pearl compact. $90.00 – 100.00.

10 Max Factor mother-of-pearl lipstick case. $35.00 – 50.00.

11 K & K gray mother-of-pearl compact with faux sapphires and rhinestones, c. 1930–40s. $50.00 – 75.00.

12 Pierced mother-of-pearl light blue and white compact with a dove mounted in center. $75.00 – 100.00.

13 Round mother-of-pearl checkerboard compact, c. 1930s. $60.00 – 75.00.

14 Volupté "Pocket watch" mother-of-pearl compact, c. 1940–50s. $60.00 – 75.00.

15 Mother-of-pearl 5"-round checkerboard compact, c. 1940s. $150.00 –200.00.

16 Maxley mother-of-pearl compact with inlaid black diagonal stripes and mother-of-pearl cameo, c. 1930s. $175.00 – 200.00.

1 Evans petit-point goldtone mesh vanity bag with metal mirror and powder and rouge compartments, c. 1940–50s. $150.00 – 225.00.

2 Evans rhinestone and white velvet vanity bag with carrying chain, metal mirror, and powder and rouge compartments, c. 1940–50s. $150.00 – 225.00.

3 Gilt mesh vanity bag with multicolored synthetic stones; metal mirror and powder compartment; c. 1930–40s. $100.00 – 150.00.

4 Tapestry vanity pouch with floral pattern on lid, c. 1920–30s. $40.00 – 60.00.

5 Rex gilt mesh vanity pouch with mini white plastic beads, c. 1930s. $40.00 – 60.00.

6 Pink satin vanity pochette with pink and green trim; mirror on outside base; c. 1920s. $75.00 – 100.00.

7 Gilt mesh vanity bag with blue synthetic stone; finger-ring chain, metal mirror, and powder compartment; c. 1930–40s. $60.00 – 100.00.

8 Evans rhinestone and black velvet vanity bag with mirror and powder and rouge compartments, c. 1940–50s. $150.00 – 225.00.

1 *Rex Fifth Avenue multicolor-striped taffeta vanity pochette with mirror on outside base, c. 1940s. $75.00 – 100.00.*

2 *Pale blue satin vanity pochette with a border of lace and colored beads, possibly handmade; mirror on outside base; c. 1920s. $75.00 – 100.00.*

3 *Silvered mesh vanity pouch with silvered repoussé disk on black enamel lid, c. 1930s. $50.00 – 75.00.*

4 *Beaded vanity pouch with silvered lid, c. 1930s. $50.00 – 75.00.*

5 *Evans oval gilt mesh, red enamel vanity pouch. $50.00 – 60.00.*

6 *Square leather vanity pouch with gilded lid. $60.00 – 80.00.*

7 *Rex Fifth Avenue navy blue taffeta vanity pochette with green polka dots; mirror on outside base; c. 1940s. $75.00 – 100.00.*

8 *Pink satin vanity pochette with lace and pink and green trim; mirror on outside base; c. 1920s. $60.00 – 80.00.*

9 *Brown fur vanity pouch with collapsible bottom. $50.00 – 75.00.*

1 Evans black velvet vanity bag with transfer picture of apple; metal mirror and powder and rouge compartments; c. 1940–50s. $200.00 – 250.00.

2 Evans gilt mesh, white enamel vanity bag with metal mirror and powder and rouge compartments, c. 1940–50s. $150.00 – 225.00.

3, 4 Evans gilt mesh vanity pouch with painted flowers on white enamel lid, c. 1930s (front and back view). $80.00 – 100.00.

5 Rex Fifth Avenue pink fabric vanity pochette; mirror at base of compact; c. 1940s. $75.00 – 100.00.

6 Volupté light blue collapsible leather vanity pouch, c. 1930s. $75.00 – 95.00.

7 Evans silvered-metal mesh vanity pouch with black enamel lid, c. 1930s. $65.00 – 80.00.

8 Gilt-mesh vanity pouch with picture of butterfly on lid, c. 1930s. $60.00 – 80.00.

9 Brown suede vanity pochette, c. 1930s. $70.00 – 90.00.

10 Blue cloissoné enameled silvered mesh vanity pouch with painted roses on lid, c. 1930s. $80.00 – 100.00.

11 Evans gilt-mesh white cloissoné vanity pouch, c. 1930s. $80.00 – 100.00.

12 Evans miniature gilt-mesh white cloissoné vanity pouch, c. 1930s. $75.00 – 95.00.

13 Evans black rhinestone vanity pouch made of bead-like material, c. 1930s (shown open). $60.00 – 80.00.

Fig. 32
*1 Blue leather one-piece horseshoe-shaped compact.
$40.00 – 60.00.*
*2 Zell Fifth Avenue blue leather compact; sides open to
reveal billfold and coin purse; c. 1940s. $70.00 – 90.00.*
*3 Maroon gold-tooled leather-covered horseshoe-shaped
compact, possibly Spain. $60.00 – 80.00.*
*4 Mondaine white leather-covered book-motif compact, c.
1930s. $75.00 – 125.00.*
*5 Mondaine blue gold-tooled leather compact, c. 1930s.
$40.00 – 80.00.*

*6 Alligator compact with pull-out mirror, possibly Spain.
$80.00 – 100.00.*
*7 Square gold-tooled leather compact, possibly Italy.
$30.00 – 50.00.*
*8 Mondaine maroon gold-tooled leather compact, c.
1930s (shown open). $60.00 – 80.00.*
9 Square leather-buckle compact, c. 1950s. $60.00 – 80.00.
*10 Lesco Bond Street small green alligator compact.
$70.00 – 90.00.*

1 *Lin-Bren green leather compact with envelope-motif coin holder on lid, c. 1940s. $70.00 – 100.00.*

2 *Gold-tooled leather compact with Venice canal scene on lid, possibly Italy. $40.00 – 60.00.*

3 *Lin-Bren green leather compact/cigarette holder combination (shown with open cigarette case); U.S. Patent No. 2,471,963; c. 1940s. $150.00 – 200.00.*

4 *Same as 3 in black leather (shown closed). $150.00 – 200.00.*

5 *Same as 3 in red leather (shown open). $150.00 – 200.00.*

6 *Maroon leather compact with sleeve for lipstick, c. 1930s. $60.00 – 90.00.*

7 *Dorette small snakeskin vanity purse with zippered compartments for powder and purse; lipstick concealed in front lid. $200.00 – 250.00.*

8 *Lady Vanity oval blue leather compact with snap closing. $40.00 – 60.00.*

9 *Square alligator compact with goldtone lipstick attached to side. $80.00 – 100.00.*

Fig 34

1 Green lizard compact with lipstick hinged on top of lid, probably Argentina. $150.00 – 200.00.
2 Gold-tooled brown leather horseshoe-shaped compact, Argentina. $50.00 – 70.00.
3 Persian gold and black compact with padded lid. $30.00 – 50.00.
4 Larue green-gold tooled leather compact designed as a book; lid contains sliding mirror (shown open). $100.00 – 125.00.
5 Brown gold-tooled leather compact, Italy. $150.00 – 200.00.
6 Mondaine green leather vanity case with carrying cord

and miniature portrait of a woman within a gold-tooled border; mirror, powder, rouge, and lipstick compartments; c. 1930–40s. $125.00 – 150.00.
7 Light brown lizard horseshoe-shaped purse-motif compact, Argentina. $60.00 – 80.00.
8 Round brown leather compact. $50.00 – 70.00.
9 Marcee handmade horseshoe-shaped gold-tooled leather compact. $80.00 – 100.00.
10 Persian gold and navy blue compact with padded lid and back. $50.00 – 70.00.

1 Croco square white leather zippered compact with decorative multicolored cord inset on lid, Israel. $50.00 – 75.00.

2 Navy blue horseshoe-shaped leather compact with gold-tooled fleur-de-lis on lid. $60.00 – 80.00.

3 Horseshoe-shaped gilt-metal compact with decoratively tooled leather inserts on lid and back, probably Argentina. $100.00 – 125.00.

4, 5 Mondaine tooled leather-covered case designed as a book, c. 1930–40s (shown open and closed). $60.00 – 100.00.

6 Horseshoe-shaped red leather zippered compact with attached sleeve for lipstick. $80.00 – 100.00.

7 Croco round light blue zippered compact with decorative multicolored cord inset on lid, Israel. $40.00 – 60.00.

8 Fur compact with coin-purse snap closure, Argentina. $75.00 – 85.00.

9 Square gold-tooled leather compact with Venice canal scene, possibly Italy. $40.00 – 60.00.

10 Nan Co-ed zippered horseshoe-shaped compact with scene of cowboy on a horse with branding-iron marks. $100.00 – 125.00.

11 Leather compact with colorful Persian scene. $40.00 – 60.00.

12 Wadsworth cobra envelope-shaped compact. $120.00 – 150.00.

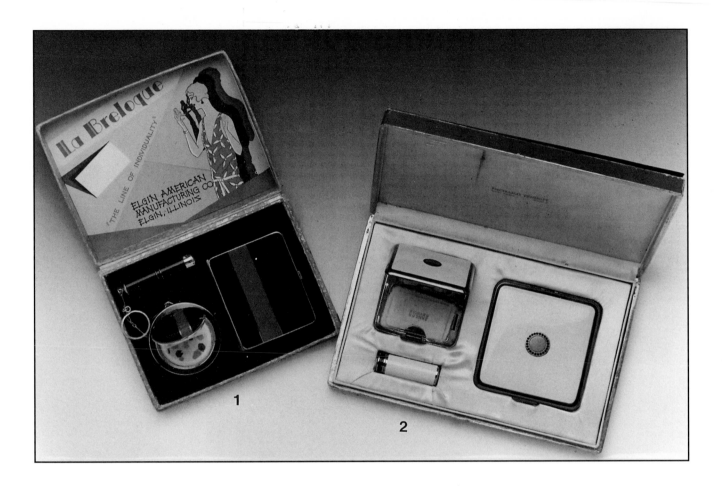

1 Elgin American "La Breloque" tango-chain red and black enameled compact; lipstick with matching cigarette case in original presentation box. $200.00 – 250.00.

2 Richard Hudnut compact in white with black enamel border; lipstick and matching cigarette case in original presentation box, c. 1920–30s. $200.00 – 250.00.

1 Ronson "Fourteencase" white Art Deco enamel combination compact/lighter/cigarette case with flannel pouch and original presentation box. $200.00 – 250.00.
2 Ronson white and brown marbleized Art Deco enamel combination compact/lighter/cigarette case, c. 1930–40s. $125.00 – 150.00.
3 Black enamel gilt-decorated combination compact/cigarette case; black enamel compact with white flower cloisonné disk on lid; c. 1930s. $125.00 – 150.00.

4 Ronson brown marbleized Art Deco enamel combination compact/lighter/cigarette case, c. 1930–40s. $125.00 – 175.00.
5 Evans light blue enamel combination compact/lighter/cigarette case with marcasite decoration on lid of compact, c. 1930s. $150.00 – 175.00.
6 Marathon black-enamel silvered-metal combination compact/lighter/cigarette case with initialed medallion on compact lid, c. 1930–40s. $150.00 – 175.00.

Fig. 38

1 Evans bronzed-metal combination compact/cigarette case with engine-turned design and white cloisonné disk on front lid, c. 1930s. $60.00 – 80.00.

2 Richard Hudnut green and black enamel metal compact and cigarette case, 1930s. $125.00 – 175.00.

3 Ronson silvered-metal compact/cigarette case combination, c. 1930–40s. $125.00 – 150.00.

4 Enameled white cloisonné side-by-side compact/cigarette case/calling card combination, c. 1930–40s (shown open). $125.00 – 150.00.

5 Enameled blue cloisonné side-by-side compact/cigarette case/calling card combination, c. 1930–40s. $125.00 – 150.00.

6 Marathon white enamel and silvered combination compact/lighter/cigarette case with enameled scene on lid of compact, c. 1930–40s. $125.00 – 150.00.

7 Lampl black enamel goldtone compact/cigarette case combination with rhinestone and green faux gemstones on lid; compact in center flanked by compartments for cigarettes; c. 1930s. $125.00 – 150.00.

8 La Mode light and dark blue enamel compact/cigarette case with pearl-beaded removable compact centered on lid of cigarette case. $100.00 – 150.00.

1 Dunhill Vanity silvered vanity case designed to resemble cigarette lighter; powder and rouge compartments; top reveals sliding lipstick; c. 1920s. $100.00 – 150.00.

2 Dunhill Vanity goldtone vanity case designed to resemble cigarette lighter; powder and rouge compartments; top reveals
sliding lipstick; U.S. Patent No. 1,639,628; c. 1920s (shown
open). $100.00 – 150.00.

3 Green and black enamel metal compact/cigarette case combination (shown open). $100.00 – 125.00.

4 Maroon marbleized plastic-covered goldtone two-sided
compact/cigarette case combination. $100.00 – 125.00.

5 Mascot brick-design engine-turned goldtone two-sided
compact/cigarette-case combination, England. $80.00 – 100.00.

6 Tan and brown enamel metal compact/cigarette case combination with white cloisonné flowered disk on lid. $80.00 – 100.00.

7 Evans silvered green enamel Art Deco miniature compact
designed to resemble cigarette lighter; top releases powder, bottom slides out to reveal lipstick. $150.00 – 200.00.

8 Ronson brown enamel goldtone compact/cigarette case combination, c. 1930–40s. $125.00 – 150.00.

9 Lampl goldtone compact/cigarette case combination with
rhinestones and green faux gemstones on lid of compact; compact in center flanked by compartments for cigarettes; c. 1930s.
$125.00 – 150.00.

10 Black enamel combination compact/lighter/cigarette case
with yellow cloisonné and painted rose on lid of compact.
$200.00 – 250.00.

1 *Illinois Watch Case Co. square goldtone compact/watch combination with three initials monogrammed on lid, c. 1930s. $100.00 – 150.00.*

2 *Evans oblong silvered-metal compact/watch combination, c. 1950s. $100.00 – 150.00.*

3 *Illinois Watch Case Co. round goldtone compact/watch combination with engraved design on lid, c. 1930–40s. $150.00 – 225.00.*

4 *Evans square goldtone compact/watch; lid designed to resemble trunk with straps, c. 1940s. $125.00 – 175.00.*

5 *Goldtone oblong compact/watch/coin holder combination with carrying chain, Germany. $125.00 – 150.00.*

6 *Black enamel silvered-metal vanity case/watch combination with powder and rouge compartments (shown open). $100.00 – 125.00.*

7 *Evans square goldtone engine-turned checkerboard compact/watch combination, c. 1940s. $125.00 – 150.00.*

8 *Elgin American round goldtone compact/watch combination with black grosgrain carrying case; lid engraved to resemble pocket watch; c. 1950s. $150.00 – 175.00.*

9 *Illinois Watch Case Co. yellow enameled bronze clamshell vanity case/watch combination with gold-plated interior and compartments for powder and rouge; c. 1930s. $150.00 – 175.00.*

1 *Elgin American silvered compact/music box combination with three gilded deer on lid; melody is "Anniversary Waltz"; black carrying case; c. 1950s. $100.00 – 150.00.*
2 *Pale yellow enamel goldtone vanity case/compass combination with powder and rouge compartments; lid contains compass and pictures of ships and their destinations; France. $100.00 – 150.00.*
3 *Elgin American gilt and satin-finish compact/compass combination with engraved scene on lid depicting the continents, c. 1950s. $150.00 – 175.00.*

4 *Marbleized brown enamel and goldtone decorated compact/thermometer combination, France. $125.00 – 175.00.*
5 *Goldtone compact with silvered music score or "Stardust" mounted on lid, c. 1920s. $100.00 – 125.00.*
6 *Black matte enamel goldtone compact/music box combination with slide-out lipstick; lid designed as piano keyboard; French melody; c. 1930s. $125.00 – 150.00.*

1 *Black enamel goldtone vanity case with U.S.N. insignia in gilt heart on lid; powder and rouge compartments; c. World War II. $80.00 – 100.00.*

2 *Navy blue and white small vanity case with nautical motif on lid; powder and rouge compartments; c. World War II. $40.00 – 60.00.*

3 *Sterling-silver compact with Marine Corps insignia on lid; gilded interior with diminishing mirror in lid and finger-ring chain; c. World War I. $200.00 – 250.00.*

4 *Wood compact with painted serviceman and girl; "Until We Meet Again" painted on lid; c. 1940s. $80.00 – 100.00.*

5 *Zell yellow marbleized plastic Kamra-Pak-style vanity case with Navy insignia on lid; powder and rouge compartments and slide-out lipstick; c. 1940s. $75.00 – 100.00.*

6 *Sterling-silver shield-shaped compact with carrying chain; Red Cross enameled insignia disk on lid; monogrammed; c. World War I. NPA.*

7 *Yellow enameled suitcase-motif vanity case with stickers depicting New York's points of interest; metal Marine Corps insignia on lid; powder and rouge compartments; c. 1940s. $125.00 – 150.00.*

8 *Brown marbleized enamel Kamra-Pak-style compact with U.S. Navy insignia on lid and sliding lipstick; Germany c. 1940s. $100.00 – 150.00.*

9 *Black enamel round clip-on compact with U.S. Navy insignia on lid, c. World War II. $125.00 – 150.00.*

Fig. 43 *Weltzunter blue marbleized enamel Kamra-Pak-style vanity case and matching cigarette lighter with silvered metal cutout map of U.S. Zone on lid; original presentation box; Germany, c. 1940s. $175.00 – 225.00.*

Fig. 44
Coty "Flying Colors" gilt-metal triple vanity case designed to resemble spread eagle wings; red, white, and blue lipstick tube in center; original presentation box and packet of Coty Airspun face powder; c. 1940s. $175.00 – 250.00.

1 Bronzed-metal compact designed as Air Force officer's cap with jeweled Armed Forces disk on top, c. 1940s. $60.00 – 100.00.

2 Khaki plastic compact designed as Army officer's cap, c. 1940s. $50.00 – 80.00.

3 Red, white, and blue plastic compact designed as Navy officer's cap, c. 1940s. $60.00 – 100.00.

4 Goldtone compact with copper Armed Forces cap mounted on lid, c. 1940s. $60.00 – 100.00.

5 Navy blue and white plastic compact designed as Navy officer's cap, c. 1940s. $50.00 – 90.00.

6 Red, white, and blue plastic compact designed as Navy officer's cap, c. 1940s (shown open). $50.00 – 90.00.

7 Black enamel goldtone heart-shaped vanity case with Armed Forces emblem on lid; powder and rouge compartments; arrow slides out to reveal lipstick; c. 1940s. $100.00 – 150.00.

8 Rex Fifth Avenue red enamel oval compact; mother-of-pearl Army hat mounted on lid, inscribed "Mother Love Son," U.S. Army; c. 1940s. $80.00 – 100.00.

9 Satin goldtone compact with copper replica of Army officer's hat mounted on lid, c. 1930s. $80.00 – 125.00.

1 *Coro black enamel horseshoe-shaped vanity case/watch combination with snap closing; powder and rouge compartments; c. 1920s. $150.00 – 200.00.*

2 *Illinois Watch Case Co. compact/watch combination, c. 1930s. $60.00 – 100.00.*

3 *Medana goldtone engine-turned Kamra-Pak-style compact/watch combination; back contains cigarette compartment; sliding lipstick case; West Germany, c. 1940–50s. $175.00 – 250.00.*

4 *Ameré goldtone engine-turned compact, Switzerland. $125.00 – 150.00.*

5 *Brown enamel compact/watch combination, Germany. $125.00 – 150.00.*

6 *American Beauty goldtone engraved vanity case/watch combination with powder and rouge compartments, c. 1940–50s. $125.00 – 150.00.*

7 *Goldtone compact/watch combination, Germany. $125.00 – 175.00.*

8 *Timepact black enamel elongated horseshoe-shaped vanity case/watch combination with powder and rouge compartments. $150.00 – 175.00.*

1 *Volupté goldtone compact with Cub Scout, Den Mother emblem. $60.00 – 80.00.*
2 *Satin goldtone Girl Scout compact. $60.00 – 80.00.*
3 *Sterling-silver octagonal miniature compact with Harvard University emblem on lid; loop for chain. $75.00. – 100.00.*
4 *Stork Club goldtone compact and lipstick. $200.00 – 225.00.*
5 *Arthur Murray presentation goldtone compact with picture of Arthur Murray Dancers on front lid. $100.00 – 150.00.*

6 *Satin-finish goldtone compact with silvered shovel mounted on lid; souvenir of ground breaking for office in Worcester, Massachusetts; presentation box. $40.00 – 60.00.*
7 *Enameled "Eastern Star" jeweled compact. $30.00 – 50.00.*
8 *Silvered "Veterans of Foreign War" vanity case with powder and rouge compartments. $40.00 – 60.00.*

1 *Goldtone compact designed as suitcase decorated with travel stickers. $160.00 – 180.00.*
2 *Silver octagonal compact with cutout map of India on lid. $150.00 – 200.00.*
3 *Goldtone compact with scenes of Paris mounted on lid. $80.00 – 120.00.*
4 *Painted brown enamel compact, Paris. $125.00 – 150.00.*
5 *Satin-finish goldtone vanity case designed as suitcase decorated with travel stickers, c. 1930s. $160.00 – 180.00.*

6 *Green enamel goldtone compact with scenes of Ireland on lid, England. $30.00 – 50.00.*
7 *Goldtone compact with scenes of Scotland on black plastic lid, England. $60.00 – 100.00.*
8 *Miref goldtone compact with "Paris, 1412" enclosed in plastic dome on lid. $80.00 – 120.00.*

1 *Silvered-metal compact with gilt design of the State of Alaska on lid. $40.00 – 60.00.*
2 *Agme goldtone compact with scenes of North America on satin-finish lid, Switzerland. $60.00 – 80.00.*
3 *Green painted enamel compact depicting the Empire State Building, New York. $50.00 – 60.00.*
4 *Compact with scene of Pennsylvania Turnpike on lid. $40.00 – 60.00.*

5 *Elgin American compact with Georgia state flag and flower on lid, c. 1940–50s. $50.00 – 75.00.*
6 *Oblong wood compact with map, state flower, and scenes of California on lid. $80.00 – 100.00.*
7 *Silvered-metal vanity case with "Souvenir of Washington, D.C." printed on lid. $30.00 – 60.00.*

1 *White plastic-covered metal compact with "The Woman's Shop, Springfield, Mass." printed on slip-cover lid. $75.00 – 100.00.*

2 *Engine-turned goldtone compact with "Compliments of The Rainbow Inn" printed on yellow marbleized plastic disk decorated with simulated sapphires, c. 1920s. $60.00 – 80.00.*

3 *Silvered-metal repoussé floral-decorated compact with shield with scene of the White House mounted on lid; loop for chain. $60.00 – 80.00.*

4 *Silvered-metal horseshoe-shaped compact with shield of "Battle Bennington Vt." mounted on lid. $60.00 – 80.00.*

5 *Artcraft round blue enamel compact with "Indian and Mohawk Trail" painted on lid. $60.00 – 80.00.*

6 *Goldtone engine-turned compact with "Summit Pikes Peak" on white plastic disk set with red stones mounted on lid. $60.00 – 80.00.*

7 *Silvered-metal compact with photograph of "Old Orchard Beach, Maine" on lid, c. 1930s. $75.00 – 100.00.*

8 *Engine-turned silvered-metal vanity case with shield of "The Pier, Old Orchard Beach, Maine" mounted on lid; powder and rouge compartments. $60.00 – 80.00.*

9 *Black enamel compact with photograph of "Bellingrath Gardens, Mobile, Ala." printed on lid, c. 1920s. $60.00 – 80.00.*

1 Engine-turned goldtone compact with "Sesquicenten-nial 1776–1926, Philadelphia, Pa." printed on plastic disk on lid. $60.00 – 80.00.

2 Wooden compact with tapestry design of 1939 New York World's Fair on lid. $80.00 – 100.00.

3 White enamel miniature flapjack compact with "A Century of Progress, 1833–1933" on silver disk mounted on lid. $70.00 – 90.00.

4 Columbia Fifth Avenue mesh vanity pouch with orange and blue scene of 1939 New York World's Fair on lid. $80.00 – 125.00.

5 Octagonal silvered-metal vanity case with copper coin inset in lid, inscribed "Sesquicentennial International Exposition, Philadelphia, 1926." $100.00 – 125.00.

6 Columbia Fifth Avenue navy blue moiré vanity pouch with orange and blue scene of 1939 New York World's Fair on lid. $80.00 – 125.00.

7 Light blue enamel metal compact with "Trylon & Peri-sphere 1939" disk mounted on lid. $70.00 – 100.00.

1 Elizabeth Arden light blue harlequin-shaped compact, c. 1940s. $125.00 – 175.00.

2 Dorothy Gray oval goldtone compact with black enamel harlequin mask on lid, c. 1940s. $80.00 – 100.00.

3 Silver Drill Instructor's hat compact with finger-ring and metal mirror. $150.00 – 250.00.

4 Pilcher silvered compact with horse's head mounted on lid, "Thoroughbred" printed below, Kentucky Derby, 1953. $80.00 – 100.00.

5 Pilcher "Slimpact" wood compact with chess knight set on inlaid checkerboard lid, c. 1940–50s. $60.00 – 80.00.

6 Pilcher wood compact with horse's head mounted on lid, c. 1940–50s. $60.00 – 80.00.

7 Lady's silvered and black metal pistol/compact, c. 1950s. NPA.

Antiqued gilt parure designed with a Fede type decoration applied to the mesh vanity pouch; locket, pillbox, screw-back earrings, necklace, and two bracelets, one with secret opening; c. 1930s. NPA.

1 Goldtone compact designed as hand mirror with decorated, engraved lid. $80.00 – 100.00.

2 Engine-turned decorated goldtone compact designed as hand mirror; ring for chain; Germany, c. 1920s. $100.00 – 125.00.

3 Engine-turned decorated goldtone compact designed as hand mirror; Germany, c. 1920s (shown open). $125.00 – 150.00.

4 Silver engraved scalloped-edged compact formed as hand mirror with lipstick in handle. $200.00 – 275.00.

5 Sterling silver compact formed as hand mirror with bloodstone cabochon thumbpiece; lipstick in bolster-shaped handle; Italy, c. 1920s. $200.00 – 275.00.

6 Sterling silver compact formed as hand mirror with coral cabochon thumbpiece; lipstick in cylindrical handle; Italy, c. 1920s. $250.00 – 350.00.

7 Blue enamel compact formed as hand mirror with painted scene on lid. $60.00 – 80.00.

8 Silvered miniature Limoges compact formed as hand mirror with painted scene on lid, France. $40.00 – 75.00.

9 Goldtone Limoges compact formed as hand mirror with painted scene on lid, France. $100.00 – 125.00.

10 Miref gilt compact formed as hand mirror with lipstick in handle; beveled mirror on both sides of compact, France. $125.00 – 150.00.

11 Antique silver-plated triangular compact designed as hand mirror with turquoise cabochon thumbpiece; lipstick in handle. $125.00 – 175.00.

12 Hoechst silver-plated compact designed as hand mirror with lipstick in handle; flannel case; probably Germany. $125.00 – 175.00.

1 Pewter-colored metal compact shaped like a hand mirror; lid decorated with stylized cutout flowers; France. $100.00 – 150.00.

2 Ivory-colored plastic miniature compact shaped like hand mirror; Germany, c. 1920s. $60.00 – 75.00.

3 Silvered miniature compact shaped like hand mirror, lid decorated with petit point; France. $40.00 – 75.00.

4 Coty plastic compact designed as hand mirror; lid decorated with Coty trademark powder puffs; lipstick in handle. $50.00 – 75.00.

5, 6 Platé "Trio-ette" plastic vanity case designed as hand mirror; powder and puff on one side, rouge on other side; lipstick in handle; c. 1940s (black case shown open, white case shown closed). $125.00 – 250.00.

7 Black and gilt enameled compact formed as hand mirror with lipstick in handle. $75.00 – 125.00.

8 Satin-finish goldtone compact shaped like hand mirror with cupid centered on lid. $40.00 – 60.00.

9 Goldtone compact shaped like hand mirror with plastic floral decoration on lid. $40.00 – 60.00.

10, 11 Blumpak plastic compact shaped like hand mirror (amber compact shown open, yellow compact shown closed). $30.00 – 50.00.

1 *Oval rose-colored velvet vanity case with cameo medallion on lid; compartments for powder, rouge, and lipstick; carrying cord with ring and ojime bead; c. 1920s. $80.00 – 100.00.*

2 *Black velvet vanity case with embroidered butterfly and edged with gold trim; compartments for powder, rouge, and lipstick; carrying cord with ring and ojime bead; c. 1920s. $80.00 – 100.00.*

3 *Fuller plastic compact with sleeve for comb mounted on lid. $40.00 – 60.00.*

4 *Elgin American red, white, and blue enamel "Drumstick Set"; compact and lipstick in drum-and-drumstick motif; original presentation box. $100.00 – 150.00.*

5 *Ivory-colored marbleized plastic compact with red trim around edge and sailing ship picture on lid; snap closure; c. 1920s. $60.00 – 80.00.*

6 *Evening in Paris wood compact with decorated lid, c. 1940s. $40.00 – 60.00.*

7 *Plastic compact with copper-etched lid depicting scene of lady and lamb; signed Biscay; France. $100.00 – 125.00.*

8 *La Faveur de Paris "Sifta-Pak" blue tooled-leather powder bag with mirrored lid and drawstring powder puff; France, c. 1920s. $60.00 – 80.00.*

9 *Elmo navy blue moiré vanity powder bag with mirror and drawstring powder puff; snap closure, c. 1920s. $60.00 – 80.00.*

10 *Pink silk double compact box with lace and gold braid trim and compartments for powder and rouge; snap closure; c. 1920s (shown open). $80.00 – 100.00.*

11 *Blue silk compact with netting and ribbon with slip-cover lid, c. 1920s. $80.00 – 100.00.*

12 *Rose silk compact with lace and braid trim and slip-cover lid, c. 1920s. $40.00 – 60.00.*

13 *Delettrez "Wildflower" pale blue paper compact with colorful floral spray on lid, c. 1940s. $50.00 – 60.00.*

14 *Harmony of Boston tan box-shaped compact with snap closure, c. 1920s (shown open). $50.00 – 60.00.*

257

1 *Zell Fifth Avenue black suede vanity clutch with compact, two lipstick tubes, and comb; metal trim on outer lid and snap closing; c. 1940s. $60.00 – 80.00.*
2 *Silver lamé vanity clutch with silver-lamé compact and lipstick, c. 1940s. $40.00 – 60.00.*
3 *Navy blue moiré and gilt vanity clutch with gilt compact, lipstick, and comb; c. 1940s. $40.00 – 60.00.*
4 *Richard Hudnut white and gold fabric vanity clutch with compact and lipstick; decorated with "Tree of Life" motif set with green stones; c. 1940s. $75.00 – 100.00.*

5 *Ciner black satin vanity clutch with rhinestone-decorated compact and lipstick, c. 1940s. $175.00 – 200.00.*
6 *Lin-Bren red lizard vanity clutch with compact and lipstick, c. 1940s. $75.00 – 100.00.*
7 *Renard black and gold fabric vanity clutch with pull-up compact and lipstick in sleeve at bottom of clutch, c. 1940. $40.00 – 60.00.*
8 *Majestic floral vanity clutch with compact, two lipstick tubes, and comb; c. 1940s. $60.00 – 80.00.*

Vanity clutches on page 258, with several shown open.

1 *Tear-shaped gilt and silvered vanity case with silvered man and horse encased in plastic dome; gilt interior, carrying chain, and compartments for powder, rouge, and lipstick. $150.00 – 200.00.*

2 *Sterling-silver hallmarked double-tier compact; upper lid reveals locket; compartment for powder in lower lid; c. 1915. $200.00 – 225.00.*

3 *Volupté black enamel gilt compact with sliding lipstick; black enamel inner and outer lids decorated with flowers. $80.00 – 125.00.*

4 *Richard Hudnut gilt compact with raised tulip design; lipstick encased in lid cover. $40.00 – 60.00.*

5 *Mondaine multicolored tooled leather vanity case designed to resemble book; compartments for powder, rouge, and cigarettes. $80.00 – 125.00.*

6 *Marathon gilt and silvered engraved vanity case with enameled disk on lid; gilt interior, carrying chain, and compartments for powder, rouge, and lipstick. $150.00 – 200.00.*

7 *E.A.M. nickel-finish tango-chain vanity; lid holds metal mirror and rouge compartment; lower half contains powder compartment. $150.00 – 200.00.*

8 *Coty octagonal polished nickel-finish vanity case; upper lid for rouge, lower opening for powder. $60.00 – 80.00.*

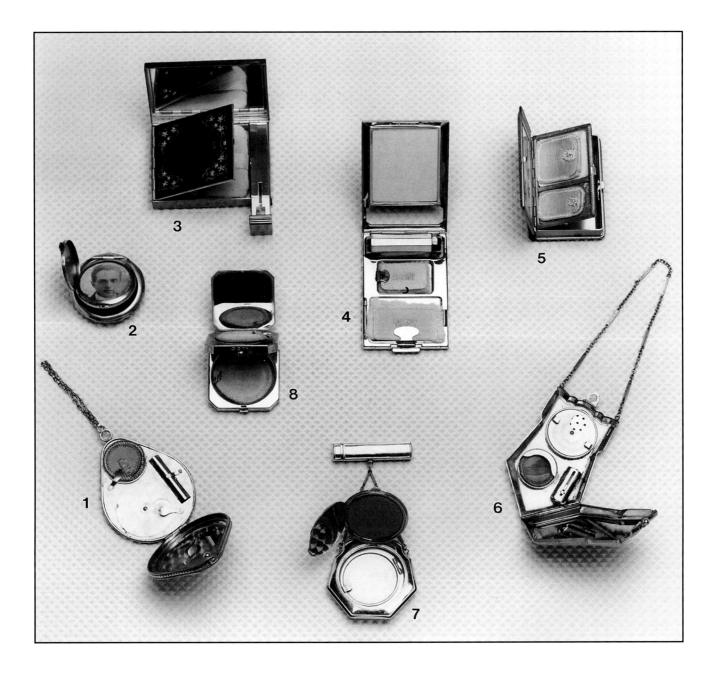

Vanity cases and compacts on page 260 shown open.

1 Brown plastic vanity case with carrying cord and tassel; powder and rouge compartments; c. 1920s (shown open). $125.00 – 175.00.

2 Butterscotch-colored plastic vanity case; writing slate on back of mirror and compartments for powder, rouge, lipstick, and comb; c. 1920s (shown open). $150.00 – 175.00.

3 Tan plastic vanity case with maroon flowers; carrying cord and compartments for powder, rouge, two lipsticks, mirror, and pocket for puff; c. 1920s (shown open). $200.00 – 250.00.

4 Tan and brown vanity case with country scene on lid; carrying cord and compartments for powder, lipstick, and perfume; c. 1920s. $200.00 – 225.00.

5 Egg-shaped yellow plastic vanity purse with cherubs; black tassel and carrying cord; powder and rouge compartments; c. 1920s. $300.00 – 350.00.

6 Gold-colored plastic vanity reticule with Oriental motif; black and gold carrying cord with ring and buckle ojime; compartment for powder and puff; c. 1920s. $100.00 – 125.00.

7 Stratton black and gold floral-decorated metal vanity reticule with fancy metal carrying chain; compartments for compact, coin purse, and comb; c. 1950s. $250.00 – 300.00.

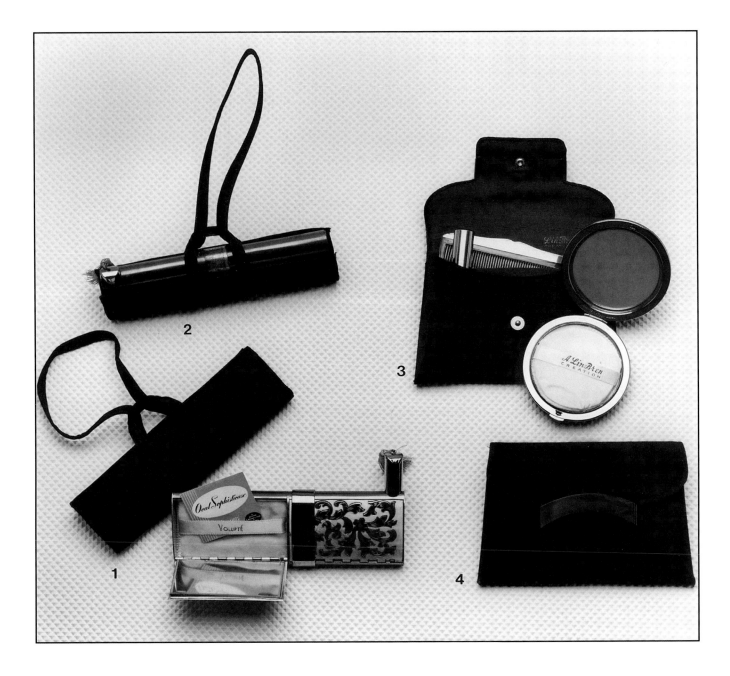

1, 2 *Volupté "Oval Sophisticase" carryall with silver-embossed gilt lid; center band slides to open compartments for powder and utilities, tassel pulls out to reveal lipstick; black faille carrying case; c. 1950s; (1 shown open, 2 shown closed). $125.00 – 150.00.*

3, 4 *Lin-Bren vanity clutch contains compact, lipstick, and comb (3, navy blue faille, shown open; 4, maroon suede, shown closed). $60.00 – 80.00.*

1 Majestic gold and black lace vanity clutch with black and gold carrying chain and compartments for compact, lipstick, and comb (shown open). $60.00 – 80.00.
2, 3 Graceline small vanity reticule with wrist chain; compartments for puff, compact, and lipstick, (2, maroon velvet, shown open; 3, multicolor woven fabric, shown closed). $50.00 – 70.00.
4 Zell gilt-padded vanity clutch with compartments for compact, lipstick, and comb (shown open). $40.00 – 60.00.

1, 2 Coty "Envelope" goldtone compact, c. 1940s. $60.00 – 80.00.

3, 4 Vanity case with compartments for powder, rouge, and cigarettes; tassel pulls out to reveal lipstick; probably England (3, blue plastic resembling cloisonné top, leather-lined interior, shown closed; 4, black silk, leather-lined interior, shown open). $100.00 – 150.00.

5, 6 Le Rage goldtone vanity case with chain-attached lipstick; center lid with enamel painted flowers reveals compartment for rouge, photo, tablets; interior reveals snap-on comb/whisk broom combination; second opening reveals powder compartment and perfume container; moiré carrying case contains perfume funnel; England, c. 1950s. NPA.

1 *Silvered-metal purse-motif vanity case with enamel bluebird and engine-turned back; contains loose powder sifter, two puffs, rouge, mirror, and carrying chain; c. 1920s. $60.00 – 80.00.*

2, 3 *Wadsworth two-sided mini vanity case with powder and rouge compartments and finger loop (2, green suede, shown open; 3, black leather, shown closed). 2, $50.00 – 75.00; 3, $40.00 – 60.00.*

4 *Coty "Buckle" goldtone vanity case with white enamel buckle, c. 1940s. $80.00 – 125.00.*

5 *Fillkwik Co. "Van-Mist" silver vanity case designed to resemble camera; compartments for powder, rouge, lipstick, and perfume; c. 1930s. $125.00 – 175.00.*

6 *Sterling silver hallmarked two-sided miniature vanity case with floral-engraved powder and rouge compartments and finger ring chain; England, c. 1900s. $125.00 – 150.00.*

7 *Jonteel repoussé silver-plated compact with finger ring chain, c. 1920s. $60.00 – 80.00.*

8, 9 *Houbigant six-sided vanity case with basket of flowers on lid; compartments for powder and rouge (8, goldtone small version; 9, silvered-metal larger version). $40.00 – 60.00 each.*

10 *Coty "Jingle Bells" goldtone compact, c. 1940s. $125.00 – 175.00.*

11 *Coty silvered-metal compact with cutout design of boy and girl, c. 1920–30s. $40.00 – 60.00.*

1 *Gun-metal clover-shaped purse-motif compact.* *$60.00 – 80.00.*

2 *Sterling silver hallmarked compact designed to resemble hand mirror; lid decorated with blue faux cloisonné; loop for chain. $75.00 – 100.00.*

3 *White enamel compact with "Yes" in green and "No" in red. $100.00 – 150.00.*

4 *Six-inch-round pink and goldtone compact with sixteen stars with faux diamonds on lid. $150.00 – 200.00.*

5 *Volupté green and yellow triangular checkerboard compact. $65.00 – 80.00.*

6 *Gold-filled compact decorated with blackbird; finger ring chain and tassel; c. 1920s. $100.00 – 125.00.*

7 *K & K small oval black enamel compact with rhinestone lipstick tube mounted on lid. $100.00 – 125.00.*

8 *Flato goldtone compact with brass key mounted on lid; red leather-like protective case. $100.00 – 125.00.*

9 *Majestic goldtone compact with comb and black faille case. $40.00 – 60.00.*

10 *Silver compact with blue and white Delft enamel windmill scene. $50.00 – 60.00.*

11 *Light and dark blue guilloche enamel 1" compact; loop for chain. $80.00 – 125.00.*

1 *La Mode gilt and black-striped enamel vanity case with black silhouette on cover; powder, rouge, and lipstick compartments; loop for chain. $100.00 – 125.00.*

2, 3 *Slim oval compact designed as a locket with chain; black silhouette on cover (2, yellow enamel, shown in presentation box; 3, red enamel with loop for chain). $100.00 – 150.00 each.*

4 *Divine lavender-striped enamel miniature compact with white silhouette on cover. $30.00 – 50.00.*

5 *Ivory-colored enamel vanity case; silver silhouette within black disk; powder and rouge compartments. $40.00 – 50.00.*

6 *La Mode ivory and black enamel vanity case with black silhouette on ivory; powder and rouge compartments and through handle. $100.00 – 150.00.*

7 *Plastic and goldtone compact with molded silhouette on plastic slip-cover lid. $40.00 – 50.00.*

8 *Black enamel and goldtone vanity case with black transfer silhouette; powder and rouge compartments. $60.00 – 80.00.*

9 *Rex Fifth Avenue blue plastic and gilt compact with white plastic silhouette on blue lid, c. 1940s. $40.00 – 60.00.*

10 *Silver and black-enamel vanity case with white silhouette; finger-ring chain; powder sifter and rouge compartment; c. 1920s. $80.00 – 125.00.*

11 *Armand red enamel compact with silhouette on lid, "Pat'd Aug. 14, 1917." $40.00 – 60.00.*

12 *Blue and clear plastic compact with white silhouette on screw-top lid. $20.00 – 30.00.*

13 *Rigaud "Mary Garden" gilt miniature compact with embossed silhouette on slip-cover lid, c. 1919. $40.00 – 60.00.*

14 *Armand silver-plated compact with engraved silhouette on lid and engine-turned back, "Pat. 7–1–24." $60.00 – 80.00.*

15 *Rigaud "Mary Garden" brass compact with embossed silhouette on cover, c. 1919. $60.00 – 80.00.*

1 *Black enamel vanity case with lipstick compartment centered on lid; powder and rouge compartments. $60.00 – 100.00.*
2 *Kigu blue enamel compact with Limoges-type locket centered on lid, c. 1940–50s. $60.00 – 100.00.*
3 *Goldtone vanity case with locket centered on lid; powder, rouge, and lipstick compartments; c. 1930s. $60.00 – 100.00.*
4 *Maroon enamel vanity case with lipstick com-* *partment centered on lid; powder and rouge compartments. $60.00 – 100.00.*
5 *Lazell goldtone vanity case with powder compartment; rouge compartment centered on lid "Pat'd. July 18, 1922." $70.00 – 125.00.*
6 *Mondaine red enamel vanity case with lipstick compartment centered on lid; compartments for powder and rouge; c. 1920–30s. $70.00 – 125.00.*
7 *Silvered-metal compact with goldtone locket centered on lid, c. 1930s. $75.00 – 150.00.*

1 Woodworth "Karess" egg-shaped vanity case in engine-turned silvered metal; edge of lid enameled with blue Greek key design; powder and rouge compartments; c. 1920s. $30.00 – 60.00.

2 Yardley goldtone vanity case with red, white, and blue embossed design on lid; powder and rouge compartments; c. 1940s. $60.00 – 75.00.

3 Alwyn blue enamel suitcase-motif compact. $80.00 – 120.00.

4 Yardley black enamel and goldtone vanity case with powder and rouge compartments and swing-out lipstick, c. 1930s. $60.00 – 75.00.

5 La Mode goldstone and enameled vanity case with powder and rouge compartments and slide-out lipsticks (shown open). $100.00 – 150.00.

6 Rosenfeld zippered goldtone compact with multicolor confetti sparkles and thread, Israel. $30.00 – 50.00.

7 Volupté "Swinglok" stippled goldtone compact with multicolored synthetic gems on swinglok, c. 1940s. $60.00 – 100.00.

8 Lucite compact mirrored on inner and outer lid, c. 1940s. $80.00 – 100.00.

1, 2 *Terri black enamel goldtone vanity case with carry-ing chain; compartments for powder, rouge, lipstick, and lip-tissues; complete eye makeup kit included; c. 1950s. $175.00 – 225.00.*

3, 4 *Rhinestone-studded vanity case; black faille carrying case incorporates sleeves for lipstick and comb; compart-ments for powder, rouge, and cigarettes (3, goldtone, shown closed; 4, black enamel, shown open). $90.00 – 110.00 each.*

5 *Rhinestone-studded black enamel double vanity case with carrying chain and compartments for powder, rouge, comb, lipstick, and cigarettes. $125.00 – 150.00.*

6, 7 *Wadsworth goldtone compact designed to resemble vanity table; collapsible cabriole legs. $150.00 – 275.00.*

8, 9 *Houbigant enameled vanity case with powder and rouge compartments and sliding comb on lid (8, black enamel, shown closed; 9, white enamel, shown open). $100.00 – 150.00.*

1, 2 *Silver-plated compact with swivel lipstick on lid, c. 1930s. $125.00 – 150.00.*

3 *Engine-turned silvered-metal compact with through handle, c. 1920s. $100.00 – 125.00.*

4 *Silvered compact with hammered surface and fleur-de-lis mounted on lid; carrying chain; c. 1920s. $100.00 – 150.00.*

5 *Silvered vanity case with carrying chain and compartments for powder, rouge, lipstick, and coins, "Pat. Aug. 9, 1921" (shown open). $125.00 – 150.00.*

6 *Silver-plated metal miniature vanity case with floral-engraved decoration on all sides; goldtone interior, through handle, and compartments for powder, rouge, and lipstick; c. 1920s. $100.00 – 125.00.*

7 *German silver engraved vanity case with carrying chain and compartments for powder, rouge, and coins; c. 1915. $100.00 – 175.00.*

8 *Silver-plated metal vanity case with engraved decoration on all sides; goldtone interior, through handle, and compartments for powder, rouge, and lipstick; c. 1920s. $125.00 – 150.00.*

9 *Silvered-metal oblong vanity case with through handle and compartments for powder, rouge, and lipstick; c. 1920s (shown open). $125.00 – 150.00.*

1 Navy blue enamel on goldtone tango-chain compact and lip-stick case with star-shaped studs mounted on a blue celestial scene. $125.00 – 175.00.

2 B.B.Co. sterling silver enameled tango-chain with light blue and cream-colored cloisonné flowers on lid, c. 1920s. $250.00 – 300.00.

3 Blue and white guilloche enamel compact with finger-ring chain, c. 1917. $100.00 – 125.00.

4 Green enamel round compact with slide-out mirror, Germany. $60.00 – 80.00.

5 Green and black enamel metal compact with finger-ring chain, c. 1920s. $100.00 – 125.00.

6 Shaded blue enamel on metal shield-shaped vanity case, c. 1920–30s. $40.00 – 60.00.

7 R & G Co. green cloisonné and silver miniature compact with painted flowers on lid; loop for chain; c. 1910. $125.00 – 175.00.

8 Yellow cloisonné locket compact with painted roses on lid; complete with chain; c. 1920s. $100.00 – 125.00.

9 Blue cloisonné purse-motif vanity case with painted flowers on lid; carrying chain and compartments for powder, rouge, and lipstick; c. 1920–30s. $150.00 – 200.00.

10 Square blue and ivory-colored enamel vanity case with carrying chain, c. 1920s. $100.00 – 125.00.

11 Green enamel tango-chain vanity with silvered-metal crown mounted on lid, c. 1920s. $100.00 – 125.00.

12 Green champlevé vermeil compact with painted ivory disk on lid; Italy, late 19th century. $125.00 – 150.00.

13 R & G Co. yellow cloisonné vanity case with painted flowers on lid, c. 1920s. $135.00 – 150.00.

1 *Vermeil sterling silver oval compact with blue cloisonné decorated lid and finger-ring chain, c. 1920s. $125.00 – 150.00.*
2 *R & G Co. sterling silver yellow cloisonné tango-chain vanity with painted flowers on lid; lipstick and perfume tube suspended from enameled and silver finger-ring chain; c. 1920s. $250.00 – 300.00.*
3 *G.L.B. Co. sterling silver yellow and blue cloisonné vanity case with painted flowers; powder sifter and rouge compartment; enameled finger ring chain; c. 1920s. $225.00 – 250.00.*
4 *Flapjack green cloisonné compact with painted flowers on lid, c. 1930s. $60.00 – 80.00.*
5 *Engine-turned silvered-metal compact with enameled disk on lid and finger ring chain, c. 1920s. $100.00 – 125.00.*
6 *May Fair engine-turned goldtone vanity case with enameled disk on lid; powder and rouge compartments; carrying cord and tassel; c. 1920s (shown open). $100.00 – 125.00.*
7 *Evans "Tap Sift" black enameled white-nickel triangular vanity case with finger ring chain, c. 1920s. $80.00 – 100.00.*

8 *D.F.B. Co. blue enamel vanity case with painted windmill scene; chain with key; powder sifter and rouge compartment, "Pat'd Feb 9, 1926." $150.00 – 250.00.*
9 *La Mode octagonal green enamel vanity case with etched basket on lid; compartments for powder and rouge and through handle; c. 1920–30s. $70.00 – 90.00.*
10 *Lavender and green champlevé vanity case with powder sifter, rouge and coin compartments; carrying chain; c. 1920s. $175.00 – 200.00.*
11 *Triangular vanity case with engine-turned decoration and lustrous simulated cloisonné disk on lid; compartments for powder and rouge; carrying chain; c. 1920–30s. $80.00 – 100.00.*
12 *Goldtone and silvered-metal vanity case with lavender cloisonné inset on lid; compartments for powder, rouge, and lipstick; carrying chain; c. 1920s. $150.00 – 200.00.*
13 *Snakeskin tango chain compact and lipstick. $125.00 – 175.00.*

1 *Rigid mesh multicolored bolster-shaped vanity bag with faux pearls and blue stones; tassel and carrying chain (shown open). $250.00 – 300.00.*

2 *Maroon enamel vanity case with compartments for powder, rouge, lipstick, comb, and eye makeup (shown open). $80.00 – 125.00.*

3 *Sterling silver hallmarked lavender cloisonné compact/ perfume combination with painted flowers; finger ring chain suspended from perfume ring. $300.00 – 350.00.*

4 *Highly finished white-nickel compact designed as hand mirror. $60.00 – 80.00.*

5 *R & G Co. "Nuwite" octagonal green enamel compact with scalework design on lid, c. 1920s. $100.00 – 125.00.*

6 *Rigid multicolored mesh purse-motif vanity case; compartments for powder, rouge, and coins; carrying chain (shown open). $150.00 – 225.00.*

7 *Daniel black leather compact with plastic dome enclosing portrait of lady, Paris. $80.00 – 100.00.*

8 *Black plastic compact with Lucite top enclosing painted picture of lady on sparkling confetti, c. 1920s. $150.00 – 175.00.*

9 *Black plastic compact with Lucite top enclosing painted "Pierrot" on sparkling confetti, c. 1920s. $125.00 – 150.00.*

10 *Evans goldtone mesh vanity bag decorated with multicolored stones; scene of man and woman on lid; satin lines; wrist chain; metal mirror and powder and rouge compartments; c. 1940–50s. $300.00 – 400.00.*

11 *Red damask bolster-shaped vanity bag with tassel and carrying chain with carved plastic ojime bead. $100.00 – 125.00.*

12 *Leather-textured blue silvered vanity case with enamel painting on lid; wrist chain; c. 1930s. $80.00 – 100.00.*

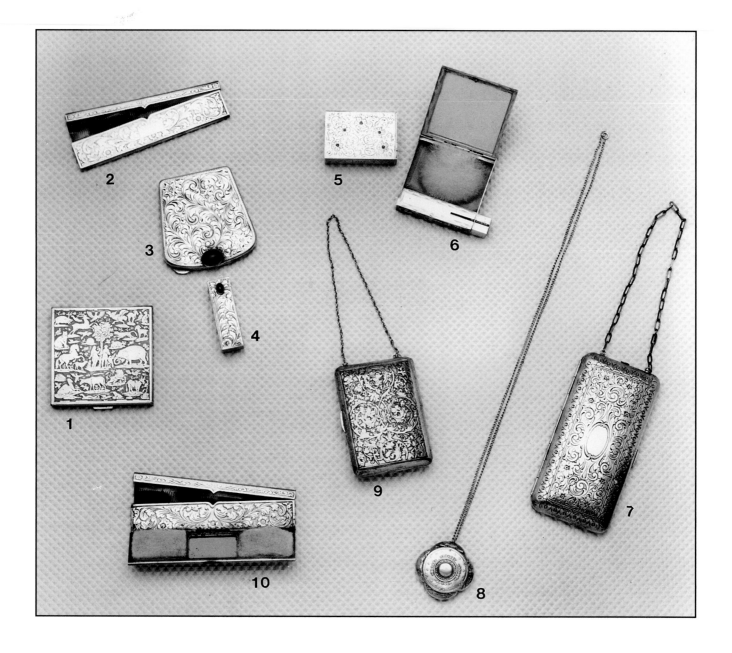

1 *Volupté silvered-metal compact embossed on all sides with "Adam and Eve" as central motif. $60.00 – 80.00.*

2, 3, 4 *Sterling silver engraved compact, lipstick, and comb set with green cabochon on compact and lipstick, Italy. $250.00 – 300.00.*

5 *Sterling silver miniature engraved vanity case with small rubies; sliding lipstick. $150.00 – 225.00.*

6 *Sterling silver engraved vanity case; sliding lipstick (shown open). $175.00 – 250.00.*

7 *German silver engraved oblong carryall with carrying chain and compartments for powder, rouge, coins, and bill-clip. $175.00 – 250.00.*

8 *Clover-shaped silvered repoussé compact/locket with chain. $80.00 – 125.00.*

9 *German silver engraved carryall with carrying chain and compartments for powder, rouge, coins, and bill-clip. $125.00 – 200.00.*

10 *Silver engraved compact/comb combination with compartments for powder and rouge in comb case. $75.00 – 125.00.*

1 *Silver filigree compact with two lids mounted with damascene scenes of India; interior lid opens to reveal powder compartment; India. $200.00 – 250.00.*

2 *Antique goldtone compact with Oriental scene on lid, Austria. $60.00 – 80.00.*

3 *Oriental brass engraved double-tier swivel vanity case (shown open). $250.00 – 300.00.*

4 *Octagonal silver compact with repoussé Siamese dancer on lid. $100.00 – 150.00.*

5 *Chinese hallmarked handmade silver filigree compact; lid lifts to reveal mirror, drawer pulls out for powder; loop for chain (shown with drawer open). NPA.*

6 *Chinese handmade silver filigree compact; multicolored lid lifts to reveal mirror, drawer pulls out for powder (shown open). NPA.*

7 *Suzuyo sterling silver compact inlaid with copper bamboo branches, Japan. $175.00 – 200.00.*

8 *Silver and black damascene compact with Siamese dancer on lid. $100.00 – 175.00.*

9 *Sunc sterling silver compact with jade cutout mounted on lid, China. $175.00 – 250.00.*

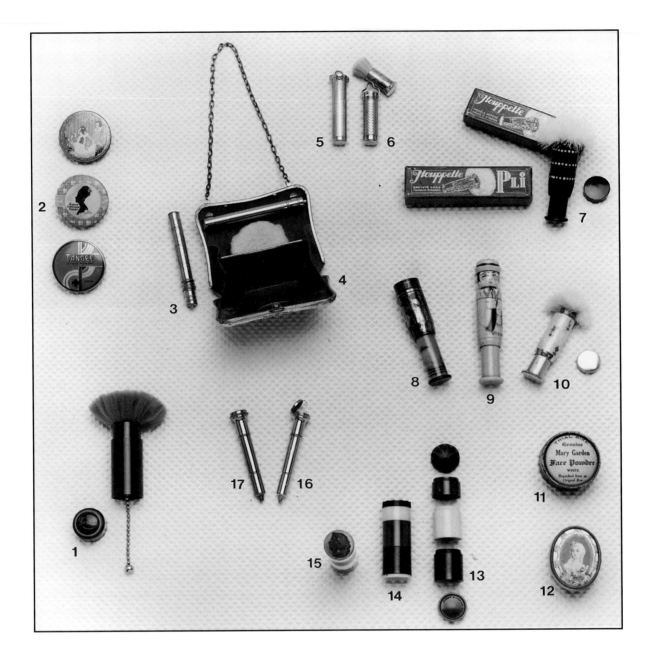

1 *Lamkin pink and black plastic powder-puff container and carrying chain, England. $50.00 – 75.00.*

2 *Three miniature powder boxes; Tangee, Armand, and Richard Hudnut; c. 1920s. $50.00 each.*

3 *Paris Fashion Co. silvered powderette, c. 1900s. $50.00 – 100.00.*

4 *Silvered repoussé vanity purse with mirror, powder puff, and powderette, "Pat'd Oct. 17, 1914". $150.00 – 225.00.*

5, 6 *Gold-filled Puf-Kase, c. 1920s (5 shown closed; 6, smaller version, shown open). $125.00 – 150.00; $100.00 – 125.00.*

7, 8 *Houppette plastic pli, France, c. 1920s (7, turqouise-beaded black, shown open; 8, goldtone decorated, shown closed). $60.00 – 100.00; $80.00 – 125.00.*

9 *Pink plastic pli painted to resemble doll; hat contains lipstick; France, c. 1920s. $150.00 – 225.00.*

10 *Sterling-silver hallmarked pli with vermeil overlay and painted cloisonné, France (shown open). $200.00 – 250.00.*

11 *Mary Garden face powder in a puff in original box, c. 1917. $25.00 – 75.00.*

12 *Richard Hudnut "Du Barry" face-powder sampler in original box; France, c. 1920s. $40.00 – 60.00.*

13, 14, 15 *Colt Purse Make-Up Kit with plastic tubular colored makeup containers, c. 1930s (13 shown open, 14 shown closed, 15 top view). $40.00 – 60.00; $40.00 – 60.00; $60.00 – 90.00.*

16, 17 *Princess Pat powderette-lipstick, c. 1920s (16, goldtone, shown open; 17, silvered, shown closed). $50.00 – 75.00 each.*

1 *Antique embossed goldtone-finish vanity case with multicolored stones; carrying chain and compartments for powder, rouge, and lipstick; turn of the century. $100.00 – 150.00.*

2 *Antique goldtone compact with filigree lid set with pearls and turqouise; jeweled tassel and carrying chain; turn of the century. $200.00 – 250.00.*

3 *Antique goldtone vanity bag lined with pink satin; multicolored silk back; filigree compact set with pearls and blue stones; jeweled tassel and carrying chain; turn of the century. $350.00 – 450.00.*

4 *Antique silvered-metal vanity bag; filigree compact set with multicolored stones; black velvet back, carrying chain, and tassel; turn of the century. $350.00 – 450.00.*

5 *Two-sided antique goldtone vanity case; filigree lids set with red stones; powder and rouge compartments; tassel conceals lipstick; carrying chain; turn of the century. $250.00 – 300.00.*

6 *Antique silvered-filigree metal vanity bag set with marcasites and blue stones; gray moire lining, jeweled tassel, and carrying chain; turn of the century. $350.00 – 450.00.*

7 *Antique goldtone filigree compact set with green stones; lipstick case bonded to top; tassel and carrying chain; turn of the century. $250.00 – 300.00.*

1 *Goldtone vanity case with filigree lid set with colored stones and green cabochon stone; red faille lining; multicolored silk back set with stones; jeweled tassel and carrying chain; compartments for powder, rouge, and lipstick; turn of the century. $300.00 – 325.00.*
2 *White cloisonné goldtone vanity reticule with lid mounted with multicolored gemstones and filigree back; silk-lined interior; tassel conceals lipstick; carrying chain; Austria, turn of the century. $400.00 – 500.00.*
3 *Embossed brass collapsible compact with edge set with multicolored cabochons; France, turn of the century (shown open). $250.00 – 300.00.*
4 *Antique goldtone tango-chain; compact and rouge have filigree lids set with green stones and micro-mosaic disks; c. 1920s. $125.00 – 175.00.*

5 *Antique goldtone compact with red stones on embossed lid; tassel and carrying chain; c. 1920s. $200.00 – 250.00.*
6 *Goldtone filigree vanity case set with pearls and yellow stones; openings on both sides for powder and rouge, lipstick attached on bottom; tassel and carrying chain. $350.00 – 400.00.*
7 *Goldtone compact with honeycomb lid set with multicolored stones; fabric back; turn of the century. $200.00 – 250.00.*
8 *E.A. Bliss Co. brass filigree purse-motif vanity case with multicolored stones and carrying chain, turn of the century. $150.00 – 200.00.*
9 *Embossed goldtone compact with multicolored stones on lid; Czechoslovakia, late 19th century. $125.00 – 200.00.*
10 *Antique goldtone compact; filigree lid incorporates lipstick holder set with blue stones; turn of the century. $250.00 – 300.00.*

1 Evans 5"-round sterling gold-wash compact with pink, yellow, and white basketweave. $200.00 – 250.00.
2 Evans 5"-round sterling compact with pink, yellow, and white basketweave (shown open). $200.00 – 250.00.
3 Evans 4"-round sterling gold-wash compact with pink, yellow, and white basketweave. $175.00 – 200.00.

4 Evans oval sterling gold-wash compact with pink, yellow, and white basketweave. $125.00 – 150.00.
5 Evans pink, yellow, and white basketweave metal carryall, c. 1940–50s (shown open). $125.00 – 150.00.

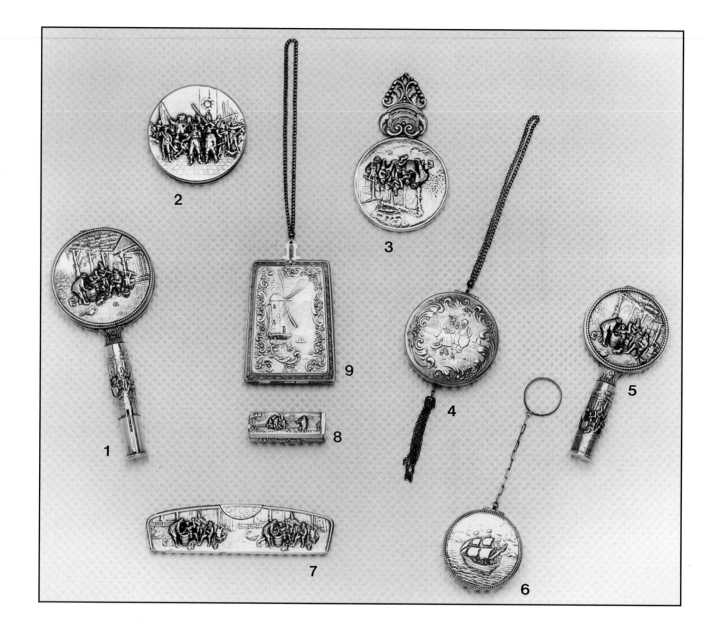

1 *S & F silver-plated compact designed to resemble hand mirror; lipstick in handle; repoussé cracker-barrel scene on lid; Denmark. $125.00 – 150.00.*

2 *Silver-plated mirror with Danish scene on lid, Denmark. $60.00 – 80.00.*

3 *Silver-plated mirror with repoussé cracker-barrel scene, Denmark. $30.00 – 50.00.*

4 *Silver-plated compact with Dutch scene on lid; tassel and carrying chain; c. 1920s. $125.00 – 150.00.*

5 *S & F silver-plated compact designed to resemble hand mirror; lipstick in handle; repoussé cracker-barrel scene on lid, Denmark. $125.00 – 150.00.*

6 *Silver-plated vanity case with sailing ship on lid; powder and rouge compartments and finger-ring chain; c. 1920s. $100.00 – 125.00.*

7 *Silver-plated comb with repoussé cracker-barrel scene, Denmark. $20.00 – 30.00.*

8 *Silver-plated lipstick with repoussé cracker-barrel scene, Denmark. $40.00 – 60.00.*

9 *Silver-plated vanity case with Dutch scene on lid; compartments for powder, rouge, and lipstick; carrying chain; c. 1920s. $150.00 – 175.00.*

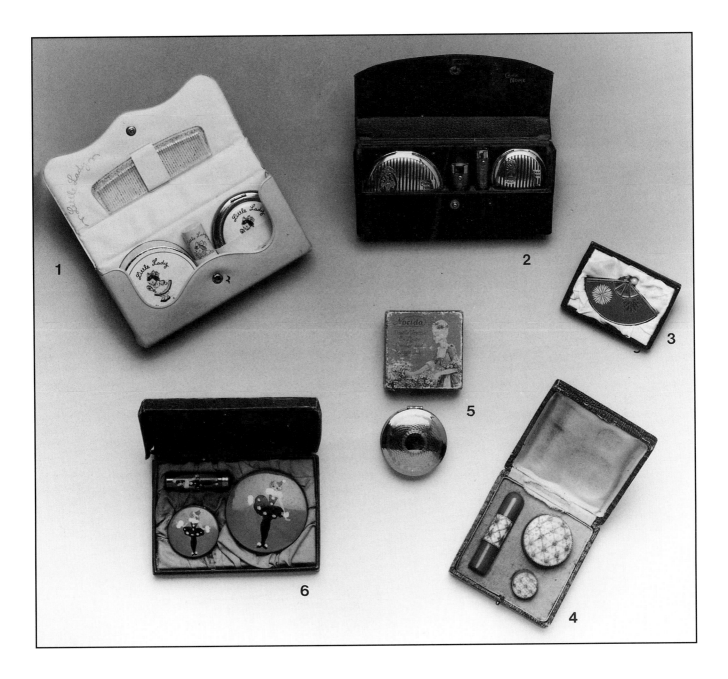

1 Little Lady child's vanity box containing compact, lipstick, powder, and comb in blue carrying case. $50.00 – 75.00.

2 Langlois "Cara Noma" blue vanity clutch containing silver-plated powder compact, rouge, lipstick, and eye makeup containers, "Pat. 7-1-24." $125.00 – 175.00.

3 Goldtone miniature red enamel fan-motif compact in original fitted presentation box, c. 1950s. $50.00 – 60.00.

4 Edouardo "Bag-Dabs" green and white plastic compact; lipstick and sachet container decorated with red flowers; original fitted presentation box; France. $125.00 – 200.00.

5 Norida nickel-silver vanity case with powder and rouge compartments in original box, "Pat. Aug. 5, 1924." $60.00 – 80.00.

6 Goldtone compact with painted clown, rouge, and lipstick set in original fitted presentation box. $80.00 – 150.00.

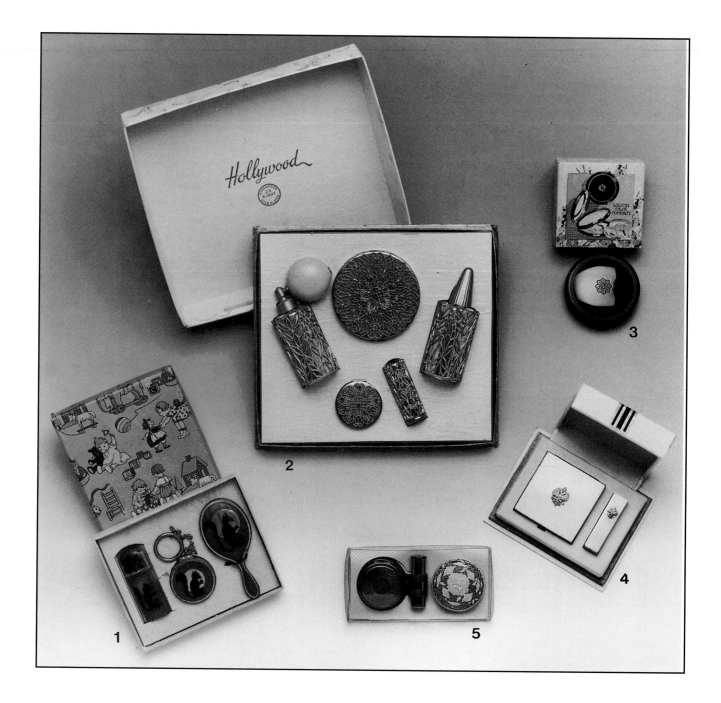

1 Annette "Chypre" child's green cosmetic set; compact with finger chain; hand mirror and perfume bottle; original fitted presentation box. $125.00 – 200.00.

2 Hollywood 24-karat gold-plated multicolored stone-studded filigree cosmetic set with compact, rouge case, lipstick, perfume bottle with atomizer, and lotion bottle in original fitted presentation box. $150.00 – 225.00.

3 Colgate & Co. "Watch Case" brown metal vanity case with powder and rouge compartments in original presentation box. $40.00 – 60.00.

4 Anna Pavlova white and gold enamel goldtone compact and lipstick case set with goldtone coat-of-arms in original fitted presentation box, c. 1930s. $100.00 – 120.00.

5 Coty "Trio" goldtone metal rouge and lipstick case; tandem set in red plastic "invitation"-size face powder; c. 1930s. $60.00 – 80.00.

1 *Goldtone compact with colorful South Seas scene encased in Lucite lid. $40.00 – 60.00.*

2 *Coty goldtone embossed book-motif compact, c. 1940s. $40.00 – 60.00.*

3 *Majestic copper-colored basketweave compact. $30.00 – 50.00.*

4 *Damascene goldtone and black metal compact, c. 1930s. $30.00 – 40.00.*

5 *Blue and white enamel plaid vanity case with powder and rouge compartments. $40.00 – 60.00.*

6 *Octagonal silvered and black enamel compact with powder sifter, c. 1920s. $75.00 – 90.00.*

7 *Black and white plastic compact. $20.00 – 30.00.*

8 *B C brass engine-turned vanity case with powder and rouge compartments, mirror and writing slate, and brass writing pencil enclosed on side lid; Germany, c. 1920s. $125.00 – 150.00.*

9 *Copper compact with black enamel bull's-eye center. $60.00 – 80.00.*

10 *Black plastic bolster-shaped vanity bag with painted blue and white flowers set with rhinestones; black carrying cord; lipstick concealed in tassel; c. 1920s. $250.00 – 300.00.*

11 *Volupté goldtone basketweave compact with red stones on lid; sliding lipstick; c. 1940s. $50.00 – 60.00.*

12 *Antique goldtone compact with goldtone leaves mounted on lid and red cabochon stone in center, c. 1930s. $40.00 – 60.00.*

1 *B.Co. green crackle plastic vanity case with enamel decoration on lid, carrying chain, and compartments for powder, rouge, and lipstick. $80.00 – 125.00.*

2 *Volupté blue enamel "Watchcase Compact," set with faux pearls with painted disk on lid and black tassel, c. 1940s. $60.00 – 80.00.*

3 *Red and black enamel tango-chain vanity with red and black enamel chain; powder sifter, rouge compartment, and metal mirror; c. 1920s. $125.00 – 150.00.*

4 *Silvered-metal compact with enameled medallion on lid and through handle, c. 1920s. $100.00 – 125.00.*

5 *Zell simulated lavender cloisonné vanity case (shown open). $40.00 – 60.00.*

6 *Marbleized brown Bakelite tango-chain vanity with red enamel disk on lid. $80.00 – 125.00.*

7 *Chrome cookie-shaped compact with loop for chain, c. 1910. $30.00 – 50.00.*

8 *Richard Hudnut black and goldtone enamel vanity case; metal mirror and powder and rouge compartments; c. 1920s. $40.00 – 60.00.*

9 *Schildkraut rhinestone compact with black faille and rhinestone carrying case. $80.00 – 100.00.*

10 *Square champlevé compact with blue, gold, and green enamel flowers and yellow cabochon stone on lid; engraved sides; Czechoslovakia. $100.00 – 125.00.*

11 *Goldtone compact with Lucite dome enclosing heather on a plaid background. $40.00 – 60.00.*

12 *Orange enamel metal vanity case with metal mirror and powder and rouge compartments; lipstick compartment centered on back lid; c. 1920s. $75.00 – 100.00.*

1 Horseshoe-shaped zippered compact with painted dancing girl on lid, signed Annette Honeywell. $50.00 – 75.00.

2 Avon oval compact with blue and green checkerboard lid. $20.00 – 30.00.

3 Royal blue ribbed-silk compact; catch set with blue stones; England. $100.00 – 125.00.

4 Dorset Fifth Avenue bolster-shaped goldtone compact. $50.00 – 60.00.

5 Terri silvered-metal vanity case with black carrying cord, c. 1950s. $60.00 – 80.00.

6 Majestic brass compact with spinning roulette wheel set on lid. $90.00 – 150.00.

7 Volupté brass and black enamel oblong vanity case with compartments for powder, rouge, lipstick, and comb. $30.00 – 50.00.

8 Wooden painted compact, c. 1940s. $40.00 – 60.00.

9 E.A.M. sterling pentagonal vanity case with goldtone engraved interior; powder and rouge compartments and carrying chain; c. 1920s (shown open). $150.00 – 175.00.

Fig. 120
Kigu brown marbleized enameled compact/camera combination; working camera incorporates compact, lipstick holder, and 16 mm film-cartridge holder; England, c. 1940–50s. NPA.

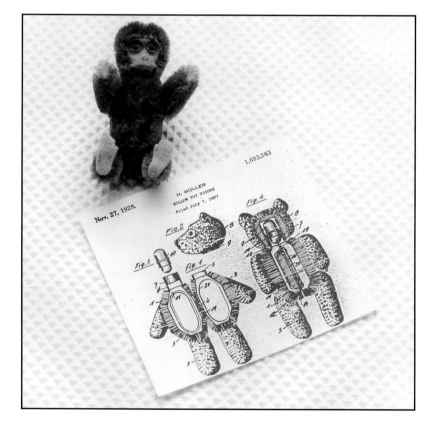

Fig. 121 *Schuco miniature monkey that opens to reveal compact and lipstick; patent shown is for hollow toy teddy bear compact/lipstick combination, c. 1920s. $400.00 – 600.00.*

Fig. 122 *Schuco monkey in Figure 121 shown open.*

1 Nickel-silver engine-turned vanity case with painted enamel flowers on lid; carrying chain and compartments for powder, lipstick, and rouge; c. 1920s. $125.00 – 200.00.

2 Woodworth "Karess" embossed silver-metal miniature vanity with compartments for powder, rouge, and lipstick, c. 1920s. $60.00 – 80.00.

3, 4 Volupté "Watchcase Compact" with picture locket on flower-decorated lid, c. 1940s (3 shown closed, 4 shown open). $70.00 – 100.00.

5 Stratton goldtone compact with crown motif, c. 1940–50s. $100.00 – 150.00.

6 Elizabeth Arden engraved goldtone powder-sifter compact, Switzerland. $60.00 – 100.00.

7 Richard Hudnut nickel-silver complimentary powder sifter, c. 1920s. $25.00 – 75.00.

8 White enamel goldtone compact with lock motif. $75.00 – 125.00.

9 Coty "Sub-Deb" red and white plastic compact, c. 1940s. $25.00 – 40.00.

10 Napier sterling-silver clamshell compact, c. 1940s. $200.00 – 250.00.

11 Givenchy goldtone clamshell compact with blue stone thumbpieces. (shown open). $100.00 – 125.00.

1 Yardley goldtone embossed vanity case; sliding mirror reveals powder and rouge compartments; England, c. 1930–40s. $60.00 – 80.00.

2 Evans oval antique goldtone compact encrusted with faux cabochon jade and pearls. $40.00 – 60.00.

3 The Rainbow Room and Grill "First Prize for Dancing" compact with picture of dancers. $80.00 – 125.00.

4 Brown plastic and goldtone compact with painted flowers on lid. $40.00 – 60.00.

5 Melba goldtone engraved vanity case with powder and lipstick compartments, tassel, and finger ring chain. $40.00 – 60.00.

6 Volupté engraved goldtone compact with swivel mirror lid. $80.00 – 125.00.

7 La Mode cloisonné flapjack vanity case. $50.00 – 70.00.

8 Goldtone and silvered miniature triangular compact with finger ring chain $40.00 – 60.00.

9 Agme goldtone compact with adjustable initials on lid, Switzerland. $80.00 – 120.00.

10 Gwenda octagonal painted foil compact. $40.00 – 80.00.

11 Cambi illuminated, enameled goldtone and plastic vanity case with powder compartment, sliding lipstick, and eye makeup in lid; France. $60.00 – 100.00.

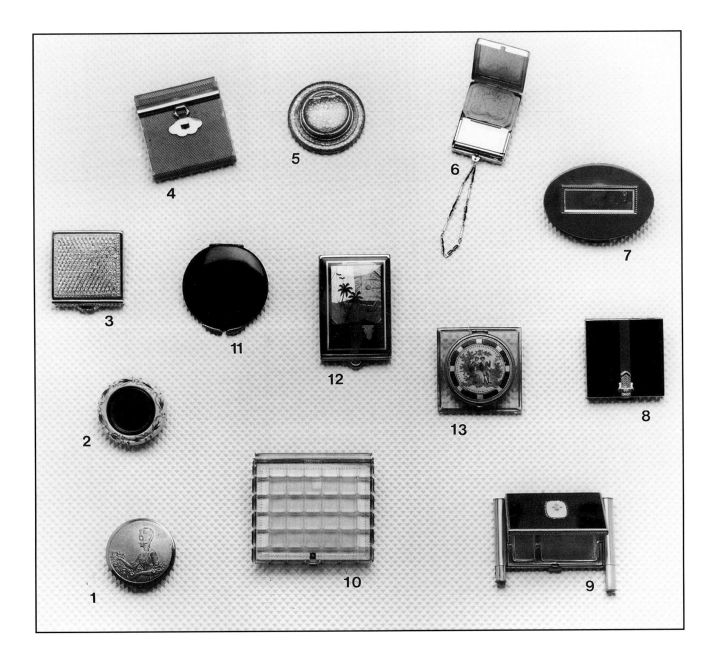

1 *Norida hammered goldtone-metal compact with powder sifter, c. 1920s. $40.00 – 60.00.*

2 *French ivory compact with mirror encircled with bluebirds on lid; "Compliments of Van Raalte" on inner lid. $30.00 – 50.00.*

3 *Rhinestone silvered-metal compact, c. 1930s. $80.00 – 100.00.*

4 *Volupté rigid goldtone mesh compact with buckle closure. $80.00 – 100.00.*

5 *Embossed goldtone cookie-shaped compact, c. 1910. $40.00 – 60.00.*

6 *Woodworth "Karess" blue enamel goldtone vanity case with carrying chain and compartments for powder, rouge, and lipstick; c. 1920s. $60.00 – 80.00.*

7 *Rex Fifth Avenue oval red enamel goldtone compact; lid inset with mirror. $80.00 – 100.00.*

8 *Volupté black enamel and goldtone buckle-motif compact. $60.00 – 80.00.*

9 *La Mode black enamel vanity case with painted enamel disk on lid; powder and rouge compartments and sliding lipstick on either side. $100.00 – 150.00.*

10 *Wadsworth crystal deep-cut cross-bar plastic compact with polished goldtone back, c. 1930s. $100.00 – 150.00.*

11 *Gucci black enamel goldtone compact. $80.00 – 100.00.*

12 *Oblong black enamel polished goldtone compact with colorful butterfly-wing scene under clear plastic on lid, c. 1930s. $75.00 – 100.00.*

13 *Compact set into square yellow plastic frame with transfer scene on lid. $50.00 – 75.00.*

1 Engine-turned brass-tone metal vanity case with multicolored stones encrusted on lid; powder and rouge compartments and carrying chain. $80.00 – 100.00.

2 Enameled silvered-metal miniature vanity case with powder sifter and rouge compartment; finger-ring chain; c. 1920s. $40.00 – 60.00.

3 Silvered-metal compact decorated with red stones. $40.00 – 60.00.

4 Black silk compact decorated with beaded pink fan, France. $60.00 – 80.00.

5 Silvered-metal compact designed in shape of a hat with repoussé cherub on lid. $100.00 – 125.00.

6 Imperial-plate goldtone-metal vanity case with flower design on lid; finger-ring chain; c. 1920s. $80.00 – 100.00.

7 Daniel satin-finish goldtone compact with three-dimensional white plastic courting scene under plastic dome. $80.00 – 125.00.

8 Engraved silvered-metal powder-vial container with puff, metal mirror, and finger-ring chain. NPA.

9 Damascene scalloped goldtone compact with windmill scene on lid. $30.00 – 40.00.

10 Engraved, embossed goldtone compact with harlequin-shaped lid decorated with two large yellow stones, France. $80.00 – 100.00.

11 Oval goldtone compact with blue plastic lid set with faux gems. $40.00 – 60.00.

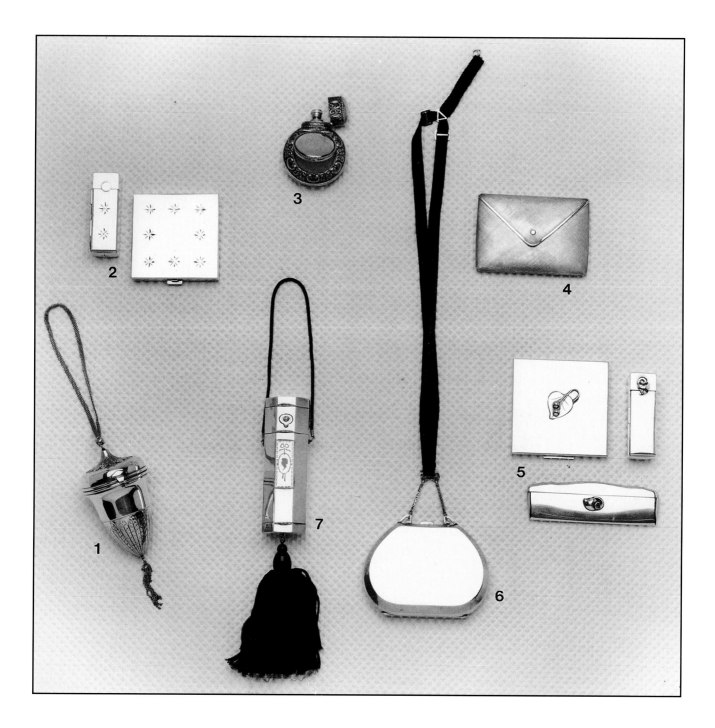

1 *Silver embossed acorn-shaped vanity case with tassel and mesh chain; powder and rouge compartments; turn of the century. $275.00 – 375.00.*
2 *Tiffany & Co. sterling-silver compact and lipstick case set with etched snowflakes. $400.00 – 500.00.*
3 *Sterling-silver compact/perfume combination with repoussé leaf design around edges; Germany, turn of the century. $325.00 – 450.00.*
4 *Tiffany & Co. sterling-silver antique-finish compact designed to resemble envelope, Italy. $250.00 – 300.00.*

5 *Sterling-silver compact, lipstick, and comb set with grape leaf; possibly Georg Jensen. $500.00 – 600.00.*
6 *Sterling hallmarked purse-motif vanity case with carrying cord; powder and rouge compartments, lipstick tube, and mirror; England, turn of the century. $350.00 – 450.00.*
7 *Sterling-silver hallmarked necessaire, silhouettes on lid and front; cord and tassel; sliding lipstick and compartments for powder, rouge, and cigarettes. NPA.*

1 *Brown marbleized enamel compact designed to resemble envelope, with cabochon blue stone on lid, Germany. $60.00 – 80.00.*

2 *Richard Hudnut "Du Barry Beauty Box" engraved goldtone vanity box with carrying chain; compartments for powder, rouge, and lipstick. $60.00 – 80.00.*

3 *Light blue plastic novelty carryall with concealed compact, lipstick, hairbrush, and comb. $125.00 – 200.00.*

4 *Flato goldtone compact with jeweled horse and carriage mounted on lid in blue velvet protective case with lipstick sleeve. $250.00 – 300.00.*

5 *Kreisler red and black enamel goldtone compact with ornate hinge and closure. $40.00 – 60.00.*

6 *Terri octagonal goldtone compact with scale-work engraved edges and dancers on lid; original fitted presentation box. $80.00 – 100.00.*

7 *Yardley goldtone vanity case with white enamel feather on lid; powder and rouge compartments and tandem lipstick; c. 1940s. $60.00 – 80.00.*

8 *Satin goldtone compact designed to resemble purse, with blue enamel disk on lid; carrying chain. $150.00 – 200.00.*

9 *Lucretia Vanderbilt blue enamel silvered-metal set decorated with silver butterflies; miniature round compact, oblong vanity case, boudoir-size face powder container, and sample-size extract container. NPA.*

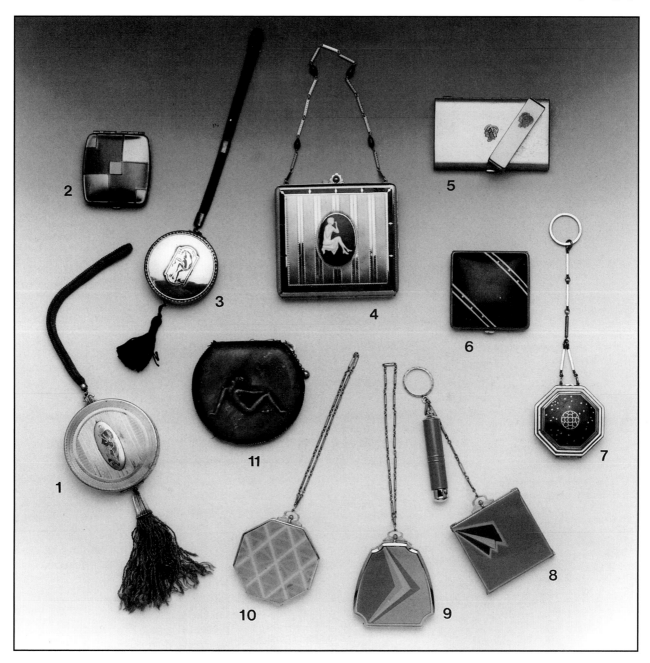

1 Silvered and goldtone vanity case with blue enamel profile of woman on lid; faded blue tassel and carrying cord; compartments for powder, rouge, and lipstick; turn of the century. $100.00 – 150.00.

2 Art Deco blue enamel and goldtone vanity case with compartments for powder and rouge. $60.00 – 80.00.

3 Sterling silver hallmarked Art Nouveau compact with silhouette of dancing woman; carrying cord and tassel. $150.00 – 175.00.

4 D.F. Briggs Co. engine-turned silvered carryall with oval disk of woman applying makeup centered and black enamel border; carrying chain and compartments for powder, rouge, lipstick, coins, and necessities. $150.00 – 200.00.

5 Chantrey bronze-colored metal vanity case and lipstick set with red and black silhouettes of man and woman. $100.00 – 125.00.

6 Black and white enamel vanity case with compartments for powder and lipstick. $60.00 – 80.00.

7 Richard Hudnut "Le Debut" octagonal vanity case with black-enamel celestial scene; powder and rouge compartments and finger-ring chain. $150.00 – 225.00.

8 E.A.M. Art Deco blue enamel tango chain with red and yellow abstract design; powder sifter and attached lipstick; finger ring chain; c. 1920s. $150.00 – 200.00.

9 E.A.M. Art Deco enameled compact with blue, yellow, and gray abstract design; powder sifter and carrying chain; c. 1920. $150.00 – 200.00.

10 Octagonal Art Deco compact with pink, yellow, and blue abstract design; powder sifter and carrying chain; c. 1920. $150.00 – 200.00.

11 Horseshoe-shaped pewter and leather zippered compact with repoussé woman on lid. NPA.

1, 2 *Goldtone and black lip-blotter tissue case with mirrored lid (1 shown closed, 2 shown open). $20.00 – 40.00 each.*

3 *Dorothy Gray engine-turned goldtone compact designed to resemble a hat, c. 1940s. $125.00 – 175.00.*

4 *Lederer "Sacs" goldtone compact with red pompon black suede beret; original presentation box, France. NPA.*

5 *Miniature red enamel goldtone bolster-shaped compact (shown open). $25.00 – 30.00.*

6 *Multicolored micro-mosaic goldtone compact, Italy. $80.00 – 100.00.*

7 *Wadsworth polished and satin-finish engraved compact designed to resemble a fan. $60.00 – 80.00.*

8 *Octagonal wood-marquetry compact inlaid with light and dark wood veneers. $75.00 – 100.00.*

9 *Brass cookie-shaped basketweave compact, c. 1920s. $60.00 – 80.00.*

10 *Langlois "Shari" green enamel and goldtone vanity case with compartments for powder, rouge, and lipstick (shown open). $80.00 – 100.00.*

11, 12 *Two goldtone and red cloisonné compacts in original silk-lined leather fitted presentation box (11 shown open, 12 shown closed). $100.00 – 125.00.*

13 *Goldtone tango chain vanity case with black painted strapwork. $100.00 – 125.00.*

1 *Antiqued silver-filigree and engraved belt chatelette with compact, pencil, perfume holder, and writing slate; Continental, 19th century. NPA.*

2 *Engraved silver compact shaped as a hand mirror with lipstick in handle; Italy, turn of the century. $150.00 – 225.00.*

3 *Whiting & Davis silvered mesh vanity bag with etched and engraved lid and braided carrying chain, c. 1920s. $400.00 – 500.00.*

4, 5 *Powder-Tier triple-tier vanity case with swivel compartments for powder, rouge, and lipstick, c. 1920s (4, sterling silver, shown open; $300.00 – 350.00; silvered metal, shown closed). $125.00 – 175.00.*

6 *Silvered compact with spider and fly repoussé on both sides; neck chain. $175.00 – 225.00.*

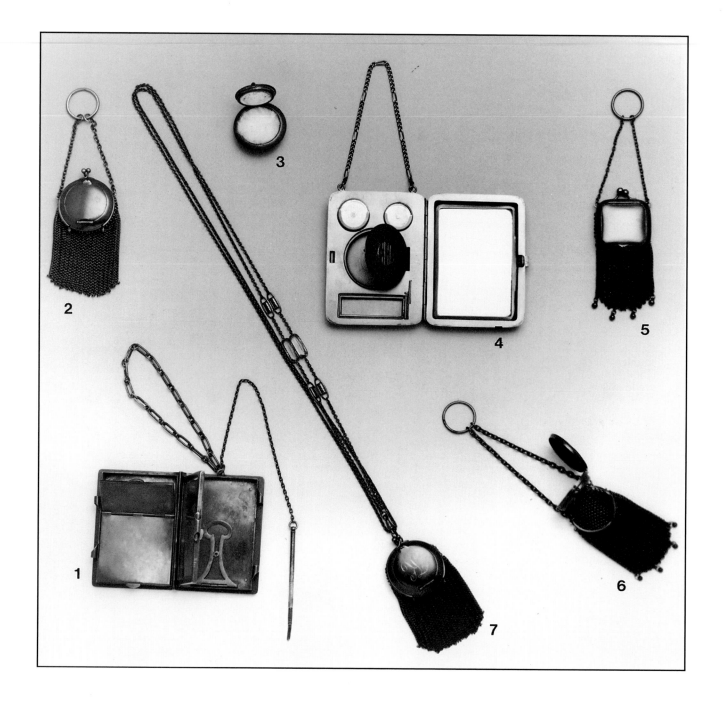

1 *Gun-metal mini carryall designed to resemble book, with four faux amethysts on lid; carrying chain and compartments for powder, rouge, bills, writing slate, and slim metal pencil (shown open). $200.00 – 225.00.*

2 *Gun-metal mini mesh vanity bag with diminishing mirror and finger ring chain, France. $150.00 – 200.00.*

3 *Gun-metal mini compact with loop for chain, Germany. $50.00 – 75.00.*

4 *Gun-metal black beaded mini carryall monogrammed ERC; carrying chain and compartments for powder, lipstick, and coins (shown open). $200.00 – 250.00.*

5 *Gun-metal mini mesh vanity bag with finger ring chain. $150.00 – 200.00.*

6 *Gun-metal mini mesh vanity bag with finger ring chain, France. $150.00 – 200.00.*

7 *Gun-metal mini mesh vanity bag with monogrammed lid; diminishing mirror and neck chain; France. $200.00 – 250.00.*

1 Volupté "Lucky Purse" satin-finish metal compact; outer lid reveals rouge; c. 1940s (shown open). $80.00 – 100.00.

2 Volupté "Lucky Purse" polished-metal tango-chain compact with multicolored stones; lipstick; c. 1940s. $150.00 – 175.00.

3 Volupté "Lucky Purse" satin-finish metal compact; outer lid reveals picture locket; c. 1940s (shown open). $80.00 – 100.00.

4 K & K polished satin-finish compact/bracelet set with pearls and blue stones; hinged bracelet. $250.00 – 300.00.

5 K & K polished satin-finish compact/bracelet; hinged bracelet (shown open). $200.00 – 250.00.

6 K & K polished satin-finish compact/bracelet set with rhinestones and red stones; hinged bracelet. $250.00 – 300.00.

7 Deva-Dassy polished goldtone compact/bracelet set with large green stones, France. $200.00 – 275.00.

1 *Hexagonal engine-turned brass tango chain compact.* $100.00 – 125.00.

2 *Sterling-silver engraved miniature compact with locket mounted on top.* $125.00 – 200.00.

3 *Brass ball compact with pair of dice under plastic dome lid.* $125.00 – 200.00.

4 *Champlevé goldtone compact with painted ivory disk on lid, Italy.* $40.00 – 60.00.

5 *Goldtone miniature compact with Limoges painting set in pearl disk on filigree lid.* $60.00 – 80.00.

6 *Green champlevé and vermeil compact, Italy.* $80.00 – 100.00.

7 *Green cloisonné and silver four-leaf-clover vanity case with painted flowers on lid; goldtone interior; metal mirror and powder sifter and rouge compartment; c. 1920s.* $100.00 – 125.00.

8 *Evans engine-turned nickel-silver triangular vanity case with yellow cloisonné lid with painted flowers; powder and rouge compartments and through handle.* $100.00 – 125.00.

9 *Terri blue plastic compact with silver dancers on metal lid.* $30.00 – 40.00.

10 *Goldtone compact with micro-mosaic flowers on lid and four stones set around base.* $60.00 – 80.00.

11 *Divine miniature orange enamel compact with white silhouette on lid.* $40.00 – 60.00.

12 *Divine miniature pink enamel compact with white picture on lid (shown open).* $40.00 – 60.00.

13 *Divine miniature yellow compact with painted picture of woman on lid.* $40.00 – 60.00.

14 *White enamel compact with molded pink and green plastic floral design on lid, c. 1930s.* $60.00 – 80.00.

15 *Flato goldtone compact with etched cat with green cabochon stone eyes on lid; lipstick sleeve in maroon velvet case; c. 1950s.* $250.00 – 350.00.

16 *Blue enamel goldtone compact with multicolored painted flowers on lid, France.* $100.00 – 125.00.

17 *Cheramy "Cappi" goldtone vanity case with powder and rouge compartments and sliding mirror, c. 1920s (shown open).* $80.00 – 100.00.

1 E.A. Bliss Co. vermeil nickel-silver compact/bracelet with etched floral decoration on lid; applied cutout leaf-shape metal band; turn of the century. $150.00 – 250.00.

2 F.J. Co. antique goldtone compact/bracelet with filigree lid and flowers on band, c. 1930s. $225.00 – 300.00.

3 La Mode satin-finish flapjack vanity case and bracelet set with rhinestone trim. $150.00 – 200.00.

4 Sterling silver hallmarked vermeil cloisonné compact/bracelet with painted flowers on lid and grosgrain band, Continental. $200.00 – 250.00.

5, 6 Mello-Glo nickel-silver "Wrist Compact" with grosgrain band, c. 1920s. $75.00 – 125.00.

7 Octagonal goldtone compact/bracelet with rhinestone and filigree overlay on lid and grosgrain band. $80.00 – 125.00.

8 Sterling-silver hallmarked blue cloisonné compact/bracelet with black grosgrain band; Continental, turn of the century. $200.00 – 250.00.

9 Black plastic compact/bracelet set with rhinestones; grosgrain band; c. 1920s. $175.00 – 200.00.

10 Silvered compact/bracelet with filigree and engraved decoration; removable pin-hinge closure; Continental, 19th century. $175.00 – 275.00.

11, 12 Marlowe Co. "Parisienne" plastic cosmetic bracelet with decorative metal band that slides to reveal two mirrors and five cosmetic compartments (11, ivory, shown closed; 12, black, shown open). $175.00 – 325.00.

1 *French ivory plastic bolster-shaped vanity case with rhinestones and blue stones; faded blue carrying cord with lipstick concealed in tassel, c. 1920s. $250.00 – 300.00.*

2 *Crystal plastic compact with blue Wedgwood disk on lid. $80.00 – 100.00.*

3 *Vani-Pak black plastic compact/cigarette case combination with sliding mirror (shown open). $80.00 – 100.00.*

4 *Black plastic vanity case with rhinestone geometric design on lid; front opens to reveal mirror and powder and rouge compartments; back contains coin pocket; black carrying cord with lipstick concealed in tassel; c. 1920s. $350.00 – 400.00.*

5 *Richelieu yellow plastic egg-shaped vanity case with monogrammed lid; powder and rouge compartments. $40.00 – 60.00.*

6 *Goldtone and orange plastic compact with filigree overlay on lid set with stones; neck chain. $100.00 – 150.00.*

7 *Oval simulated-tortoise shell plastic compact with raised grape and leaf design on lid; sterling-silver catches; c. 1940s. $60.00 – 80.00.*

1 K & K brass-colored, engine-tooled, basket-shaped compact with dice enclosed in plastic domed lid; embossed swinging handle. $125.00 – 200.00.

2 Kigu engraved brass-colored, basket-shaped compact with filigree flowers centered with faux pearl on lid; embossed swinging handle; England, c. 1940–50s. $125.00 – 200.00.

3 K & K brass-colored, engine-tooled, basket-shaped compact with embossed swinging handle (shown open). $80.00 – 100.00.

4 K & K brass-colored, engine-tooled, basket-shaped compact with satin-finish lid and embossed swinging handle. $80.00 – 125.00.

5 K & K brass-colored, engine-tooled, basket-shaped compact with multicolored silk flowers enclosed in plastic domed lid; embossed swinging handle. $125.00 – 200.00.

6, 7 Brass walnut-motif compact; inner partition incorporates writing slate and diminishing mirror; compartments for powder and combination hinged scent bottle and pin holder; loop for chain; 19th century (6 shown open, 7 shown closed). $200.00 – 250.00.

8 Silver walnut-motif compact; inner partition has picture locket and diminishing mirror; compartments for powder and hinged scent bottle; loop for chain (shown open). $250.00 – 350.00.

9 Zell goldtone engraved basket-motif compact with engraved pink and green flowers and embossed rigid handle. $100.00 – 150.00.

10 Polished goldtone basket compact with red, white, and green painted flowers on lid and engraved swinging handle. $125.00 – 175.00.

1 Blue plastic sphere-shaped compact with multicolored plastic flowers; carrying cord and tassel. $150.00 – 250.00.
2 Polished goldtone ball-shaped compact with roulette wheel enclosed in plastic domed lid. $125.00 – 200.00.
3 Green lizard oval compact with brass decoration and closure and lizard wrist strap. NPA.
4 Ebony enamel "eight ball" compact. $125.00 – 200.00.
5 Kigu brass musical globe compact, England, c. 1940–50s. $350.00 – 450.00.
6 Henriette brass compact, c. 1930s (shown open). $60.00 – 80.00.

7 Vogue Vanities "PomPom" ivory enamel ball compact decorated with painted flowers; powder sifter and multi-colored tassel; England. $100.00 – 125.00.
8 Enameled red, white, and blue air-balloon-motif compact; balloon basket contains rouge. NPA.
9 Asprey sterling silver hallmarked miniature ball compact with vermeil blue enamel; loop for chain. $150.00 – 250.00.
10 Henriette polished brass-ball compact with multicolored flowers enclosed in plastic domed lid, c. 1930s. $125.00 – 200.00.

1 Stratton scalloped oblong multicolor enamel goldtone compact with lipstick in lid. $60.00 – 80.00.

2 Volupté goldtone carryall with multicolored enameled animals on lid; compartments for powder, rouge, cigarettes, and comb. $125.00 – 150.00.

3 K & K satin and polished goldtone diamond-shaped compact. $40.00 – 60.00.

4 Coro half-moon-shaped goldtone compact with enameled Persian design on lid. $40.00 – 60.00.

5 Coro half-moon-shaped satin and polished goldtone compact (shown open). $40.00 – 60.00.

6 Miref engine-turned goldtone compact designed to resemble pocket watch; carrying ring; France. $100.00 – 150.00.

7 Rex Fifth Avenue red, white, and blue enamel oval compact with military emblem on lid. $50.00 – 75.00.

8 Volupté scalloped goldtone compact with black enamel border and finger-ring cord. $40.00 – 60.00.

9 Black silk vanity case with embroidered birds on lid; blue beaded tassel with green ojime bead and carrying ring; compartments for powder, rouge, and lipstick; c. 1920s. $150.00 – 225.00.

10 Shaded yellow enamel horseshoe-shaped vanity case with coat-of-arms on lid; powder and rouge compartments. $40.00 – 60.00.

11 Zell Fifth Avenue goldtone compact with picture locket in lid. $40.00 – 60.00.

1 Engine-turned silvered-metal vanity case with powder sifter, rouge compartment, and finger ring chain; c. 1920 – 1930s. $80.00 – 100.00.

2 Etched silvered-metal compact with rhinestone decoration around rim and finger ring chain, c. 1920 – 30s. $80.00 – 100.00.

3 Silver-plated compact with finger ring chain, c. 1920 – 1930s. $40.00 – 60.00.

4 Rounded-oblong silvered and goldtone vanity case with powder sifter, rouge compartment, and finger ring chain, c. 1920 – 1930s. $80.00 – 100.00.

5 Engine-turned goldtone vanity case with blue and white enamel flowers set with cabochon blue stones; powder sifter, rouge compartments, and finger ring chain; c. 1920 – 1930s. $100.00 – 125.00.

6 Engine-turned nickel-finish octagonal compact with green enamel disk on lid and finger ring chain, c. 1920 – 1930s. $80.00 – 100.00.

7 May Fair goldtone vanity case with yellow cloisonné disk on lid; compartments for powder and rouge and finger ring chain; c. 1920 – 1930s. $80.00 – 100.00.

8 Silvered goldtone oblong octagonal vanity case with powder and rouge compartments and finger ring chain, c. 1920 – 1930s. $60.00 – 80.00.

9 Silver-plated engine-turned vanity case with green enamel disk on lid; powder sifter, rouge compartment, lipstick, and finger ring chain; c. 1920 – 1930s. $80.00 – 100.00.

10 Engine-turned silvered-metal vanity case with yellow cloisonné on lid; powder and rouge compartments and finger ring chain; c. 1920 – 1930s. $90.00 – 100.00.

11 Sterling silver hallmarked double-sided vanity case with powder and rouge compartments and finger ring chain; Continental. $200.00 – 250.00.

1 *Goldtone compact with painted peacock on plastic disk set with red stones. $40.00 – 60.00.*

2 *Melba miniature oblong compact with enameled scene on lid. $40.00 – 60.00.*

3 *Woodworth "Karess" polished goldtone vanity case with powder and rouge compartments, c. 1920s. $30.00 – 50.00.*

4 *Navy blue enamel silvered-metal vanity case with marcasite flower on lid; lid opens to reveal pop-up-mirror and compartments for powder, rouge, and lipstick. $60.00 – 80.00.*

5 *Pale yellow vanity case with raised mountain scenes; tassel and carrying cord; compartments for powder, rouge, and lipstick; c. 1920s. $175.00 – 225.00.*

6 *Evans goldtone tap-sift powder compact with red enamel goldtone lid. $40.00 – 60.00.*

7 *Multicolored damask compact with wallet-type closure and plastic ring on lid, France. $40.00 – 60.00.*

8 *Estée Lauder Lucite compact with monogrammed metal lid. $40.00 – 60.00.*

9 *Silvered-metal vanity case with abalone disk; "Chicago, Ill" printed on cover; c. 1920s. $60.00 – 80.00.*

10 *Oblong engine-turned silvered-metal vanity case with raised basket on lid; sliding mirror reveals powder and rouge compartments. $100.00 – 125.00.*

1 *Mary Dunhill satin goldtone compact with hinges and thumbpiece set with rhinestones and green stones. $60.00 – 80.00.*

2, 3 *Jet set, compact and matching pillbox. $40.00 –60.00 set.*

4 *Volupté brown oblong vanity case with compartments for powder, rouge, pills, and comb (shown open). $40.00 – 60.00 set.*

5 *Silvered compact with purple enamel lid set with rhinestones. $50.00 – 60.00.*

6 *Dorothy Gray blue enamel and silvered compact with mirror on outside lid. $40.00 – 60.00.*

7 *Engine-turned nickel-finish compact/cigarette case/lighter combination with raised giraffe and palm trees on lid. $125.00 – 175.00.*

8 *Sterling silver mini compact with yellow enameled lid decorated with flowers and finger-ring chain. $60.00 – 75.00.*

9 *Harriet Hubbard Ayer engine-turned goldtone vanity case with center-opening compartments for powder, rouge, and lipstick (shown open). $60.00 – 80.00.*

10 *Double-sided painted filigree metal vanity case set with colored stones; powder and rouge compartment and hanging bead chain. $175.00 – 225.00.*

11 *Brown plastic compact with lid inset with embroidery under plastic; interior and exterior mirrors. $60.00 – 80.00.*

1 Triangular goldtone compact with raised elephants. $40.00 – 60.00.

2 Wadsworth bolster-shaped black enamel goldtone vanity case with compartments for powder, lipstick, and cigarettes (shown open). $100.00 – 150.00.

3 Volupté satin and polished goldtone strapwork-design compact with raised flowers and small orange stones on lid. $40.00 – 60.00.

4 Richard Hudnut marbleized blue plastic vanity case with silver-plated engraved lid; powder and rouge compartments; original fitted presentation box. $80.00 – 100.00.

5 Painted plastic compact with ballet scene on lid. $60.00 – 80.00.

6, 7 Stratton blue enamel scalloped compact and matching lipstick holder. $60.00 – 80.00 set.

8 Beaded compact with multicolored beaded flowers on white beaded background, France. $75.00 – 100.00.

9 Polished goldtone oblong vanity case with leaves on lid; powder and rouge compartments. $40.00 – 60.00.

10 Vitoge polished goldtone compact and lipstick case with four-leaf clovers; protective carrying case. $80.00 – 125.00.

11 Elgin American silvered compact with engraved lid. $40.00 – 60.00.

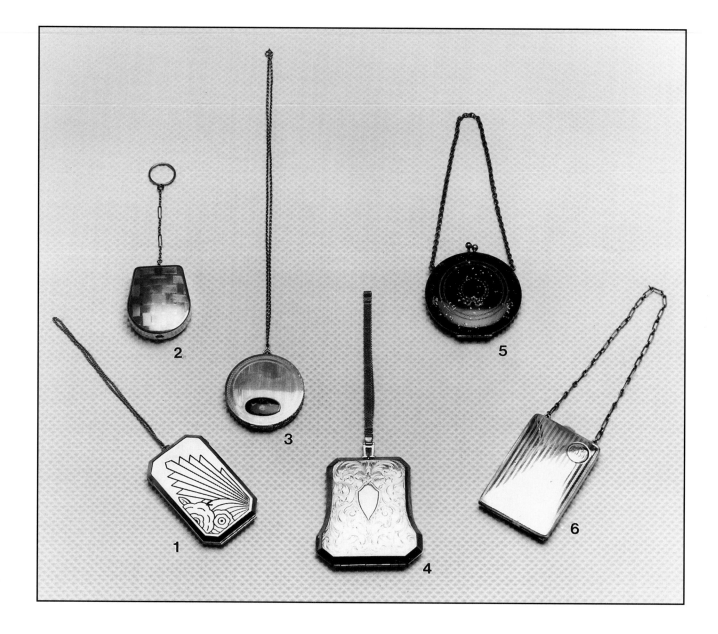

1 Melba goldtone vanity case with blue enameled flower design on lid; carrying chain and compartments for powder, rouge, and lipstick. $80.00 – 125.00.

2 Silvered-metal horseshoe-shaped vanity case with basketweave design on lid; powder and rouge compartments, swivel mirror, and finger ring chain; c. 1920s. $60.00 – 80.00.

3 D.F. Briggs Co. gold-filled engine-turned vanity case with enamel disk on lid; carrying chain and compartments for powder, rouge, lipstick, and eye makeup. $80.00 – 100.00.

4 Goldtone engraved vanity case with mesh carrying chain and compartments for powder, rouge, lipstick, and coins. $125.00 – 150.00.

5 Goldtone and green enamel vanity case with goldtone interior and green cabochon thumbpieces; carrying chain and compartments for powder and coins. $100.00 – 125.00.

6 Sterling silver hallmarked engine-turned vanity case with monogrammed lid; carrying chain and compartments for powder, coins, and bills; Continental. $150.00 – 225.00.

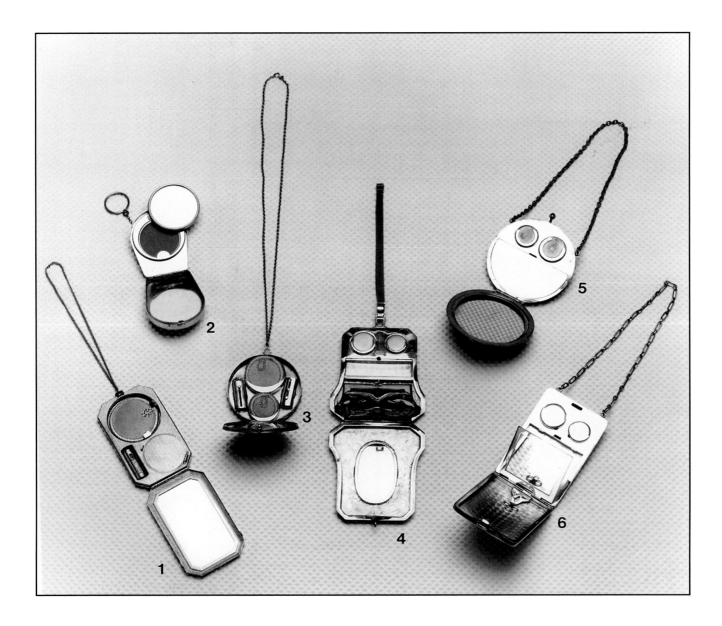

Vanity cases on page 310 shown open.

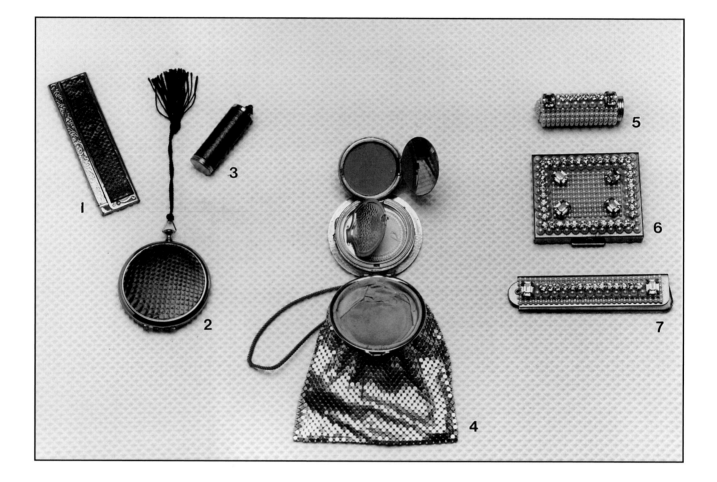

1, 2, 3 *Zell Fifth Avenue brown lizard compact, lipstick, and comb set; compact designed to resemble pocket watch. $200.00 – 250.00 set.*
4 *Silvered-mesh vanity bag with powder and rouge compartments and carrying chain (shown open). $250.00 – 300.00.*

5, 6, 7 *Compact, lipstick, and comb set decorated with pearls, rhinestones, and blue stones. $125.00 – 150.00 set.*

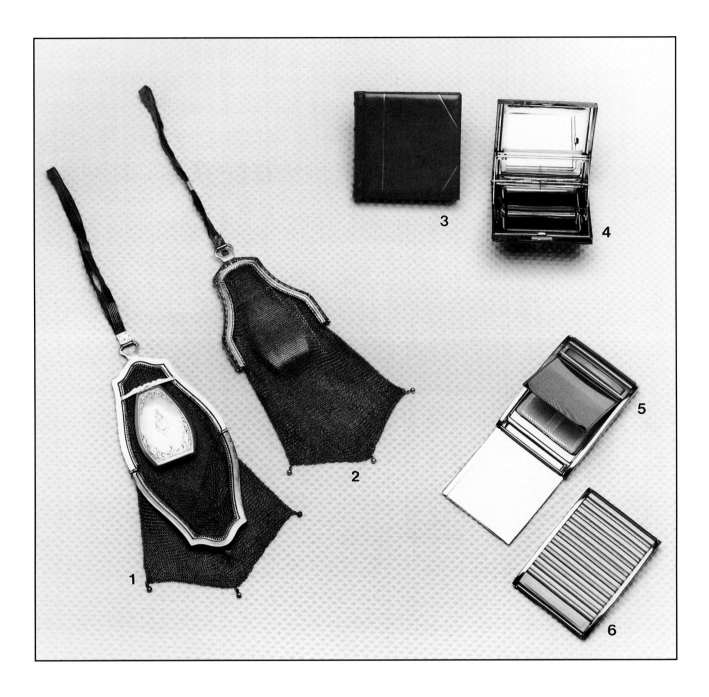

1, 2 *W B silvered-metal mesh vanity bag with compact suspended on bar inside bag, c. 1920s (1 shown open, 2 shown closed). $350.00 – 450.00.*

3, 4 *Dunhill "Clearview" brown leather windshield-wiper compact designed to resemble book, c. 1930s (3 shown closed, 4 shown open). $80.00 – 100.00.*

5, 6 *Blue enamel and goldtone roll-top compact; Germany, c. 1940s (5 shown open, 6 shown closed). $100.00 – 125.00.*

A Sampling
of Important Patents

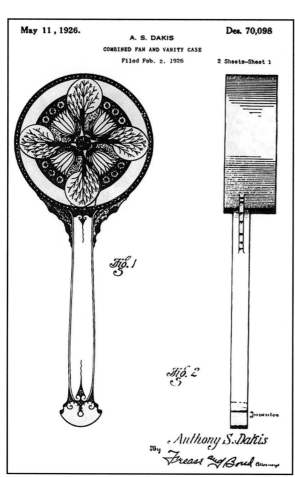

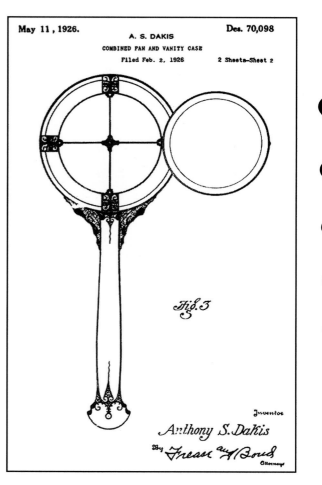

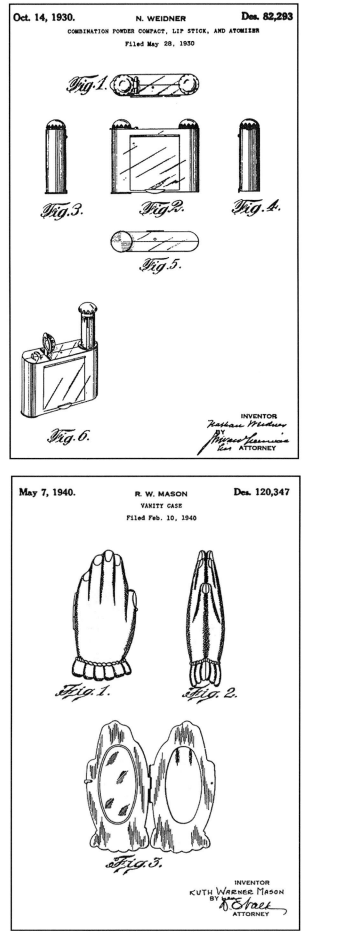

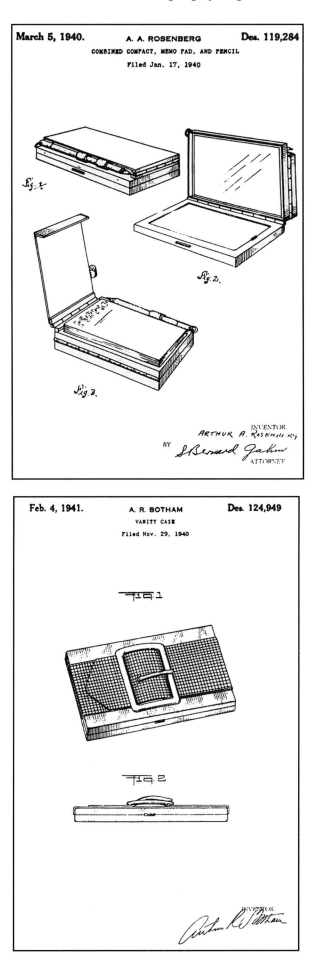

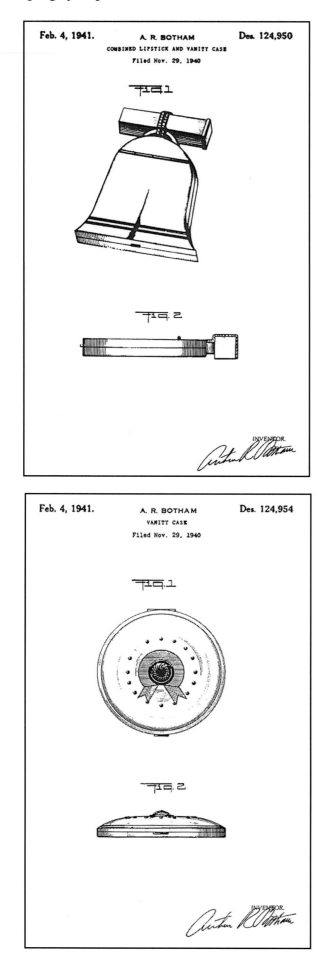

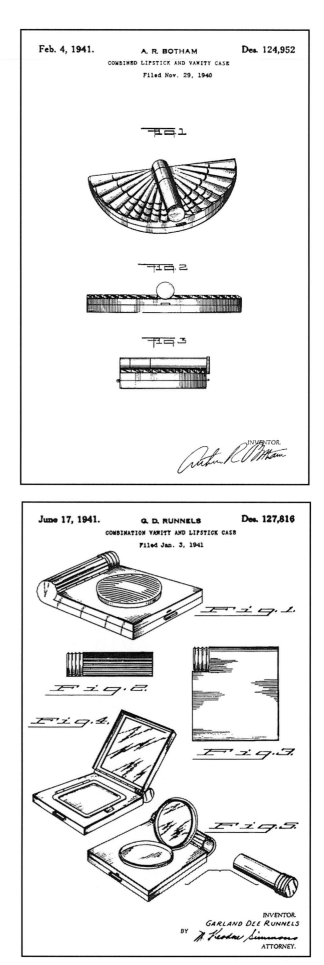

316

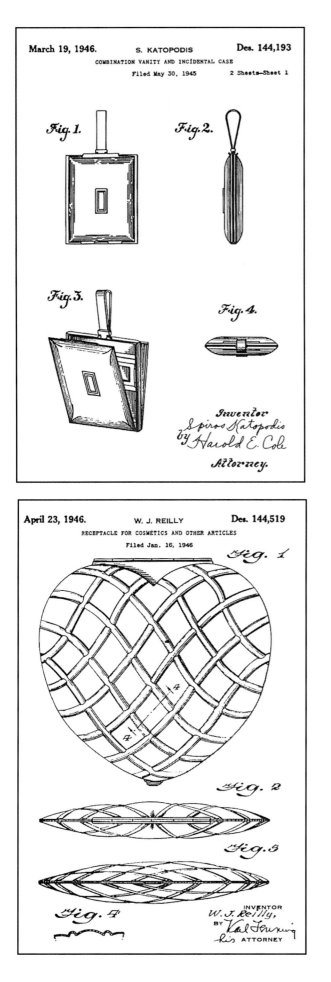

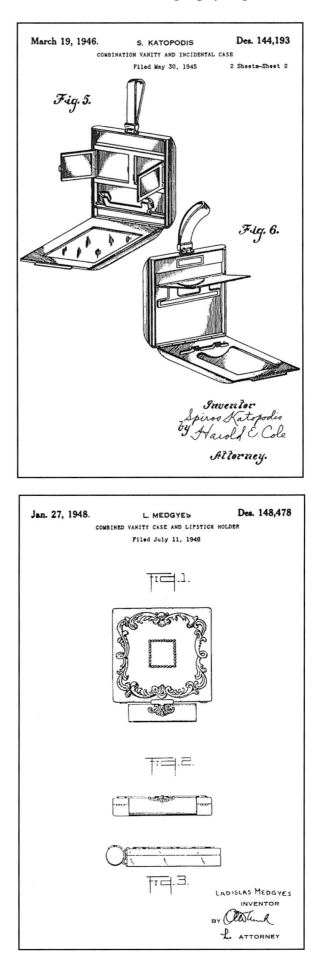

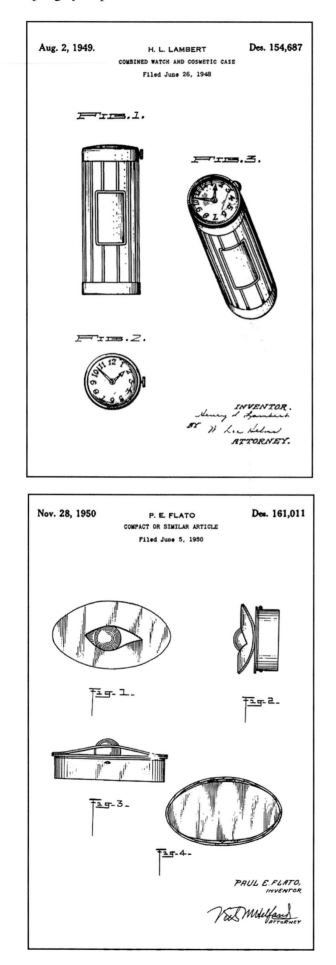

Aug. 2, 1949.

H. L. LAMBERT

Des. 154,687

COMBINED WATCH AND COSMETIC CASE

Filed June 26, 1948

FIG.1.

FIG.3.

FIG.2.

INVENTOR.
Henry L. Lambert
BY W. Lee Helms
ATTORNEY.

Nov. 28, 1950

P. E. FLATO

Des. 161,011

COMPACT OR SIMILAR ARTICLE

Filed June 5, 1950

Fig.1.

Fig.2.

Fig.3.

Fig.4.

PAUL E. FLATO,
INVENTOR.

ATTORNEY

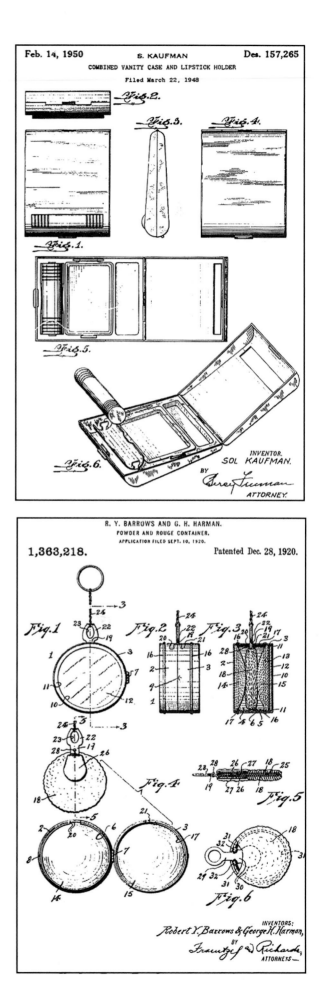

Feb. 14, 1950

S. KAUFMAN

Des. 157,265

COMBINED VANITY CASE AND LIPSTICK HOLDER

Filed March 22, 1948

Fig.2.

Fig.3.

Fig.4.

Fig.1.

Fig.5.

Fig.6.

INVENTOR.
SOL KAUFMAN.

BY
ATTORNEY.

R. Y. BARROWS AND G. H. HARMAN.

POWDER AND ROUGE CONTAINER.

APPLICATION FILED SEPT. 10, 1920.

1,363,218.

Patented Dec. 28, 1920.

Fig.1

Fig.2

Fig.3

Fig.4

Fig.5

Fig.6

INVENTORS:
Robert Y. Barrows & George H. Harman,
BY
ATTORNEYS.

318

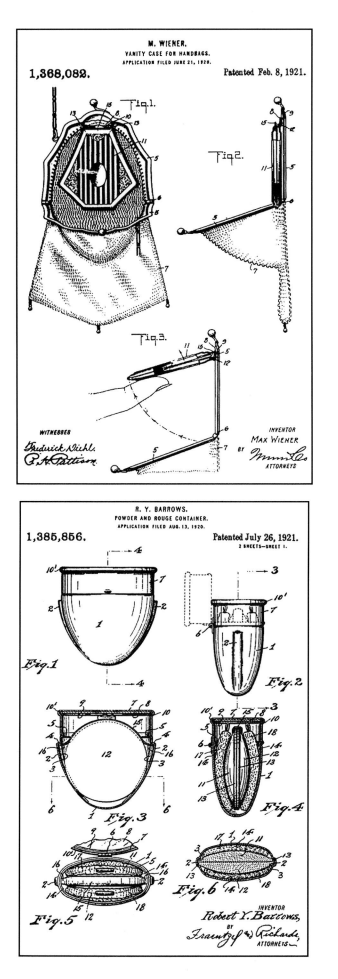

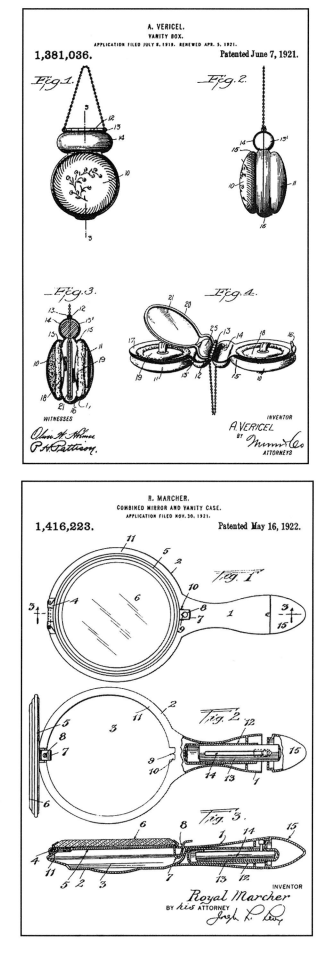

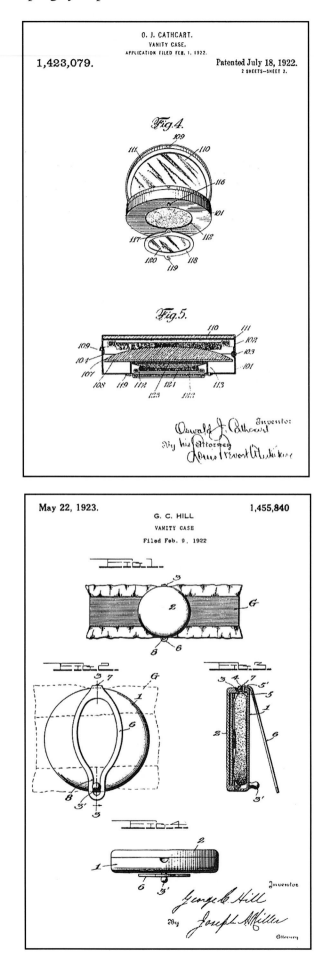

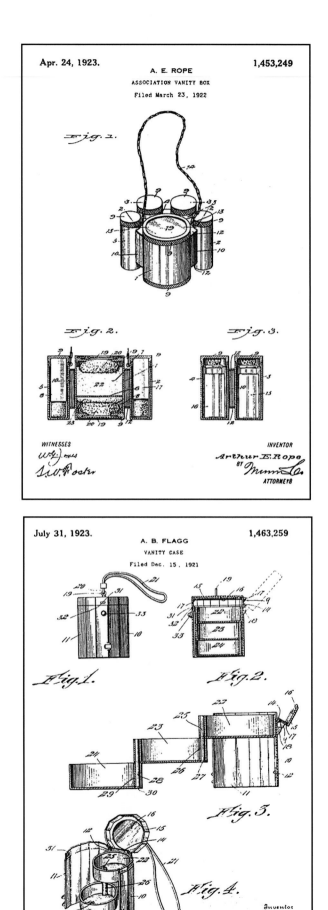

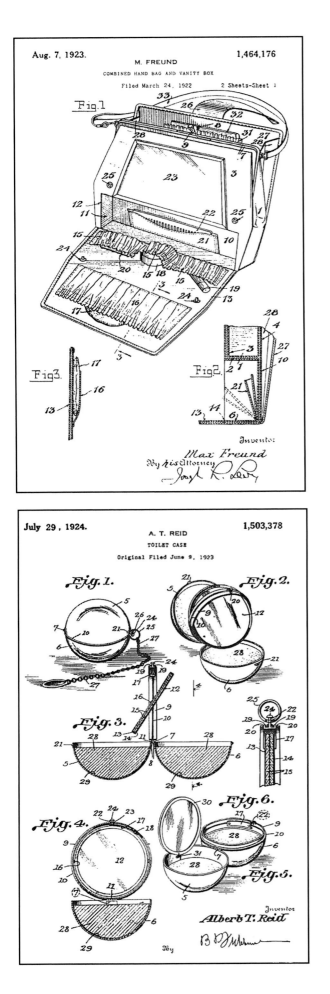

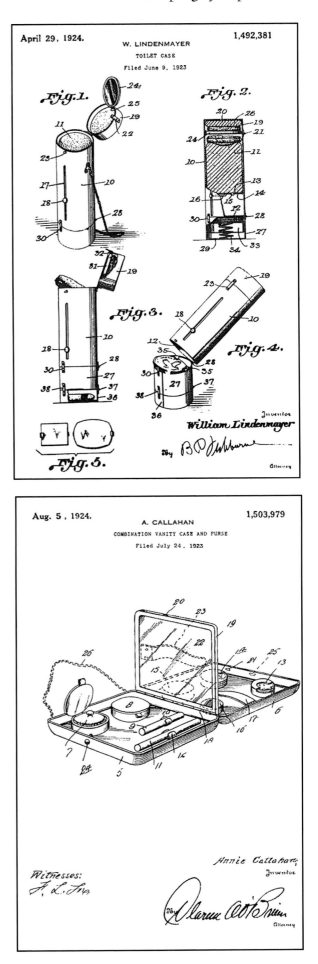

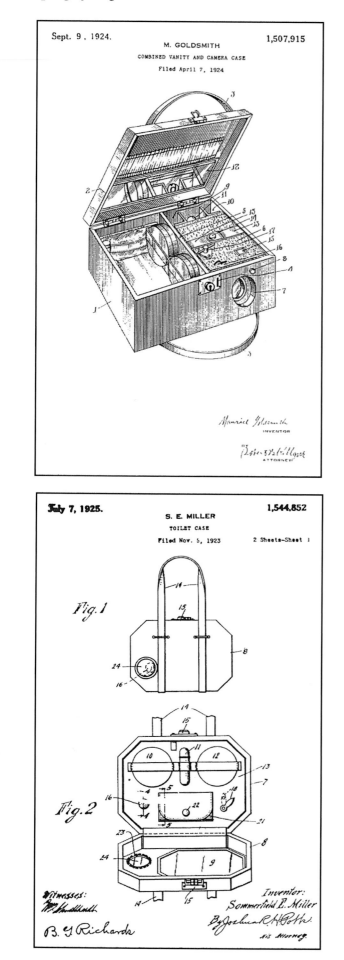

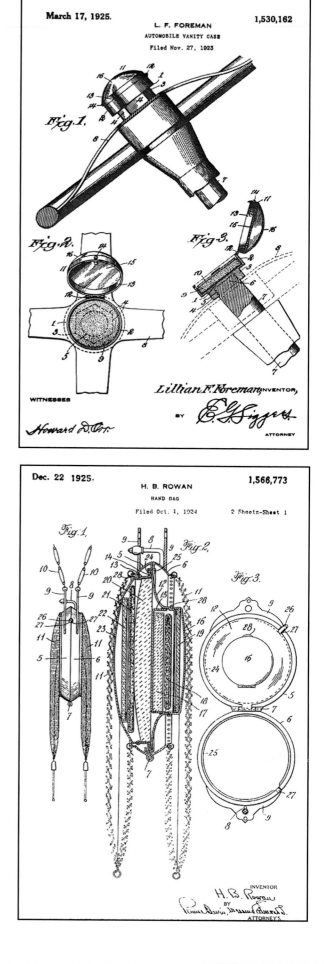

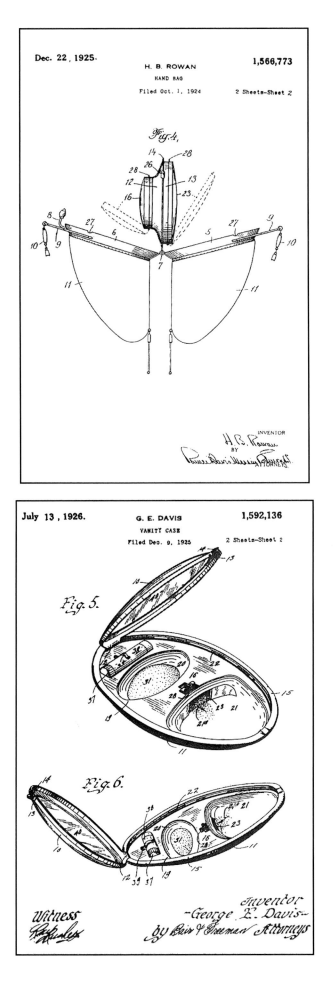

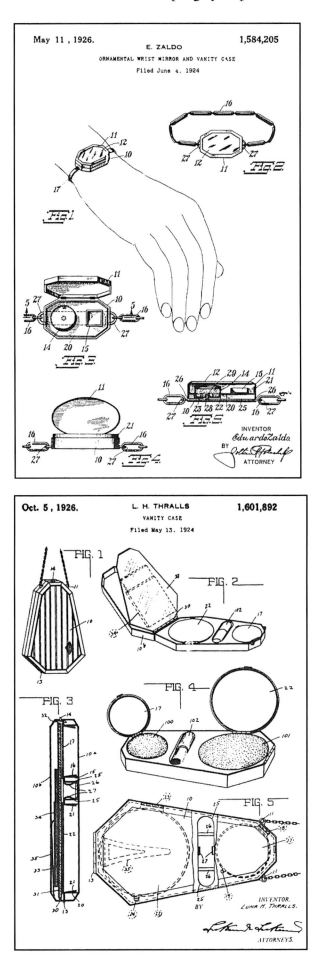

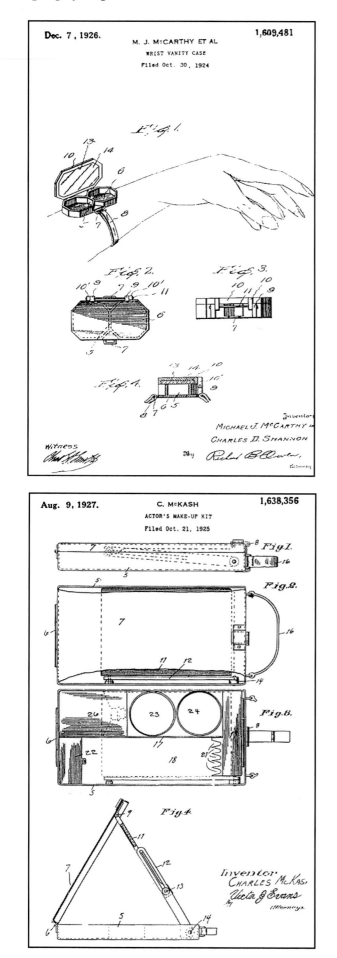

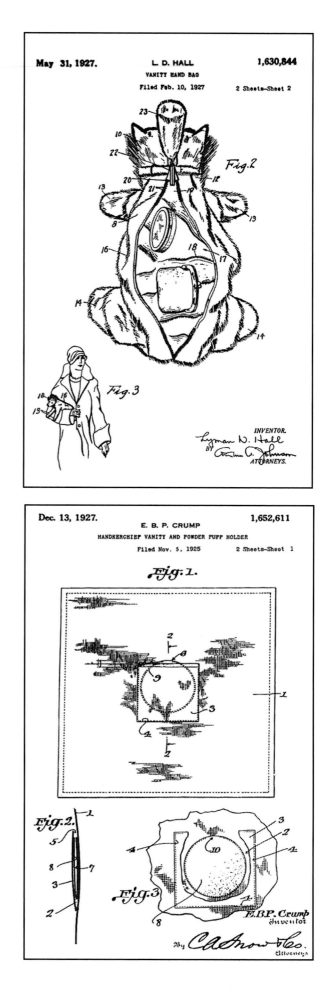

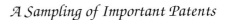

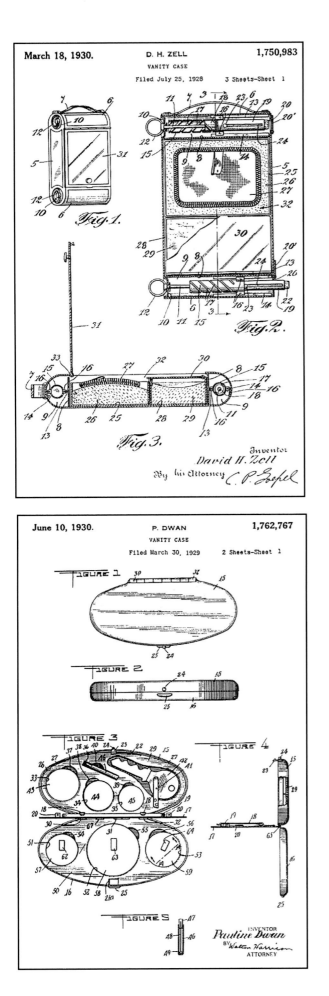

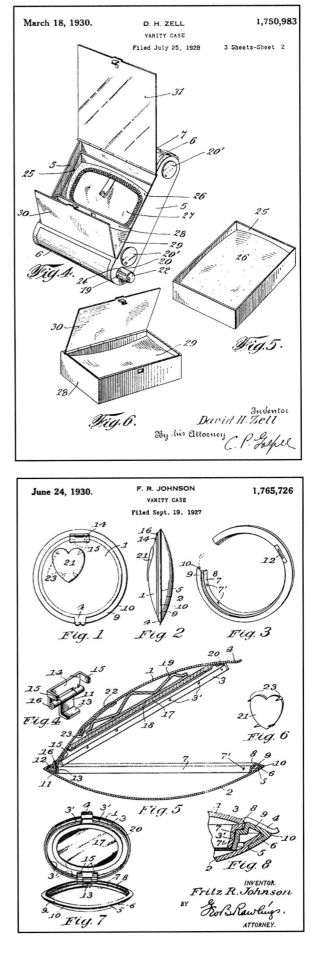

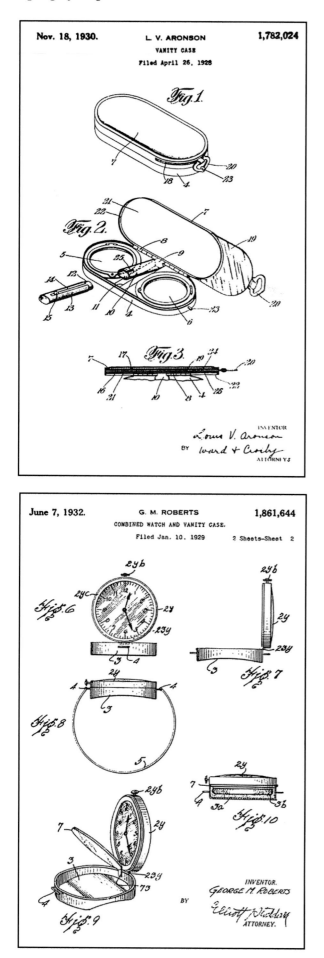

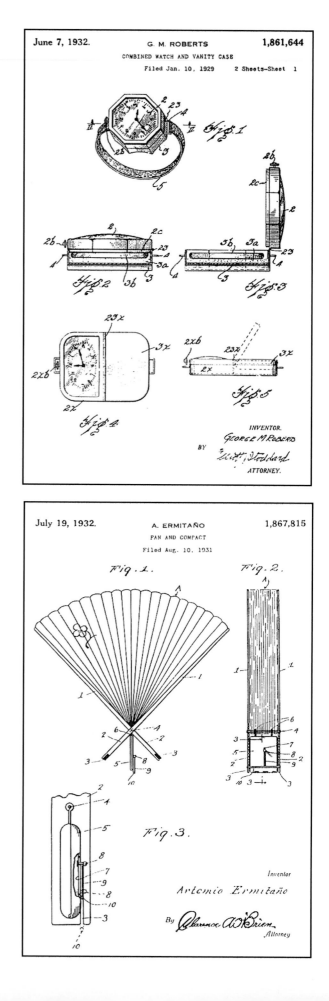

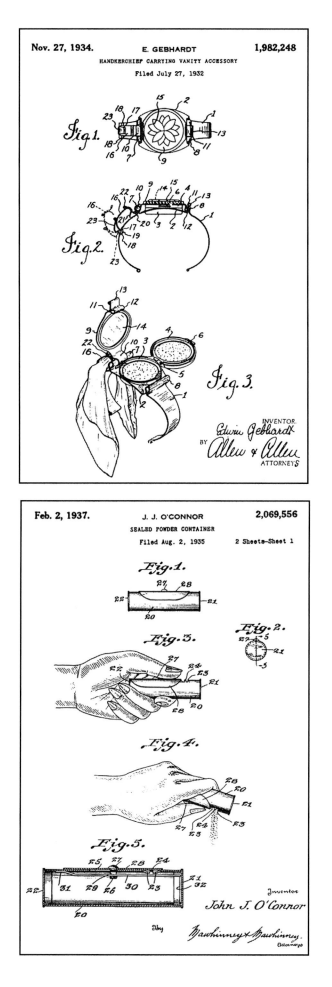

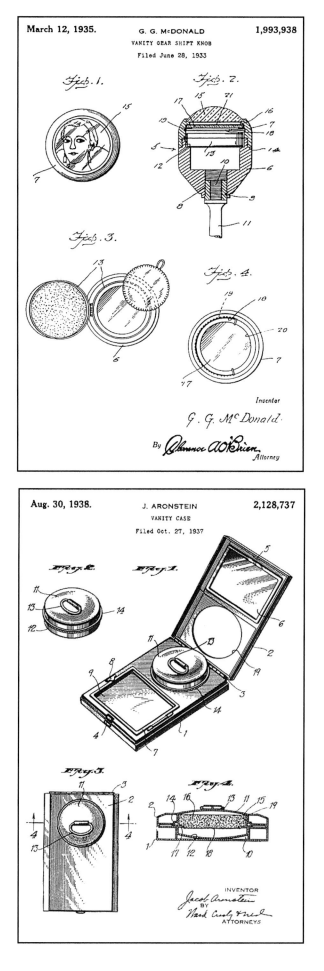

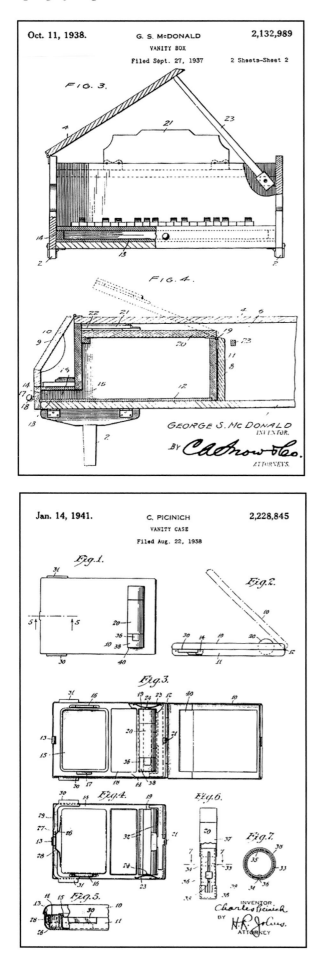

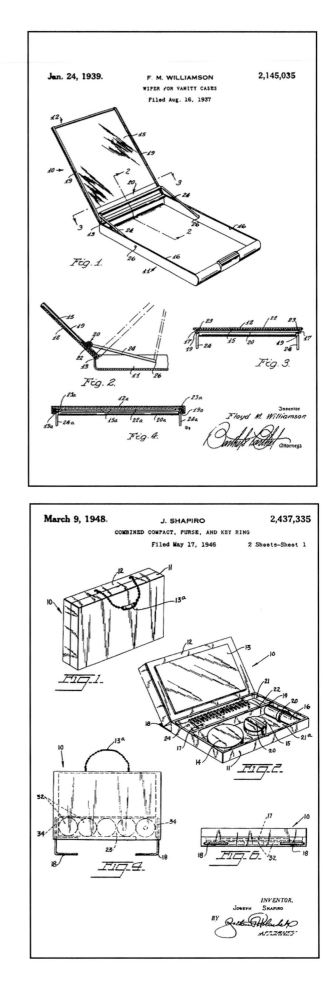

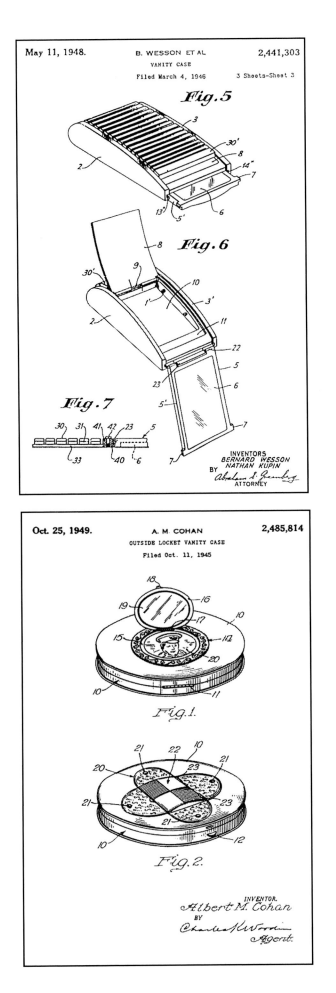

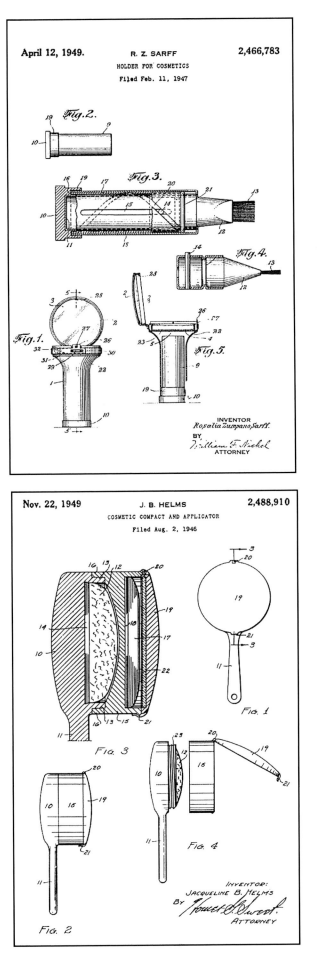

Invention Patents

Invention patents cover the unique mechanical workings of inventions which produce utilitarian results. An invention patent is in effect, with exclusive rights for the inventor, for 17 years from date of issuance.

A GUIDE FOR DATING INVENTION PATENT NUMBERS

Patent		Numbers	Date	Patent	Numbers	Date
1	thru	109	1836	488,976	511,743	1893
110		545	1837	511,744	531,618	1894
546		1,060	1838	531,619	552,501	1895
1,061		1,464	1839	552,502	574,368	1896
1,465		1,922	1840	574,369	596,466	1897
1,923		2,412	1841	596,467	616,870	1898
2,413		2,900	1842	616,871	640,166	1899
2,901		3,394	1843	640,167	664,826	1900
3,395		3,872	1844	664,827	690,384	1901
3,873		4,347	1845	690,385	717,520	1902
4,348		4,913	1846	717,521	748,566	1903
4,914		5,408	1847	748,567	778,833	1904
5,409		5,992	1848	778,834	808,617	1905
5,993		6,980	1849	808,618	839,798	1906
6,981		7,864	1850	839,799	875,678	1907
7,865		8,621	1851	875,679	908,435	1908
8,622		9,511	1852	908,436	945,009	1909
9,512		10,357	1853	945,010	980,177	1910
10,358		12,116	1854	980,178	1,013,094	1911
12,117		14,008	1855	1,013,095	1,049,325	1912
14,009		16,323	1856	1,049,326	1,083,266	1913
16,324		19,009	1857	1,083,267	1,123,211	1914
19,010		22,476	1858	1,123,212	1,166,418	1915
22,477		26,641	1859	1,166,419	1,210,388	1916
26,642		31,004	1860	1,210,389	1,251,457	1917
31,005		34,044	1861	1,251,458	1,290,026	1918
34,045		37,265	1862	1,290,027	1,326,898	1919
37,266		41,046	1863	1,326,899	1,364,062	1920
41,047		45,684	1864	1,364,063	1,401,947	1921
45,685		51,783	1865	1,401,948	1,440,361	1922
51,784		60,657	1866	1,440,362	1,478,995	1923
60,658		72,958	1867	1,478,996	1,521,589	1924
72,959		85,502	1868	1,521,590	1,568,039	1925
85,503		98,459	1869	1,568,040	1,612,789	1926
98,460		110,616	1870	1,612,790	1,654,520	1927
110,617		122,303	1871	1,654,521	1,696,896	1928
122,304		134,503	1872	1,696,897	1,742,180	1929
134,504		146,119	1873	1,742,181	1,787,423	1930
146,120		158,349	1874	1,787,424	1,839,189	1931
158,350		171,640	1875	1,839,190	1,892,662	1932
171,641		185,812	1876	1,892,663	1,941,448	1933
185,813		198,732	1877	1,941,449	1,985,877	1934
198,733		211,077	1878	1,985,878	2,026,515	1935
211,078		223,210	1879	2,026,516	2,066,308	1936
223,211		236,136	1880	2,066,309	2,104,003	1937
236,137		251,684	1881	2,104,004	2,142,079	1938
251,685		269,819	1882	2,142,080	2,185,169	1939
269,820		291,015	1883	2,185,170	2,227,417	1940
291,016		310,162	1884	2,227,418	2,268,539	1941
310,163		333,493	1885	2,268,540	2,307,006	1942
333,494		355,290	1886	2,307,007	2,338,080	1943
355,291		375,719	1887	2,338,081	2,366,153	1944
375,720		395,304	1888	2,366,154	2,391,855	1945
395,305		418,664	1889	2,391,856	2,413,674	1946
418,665		443,986	1890	2,413,675	2,433,823	1947
443,987		466,314	1891	2,433,824	2,457,796	1948
466,315		488,975	1892	2,457,797	2,492,943	1949

Patent	Numbers	Date	Patent	Numbers	Date
2,492,944	2,536,015	1950	2,966,681	3,015,102	1961
2,536,016	2,580,378	1951	3,015,103	3,070,800	1962
2,580,379	2,624,045	1952	3,070,801	3,116,486	1963
2,624,046	2,664,561	1953	3,116,487	3,163,864	1964
2,664,562	2,698,433	1954	3,163,865	3,226,728	1965
2,698,434	2,728,912	1955	3,216,729	3,295,142	1966
2,728,913	2,775,761	1956	3,295,143	3,360,799	1967
2,775,762	2,818,566	1957	3,360,800	3,419,096	1968
2,818,567	2,866,972	1958	3,419,907	3,487,469	1969
2,866,973	2,919,442	1959	3,487,470	3,551,908	1970
2,919,443	2,966,680	1960			

Design Patents

Design patents cover unique, ornamental exterior shapes or structures of an invention. A Design patent is in effect, with exclusive rights for the inventor, for 14 years from date of issuance.

A GUIDE FOR DATING DESIGN PATENT NUMBERS
Design patent numbers are preceded with the letters D or DES

Patent Numbers			Date	Patent Numbers		Date
1	thru	14	1843	17,046	17,994	1887
15		26	1844	17,995	18,829	1888
27		43	1845	18,830	19,552	1889
44		102	1846	19,553	20,438	1890
103		162	1847	20,439	21,274	1891
163		208	1848	21,275	22,091	1892
209		257	1849	22,092	22,993	1893
258		340	1850	22,994	23,921	1894
341		430	1851	23,922	25,036	1895
431		539	1852	25,037	26,481	1896
540		625	1853	26,482	28,112	1897
626		682	1854	28,113	29,915	1898
683		752	1855	29,916	32,054	1899
753		859	1856	32,055	33,812	1900
860		972	1857	33,813	35,546	1901
973		1,074	1858	35,547	36,186	1902
1,075		1,182	1859	36,187	36,722	1903
1,183		1,365	1860	36,723	37,279	1904
1,366		1,507	1861	37,280	37,765	1905
1,508		1,702	1862	37,766	38,390	1906
1,703		1,878	1863	38,391	38,979	1907
1,879		2,017	1864	38,980	39,736	1908
2,018		2,238	1865	39,737	40,423	1909
2,239		2,532	1866	40,424	41,062	1910
2,533		2,857	1867	41,063	42,072	1911
2,858		3,303	1868	42,073	43,414	1912
3,304		3,809	1869	43,415	45,097	1913
3,810		4,546	1870	46,098	46,812	1914
4,547		5,451	1871	46,813	48,357	1915
5,452		6,335	1872	48,358	50,116	1916
6,336		7,082	1873	50,117	51,628	1917
7,083		7,968	1874	51,629	52,835	1918
7,969		8,883	1875	52,836	54,358	1919
8,884		9,685	1876	54,359	56,843	1920
9,686		10,384	1877	56,844	60,120	1921
10,385		10,974	1878	60,121	61,747	1922
10,975		11,566	1879	61,748	63,674	1923
11,567		12,081	1880	63,675	66,345	1924
12,082		12,646	1881	66,346	69,169	1925
12,647		13,507	1882	69,170	71,771	1926
13,508		14,527	1883	71,772	74,158	1927
14,528		15,677	1884	74,159	77,346	1928
15,678		16,450	1885	77,347	80,253	1929
16,451		17,045	1886	80,254	82,965	1930

Patent Numbers		Date	Patent Numbers		Date
82,966	85,902	1931	161,404	165,567	1951
85,903	88,846	1932	165,568	168,526	1952
88,847	91,257	1933	168,527	171,240	1953
91,258	94,178	1934	171,241	173,776	1954
94,179	98,044	1935	173,777	176,489	1955
98,045	102,600	1936	176,490	179,466	1956
102,601	107,737	1937	179,467	181,828	1957
107,738	112,764	1938	181,829	184,203	1958
112,765	118,357	1939	184,204	186,972	1959
118,358	124,502	1940	186,973	189,515	1960
124,503	130,988	1941	189,516	192,003	1961
130,989	134,716	1942	192,004	194,303	1962
134,717	136,945	1943	194,304	197,268	1963
136,946	139,861	1944	197,269	199,994	1964
139,862	143,385	1945	199,995	203,378	1965
143,386	146,164	1946	203,379	206,566	1966
146,165	148,266	1947	206,567	209,731	1967
148,267	152,234	1948	209,732	213,083	1968
152,235	156,685	1949	213,084	216,418	1969
156,686	161,403	1950	216,419	219,636	1970

Manufacturing Information

LIST OF MATERIALS

Alligator	Gun-metal	Precious gems
Aluminum	Ivory	Rhinestones
Bakelite	Jade	Satin
Beads	Lace	Sequins
Bird feathers	Lacquer	Shagreen
Brass	Leather	Shell
Brocade	Lizard	Silk
Bronze	Lucite	Silver
Butterfly wings	Marcasite	Snakeskin
Celluloid	Mesh	Steel
Chrome	Moiré	Suede
Delft	Mosaic	Synthetic stones
Fur	Mother-of-pearl	Taffeta
Gemstones	Paper	Tortoiseshell
German silver	Pearl	Velvet
Glass	Pewter	Wedgwood
Gold	Plastic	Wood
Grosgrain	Porcelain	Wool

COMPACT MANUFACTURERS AND TRADE NAMES

A. Bourjois & Co., Inc.
A. L. Siegel Co. (Handysift)
A. S. Brown (England)
AC Belkin Company
Adrienne
AGME (Switzerland)
Aklar
Alpacca (Germany)
Alpaccahoka
Alwyn
Ameré (Switzerland)
American Beauty
American Maid
Amita
Anna Pavlova
Annette
Ansico
Antoine
Arden, Elizabeth
Armand
Armond Co.
Arpels
Artcraft
Asprey
Aveon, NY
Avon
B. B. Co
B & B Co.
B. Co.
BC
Bag-Dabs
Bagirette
Baird North
Barbara Gould
Beauty-Full
Belais
Bertie (Paris)
BG
Bigney
Blanchette DeCorday
Black, Starr and Frost
Bliss Brothers
E. A. Bliss Co.
Blumpak
Bond Street, Laaco
Bonnjolie
Botony Lanolin
Boucheron
Bourdier (Paris)
Bree
D. F. Briggs
Britemode
Broderie Main (France)
Buccellati
Buchner
C & N
C. Fauré
Cambi (France)
Campus Make Up
Cappi (Cheramy)
Cara Mia
Cara Noma
Cartier (Paris, London, New York)
Chament
Chanel

Chantrey
Charbert
Charlton
Charles of the Ritz
Chaumet
Cheramy
Chez ReLew
Cigogne, Inc.
Ciner
Clarece Jane
Cleopatra Vanity, Rex Co.
Clercygne-Pierrette (Paris)
Clover
Colgate & Co.
Colleen Moore Cosmetics
Colt Purse Make-Up Kit
Columbia Creation
Columbia Fifth Ave.
Compant
Concord
Coro
Coty
Crafters (Chicago)
Creme-Puff
Croco (Israel)
Crysta
D. B. H. Sterling (England)
D. F. B. CO.
Daniel (Paris)
Darnee (New York)
Dassy (France)
De Mendor-Lazell
De Meridor
Deerie
Deletron
Delettrez
Dermay
Deva (France)
Deva-Dassy
Divine
Djer-Kiss
Donmark Creations
Dorette
Dorine
Dorothy Gray
Dorset, 5th Ave. (New York)
Dorset, Rex 5th Ave. (New York)
Doucette
Dovell Co.
Dover Briars
Dreisen & Co.
DuBarry
Dunhill Vanity
Dunhill, N. Y.
Duro Gloss
E.A.M. (*see Elgin American*)
E.P.M.S.
Edna Wallace Hopper
Edouardo
Edwards' Bag,. Ltd.
Egme (England)
Eisenberg
Elgin American Co., Inc.
　(*also owned Clarece Jane*)
　　E.A.M.

Elgin Vanity
Elgina
Elginite
Elzabbeth Arden
Elmo
Enco
Entiérement
Esté Lauder
Evans
Evanshire
Evening In Paris
Eversmart Manicure Compact
F & Co.
F & J
F M Co.
F & B
F. H. Sadler
F. J. Co.
Fabergé (Russian)
Fiancee
Fifth Avenue
Fillkwik Co.
Fitch
Fladium (France)
Flamond (France)
FM Co.
Foreum
Foster
Foster & Bailey
Framies
Framus
Fuller
G. L. B. Co.
Gaess & Hollander
Gainsborough
Garden Court
Gayanne
Georg Jensen (Denmark and New York)
Gibbs
Girey (U.S.A.)
Givenchy
Graceline
Gucci (Italy)
Gwenda (England)
H.F.B.
Hammacher Schlemmer
Hampton
Harmony of Boston
Harriet Hubbard Ayer
Hattie Carnegie
Helana Roma Firenze
Helena Rubinstein
Helene Curtis
Henriette (U.S.A.)
Hingeco (Rhode Island)
Hoechst
Hollywood
Houbigant
Houppette
Illinois Watch Case Co. (Welwood Watch)
Ingram Co.
International Silver
Ivan Britzin (Moscow)

J. F. Creations J.F.B. Co.
J. M. Fisher Co.
J. M. F. Co.
Janesich
Jaquet
Jason Wherler & Sons Mfg.
Jean Panand
Jean Pesprés
Jonteel
JRS (Denmark)
Jules Richard
K & K (Kotler & Kopet, Inc.)
Karess
Karnee
Kaycroft
Kigu of London
Kissproof
Komai/Amita (Japan)
Komdi (Kyota, Japan)
Krank
Kreisler
Kyrill
L. T. Piver (Paris)
La Bohéme
La Faveur de Paris
La Jaynees
La Mode
La Mode (R & G. Co. Sterling)
La Ray, Inc.
La Santo
La Vedelte
La-May Vanity
Labco
Lablache
Lacherche (Paris)
Lady Esther (Chicago)
Lady Lee
Lady Vanity
Lamkin
Lampl
Lanado
Lanchére
Langlois (New York)
Larue
Larvé
Lazell
Le Debut
Le Rage (England)
Le Tresor
Lee Fran
Lederer (Paris)
Lenthéric
Leon
Léon Farchery (Paris)
Lesco (bond Street)
Liberty of London
Lilly Daché
LIN-BREN
Linc Vautrin
Little Lady
LOOS PACT
Lubin
Lucien Lelong
Lucky Purse
Lucretia Vanderbilt (New York)

Luschous
Lushus
Luxor Limited (Chicago)
Lyric
M.M.R's
Ma Poudre
Marenello Co.
Majestic (New York)
Man Five
Manna (Naples)
Mara
Marathon
Marcee
Marhill
Marie Earle
Marion Bialac (New York)
Mark Cross
Marlene
Marlowe Co.
Marly (Les Parfums)
Mary Dunhill
Mary Dunhill Co.
Mary Garden
Mary Garden, Rigaud (Paris)
Mary Lewis
Mascot A.S.B.
Maubousson, Park and 55th (N.Y.)
Mavco
Mavis
Max Factor
Maxim
Maxley K.K.
May Co. (Calif.)
May-Fair
Medana (West Germany)
Melba Compacte
Melissa (England)
Mello-Glo
Metalfield
Milrone
Mignon
Mingeco (U.S.A)
Minois
Miref
Mireve
Misof of Paris
MMR Company (1920)
MMR Red Seal
Molinard (France)
Mondaine

Montré a Poudre (France)
Morss
Movado
Murat
Nan Co-Ed
Napier
New Light-Nissei Co., Ltd. (Tokyo)
Norida
Novex
Nylotis (Nyal Co.)
Nymfaun
Old Spice
Opaline
Osaka (Japan)
Ostertag (Paris)
Paris Fashion Co.
Parklane LSM
Patrys (Paris)
Pattie Duette Vivaudou
Paul Flato
Personal Beauty Ware
Pilcher Mfg. Co., Inc.
Platé
PN Co. (Chicago)
Pomone
Pompeian
Poster
Powder-Tier
Primrose House
Prince Matchabelli
Princess Marcella Borghese
Princess Pat
Profile Et Modile (France)
Puf-Kase
Pygmalion (England)
Quinlon
Quinto
R & G Co.
RAC
Raymond Templier
Regent
Regent of London
Remé (Switzerland)
Renard (New York)
Revels Glamour Kit
Revlon
Rex Products Corp.
RH Co.
RHO-JAN
Richard Hudnot

Ricard Limoges (France)
Richelieu
Rigaud
RION (Brazil)
RITZ
Robin Handbag
Roger & Gallet
ROGER EDET
Ronson
Rosenfeld (Israel)
Rowenta
Rumpp
S and F
S.G.D.G (France)
Sabor (France)
Sam Fink
Samaral (Madrid)
Schildkraut 5th Ave.
Schleps & Hausemann
Schlumberger
Schuco
Segal
Seventeen Toiletries
Shari
Shields MFG Inc.
Shields Inc.
Silroy
Silvaray
Stadium Girl
Starlet Compact
Stearns of Detroit and Paris
Stratnoid (England)
Stratton (England)
Sue et Mave
Sunc (China)
Suncer Flanjack (Austria)
Superb (USA)
Suzuyo (Sterling-Oriental)
Swinglok
Tangee
Tattoo
Tre-Jur
Terri Vanities
The D. L. Avld Co. (Columbus, Ohio)
The Marhill Co. Inc.
Tien
Tiffany & Co. (New York and Paris)
Timepact
Tokalon (Paris)
Ton Ton 5th Ave.

Trabert & Hoeffec, Inc.
Tradition
Trio-Ette
Tu Adore
Tussy
Tyrolean
Vade Mecum
Van Cleef & Arpels (Fifth Avenue,
New York, Paris, Palm Beach,
London)
Van-Mist
Vanace Fifth Ave.
Vanderbilt
Vani-Pac
Vanstyle (U.S.A.)
Vantine
Vashé
Venine
Venus
Venus-Ray Spotlight
Verdura (New York)
Viegay
Vitoge
Vivaudou, Inc.
Vogue Vanities
Volante-Dure
Volupté Inc.
W & H Co.
W. B. Mfg. Co.
W. M. Co.
Wadsworth
Wadsworth Watch Case Co.
Wand Art
Warner of California
Webster Co.
Weltzuner
Whiting
Whiting and Davis Co.
Wiesner of Miami
Wilardy
Woodbury
Woodworth
Yardley
Yurat
Yves Saint Laurent
Zell 5th Ave.
Ziegfeld Girl
ZP Okasa

Glossary

alloy – Base metal fused with a precious ore to change its color or to harden it.

Art Deco – (1920–1930). An angular style of geometric patterns and abstract designs that originated in France.

Art Nouveau – (1890 – 1910). A free-flowing style introduced in England, with emphasis on curved lines, natural motifs, and women with long flowing hair.

Bakelite – Trademark for an opaque synthetic plastic developed in 1909.

bar brooche – A narrow, horizontal decorated pin.

baroque pearl – Pearls with an irregular shape.

base metal – All metals other than the three primary precious metals: silver, gold, and platinum.

basse-taille – A decorative enameling technique in which the metal is etched, engraved, or cut and then filled with transparent enamels. Also known as translucent enameling.

brass – An alloy composed of two-thirds copper and one-third zinc.

brocade – Silk fabric with a woven raised design.

bronze – A reddish-brown alloy of copper and tin.

cabochon – A highly polished dome-shaped stone with no facets.

cabriole – An elongated S-shaped support.

cameo – A gem, shell, or stone with a design or figure carved in relief against a background of a darker or lighter color.

carryall – Mass-produced version of a minaudiére.

celluloid – Trademark for a type of plastic developed in 1868.

champlevé – An enameling technique in which cut-out or depressed areas in the metal are filled with enamel.

chatelaine – An ornamental clasp from which five to nine chains are suspended to accommodate various small objects.

chatelette – A chatelaine with shorter and fewer chains.

chinoiserie – European decoration with a Chinese motif.

chrome – A hard, brittle gray metal used to plate other metal with a bright mirror-like finish.

circa – Approximate date an item was manufactured.

clip – A hinged support on the back of a pin or brooch that clips onto an article of clothing.

cloisonné – A enameling technique in which narrow strips of gold or silver wire are soldered to a metal base to form compartments (cloisons), which are then filled with enamel.

compact – A small portable makeup container consisting of a mirror, powder, and puff.

damascene – Decorative inlaid pattern of gold or silver on metal.

déposé – French word for patent or copyright.

enamel – A form of powdered colored glass that is fused onto metal surfaces for decoration.

engraving – A pattern or design cut into the surface of a hard material with a sharp instrument.

fede – A decorative form consisting of a pair of clasped right hands symbolizing faith and trust.

flapjack – A slim, thin compact resembling a "flap-jack" pancake.

French ivory – Trademark for plastic imitation ivory.

German silver – A white alloy of nickle, zinc, and copper. Also called nickle silver, although contains no silver.

gilt or gild – To cover a base metal with a thin layer of gold or gold color.

gold – A soft precious metal usually combined with copper or nickle, depending on the color and hardness desired.

gold filled – A base metal (usually copper) plated with gold, usually by electroplating.

grosgrain – A stiffly corded silk fabric.

guilloché enamel – An engraved decoration on metal, usually geometric or floral, covered with a translucent enamel.

hallmark – A mark stamped on some objects of gold and silver to denote the quality, purity, origin, and manufacturer. First used in Great Britain.

inlay – A decorative technique in which a design in metal is etched or cut out and another hard material inserted in the recessed pattern to make a flat or even shape.

intaglio – A form of engraving or carving that gives the object a hollow, three-dimensional effect. The reverse of a cameo.

jet – A glossy black variety of hard coal. A name commonly used for imitation or genuine black stones.

karat – A term denoting the amount of pure gold in an article. 24 karats equals pure gold; 18 karats equals 18 parts pure gold and 6 parts of another metal.

Limoges – A translucent enamel of colorful portraits or scenes on copper that originated in Limoges, France.

lusterware – A glaze used on pottery to give a metallic or iridescent appearance.

marcasite – Natural marcasite is crystallized white iron pyrites. Imitation marcasite is made of cut steel that is formed and faceted.

minaudiére – A rigid metal, usually box-shaped evening bag with compartments for powder, lipstick , rouge, mirror, coins, and cigarettes.

mosaic – A picture or design composed of small vari-colored stones or glass. A micro-mosaic is created with tiny pieces of glass or stones.

mother-of-pearl – The hard, smooth iridescent lining of pearl oyster shells.

motif – In the style of or resembling.

necessaire – Bolster-shaped version of the minaudiére with fewer compartments.

obelisk – A four-sided tapering shaft with a pyramidal top.

ojime – A sliding bead or button on a cord used to tighten or loosen an inro.

parure – A set of matching pieces of jewelry.

petit point – One-half the cross of a cross-stitch done in fine thread on a fine canvas.

pewter – A silver-white alloy of tin and lead.

plastic – synthetic material, such as Bakelite, celluloid, or Lucite, that is molded by heat into a variety of shapes and colors. Natural, organic plastics (amber, ivory, tortoiseshell, and horn) can be softened and molded or pressed into shape.

pli – A makeup tube containing powder and a puff-brush.

plique-à-jour – An enameling technique in which transparent enamel is placed across soldered bands of metal to produce a stained-glass effect.

reticule – A small handbag that is held in the hand or carried over the arm.

rhinestone – A form of rock crystal faceted to resemble diamonds.

seed pearl – a small pearl.

shagreen – Green-dyed leather made from the skin of a shark.

silver – A precious metal usually combined with copper for hardness.

Sterling silver – The purest alloy of silver, containing 0.925 parts of silver and 0.075 parts of copper.

strapwork – A pattern of crossed and interwoven bands that resemble straps.

synthetic stone – Man-made imitations of precious or semiprecious stones.

taffeta – A bright, shiny thin silk fabric.

tango chain – A short chain that attaches a compact and lipstick case.

thumbpiece – A small knob that releases a catch when pressed.

tooling – A design in leather produced by a heated tool.

tortoise shell – The translucent shell of a tortoise, which can be molded by heat.

transfer – A commercial pattern or design applied to another surface.

vanity bag – A dainty mesh evening bag incorporating a compact as an integral part of the bag.

vanity box – Fitted traveling cosmetic box.

vanity case – A compact that contains rouge and/or lipstick.

vanity clutch – A fitted cosmetic bag with sleeves attached to the inside lining to accommodate compact, lipstick, and rouge.

vanity pochette – Drawstring powder pouch with a mirror at the base.

vanity purse – Leather, fabric, metal, or beaded purse incorporating a vanity case as an integral part of the purse.

velvet – A fabric made of silk with a smooth pile surface.

vermeil – A layer of gold over silver, copper, or bronze.

vinaigrette – A small ornamental receptable that contains scented vinegar or ammonia.

Bibiliography

BOOKS

Andacht, Sandra. *Oriental Antiques and Art.*
Greensboro, NC: Wallace-Homestead Book Company, 1987.

Baker, Lillian. *100 Years of Collectible Jewelry.*
Paducah, KY: Collector Books, 1978.

Baker, Lillian. *Fifty Years of Collectible Fashion Jewelry 1925 – 1975.*
Paducah, KY: Collector Books, 1978.

Battersby, Martin. *The Decorative Twenties.*
NY: Walker and Company, 1971.

Battersby, Martin. *The Decorative Thirties.*
NY: Collier Books, 1971.

Carter, Rosalynn. *The First Lady from Plains.*
Boston, MA: Houghton Mifflin, 1984.

Chandro, Moti. *Journal of the Indian Society of Oriental Art.*
Tagore, Abanindranath, Kramrisch, Stella, Editors. Vol. VIII, – 1940.

Dike, Catherine. *Cane Curiosa.*
Switzerland: 1983. Imprimerie Rod S.A., Rolle.

Encyclopedia Britannica.
William Benton, Publisher, 1970.

de Fontenoy, The Marquise. *Eve's Glossary.*
Chicago & New York: Herbert Stone & Co., MDCCCXCVII.

Gerson, Roselyn. *Vintage Vanity Bags & Purses.*
Paducah, KY: Collector Books, 1994.

Edwards, Juliette. *Compacts.*
Surrey, England: 1994.

Haertig, Evelyn. *Antique Combs & Purses.*
Carmel, CA: Gallery of Graphics Press, 1983.

Hainworth, Henry. *A Collectors Dictionary.*
London, Boston, and Henley: Rutlege & Kegan Paul, 1981.

Heide, Robert and John Gilman. *Dime-store Dream Parade.*
New York: E. P. Dutton, 1983.

Hillier, Bevis. *The Style of the Century 1900 – 1980.*
New York: E. P. Dutton, Inc. 1983.

Hillier, Bevis. *The World of Art Deco.*
New York: Studio-Vista Dutton, 1971.

Hillier, Bevis. *Art Deco of the 20's & 30's.*
New York: Studio-Vista Dutton, 1968.

The History of Coty.
235 East 42nd Street, New York, NY. 10017.

Holiner, Richard. *Antique Purses.*
Paducah, KY: Collector Books, 1982.

Kaplan, Arthur Guy. *Official Price Guide to Antique Jewelry*, First Edition.
Orlando, FL: The House of Collectibles, Inc., 1982.

Kaplan, Arthur Guy. *Official Price Guide to Antique Jewelry*, Fifth Edition.
Westminster, MD: The House of Collectibles, 1985.

Kelley, Lyngerda & Nancy Schiffer. *Plastic Jewelry.*
PA: Schiffer Publishing Ltd., 1987.

Klein, Dan, Nancy A. McClelland, Malcolm Haslam. *In the Deco Style.*
New York: Rizzoli, 1986.

Lester, Katharine Morris and Bess Viola Oerke. *Accessories of Dress.*
Peoria, IL: Charles A. Bennett Co. Inc., 1940.

Loring, John. *Tiffany's 150 Years.*
New York: Doubleday & Co. Inc., 1987.

McClinton, Katharine Morrison. *Art Deco. A Guide For Collectors.*
NY: Clarkson N. Potter, Inc., 1972.

Mebane, John. *Collecting Nostalgia: The First Guide to the Antiques of the 30's and 40's.*
New York: Castleton Books, Inc., 1972.

Patterson, Jerry E. *Matchsafes.*
Washington, DC: Smithsonian Institution, 1981.

Sloane, Jean. *Perfume and Scent Bottle Collecting.*
Lombard, IL: Wallace-Homestead Book Company, 1986.

Whiting & Davis Co. *Tercentenary Booklet 1876 – 1930.*
Plainville, MA.

ARTICLES

Andre, Mila. "Ancient Egypt's Afterlife at the Met." *Daily News* (August 14, 1994).

Barta, Cynthia. "In the Palm of Your Hand, A Short History of Cosmetic Use and Compacts in the 20th Century."
The Echoes Report (June, 1994).

Baker, Stanely L. "Collecting Compacts." *The Antique Trader Weekly* (July 27, 1977).

Bader, Terry. "Musical Compacts Repaired." *Powder Puff*, Vol. 7, #3 (Spring, 1994).

Bayer, Patricia. "Collecting Compacts." *Antiques World* (April, 1979).

Berg, Rona. "The Art of Beauty." *New York Times Magazine* (October 18, 1992).

Biallot, Suzanne. "Compact Dreams." *Town & Country* (April, 1994).

Brous, Elizabeth. "Beauty Clips." *Vogue* (December, 1993).

Cohen, Marion. "Male Compact Collector." *Powder Puff*, Vol. 5, #1 (Fall, 1991).

Drake, Laurie. "The Powder and the Glory." *Self* (March, 1994).

Gerson, Roselyn. "Open and Shut Cases: The Wonderful World of Ladies' Compacts." *American Country Collectibles* (Winter, 1994/5).

Gerson, Roselyn. "Ladies' Vintage Compacts." *Vintage Fashions* (August, 1990).

Gerson, Roselyn. "Vintage Compacts: Coming of Age." *Lady's Gallery* Vol. 1 Issue 1.

Gottschalk, Mary. "Compact Packages." *San Juan Mercury News* (December 18, 1994).

Greiner, Carol. "Dial 911." *Powder Puff*, Vol. 7, #4 (Summer, 1994).

Hillier, Bevis. "Powder Compacts." *Country Living Magazine* (England) (October, 1994).

Hillier, Bevis, "Open and Shut Cases." *Los Angeles Times Magazine* (December 29, 1985).

Hutchinson, Diana. "Compact and Bijou." *Daily Mail*, London, England (July 7, 1994).

Jailer-Chamberlain, Mildred. "Celebrity Jewelry." *Antique Week* (July 5, 1993).

Johnson, Frances. "Compacts, Objects of Beauty." *Antiques and Collecting Magazine* (July, 1994).

Kirsch, Francine. "Something from the Boys." *The Antique Trader Weekly* (November 24, 1993).

Klyde, Hilda. "Locating Ladies' Compacts in London." *Powder Puff*, Vol. 7, #2 (Winter, 1994).

Kovel. "Hotline." *Kovels on Antiques and Collectibles* (April, 1993, October, 1994).

"'Make-up' a Collection." *Kovels on Antiques and Collectibles*, Vol. 11 #6 (Feb. 15, 1985).

Litts, Elyce. "That Mondaine Lady." *Powder Puff*, Vol. 8, #1 (Fall, 1994).

Litts, Elyce. "Compact Findings." *The Antique Trader Weekly* (Dec. 2, 1987).

Lord, Shirley. Beauty Clips." *Vogue* (February, 1994).

Moen, Vicki. "Texas Fair Compact Category." *Powder Puff*, Vol. 8, #1 (Fall, 1994).

Montag, Joan & Reine. "Rare Red Enamel." *Powder Puff*, Vol. 3, #2 (Winter, 1990).

Palivos, Tomi. "Antique Addict." *Powder Puff* Vol. 7, #3 (Spring, 1994).

Reif, Rita. "Cartier Hunts its Own Eggs and Other Treasures." *New York Times* (April 3, 1994).

Rosen, Marc. "On Design." *Beauty Fashion* (February, 1994).

Schmid, Wendy. "Making Up." *Vogue* (August, 1994).

Wacker, Ruth. "Seek and ye Shall Find." *Powder Puff*, Vol. 7, #4 (Summer, 1994).

Weinstein, Sheryl. "The New Collectibles: Powder Compacts." *Woman's Day* (February 22, 1994).

CATALOGS

"American Jewelry." Christy's New York, October 21, 1992.

"The American Perfumer" New York, NY, Dec. 1920.

Baird-North Co. Providence, RI, 1917.

"Year Book 1926." Baird-North Co. Providence, RI

"Exquisite Accessories." Elgin American Catalog 1952 – 1953. Elgin American Watch Case Co. Elgin, IL, September 1, 1952.

"Your Bargain Book." F. H. Sadler Co. Fall and Winter 1927 – 1928. New York Styles.

Holsman Company Chicago IL.
"Important Jewelry." Christy's New York, December 6, 1994.

Joseph Hagn Company Catalog. Spring-Summer 1938, Chicago, IL.

Catalogue #109 Fall & Winter 1928 – 1929, Montgomery Ward & Co. Baltimore, MD.

Catalogue #97 Golden Jubilee 1872 – 1922, Chicago IL.

"The Pohlson Colonial Gifts." Pohlson Galleries Pawtucket, RI, 1920s.

Sears Roebuck Catalogues. 1897, 1908, 1923, 1927, 1928, 1930, 1935, 1949 Editions. Chicago IL.

"Gifts from the Shepard Stores." Shepard Stores Boston, MA, 1923.

MAGAZINES and NEWSPAPERS

New York Times, July 4, 1993.

Vogue, August 1993.

Mirabella, May 1993.

Beauty Fashion, May 1993 and October 1993.

Toilet Requisites, December 1921.

Woman & Beauty Magazine, IPC England, November 1931.

True Confessions, June 1946.

Woman's World, 1925.

Eastman Kodak Trade Circular, 1928.

Fortune August, 1930.

Glamour, November 1948.

Good Housekeeping, Dec. 1928 and Dec. 1941.

Harper's Bazaar, Dec. 1943.

McCall's Magazine, June 1929.

Metropolitan Home, New York, 1987.

Pictorial Review – Oct. 1924, Sept. 1925, April 1927, June 1928, Jan. 1931, and Sept 1931.

Redbook, Dec. 1951 and Nov. 1954.

The Delineator, April 1919.

The Ladies Home Journal, Dec. 1921, March 1922, March 1924, Dec. 1924, June 1925, and April 1942.

Theatre Magazine, 1919, 1920, 1926, 1927, and 1928.

Woman's Home Companion, Dec. 1933.

Index

VINTAGE
Vanity Bags
Purses

AN IDENTIFICATION & VALUE GUIDE

By Roselyn Gerson

Over 300 full-color photos

History, patents, manufacturers & more!

Necessaires, minaudiers & chatelaines

Well researched & written

Wonderful text & photos

Vintage advertisements

8½ x 11, 272 Pgs., hardbound, $24.95

The first of its kind, this beautiful book deals exclusively with ladies' vanity bags, purses & carryalls. A complete pictorial reference guide, it is the definitive source for history, values, patents, origins, composition & manufacturers of these many whimsical yet functional accessories. More than 300 gorgeous color photos in addition to hundreds of vintage ads feature all types of bags — from traditional mesh & beaded bags to the funky 1950s Lucite box-shape. A beautiful reference & value guide such as this will appeal to collectors & dealers of compacts, mesh & plastic bags, cigarette cases, lighters, music boxes & vintage clothing, as well as anyone interested in a look at the history of ladies' fashion.

Schroeder's
ANTIQUES
Price Guide

. . is the #1 best-selling antiques & collectibles value guide on the market today, and here's why . . .

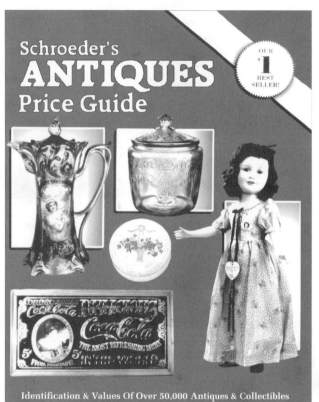

Schroeder's
ANTIQUES
Price Guide

OUR #1 BEST SELLER!

Identification & Values Of Over 50,000 Antiques & Collectibles

8½ x 11, 608 Pages, $14.95

• *More than 300 advisors, well-known dealers, and top-notch collectors work together with our editors to bring you accurate information regarding pricing and identification.*

• *More than 45,000 items in almost 500 categories are listed along with hundreds of sharp original photos that illustrate not only the rare and unusual, but the common, popular collectibles as well.*

• *Each large close-up shot shows important details clearly. Every subject is represented with histories and background information, a feature not found in any of our competitors' publications.*

• *Our editors keep abreast of newly developing trends, often adding several new categories a year as the need arises.*

If it merits the interest of today's collector, you'll find it in *Schroeder's*. And you can feel confident that the information we publish is up to date and accurate. Our advisors thoroughly check each category to spot inconsistencies, listings that may not be entirely reflective of market dealings, and lines too vague to be of merit. Only the best of the lot remains for publication.

Without doubt, you'll find
SCHROEDER'S ANTIQUES PRICE GUIDE
the only one to buy for
reliable information and values.

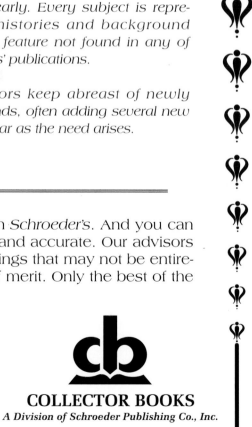

COLLECTOR BOOKS
A Division of Schroeder Publishing Co., Inc.